Praise for *Francis and Clare.*

"Brady succeeds in presenting a . Francis and Clare. This impressively researched biography casts its subjects in a new light." —*Publishers Weekly*

"Brady chronicles the turbulent journeys of the two saints...the author brings to vivid life the religious and political tumult of the time—which included the Crusades—and astutely articulates the various lines of theological division. Furthermore, the book is lucidly written, a scrupulously thorough account enlivened by what Brady calls "novelistic details," the minutiae, however imagined, that immerse readers in the drama." —*Kirkus Reviews*

"The story of Francis and Clare is surprisingly modern. We learn enough about them in Ms. Brady's narrative to appreciate their quirks and powerfully independent personalities. Sometimes their story is dramatized, which is not to say that the biographer makes up scenes or events, but from documents and testimony she is able to recreate certain days in the lives of her subjects." —Carl Rollyson, *The New York Sun*

Praise for the author's *Ida Tarbell: Portrait Of A Muckraker*

"Kathleen Brady's triumphant portrait of Ida Tarbell will last for generations. No other biography of Ida Tarbell is likely to provide a more vivid look at this endlessly fascinating woman."

—Doris Kearns Goodwin
best-selling author of *The Bully Pulpit: Theodore Roosevelt, William Howard Taft, and the Golden Age of Journalism*

"This eminently balanced biography is more than a valentine."
—*The New York Times*

Praise for the author's *Lucille: The Life Of Lucille Ball*

"Brady is meticulous in her reconstruction of the life of a contract player in the studio system of the thirties and forties . . . and superb at capturing the loose-goose chaos of early television production." —*The Toronto Globe and Mail*

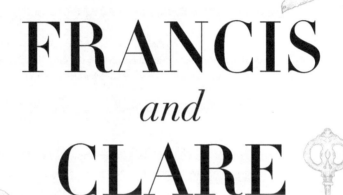

FRANCIS
and
CLARE

The Struggles of the
Saints of Assisi

KATHLEEN BRADY

LODWIN PRESS

Published in the United States by Lodwin Press, New York.

PUBLISHER'S CATALOGING-IN-PUBLICATION DATA
provided by Five Rainbows Cataloging Services

Names: Brady, Kathleen, author.
Title: Clare and Francis : the struggles of the Saints of Assisi / Kathleen Brady.
Description: New York : Lodwin Press, 2021. | Includes bibliographical
references and index.
Identifiers: ISBN 978-1-7375498-0-2 (paperback) | ISBN 978-1-7375498-2-6 (ebook)
Subjects: LCSH: Clare, of Assisi, Saint, 1194-1253. | Francis, of Assisi, Saint, 1182-1226. |
    Christian saints—Italy—Assisi—Biography. | Christian women saints—Italy—Assisi—
    Biography. | Women—Biography. | Assisi (Italy)—Biography. | BISAC: BIOGRAPHY
    & AUTOBIOGRAPHY / Religious. | BIOGRAPHY & AUTOBIOGRAPHY /
    Historical. | BIOGRAPHY & AUTOBIOGRAPHY / Women.
Classification: LCC BX4700.C6 B73 2021 (print) | LCC BX4700.C6 (ebook) |
    DDC 271/.302—dc23.

www.francisandclarethestrugglesofthesaintsofassisi.com

For information about special discounts available for
bulk purchases, sales promotions, fund-raising, and educational needs,
contact the author at brady@kathleenbrady.net

Book design by Kathryn Holeman

For those who struggle with their faith

Acknowledgments

I am grateful for the tireless support of friends and family with whom I shared news about this project. These include Stephen F. Brown, Mary Bridget Schuchman Cassidy, Shelby Coleman, Caroline Golden, Barbara Fowler Hoeper, Judy Toolan Leane, Anne Riccitelli, Ina Saltz, Anastasia Toufexis, Mary Ann Walk, Chris Leonard, Alexandra Eames, Ric Wyman, and the Bradys: Larry, Debbie, David, and Benjamin, who got me back to Assisi. Special thanks to a trio of personal and professional friends Sidney S. Stark, Paul Pitcoff, and Kathleen McGraw who read some of the pages, and to Kathryn Holeman, illustrator, book designer, and person extraordinaire.

Thanks go as always to remarkable and tireless research librarians at the New York Public Library, Paul Friedman in particular; and to Debra Cashion of the Pius XII Memorial Library at St. Louis University who led me to an essential source.

Finally, I am indebted to five treasured persons who supported my work but sadly did not live to see its publication: Patricia Bosworth, Brother Ed Coughlin OFM, Kenneth Silverman, Patricia Kennealy Morrison, and Nicholas Von Hoffman.

Prologue

SOME YEARS AGO an unusual display in the window of a fashionable florist shop just off Madison Avenue held me in thrall. It was a carved wooden santos, a hand-hewn figure of a saint. The body was spindly, bare, little more than an armature, but the face was specific, austere, and intense. In its eyes were battles and deprivation, conquest, and strife. That such a tony Manhattan shop would feature a difficult and fearsome saint made sense to me. Surely it was Ignatius of Loyola, a warrior and founder of the Jesuits, or Simeon Stylites who lived on top of a pillar to escape the pilgrims who flocked to him.

I had to speak to the shop owner who displayed such sophisticated knowledge of the church. I wanted to find out who the uncommon figure in the window was supposed to be. Saints—all of them—nobles, peasants, martyrs who endured so much—had captured my imagination early on. When I was a teenager, religion had tranquilized me. I walked to Mass every morning after the school year ended. Through sweltering Arkansas summers, as floor fan breezes cooled the cavernous expanse of a nearly empty church, I turned the pages of my missal to the brief profile of the virgin, confessor, or bishop being honored that day, much as I now open the obituaries of the *New York Times* to read of the scientists, athletes, and celebrities who have departed this life. The face of the santos unlocked so many memories.

Entering the shop I boldly announced, "How fabulous that you have a statue of Ignatius of Loyola in your window! Or is it Saint

Simeon?" The proprietor was incredulous. "Are you crazy?" he sputtered. "It is Francis of Assisi!" I was stunned, in part because he had been so rude.

"Without their robes, all saints look alike," I said, retreating outside for another look. Sure enough, a bird perched on one wooden santos hand and a long spiky flower bloomed in the other. Both attributes of Francis were there for anyone to see, but I had missed them because the spirit burning in those eyes had obscured everything else.

As I hurried up the street, embarrassment gave way to insight. To have survived through the ages as a distinct personality, to have eclipsed all others who preached Christ's love, Francis had to have been as fierce and unrelenting as the Inquisitors had been in pursuing Infidels. I proceeded directly to the New York Society Library a dozen blocks uptown and entered the stacks. I found Paul Sabatier's 1894 biography of Francis, a late nineteenth century work that took a French Protestant's skeptical view of the Roman Catholic hierarchy but had a loving regard for Francis. Then I read the folkloric, pious stories from the classic *Little Flowers of Saint Francis* that showed him as God's chosen fool. My eyes swam as the antic tales of outlandish miracles brought back memories of how two disruptive experiences brought my faith to an end.

The first was the time I turned to a fatherly Franciscan priest for help in a crisis. I saw that while he wanted to help a weeping young woman, he was very ill at ease. He looked like he was trying to figure out how soon the encounter would be over.

I forgot what he told me—"this shall pass" was probably it. In any event, he did distract me from my troubles. The situation revealed to me that to priests—not just this one, all of them, even the best—women were a group apart. I saw that all my life I had meant far less to the church than the church had meant to me.

Yet still I went to Mass. Every day. And to communion as well—of course to communion, the Eucharist, the presence of God come to live within me. After I moved to New York City I attended Mass only on Sundays, although I often dropped in to one open church or another on weekdays to order my thoughts after a problem in the newsroom or when I needed to figure out how to structure the story I would write that day. Other people were taking Valium or sipping wine at lunch. Not me. I had the holy water font.

Then came the sermon on Mother's Day. The priest, as he slowly drew out his every syllable, imparted the story of how Mary, the Blessed Mother, had raised her son Jesus, feeding him, teaching him, guiding him, and standing near him as he died on the cross. Really, Mother's Day was her day, he said. She, more than the woman who raised us, was our mother, he said. Equally as important was that she was a virgin. "It is also for her spotless virginity that we honor her today," he said.

I looked down at my shoes, which were blue and white—Mary's colors. They were trying to step into the aisle and walk out the door, even as my hands gripped the back of the pew in front of me to keep me fixed in place. After all these years, probably with the help of new perspectives I was gaining from feminist writing, I heard it: a woman would need to be a virgin for the church to acknowledge her motherhood as truly honorable. Suddenly it was all too much for me. What else did the church have wrong? A week later when my alarm clock roused me to Mass, I heard a voice say clearly, "There is no point in going." The mattress springs squeaked as I rolled over and went back to sleep.

The next day I found that I had become a strict rationalist and that I was completely at peace. I believed in nothing that did not have physical form. The loss of heaven or the hope of seeing the departed once again did not matter to me. The surprising thing was that I felt kinship with strangers. Until then I thought I had empathy only because Jesus insisted upon it. Now I liked people because they were all that there was. When I held the door open for a person walking in behind me, I wasn't being polite. I was being kind. Jesus and his wisdom still mattered to me, but when I went into a church I felt like one who returns to an alma mater and marvels that they had ever been so young. I had claimed my power.

A few years later, a dear friend persuaded me to listen to the ideas that were changing her life. I went to a talk where a pale young American wearing the white garb of an Indian guru said that all people and creation made up the being that is God. That made sense to me. I believed every word that he said. Together we were all It. We might experience our existence in time, space, and three dimensions, but beyond these limitations of perception, together we are all It, a giant force field. There was a God. I cannot explain this conversion logically. I accept it as grace, a gift. My rationalism was revealed to me as a spiritual journey, a hacking through overgrowth that led to a clearer path. Yet after all that, there I was in the library stacks immersed in Francis who lived by many beliefs I had shed through a years-long process.

But even as my preoccupation with Francis grew, I resisted it. That I was delving back into the world of Catholicism appalled me as much as it energized me. I reread *The Little Flowers* and I made myself take notes. I found a biography by Thomas of Celano written soon after Francis's death that made him more believable. Thomas mentioned Clare, the woman who led the women in his movement, and he was full of praise for her; but to me she seemed to be another bygone holy woman who sought nothing more than to be hungry and poor. When I decided to write a biography of Francis I planned to give her very short shrift, but over the years of research and writing, I slowly discovered the real woman who had been misrepresented by a cheerless portrait. One cannot tell the full story of Francis without the story of Clare, no more than one can tell the story of Clare without Francis. His greatest shame was allowing the church to betray his promises to her. She used her association with him to wage a decades-long fight with the papacy, upending some of its plans and blindsiding the pope who thought he had confined her in a cloister.

As I grew in knowledge, I evaluated the materials by considering who wrote a particular text and when, giving weight to those who knew Francis personally and wrote closest to his time. Context was essential: the gist of the event described, the commentary surrounding it, and the bias of the author or sources. Many made an effort to portray Francis as the New Christ, which led to neatly shaping his story to encompass a dozen original disciples, a multiplication of loaves, and a Judas or two in his midst, things that might have been true but needed to be scrutinized. I gave weight to anecdotes that seem more human than spiritually uplifting, such as the healthy Francis waking up all his companions to have them eat with the one who was in agony from hunger; or the ailing Francis rescuing the fur pelt that kept him warm while his comrades rushed in to extinguish the flames of his burning cell; or the lonely, bedridden Clare talking to a cat. Francis and Clare also came into sharper focus as I learned more about the world of their time, including the trade fairs of Champagne, mobilization for the Crusades, and the rounding up of women who created their own ways to lead lives of prayer and service outside of church-sanctioned convents.

Just as Paul Sabatier had galvanized me that day in the library, he launched a new round of Franciscan scholarship at the close of the nineteenth century. He posed what has come to be known as the Franciscan Question, the analysis of sources to determine which are likely to be the most authentic and fact-based and thus offer the truest picture of Francis and his order, including Clare. While it is impossible to be sure of the exact dates of certain events, I have organized the timing of a few incidents according to what is most credible.

Throughout the book I have occasionally included novelistic details that cannot be found in the early biographies of Francis or Clare. I take my justification from the fine biographer Geoffrey C. Ward. When I was a co-chair of the Biography Seminar at New York

University, he read to us from his work on Franklin D. Roosevelt. In one highly descriptive phrase he wrote that when FDR stood on crutches his knuckles were white and his legs were dangerously splayed out for balance. After his talk, when I asked how he could possibly know this, he said that as a boy he had had polio and he knew exactly how the human body looked and felt when it relied on crutches.

Thus inspired, I describe such scenes as the sights and smells of the dungeon in Perugia where Francis found himself imprisoned and how when Clare awakened at Saint Damian, roosters crowed in the distance and the glow of early dawn filled the narrow-arched window of the loft. I say that at Portiuncula Francis "listened to its birdsong and inhaled the tang of pine when the air was hot. In late afternoon he watched wisps of inky clouds float across the pewter sky and saw the hilltops glow red as the sun bade them farewell for the night." This is what I experienced in the woods of Umbria and I believe that it is safe to say that Clare and Francis felt something like that too.

I would have happily omitted miracles from my narrative, which I now think would have been like writing about Francis and Clare while leaving out God. I had to include them. Too many people testified that Francis or Clare had cured the sick and injured and had sat with angels or the divine. Clare's powers were such that Francis sent men with mental afflictions to her for help. Like Scrooge, who tried to explain away the sight of Marley's ghost as "an undigested bit of beef" or "a fragment of an underdone potato," I was tempted to see these phenomena as psychosomatic ills or hallucinations brought on by bad food. I have had experiences I consider to be miraculous, but I can also account for them by improbable coincidences. Clare's calming presence could have explained how she cured the boy who was convulsing with a pebble up his nose—he finally stood still long enough to exhale the little stone—but what about her healing an open sore that had festered for years? How was it that after days of agonizing labor a woman safely gave birth when the reins that Francis had held were placed upon her stomach? In the fourth century, Saint Augustine of Hippo said that miracles were not contrary to nature, only to what we know of nature. God was as real to medievals as the law of gravity is to us. Perhaps where we see dust motes floating in a sunbeam, they would have discerned the Christ Child coming into the room. I like best an explanation that a Franciscan priest gave me: "God does not create miracles. It is the love of God that creates miracles."

Whether or not the miracles of Francis and Clare actually happened as reported, medievals believed them to be true and they acted in accordance. However, since this is a book written in the twenty-first century, we must look to science. The closest science comes to dealing with the phenomenon of miracles is the placebo effect, a beneficial result produced by an ineffective means such as a sugar pill that can only be attributed to a patient's belief in that treatment.

Ted J. Kaptchuk, professor of medicine and of global health and social medicine at Harvard Medical School, as well as the author of *The Web that Has No Weaver: Understanding Chinese Medicine*, has conducted studies that indicate that the placebo effect, or unexplained cure, is a result of the act of caring and the sufferer's faith in that care. The encounter, whether it involves an acupuncture needle, a story told in a Navaho chantway ritual, or an approved Western medicine treatment, evokes a healing response. His conclusions go some way toward a rational explanation for miracle cures.

This book is the story of two people who were betrayed by their faith but believed in it still. Beyond the framework of religion, it is about individual power versus the control of society. For me personally, writing this book has left me pondering a bit of Roman Catholic canon law, according to which there are no lapsed Catholics. Law 849 states that baptism conveys an indelible spiritual mark that forever unites them, not just to Christ, but to the Catholic Church.

Mine is not a book of devotion, although it is the work of some twenty years of commitment to the earthly lives and struggles of Francis and Clare of Assisi. It is a sympathetic, twenty-first century examination of two real people who lived in the 1200s and captured, to this day, the imagination of the Western world. Francis did indeed love animals, and Clare did find in poverty an authentic life, but I found so much more to their lives than I imagined when I started my quest and many more reasons to admire them.

PART I

1

A Woman Set Apart

In July 1194 the young Lady Ortulana of Assisi knelt before the cross in the Cathedral of Saint Rufino heavy with child and overcome by fears. The faces of friends and cousins who had died in childbirth haunted her, along with thoughts of the motherless sons and daughters who had been raised by kinswomen, children loved by all but never loved enough. As she breathed into her terror, fanning as much as quelling it, she heard a voice clearly say, "Lady, do not be afraid. You will joyfully bring forth a clear light that will illuminate the world." Soon afterward she gave birth to a daughter she named Clare, or Chiara, the luminous one.

Because Clare was not a son, her birth would have been a disappointment. Still, she was bathed and wrapped tightly, like a miniature mummy, to assure that her bones would grow straight. She was placed in a cradle and rocked head to foot in the Umbrian way so that her toes were first above her head, then her head above her tiny feet. As Clare grew, Ortulana told her the story of the voice that announced that she would be a light to the world. And, true enough, the little girl developed a sense of purpose and a certainty that set her apart.

By the beginning of the thirteenth century, Assisi was a prosperous if minor city on the western slope of Mount Subasio in the Apennine chain about eighty miles north of Rome. It drew most of its wealth from vineyards, fruit and olive orchards, and fields of

cereals in the Spoleto Valley below. Some twenty-five hundred souls
lived on the six acres of sloping ground within and around its thick
city walls. Tradesmen and artisans serving mostly local needs clustered around its market square, lawyers and civil officials dwelled in
the bishop's quarter, and nobles lived in the quarter called Broken
Wall on the city's highest point surrounding the Cathedral of Saint
Rufino, Assisi's patron saint.

Little is known of Clare's mother's family other than that they
were distantly related to Constance, the wife of the Holy Roman
Emperor Henry VI. Ortuluna and her husband Favarone came from
separate branches of a lineage that can be traced to an eighth century administrator of the Duchy of Spoleto, one Lord Taciperticone,
whose name indicates that he would have been a tall, lanky man of
few words. Favarone was of the Offreducci clan. His marriage to
Ortulana was surely arranged, but theirs was probably one of the
less important alliances in their families. As a younger son, Favarone
could not have commanded one of the wealthier, most desirable
brides in the marriage market. When they wed, he was probably
twenty-five and she around fifteen.

Ortulana was, according to all accounts, pious and adventurous.
One cannot know, however, whether her piety surpassed that of others in an age when the presence of God and the menace of the devil
were as real as the personalities of one's own household. She was
willing to join groups of pilgrims who undertook the rigors and dangers of travel in the hopes of earning a cure, a particular blessing or
favor, the forgiveness of sins, or to simply venerate the saint. In the
course of her life she made all the important pilgrimages of the age.
She journeyed to Rome, to the shrine of Saint James in Compostela
in Galacia, the northwest region of the Iberian Peninsula, and to the
shrine of Saint Michael the Archangel atop an isolated mountain on
the heel of Italy's boot.

Favarone's character is still less clear. According to surviving accounts, Clare's closest female friends knew Ortulana well from their earliest childhoods, but they said they were hardly acquainted with her father. A longtime neighbor described him as "noble, great and powerful in the city—he and the others of his household." Perhaps he was unknown to them because the women were sequestered from men who were not close relatives. It is equally likely that Favarone was often away, involved in various military disputes and campaigns under the command of greater nobles to whom the family owed allegiance.

Favarone's family had two foes. The first was Pope Innocent III, who claimed that as pontiff he was the lawful ruler of central Italy: what is today Umbria, Lazio, Marche, and parts of Emilia-Romagna. The papacy contended that the Emperor Constantine had ceded these territories to the church in the fourth century. Those who supported the claims of the Papal States were known as Guelfs.[†] However, Favarone's family supported the claims of the Holy Roman Empire to that same territory, making them members of the Ghibelline party. The names were taken from dynasties that championed one or the other. The Holy Roman Emperor Henry VI had recently died, but his infant son Frederick, who like Clare had been baptized at the Cathedral of Saint Rufino, succeeded him. Baby Frederick ruled Assisi nominally in the person of Conrad of Lützenfeld, who was an accomplished general but so incompetent a governor that he was nicknamed "Fly in the Brain." In 1198, when Clare was four, Conrad switched sides. Believing that the imperial armies were too fragmented after Henry's death to hold out against papal forces, he led a retinue of knights, which may have included Clare's father, out of Assisi through steep mountain passes to the city of Narni fifty miles away so that he and his vassals could swear allegiance to the new pope, the charismatic Innocent III.

---

† In the fifteenth century, the humanist and literary critic Lorenzo Valla proved that the vernacular style of The Donation of Constantine manuscript established it as a forgery from the eighth century.

The removal of the military from Assisi left Clare's family and their fellow nobles vulnerable to their second but more immediate enemy, the city's common people. As in other cities on the Italian peninsula, this class had banded together into a commune, or municipal government, led by rising merchants, artisans, and tradesmen. As this body grew in prosperity, its members had come to resent paying the tolls and tribute that the nobles exacted each time they crossed a bridge or travelled a road on hereditary noble lands. These levies dated from the Roman Empire and remained in place to benefit whoever was in power. At this time, the lords and nobles tried to keep their hold on the merchants and others who regularly used the roads by charging for the right to pass. By making the lower orders pay often, and delaying their progress, the nobility reminded them that there were limits to how far they could rise. While the merchants took for granted that the nobles were of a higher rank, they wanted to abolish all practices that interfered with trade.

With Conrad and his forces away in Narni, the common people of Assisi stormed the Rock, his fortress on Mount Subasio overlooking Assisi, and destroyed it stone by stone. They then attacked the nobles' homes and property, including that of the Offreducci. Conrad, who apparently had no sense that the commune was ready to go to war, had taken his best fighting men with him. The nobility who remained, like Clare's extended family of women, children, and males who were too young or too old to go, were unable to defend themselves. Their houses were severely damaged as they cowered within. At age four, Clare was surely clinging to her mother or to her nurse while the savage cries of war and pillage echoed through the streets. Francis of Assisi, then around age sixteen, was likely to have been one of the marauders.

Assisi's nobles, including Clare's family, were driven to seek refuge in Perugia, which lay about fifteen miles away to the west on an opposing hilltop across the shallow River Tiber. On January 18, 1200, Girardo di Gislerio became the first noble to apply for citizenship there. He swore allegiance to its consuls and transferred his holdings in nearby Collestrada to their jurisdiction, removing them from Assisi tax rolls. Five days later others followed suit, including Clare's family. Perugia was no easy haven for them, however. According to an old proverb, its citizens were so extreme that they were either angels or devils. Certainly, they were proud. Some believed that their ancestors originated in Troy, others that Slavic and Persian kings under the command of the Emperor Justinian had built their city in the fifth century. Perugia had been the archenemy of Assisi for two millennia, ever since the city had been a capital of the Etruscans, while Assisi was an outpost of the Umbrian tribe that warred against them. In the first fifteen years of the thirteenth century, when communes were rising in other Italian cities, the nobles and merchants of Perugia continued to live together in relative peace. Their common concern was that the peasants would revolt against them all. To gain reinforcements, in December 1188 they declared that they would welcome outside nobles who were willing to provide service to Perugia in peace and war, provided they aided neither the pope nor the emperor. In 1200, after the Assisi uprising, the Offreducci felt they had no alternative but to accept this hand of peace. As a practical matter of survival, Monaldo, Clare's uncle and the head of the Favarone family, took up citizenship in Perugia, which put her whole family under the city's protection, and its debt.

Clare was old enough to feel the danger around her. A miniature painted about that time conveys a sense of what the journey from Assisi would have been like. This scene actually portrays the Apocalypse, but it could just as easily be the noble Offreducci approaching the forbidding gates of Perugia, which date from the time of the Caesars and stand in part to this day. The painting depicts a pair of knights and a soldier armed with a lance protecting a horse-drawn cart filled with ladies. Near them, a hooded man with two toddlers strapped to his back walks before a woman with a cradle on her head. Two small children holding a pitcher and a spoon clutch her skirt. All trudge on away from the protective walls of their city, dazed but determined.

The Perugia that became Clare's childhood home was a city of some seven hundred towers divided into five wards, each with its own symbol, each named for the city's ancient portals. Noble families lived in three of them: Susanna Gate, Angel Gate, or Sun Gate, respectively under the sign of the bear, the horse or the star. From the gate of each quarter, a main street lined by clusters of houses and shops ran to the Grand Plaza in the center of the city, where the Church of Saint Severus, the bishop's palace, and the Cathedral of Saint Lawrence were located. In this plaza, public business was conducted. There the official measurements of the *canna, braccio,* and *piede* were marked so that merchants and customers could settle disputes in full view. On its porticoes, magistrates and citizens discussed the concerns of the day, such as peace and war.

As for the world of the young Clare, she "never studied letters," but she learned to do needlework and spin yarn on a hand-held distaff, as was the custom for all medieval women. At seven, she reached the age of responsibility—old enough to express her intentions, her feelings and thoughts; old enough to know right from wrong and to choose between them. She was also old enough to examine her conscience, confess her sins, and receive the Eucharist, the body and blood of Christ in the appearance of a piece of bread, which was a profound experience for any believer.

God so captured her imagination, and was such a refuge to her, that no earthly joy or promise was comparable. As she grew, she spent an increasing amount of time in her devotions, counting on pebbles the number of prayers she said. Fasting, kindness to the poor, and good works may have helped her transcend the anxiety that was all around her.

Soon after their arrival in Perugia, the family expanded. Ortulana gave birth to another child, presenting Clare with a baby sister. Surely this second daughter was another disappointment, but they named her Catherine after the powerful Saint Catherine of Alexandria. By the time Clare's mother became pregnant again, Clare was old enough to feel the tension surrounding pregnancy, which put a woman's life in jeopardy. Ortulana's third child was safely delivered, but it was yet another daughter, whom they named Beatrice. The year of this girl's birth is unknown; nor do we know if Ortulana gave birth to other children. If so, they did not likely survive childhood.

Clare loved her two little sisters and delighted in watching them grow. As the oldest, she encouraged their first steps, praised their first words, and learned how to make them smile, forging bonds of affection and dependence that would endure throughout their lives, surpassing most other earthly attachments. She was close to two cousins, as well, the sisters Bona and Pacifica Guelfuccio, whose family had also fled Assisi. Pacifica was probably at least ten years older than Clare, having accompanied Ortulana on pilgrimage before Clare's birth. Clare also made a best friend named Benvenuta, a little girl born in Perugia whose family shared quarters with the Offreducci, but surviving records indicate that she was probably not of noble birth.

The little girls may well have stood together on a balcony with Ortulana and other women to watch and cheer as the men of Perugia assembled for war against Assisi in November 1202. Since taking in the nobles of Assisi, Perugia had been demanding that Assisi pay restitution and rebuild property damaged or destroyed when that city's commune drove out those of noble blood. The noble refugees did not prove to be trustworthy, nor did they consider Perugia's needs to be their own, yet Perugia pressed their claims for compensation through a series of skirmishes, raids, and ambushes on Assisi. Finally, it called on that city to meet the forces of Perugia in a full and decisive battle on the fields of Collestrada in the valley between them.

With church bells tolling, eight-year-old Clare may have scanned the procession of knights on horse in gleaming armor, searching out her father and uncles as they gathered in the main plaza to join foot soldiers and archers with deadly crossbows. Then they all filed through the streets, their swords and shields clanging. Dogs snapped and barked, not knowing whether to drive off these menacing figures or join in their hunt as they headed down the well-worn road to meet the enemy. When the city gates slammed shut after them, prayers began. Along with the others trembling in fear, Clare begged God to give them victory in battle, to save them all from harm.

As the city prayed, the archers of Perugia came in range of the enemy and let their flinty arrows fly. The Offreducci and other knights raised their swords and surged down the hill to meet the Assisiani, slaughtering those who did not run away, sparing only those whose armor and weapons indicated they were wealthy enough to fetch ransoms.

The Perugini returned home at day's end exhausted but victorious, dragging and shoving their hapless prisoners toward the dungeon where they would await death or delivery. Among them was the firebrand Francis Bernadone, the future Saint Francis of Assisi, just twenty years of age. Might tiny Clare have been peeping from a balcony as the women of Perugia pelted him and his wounded comrades with refuse and excrement in the name of Perugini killed or injured?

The defeat of the commune of Assisi promised to return Clare's family to their ancestral home, but delay followed delay, and the years dragged on. Clare was raised by people who felt exiled, displaced, aggrieved. Favarone and Ortulana knew Assisi as the place where they belonged, but Clare may have remembered it only as a place of terror while she felt a bond with the city and walls of Perugia that had sheltered her. Finally in 1205 Clare's uncle Monaldo, who had never been a true citizen of Perugia in his heart, decided to accept the family's losses and return home to their damaged compounds around the Cathedral of Saint Rufino. The Assisiani, both highborn and low, had simply had enough, and so they decided to reconcile for the good of all of them.

On November 9, 1210, the people of Assisi, including the merchants and the feudal nobility such as Clare's family, came together to sign the Peace Pact. All pledged not to make separate alliances with pope or emperor but to do all they could do for the honor, safety, and advantage of Assisi. The commune agreed to cover the costs of the war and repairs to the nobles' property. Most serfs were freed. In addition, citizens of nearby territories were invited to move within the city's walls so as to build up the city's population and strength. Clare's uncle Scipione deeded to the commune an olive grove with ancient ruins so they might rebuild the fountains, springs, and baths that had been splendid in Roman times.At last the Offreducci felt safe to return to the place that was home to the adults but unknown to Clare. Now sixteen, Clare left Perugia tearfully, wrenching herself from Benvenuta and other young women with whom she had grown up.

The home the family returned to in Assisi no longer stands, but it was an imposing structure with quarters for each of the five Offreducci brothers and their families. Such compounds typically held as many as forty or more persons, including servants, poor relations, illegitimate children, and other dependents. "Their household was one of the largest in the city," the family watchman would later note, "and great sums were spent there." Embroidered textiles hung on the interior walls. Lavender and rosemary freshened their linens and sweetened the air. At night, when the sun faded from the narrow windows, oil lamps and candles made of animal fat pierced the darkness but, for the most part, the family slept when the sun set and rose with the dawn.

At mealtimes, Clare joined the others in the common room at a long trestle table where places were set with trenchers. These dense slices of dry bread, slathered with smoked pork or spiced game and thick sauces, served as plates. Empty bowls were placed in the middle of the table to receive leftover food that could be given as alms. Clare routinely placed most of her share of the meal there, then sat waiting for the others to finish. "She saved the food they were given to eat, put it aside, and then sent it to the poor," the family watchman recalled.

Clare continued praying and fasting in Assisi as she had in Perugia. While girls her age strove to improve their complexions with herbal acne remedies like distilled water from cowslip leaves, Clare sought the remission of sins by fasting and wearing a hair shirt next to her skin.

The eminent feminist scholar and medieval historian Caroline Bynum has written that no matter how lofty a medieval adolescent's stated intentions might be, no matter how great her devotions, a girl whose religious practices were so extreme that she starved herself for the love of God in the devout Middle Ages was also rejecting, in a way that made her above reproof, everything her family represented or strove for. Girls posed a problem for their families, particularly families lacking sons. Records of the thirteenth century show that women's life expectancies were greater than those of men since wars and fighting killed off males even faster than childbirth claimed wives. Surplus women abounded. Fathers had to increase dowries, which included clothes and jewels, to make their daughters more attractive to a limited pool of suitors. Fathers pushed early marriages to shift the burden of supporting their daughters onto their hus-bands. Girls typically married between the ages of fifteen and seven-teen, men typically after twenty-five. Bynum believes daughters felt these pressures and resented them, felt guilty about their strain on a family's resources, and were also angry that once a dowry was paid, their family's obligation to them was done.

Eating itself was a rite of family life, and food was rich in mean-ing. To reject it was a shocking thing. Bynum writes that in an era when food was hard-earned from soil and climate, and famine was a constant threat, medieval people treasured the grains, fruits, and plants that had sprouted from the earth. Most knew the orchard that produced the olives they ate and the field where their barley had been seeded. The harvest was a time of festival and a hedge against the barren winter ahead. Householders or the servants who were essential to their lives laid up stores of root vegetables and preserved what they could in salt and oil and looked forward to the time when planting began again.

Food was the one resource that women controlled. It was their source of power in the medieval world. Food and the women themselves were sources of life. Women were responsible for a family's sustenance, even in upper classes where noblewomen supervised female servants who prepared it. Women who nursed babies produced food from their bodies for their children. In fasting, Clare not only showed devotion, she showed defiance. What motivated the medieval female adolescent to fast was not a desire for holiness, but unacknowledged rage.

By sixteen, Clare had been of marriageable age for some time. Not only was Clare beautiful, but as the eldest daughter of a man without a son she had the greatest claim to Favarone's property. A young noble Ranieri de Bernardo became her prominent suitor. She rejected him, however, saying that she planned to devote herself to spiritual life and to remain a virgin consecrated to God. Decades later, during her canonization process, Ranieri would testify that he had asked her to marry him many times, but she always refused him. He had continued to hold out hope, he said, but Clare could not be persuaded. She was adamant and showed no sign of relenting. She continued to tell him that she had no interest in his proposals; she wished to have no conversation with him unless they spoke about the greatness of God. One has the sense of a young woman who felt herself cornered—increasingly desperate to rid herself not only of an unwanted suitor but of the topic of marriage altogether.

Clare did indeed have the right to refuse him. Only a few decades before Clare's birth, Pope Alexander III had issued a series of decrees stating that if a marriage was to be valid, the bride and groom must each, and separately, speak out their consent. Thus, feudal lords had lost control over the marriages of their serfs and subordinates, while fathers could no longer force a son or daughter into a marriage they did not wish. Of course, even so, only those with the strongest wills could resist familial pressure to agree to an unwanted match.

Custom would not have allowed Clare to remain unmarried and live in the family home, but radical options were available to her if she wished to remain unwed. One was the nearby Benedictine convent Saint Paul of the Abbesses, intended for the daughters of wealthy families. A more controversial possibility was to join a community of unmarried women in the town of Panzo, just north of Assisi. This innovative living arrangement began to appear throughout Europe in the middle of the eleventh century. It offered some surplus women without husbands a way to survive with dignity. For others, it was a way to avoid unwanted marriage or the dangers of childbirth. At least in the beginning, the women's independence and self-sufficiency attracted suspicion and scorn. Those who banded together to live religious lives without taking strict religious vows were called "bizoke" in central Italy during Clare's lifetime. To history they are known as Beguines. One theory of the origin of the term is that it was derived from Albigensian, the name of a heretical sect that attracted so many followers that it became a serious threat to the church. But the Beguines in fact were Roman Catholic women loyal to church teachings but intent on creating a life for themselves outside the control of priests or husbands.

Ortulana and Favarone would not hear of any alternative to marriage, however. They wanted Clare to marry Ranieri, and with the help of relatives who must have included her belligerent uncle Monaldo, they pressured the unyielding young woman. Meanwhile, she was not the only young person giving the family trouble. Clare's cousin Rufino, son of her uncle Scipione, had distributed his share of the family wealth to the poor and joined a band of beggars called the Lesser Brothers, who were led by a merchant's son who had lost his reason, fallen out with his father, and now preached the Gospel.

Rufino's defection started with a piece of dung. While on business for his father he saw a man named Barbaro swear at a comrade. Rufino was used to shouting and fighting, although it never failed to frighten him. The surprise for Rufino was what came next. The angry Barbaro turned pale with remorse, stepped back from his antagonist, and fell to the ground. He reached for an animal dropping and placed it in his mouth as if it were bread. "Let the tongue that poured out the poison of anger upon my brother eat dung," he said in abject apology.

Rufino had never seen anger melt in such a fashion, and decided to learn more about the Lesser Brothers, who begged for their food, slept on the ground, and seemed truly happy. In the months that followed, Rufino visited and prayed often with them and their leader Francis, son of the merchant Bernadone. He was not impulsive like Francis and he took time to gather his courage but finally, confidently, he joined them.

Francis saw in Rufino a man who needed to be freed from the anxieties that had plagued him in the world and nipped at him still. Since Francis had overcome his own great fear of lepers by kissing one, he believed that a similar shock would help his new brother. He told Rufino to face his fear of people by preaching to them in one of Assisi's churches. And so on a Sunday in 1211, worshippers found one of their noblemen standing in the pulpit, bare-chested and clad only in his breeches for all to see. He was so terrified that when he began to speak, words failed and nothing emerged from his mouth but gurgles and pips.

Scornful laughter ricocheted from the pink limestone walls, sparkling on shafts of clear morning light from the pierced windows and dancing on the flickering flames of overhead oil lamps. Veteran Crusaders, scarred from the blows of the Saracens, laughed. Young men dreaming of wealth laughed. Privileged young women, with nothing to concern them but their prospective husbands, giggled as well. Rich and poor, noble and common, all were united in laughing at the ridiculous Rufino.

Someone shouted, "Look, they're doing so much penance they're going crazy!" and the laughter grew. Then, like a child learning to talk, Rufino gained control. His gasps turned to syllables, then to words, then to sentences that were coherent. It was the first time the worshippers had heard pious words—or indeed a strong statement of any sort—from Rufino. "Dear people, flee the world," he stammered. "Give up sin. Restore to others what belongs to them if you want to escape hell. But keep God's commandments and love God and your neighbor if you want to go to heaven."

At the back of the church, a short gaunt man of about thirty years appeared, as naked as Rufino, his face white and strained. After sending Rufino to Assisi, Francis had thought better of his idea and rushed to Assisi. When he arrived, Francis had followed the howls that were pulsing through Assisi's empty streets that Sunday morning, knowing the guffaws would lead to the man he was seeking. He drew the stares first of the people in the back as he passed, then of those closer to the front. Rufino continued in his talk. "...And do penance," he urged in halting words, "because the Kingdom of Heaven is drawing near."

Stepping up to the pulpit, Francis put his arm around Rufino and led him down to the safety of the shadows. Then he returned to the lectern himself and stood as if to display himself for their judgment. Once he had been the hope of Assisi's merchant class, a ready fighter who harassed Rufino's kinsmen and sacked their property. Then he had taken up residence in a decrepit church, begun begging in the streets, and retired to a cave where he had become a magnet for other fools like himself, including the pitiful Rufino. But the Francis who stood before them was not a madman. He was a calm and commanding presence. He spoke of Christ, who had been stripped naked, whipped, and paraded before a jeering crowd of the very people who had cheered him as a king just days before. The world had hated Christ, Francis pointed out, so who could trust the judgment of the world?

As he spoke, Francis made the Lord so real to them that he shamed the scoffers, touched their hearts, and transmuted their emotions, so that their laughter soon faded to solemnity, and, for many, puddled into tears. Finally, when he was done, he blessed them all. With the recovering Rufino, he departed.

Around the time of Rufino's dubious preaching cure, Francis sent word to Clare saying that he would like to meet her. Perhaps Rufino had told him of her character and strength, her determination not to marry and her dedication to help, as best she could, the poor. Exactly how Francis's invitation came to her is lost to history. Perhaps Rufino, prodded by Francis, appeared at the family home and conveyed the message through a trusted servant. However it may have happened, Clare agreed to meet the former merchant and she went secretly to him, without her parents' knowledge, accompanied by the sisters Bona and Pacifica, the latter being old enough to act as chaperone. Francis, for his part, brought with him his companion Philip, sometimes called Philip the Tall. The place would have been one where the girls were free to go without compromising their honor and also where Francis and his companions would not arouse suspicion or curiosity. Most likely they met in and around the Cathedral of Saint Rufino. Its priests, or canons, allowed Francis to stay in the crypt or in a small building in its garden whenever he came to the city.

One pictures Clare and Francis meeting face to face, she a young woman in a heavy, long silk tunic and veil befitting her rank, and he, unkempt and close to thirty, in a patched cloak he received from a freed serf. Clare was five feet tall, almost average height for a woman, but only an inch shorter than he. Her features were a bit uneven and her jaw was strong despite her oval face. Her long, wavy blond hair fell loose as was the custom for unmarried girls. Her smooth young hands were as yet unscarred by manual work and she kept them folded in her lap. As Francis talked, her deep-set blue eyes grew animated, and she smiled.

In contrast to the fair Clare, Francis was short and dark. Descriptions and images painted during his life portray a thin face with straight dark eyebrows and small straight lips surrounded by a black beard. His physique was slight and wiry, even in an era when the average male was five feet five. Clare was not afraid of him, nor was she appalled by his appearance and demeanor. Instead, she saw in him her true life calling. She decided to follow the simple instructions he took from the Gospel: "Sell what you have and give to the poor." (Matthew 19:21) "If anyone wishes to come after Me, let him deny himself and take up his cross and follow Me." (Matthew 16:24) "Take nothing for your journey." (Luke 9:3).

Clare found the prospect of serving the poor far more engaging than the comforts and honors of her own privileged position. Property, servants, and luxuries presented her with a confusing array of distracting choices. Renunciation, on the other hand, expanded her sense of her own importance in life, and left her with nothing to worry over as she escaped her parents and concentrated her will on the exacting circumstances around her. Poverty is anything but simple. Whether or not she knew it then, poverty demands one's wit, talent, and strength in the complex business of survival. Perhaps Clare longed for a life that required such things of her.

Over many months she continued to meet Francis in secret as he elaborated his vision of a community of women living the life of the Gospel, preaching, and helping the poor and the sick of Assisi. Communities of laymen and women, many of them living side by side under vows of poverty and chastity, were already growing in the cities of Europe. Since the eleventh century, beginning with some monks and priests, many lay people grew critical of the church for such things as the lax morals of its priests and bishops who bought their appointments. Reformers wanted to return to the spiritual ways of the first Christians as told in the gospels. Francis had undoubtedly encountered many of these people during his travels, first as a merchant and then as a wandering preacher himself.

Among his models were the Waldensians, who were followers of Peter Waldo, a rich merchant of Lyons who had distributed his money to the poor and had begun preaching around 1160, half a century before Clare met Francis. Waldensian women preached alongside the men. As their good works in helping the poor and the simplicity of their lives won them many converts and sympathizers, communities sprang up in the territories of today's France and Germany. But they ran afoul of the church when they pointed out the sinful lives of many priests and when they rejected the idea that Christ was present in the Eucharist. They adopted the Our Father as their only prayer because it came directly from Christ without the taint of priestly corruption.

Since Francis sought to avoid conflict, he was more interested in praising the clergy than in condemning them or anyone else. Another lay group still more to his liking was the Humiliati, who were centered around Milan in Lombardy. Supporting themselves as weavers of wool, the Humiliati were faithful to the church and under its protection. In 1200, Pope Innocent III approved their three orders or divisions. One consisted of cloistered men who wore the tonsure and were allowed to leave the group and return to the world at will. A second order consisted of married people living with their families and engaging in trades but living in strict observance of the Gospels. Yet another—and perhaps it was this one that inspired Francis to seek out someone like Clare who did not wish to wed—consisted of lay men and women living in separate communities but following the pure life of the Gospels.

Francis, however, had made the lepers part of his brothers' daily lives. They not only brought them food and gave them words of encouragement, they lived with them both in Assisi and wherever the brothers wandered. He expected the women in his movement to do the same. After a year of meetings and discussions with Francis,

Clare decided to join him and become a Lesser Sister, a counterpart to his brothers. Pacifica agreed to join her.

In preparation and over the objections of her family, Clare exercised her legal right to sell her inheritance as well as a portion of that of her younger sisters, which reduced their value in the marriage market. Family members offered to buy her jewelry, which probably consisted of pieces of gold or silver set with stones, but as they did not meet her price, she sold it instead to someone who offered more money, possibly a wealthy supporter of Francis, like Guido, the Bishop of Assisi—a confidant of Francis and a protector of the Lesser Brothers.

Clare used the proceeds to build her future home. She entrusted the money to Bona, who conveyed it to Francis for the restoration of the Church of Saint Damian. Established centuries before by religious hermits, this simple little structure had been taken over by priests and slowly fell into ruin. In 1205 it became the place of Francis's conversion to the life of the Gospel. The young merchant had gone there to pray for guidance and heard God say, "Repair my church." Francis took the words literally and believed he was meant to restore its walls, using what materials he could find, buy, or beg. Slowly, however, he came to understand that he had a wider mission to the world.

Francis decided that his beloved Church of Saint Damian would be the place for Clare and the Lesser Sisters to live. When visitors, not all of them supportive, found him working on its walls again, he looked up from his labors and announced, "I am building a house for fine ladies." His plan was to turn the church into a hospice-like dwelling with a sleeping loft above a large room taking up the entire ground floor. This had slits instead of windows for air and minimal light, the better for the lepers' privacy and comfort. The design was ambitious enough that he probably had the advice of an experienced builder, possibly one of his own brothers who had joined him after a life as a mason or carpenter. He had probably learned something of masonry when he repaired the nobles' houses, which was required by the Peace Pact.

Archeologists who have studied his renovations at Saint Damian suggest that he removed floor tiles from the crypt. These may have been what he offered as a reward for the gift of building stones. Singing hymns of praise, Francis walked through Assisi asking citizens in the streets and squares to give him building stones to repair the church. "Whoever gives me one stone will have one reward," he announced. "For two stones, two rewards, for three, three rewards."

As Francis completed his work, Clare and Pacifica prepared to leave their families and their old way of life. Clare persuaded Bona to go on a Lenten pilgrimage to the far-off shrine of Saint James the Great, most likely in the company of Clare's mother. Safely away from Assisi, Ortulana could not be held responsible when Clare and Pacifica escaped the family home, nor could Bona accidentally betray them or be implicated in what the older girls had done. Thus Clare, Pacifica, Francis, and his brothers were left free to plan a course of action.

Clare attended Mass the morning of Palm Sunday in May of 1212. By long tradition, marriageable young women on that holy day made the procession through the church in a commemoration of Christ's entry into Jerusalem. Their more immediate purpose, however, was to exhibit themselves, their availability, and their wealth to suitors. While the other girls went to the altar to receive blessed olive branches and display their charms, Clare remained in her seat. Bishop Guido himself brought a palm branch to Clare, possibly as a signal or possibly to take the opportunity to tell her that it was time to act.

That night, when the house finally quieted and everyone was in bed, Clare and Pacifica crept to a side door. It was usually barricaded with wooden beams and an iron bar, but they were able to push it open. They stole down the slope toward the darkened lower town, then out the Moiano Gate that led through groves of gnarled and twisted olive trees to the plain below. Surely at least one of the brothers joined them at some point, most likely Rufino who would have been able to hide in the family home and help them with the locked door. The fugitives hurried toward the distant light of Saint Mary of the Angels two miles south of Assisi, a tiny church affectionately called Portiuncula or The Little Portion, where the brothers made their home. Francis's first followers greeted Clare and Pacifica with flaming torches that illuminated them all as Clare and Pacifica vowed that they would live according to the Gospels and be obedient to Francis and to the church.

In an ancient custom symbolizing total surrender to God and the rejection of earthly vanity, Clare stood as Francis took a pair of scissors and sheared off her long tresses, which dropped in heavy locks to the ground. Francis then cut Pacifica's hair and proclaimed both of them Lesser Sisters and penitents like the brothers under the protection of Francis. Elated by the solemnity of the occasion, the two women proceeded with an escort of brothers to Saint Paul of the Abbesses, the Benedictine convent for women from wealthy families an hour's walk away on the outskirts of Bastia, near the Chiagio river. In 1201, about a decade earlier, Pope Innocent III had given these nuns the right of asylum, proclaiming that any violence committed there would be punished by excommunication. And so, in this nunnery for the daughters of nobles, Clare and Pacifica were left to await the consequences of their actions.

The next morning the Offreducci discovered that Clare and Pacifica had disappeared. While their frantic families set about to find them the next morning, the young women passed their time acting as servants to the nuns from noble families. Having sold her inheritance, Clare arrived as an indigent woman, and as such was to do the work of the place, whether it was drawing water or carrying slops from the kitchen, all the time mindful that trouble was looming.

Clare might have taken special comfort in Psalm 34, part of the liturgy for that day of Holy Week: "Brandish the lance, and block the way in the face of my pursuers; say to my soul, 'I am your Salvation.'" The next day, a Tuesday, she found again the words of the Psalmist: "When they were troublesome to me, I was clothed with haircloth, and I humbled my soul with fasting and poured forth prayers within my bosom. Judge, O Lord, those who wrong me; war against those who make war upon me. Take up the shield and buckler and rise up in my defense."

That afternoon, Clare's uncles and cousins appeared in full armor at the convent door to take her home. Agreeing to meet them in the chapel, Clare rejected their insistence that she return. When they moved to seize her bodily, Clare rushed to the altar and claimed the law of sanctuary. She pulled the veil from her head to reveal her shorn hair, the sign of her religious vows. Frightened and desperate, Clare clung to the altar, a place where no one who wished to remain in the grace of God might lay hands on her. The Benedictine nuns now intervened to end the ruckus and persuaded the men to leave, probably by reminding them that the convent was under the special protection of the pope, who had the power to excommunicate anyone who did violence there.

Clare's actions indicate that her escape from her family was carefully planned according to church and civil laws, very likely under the guidance of Bernard of Quintavalle, a wealthy lawyer from Assisi who had been one of the first to join Francis and was on hand for Clare's stay at the convent. Bernard's next task was to get her out. Since Clare and Pacifica had not joined the Benedictines, the power of the convent to protect them was limited and so Francis, Philip the Tall, and Bernard took Clare and Pacifica to new lodgings with the Beguines in Panzo about four miles away. Surely the two women were disguised for the journey, perhaps as two Lesser Brothers. The men were incapable of fighting off armed knights, but Bernard of

Quintavalle could use his knowledge of church and local statutes to plot every move so that Clare and Pacifica would be protected by canon law.

Francis returned to Portiuncula and Clare and Pacifica adopted the Beguines' routine, but they were eager for their own place to be finished so they could begin their own work. As the reality of her new life dawned on her, Clare discovered just how painfully she missed her younger sister Catherine and prayed to God to inspire the girl to leave the world and join her and Pacifica. This prayer was quickly answered, perhaps because Catherine found herself ensnared in hasty plans to marry her off before she too could flee. For whatever reason, and by whatever means, sixteen days after Clare's escape Catherine reached Clare and declared herself ready to leave the world with her. Beside herself with joy, Clare embraced her. "I thank God, most sweet sister," she said, "that He has heard my concern for you." The girls rejoiced, but they were by no means safe.

The story of what followed paints a family portrait, however typical it might be, that does much to explain the resolve of its women. Certainly it indicates why Clare wanted to control her own destiny and took refuge in a greater power than family authority. It also provides concrete reasons why young women would be eager to forgo marriage and motherhood as well as earthly comfort. When the men of the family, including her father, uncles, and cousins, realized that Catherine had disappeared, they knew where to find her. A dozen male relatives travelled to the Beguines' dwelling which, having no consecrated altar, enjoyed no papal protection. Still, the men pretended to be resigned and reasonable so that the Beguines invited them inside. But when Clare, Catherine, and possibly Pacifica were brought before them, they demanded of Catherine, who had taken no religious vows, "Why have you come to this place? Get ready to return immediately with us."

One of them, perhaps the sisters' father Favarone, grabbed Catherine's hair, which was as yet unshorn, and began dragging her toward the door. The other men fell upon her. Shoved, kicked, beaten and pummeled, Catherine cried out in terror to Clare. "Dear sister, help me! Do not let me be taken from Christ the Lord!"

But Clare could only fall down weeping and praying as the attackers tore Catherine from the house. They dragged her down a sloping path, ripping her veil and tunic and yanking out hanks of her hair that they dropped in the road. Men and women working in the fields and vineyards heard the ruckus and ran forward, ready to help the nobles capture the hapless girl. But however eager these laborers were to ingratiate themselves to the knights of the Offreducci family, and however strong they might have been, they were unable to carry the battered girl over a flowing stream. Perhaps Catherine's assailants had injured each other in their frenzy because for some reason no one could move her. Taken aback, someone scoffed with meaningless bravado, "She has been eating lead all night. No wonder she is so heavy!" Then, as Catherine's enraged uncle Monaldo prepared to strike her, a pain shot through his raised hand, leaving him immobilized with his arm above his head.

Meanwhile, Clare collected herself from her fright, rose from the floor, and ran down the path after them. She found Catherine inert at the foot of the hill encircled by menacing peasants, armed men, and their uncle Monaldo, now frozen, whether by his own conscience or a heart attack, with a pain he would suffer for days. Monaldo had no choice but to leave Catherine to Clare while his stunned men led him back to Assisi and the peasants scattered. After her foes were out of sight and unlikely to return, Catherine revived. Clare helped her arrange her torn and bloody clothing and supported her as they walked slowly up the hill back to the Beguines.

Imagine Francis's feelings when he joined the women in Panzo. Whenever he learned the story, after hearing of Catherine's courage he declared that henceforth she was to be known as Agnes. This adolescent girl was his only female follower who was recorded as having been physically beaten, so Francis almost certainly named her after Saint Agnes of Rome, an adolescent virgin martyr who was celebrated for bravely facing torture by fire or decapitation in the fourth century.

Francis imparted his blessing over the bloodied scalp of the new Agnes, cut off what remained of her hair, and then proclaimed Clare's younger sister consecrated to the service of God under his protection and that of the church. A few days later, the three Lesser Sisters moved for a third and final time, again possibly in darkness and disguised as men, to Saint Damian, their own house, built in part with the proceeds of Clare's dowry as well as what she had appropriated from those of her sisters. There at Saint Damian—even as forces gathered that would obscure the record of her deeds—the light of Clare began to glow.

2

The Young Francis

I N THE DAYS when Clare's noble family schemed and battled to preserve its wealth and privileges, the winds of fortune favored Francis's father, Peter Bernadone. The grandson of a serf, he was sufficiently appealing in mind and person to win the hand of Pica, a prosperous widow with a two-year-old son named Angelo, around the year 1180. Probably her late husband, a well-established textile merchant for whom Peter worked, had been much older than she. In marrying Pica, Peter gained control of the business and capital she inherited when she became a widow, as well as the use of the dowry she had brought to her first marriage.

In 1182 or thereabouts, Peter also gained his own son, whom his wife named John. Possibly Pica named the boy after her own late father, since naming a baby after someone who had died was the custom of the time, known as "remaking," or recalling the person to the living. John was soon baptized at the Cathedral of Saint Rufino, where a priest blessed him and placed a small amount of salt on his tongue, an exorcism that forced the baby to drool away any lurking demons. Then John was immersed in a carved stone holy water font three times and baptized in the name of the Father, Son, and Holy Ghost. This not only absolved him of original sin but made him a citizen of Assisi and established a lasting bond with all who had ever been baptized there.

Some accounts say that at the time of the baby's birth Peter was away from home, possibly engaged in business at one of the great trade fairs in France, and that when he met his infant son on his return to Assisi he renamed the boy Francesco or Francis. Others say that later in life the boy's own love of the French language inspired the change. Whether or not he grew up being called John, the world would come to know him as Francis of Assisi.

His charm was great, his circumstances fortuitous. He was whimsical, wheedling, and so indulged that he did whatever he wished to do before anyone could tell him otherwise. Francis rejected foods that he declared to be foul, and when he chose not to eat, neither his nurse nor his mother had the power to coax him to open his mouth. If turnips, beets, or carrots did not please him, he could choose pork or carp, pike, eels, and trout, fish that were carted in tubs of water from Lake Trasimeno to the family table. They were served along with light bread made of wheat, rather than the inferior grains such as spelt or sorghum that poorer folk relied on.

The family—Peter, Pica, Francis, and his half-brother Angelo, who was his elder by about four years—lived in relative luxury in the Badia district around the Benedictine monastery. The exact location of their house is debated, and it is possible they changed dwellings during Francis's childhood, but tax records show that Peter's assessment was in the top third of the neighborhood. This indicates that the building was imposing, with an outside staircase winding past balcony windows to a tower. Arnaldo Fortini, historian of Assisi, places the house just west of the busy forum on Portico Street next to the Church of Saint Paul. If so, the family would have faced the giant Benedictine monastery with its thick walls pierced by narrow slits and its bells that tolled each hour to regulate the life of Assisi.

On the other side of the Bernadone house, separated by a passageway, stood the Church of Saint Nicholas, which jutted into the forum where vendors set up their stalls. Peter's shop would have been at street level. The family lived, slept and ate on the second floor where a fire blazed in the hearth day and night, giving light as well as warmth. The interior was dark. The small, grudging windows were fitted not with glass but with oiled parchment that filtered out much of the sun, and the oil lamp that hung from the ceiling burned dimly even in blackest night. Rush mats sprinkled with sweet woodruff imparted the fragrance of vanilla and new-cut hay. Panels of embroidered linen hung from the stone walls. At mealtimes a servant set up a long trestle table in the middle of the room and covered it with cloth and bowls. In the kitchen, which shared its chimney with the main room, kettles and cauldrons hung from the hearth and live fish swam in a leather tank next to a wooden pickling tub.

A prosperous couple of the merchant class such as the Bernadones would have had a heavy canopied oak bed with a mattress of feathers. Elaborately carved, footed chests preserved their linens safe above the damp and clammy floors. Servants and their mistresses waged ceaseless war against fleas and bedbugs, covering mattresses with white sheepskin so that they might better pick out the tiny vermin. When other techniques failed, which they inevitably did, the women set out lures of rags soaked with honey.

At sunrise, when the watchman unbarred the city gates and the town crier began to make his rounds, Francis and his brother Angelo could awaken to the lowing of the cows and the bleating of the sheep being driven to pastures outside the city walls. They could run to their mother's room and watch her comb and plait her long dark hair before they broke the night's fast with a piece of toasted bread or one soaked in watered wine, while the servants began the work of preparing for the main midday meal. Food preparations were endless—the servants peeled, cut, chopped, and minced, then boiled, stewed, and baked all day.

On market days, a knowledgeable woman like Pica would guard her purse wisely. At a poultry stall she looked for the youngest, plumpest fowl. Once her selection was made, the butcher decapitated it on the spot. At the bakery she brought bread whose weight and price were fixed by law and marked with the baker's own seal. A woman of Pica's status would also supervise the care of the family's clothes, have the woolens cleaned with lye, and stains rubbed with chicken feathers rinsed in hot water. She would also tend the household garden of lettuce, sorrel, beets, and scallions.

Only in the streets did the small Francis encounter the harshness and the hubbub of life. Merchants selling copper pots, wooden buckets, and porcelain mortars with pestles shouted out the merits of their products, and loudly shared their latest personal news, while carpenters sang familiar tunes to accompany the pounding of their hammers. Horses and donkeys crowded the streets, bringing produce and other goods, jostling the people and fouling the pavement stones. Hooded monks with clasped hands hidden in their sleeves made their way to the bishop's house to haggle over his share of their tithes and land. When his parents brought Francis out to the streets, if they heard even a distant sound of a leper's bell, they quickly and sometimes roughly snatched him away from approaching danger. But they could not shield him from the disturbing sight of the many ragged beggars and crippled crones. The first few years of Francis's life were a time of famine. Storms raged through the land, felling men and oxen, snapping trees into twigs and flooding crops. Food was scarce and many starved, but the disasters touched the Bernadones less than other people. Merchants like Peter had ways of coping. They brought home apples, olives, and other foodstuffs in their caravans while others ate whatever grasses and clover had survived the floods.

Peter invested his profits from trade by buying land from nobles who wanted to turn their holdings into usable goods and money. His extensive holdings included fertile property along the River Tiber and up on Mount Subasio, where thyme grew plentifully. He also acquired olive groves in the valleys as well as acreage irrigated by bubbling streams.

In the late summer months, the family escaped the heat in town by going to the cooling brooks and shady trees of their farm along the River Torto. They locked tight their house in Assisi and left the shop in the care of a trusted assistant. Then they travelled by cart over the Todero bridge, past the tower of Saint Savino, and across the stream known as the Path of the Pool. At each crossing, and finally at the castle of the noble Bassano near their property, Peter had to pay a toll to whoever controlled the road. These levies dated from the Roman Empire and remained in place to benefit whoever was in power. At this time, the local nobles disdained the rise of bold and acquisitive upstarts like Peter Bernadone. They tried to keep their hold on the merchants and others who regularly used the roads by charging for the right to pass.

On October 2, 1187, when Francis was about five, Jerusalem was captured by Saladin, the sultan of Egypt, Syria, Yemen, and Palestine, and his Muslim army. When Europeans learned of it, they wept openly in the streets, as if every tragedy they had ever experienced in their own lives had struck again. It was said that on hearing the news, Pope Urban III suffered a seizure and died. Jerusalem was the heart of Christianity, the city that God had entrusted to Christ's followers since the end of the First Crusade nearly nine decades earlier. Jerusalem was the mirror of His glory, and the center of Christendom's maps. The faithful felt that if Jerusalem was lost, then no one might be saved. Troubadours and jongleurs abandoned songs of love in favor of laments about the devastation that had come upon the people of God. By night and day priests in the churches chanted Psalm 78: "Oh God, the heathens are come into thine inheritance, they have defiled thy holy temple..." Surely Francis in his imagination became a Crusader, taking back the True Cross and winning glory for all time.

At about this time he entered school at the Church of Saint George. His father and others of the rising merchant class paid to have their sons learn to read and write basic Latin so that they might make and understand contracts. In later years, messages that Francis wrote in his own hand show him to have used a script that was common in the Apennine mountain areas at this time, particularly among the legal professions. He was painstaking in forming his letters, pressing parchment firmly with a wide and rigid nib, and setting off each letter with wide and uneven spaces. Above all, Francis as a boy would have been required to become proficient at counting and sums. He would have been taught the new Arabic concept of zero as well as their numerals, which Italian merchants had introduced to Europe. He surely learned to use the abacus, making beads dance and slap against each other so that they played a little tune as he figured up his sums.

Francis's first schoolmaster was named John of Sasso, or Giovanni di Sasso, who owned vineyards and land in nearby Panzo and Correggiano and who also ran the church and hospital of Saint George in Assisi. As Francis trudged down the Street of the Block and Chain from his house toward the Gate of Saint George on the way to school, he might pass shepherds wrapped in animal skins leading their goats up the road, gallant youths staggering home from a night of carousing, and servants bearing clucking chickens and soft white rabbits in their baskets.

Early in Francis's school year, which began after Easter, came the feast of Saint George, Slayer of Dragons, on April 23, when winter was finally over and the roads became less muddy. Banners of red and blue, the colors of Assisi, hung from every window and balcony. Gaily pealing church bells and blaring trumpets called the people, all dressed in their finest raiment, to the Mass of the Knights. Every noble warrior in the area attended. Inside, candlelight danced in the thicket of gleaming swords and lances, and the snorts and neighs of horses blended with the hymns of the service.

In the afternoon, knights put on their heavy armor, took up clubs, lances, and shields, and staged a contest in the Roman amphitheater just outside the city's ancient northwest walls. The men of the town, refreshed by the noon meal and emboldened by drink, joined in behind them, carrying stones and wooden sticks. When Francis was a boy, the number of contenders was so great that the games not only filled the ancient arena, they spilled down to the meadows just outside the city walls. The men divided into two teams, half from the upper town, the others from the lower one on the city's western slopes. A herald sounded his horn and the battle began, mildly at first. With the two sides far apart, small stones arced through the air, then insults. Each year the game turned into a melee, yet when boys were eight, they were allowed to join in, keeping well to the rear behind their battling elders.

At the end of the year, as if to burn off the early winter gloom before the solstice, came the December Liberties, a licentious festival held, paradoxically, in Francis's parish Church of Saint Nicholas. For two weeks everything was upended—the altar became an auction block, lewd women danced in sacred places, husbands became public lechers, and masters served servants. Fortini reports that the altar was also used as a dining table where wine flowed so freely that an orgy spilled out to the public streets. Half-naked women, their hands and ankles bound, were crowned with flowers and tossed into carts to be wheeled and sold to the highest bidder.

This ancient festival was the custom in cities throughout the Italian peninsula from Roman times, when it was known as the Saturnalia. In the Christian era, civic officials, including local bishops, declared that its purpose was to instill humility by overturning the usual hierarchy. It began on December 6, the feast of Saint Nicholas, patron saint of merchants. He had been the Bishop of Myra, in what is now southern Turkey, in the fourth century AD, and he died on December 6 in 345 or 352. Little else is known about him other than that as a young man he made a pilgrimage to Egypt and Palestine and soon afterward became bishop. During the persecutions of the Emperor Diocletian he was imprisoned, but when the Edict of Milan made Christianity legal in 313, Nicholas was released. Nicholas was credited with many miracles both before and after his death. He grew to be so popular in both the Roman and Greek churches over the centuries that he became the patron saint of seamen, travelers, bakers, and children, which was the origin of jolly old Saint Nick. Italian merchants appropriated him as their own by stealing his body from Myra in 1087, with the help of fishermen from the city of Bari in the heel of Italy. After their escapade, they enshrined his body in a cathedral they built there.

On Saint Nicholas's feast day the year that Francis turned fourteen—that age of nascent beards, spotted faces, and cracking voices—he was expected to participate in the December Liberties. The boys of the town would elect a son of a rich and influential man to be their own "bishop," a boy to lead them into their introduction to the bawdier aspects of being a man, with society's permission to strut with pride and boastfulness, to dominate women, and to command everything within closed doors. Meanwhile, the real bishop decamped for his house outside the city walls, taking with him the Sacred Host, which the faithful believed to be God Himself in the appearance of a wafer of bread. Thus the prelate removed himself from the goings-on at the same time he was complicit with them.

The feast began at dusk the night of December 6, and with it the boy bishop's weeks of rule. He was dressed in a copy of the bishop's alb and miter, given a crook of office, and was installed in a seat in the church high above the swirling activity. Thomas of Celano, Francis's contemporary and first biographer who knew the Assisians of Francis's day, was probably alluding to these rites when he described the wickedness of the parents of Assisi. He wrote of the city's children in the first chapter of his first work on Francis: "But when they begin to enter the portals of adolescence, how do you think they will turn out? Then, indeed, tossed about amid every kind of debauchery, they give themselves over completely to shameful practices, in as much as they are permitted to do as they please. For once they have become the slaves of sin by a voluntary servitude, they give over all their members to be instruments of wickedness and showing forth in themselves nothing of the Christian religion either in their lives or in their conduct..."

Thomas of Celano continued: "These are the wretched circumstances among which the man whom we venerate today as a saint, for he is truly a saint, lived in his youth...indeed he outdid all his contemporaries in vanities and he came to be a promoter of evil and was more abundantly zealous for all kinds of foolishness."

When the revels concluded on December 28, the Feast of Innocents, the boy bishop, on his father's horse, rode out with his retinue to the actual bishop. Surely smirking with knowledge of what the weeks had entailed, the elder man poured him wine and inquired about the number of souls he had baptized, and asked for the boy's mock blessing. The December Liberties over, the boys returned home, with childish innocence behind them.

The adolescent Francis was undersized, with a plain, unremarkable face, except when he was in action, or so we can believe from the few descriptions we have of his appearance when he was a grown man. He joined Angelo, and possibly his mother Pica, in working in the shop. Although women played no role in city government, those who owned property belonged to the commune. Women did have legal rights, could participate in business, and belong to guilds.

Each morning one of the two brothers removed the bar from inside the window of the shop and raised the shutter to start the day's business. The rules of the merchant guild directed their every movement, standardizing the members' actions so as to deny an advantage to anyone. All sellers of cloth were to display goods in a showcase or spread them on the counter. When a sale was made, the merchant unrolled the fabric and measured it with the official *canna*, or metal measurement stick, of Assisi. Whatever the length might be in another city, in Assisi the *canna* for silk was twenty-three inches, for wool twenty-seven, and for linen forty-one. If there was ever any doubt that a merchant used a true measure, his *canne* were taken to the People's Tower in the forum and measured against the standard ones embedded there.

Obeying these regulations, meeting these guarantees, and submitting to these practices were the responsibilities that came with the guilds' control of all the various trades and crafts. Guilds began to develop in the early Middle Ages when, after earlier centuries of barbarian invasions and scarcity, Europe opened like a scarlet poppy in the brightness of spring. Starting around 1000 AD, the climate changed, the earth warmed, and more benign temperatures fostered a safer, better-nourished, and more comfortable society where people could thrive rather than just subsist. This relative spike in Europe's temperatures, which might have resulted from a lack of volcanic activity, is sometimes called the Medieval Climate Anomaly, a period that was two to four Fahrenheit degrees warmer than those of the early twentieth century. In this era, Greenland was green. The population grew rapidly. Estimations of how many people might have lived in medieval Europe at any point vary widely. It seems there were as few as twenty-five thousand in the year 1000 and perhaps more than seventy-five thousand in 1300. Whatever the actual numbers may be, it is agreed that there was a doubling.

With this came an increase in economic activity and significant cultural and political change, including the expansion of cities. In the new commercial climate, traders and craftsmen found that they had common complaints, challenges, and interests. They banded together into guilds to regulate production, minimize competition, negotiate equitable prices, and maintain high standards. Members paid to belong. An important aspect of guaranteeing quality was the establishment of journeymen and apprentice programs to teach craftsmanship. Fines were imposed on those who traded outside the guild or violated the charter, but members were also protected. The guild cared for those who fell sick, and when that failed, burials were arranged and orphans were provided for. Members and their goods, horses, and wagons were also protected when they travelled, especially to trade fairs. They also promised upward mobility and muted class distinctions, which might be why one-time apprentices often married their masters' widows, as Peter Bernadone must have done.

In Francis's era, these guilds were at the height of their power because they functioned best in small, relatively contained markets. Commerce was organized and arranged, for the most part, without the involvement of church authorities or the nobility. As soon these societies gained the exclusive right to do business in a town, they began to govern it. While guilds developed all over Europe, the Italians were the best organized, and the Italian peninsula with eleven million people was the most urbanized area of the continent.

In the daily life of a merchant like young Francis, monotony surely alternated with commotion when several customers would appear demanding attention, some knowing what they wanted, others waiting to be shown. Occasionally a person of means might appear and spend so much on himself and his retinue that he would double a week's receivables. At night the Bernadones, like other businessmen, toted up accounts. Medieval shops had counting rooms behind their selling areas where in the dim light figures were checked, and silver alloy coins minted in Lucca were placed along with letters of credit—a recent innovation—in the corner strong box and secured with a huge black lock.

On slow days, in the timeless manner of business, anxiety rose. Bad weather or fickle luck might prevent customers from appearing for days. A merchant's debts were steady, but his income was not. Profits and debts from property were balanced against accounts from their textile trade. As clever as they could be as businessmen, merchants were at the mercy of rain and sun, drought and locusts, the resources of their customers, the health of wool-producing sheep, on whether the pope and emperor were at peace, and on what a lord would charge for the use of his roads.

Travel was part of any merchant's business. Even in the thirteenth century, they needed new goods to tempt old customers and to attract new ones. They also needed to see what was developing in the world. For two centuries, since the First Crusade captured Jerusalem in 1096, knights had returned from the Levant bringing new and exotic fabrics, medicinal and culinary spices, and fragrant incenses from the East. Europeans, including those of the Italian peninsula, were eager for such new delights as silk, sugar, and dates.

One Norse merchant of the era gave his son counsel that Peter might as easily have imparted to Francis: "A trader faces many dangers, often far from home and among people who are alien, even if they follow the True Faith. Always be agreeable and discreet and, if it is possible for you, be quiet, even as you are on the alert. Do not allow yourself to be thought a coward, but be slow to take revenge. Learn to read the skies, even when you travel by land. Every day, learn something that will profit you, something that you can turn to coin. Take care in choosing business associates and ask Almighty God, the Virgin, and Saint Nicholas, patron of merchants, to be your guide."

As a young merchant Francis entered a wider world. His father specialized in fine cloth from Flanders, where Champenois, a medieval form of French, was spoken. Through this trade Francis acquired a love for and delight in the language, although he did not speak it well. Surely it was as a young merchant that he took the first of many lifelong trips outside Assisi to travel with his father or one of his father's agents to the Champagne fairs.

Shortly before Francis was born, Henry I of Champagne, known as "The Liberal," who governed the province from 1152 to 1180, instituted the fairs of Champagne. He had taken stock of his immense land with its poor growing soil, swamps, and dense forests and decided that since agriculture was largely impossible, commerce would be its source of wealth. Champagne was situated in the middle of the richer domains—Flanders to the north, Lorraine to the east, Burgundy to the south, and the French lands to the west. All were safe and well-administered. His principality was the chalky, disadvantaged center that lay at the heart of all of it. Henry I saw that he could draw in their prosperity by hosting a series of six fairs in the towns of Troyes, Provins, Lagny-sur-Marne, and Bar-sur-Auge throughout the year. He assured the merchants safe conduct for themselves and their merchandise, not only in Champagne but along the routes they travelled. If merchandise was lost or injuries were suffered, he would give them recompense. Italian and Flemish merchants enthusiastically accepted his invitation. The Italians, who were the most practiced in the innovation of banking, purchased wool, silk, gold, silver, skins, and wares from the Levant at the fairs. Thanks to periods of truce, and despite years of war, a market for luxurious goods from the Muslim world developed during the era of the Crusades. Italians, notably the Bernadones, were also especially interested in purchasing fabric from Flanders and raw goods from France that they improved through various cleaning, dyeing, and texturing processes.

Getting to the Champagne fair was an enterprise in itself. If Francis and his party travelled by land, they would have gone up the Via Francigena, the ancient road that led from Rome through Tuscany and Lombardy to France and on to Canterbury. To reach the "hot fair" in Troyes that began on the feast of Saint John on June 24, they would have left Assisi in mid-May when the hilly lands had drained and the mud had hardened. With their pack horses loaded with goods, including the dark dye for which Umbrians were noted, and root vegetables to cook along the way, they would have left the city through the Saint Antino gate, the old Roman portal that opened to the plain, and rode past silvery olive trees to the foot of Mount Subasio. There they could join a caravan from Orvieto, and travel up along the Tiber River toward Florence to one of several passes in the Alps, through precipices, crevasses and lingering snow drifts.

As they journeyed, they were joined by merchants of other Italian cities speaking their different dialects. The Florentines were the most sophisticated and talked only of commerce. They were far more interested in credit and exchange rates than whatever wares they were engaged in. Those from Arezzo had a hearty friendliness and a false frivolity that covered the fact that they trusted no one but each other. The Bolognese were knowledgeable in many things: points of the law, the stars, or even disputes in theology. They digressed about such matters just for the pleasure of talking. The clever Venetians avoided all of them by taking the longer route across the Tyrol and the length of Switzerland to enter France.

When garrulous merchants grew tired of their own voices, they listened to the sounds of whirling brooks or the falling of tree limbs through the cool mountain air. Descending the western slopes of the Alps, and packing away their woolen caps and leggings, they journeyed to Lyon, where they merged with merchants from the Iberian Peninsula and Languedoc for the final leg north through the Saône Valley. Led by a standard bearer and accompanied by crossbowmen and pike carriers guarding their flanks, they wound through the heavy woodlands of Champagne. Finally, after a journey that might have taken six weeks, they saw the sand-colored walls of Troyes, which were a formidable twenty feet high and eight feet thick.

About ten thousand people lived there permanently, but visitors multiplied the population. Stalls of wool and spices were set up in the permanent halls in the section of the city that housed the fair. The air was filled with the clinking of coins, the shouts of those who feared being short changed, the stinging scent of cinnamon, and insinuating jasmine smoking on incense braziers. Merchants' eyes widened and hearts raced to see piles of richly colored velvets and satins, thick wools, and gossamer silks. Notaries, clerks, and bankers scurried throughout the stalls, drawing up contracts. Some bartered, some accepted letters of credit, and some lent money, even as money changers raked in florins, lire, ducats and the *bisanti* of the Saracen, or Arab Muslims.

Every three hours bells tolled, marking times for prayer and reminding merchants of how much daylight was left for business. When he was given time to roam the city, Francis saw the citizens of the world passing under the universal language of shop signs: three gilded balls—intended to be pills—denoting the apothecary, a white pole with red stripes for the barber, a unicorn for the goldsmith, and a horse head for the harness maker. Growing up in the textile trade, Francis would surely have studied the various costumes—the fez of Spain, the soft chapeaux of the French, and how they differed from the brimmed caps of England. He would also have seen a gigantic construction project. Around 1200, when Francis would have been in Troyes, Bishop Hervé was rebuilding the city's cathedral that had been destroyed by fire in 1188. Its shell was set in place and thick poles were lashed together to form scaffolding. Inside, a crane that was powered by yoked oxen trudging in a circular path lifted building stones. Its dimensions were so vast that it was nearly twice the size of Assisi's Cathedral of Saint Rufino.

As much as it was a marketplace, the international fair was also a hotbed of ideas, customs, and culture that drew troubadours who travelled Europe, particularly southern France and the Italian peninsula. Troubadours were essentially poets or composers, who often employed jongleurs to perform their songs. In warm months they journeyed from noble house to noble house entertaining patrons and seeking new ones. In winter they settled in friendly courts to sing away the winter tedium. They came from all orders of society: craftsmen, prelates, knights, or bakers.

At the fairs, Francis would have heard the tales of the Round Table by Chrétien of Troyes. His stories of magical Arthur, conflicted Lancelot, valiant Percival, their adventures and ordeals, and their quest for the Holy Grail had spread throughout Europe. Even in Assisi, girls of Francis's generation were named after Queen Guinevere. Jongleurs in French lands and elsewhere would have made the ideals of chivalry—military skill, courage, zeal for justice, generosity and loyal service—especially vivid. The imaginative Francis took them as his code of conduct. Of all the stories he heard, he loved best the French epic poem *The Song of Roland* that told the tragic, although fictitious, exploits of Charlemagne's troops on the Iberian Peninsula, their readiness to face death, and their call—too late—for rescue.

After he returned to Assisi, Francis joined a group of young male and female singers and dancers who entertained during city festivals. They sang of greed and loneliness, of the fragility of life, and of joy and despair, but their crowd-pleasers were songs of lust and longing. They called the baker, the dyer, and the merchant into their revels in early May. The streets were strewn with rushes, mint, and lilies. Francis's troupe crowned themselves with early flowering vines. The men dressed in velvet against the lingering chill while the young women tied their white mantles from one shoulder, as if they had cast off winter's snow.

One song of the time began with a young woman lying safely on her bed in her father's castle. Her quick feet darted and turned as she rested her chin on her folded hands like a maiden falling asleep. Meanwhile, a young man took the role of a blackbird who comes through her window and sings in her ear, telling her of life and love. The girl awakens and dances into the imaginary street to wait for the unknown love that would pull her into life.

Piping, bowing, dancing under banners hung overhead from balcony to balcony, the blackbird then sang:

Come loving damsel,
My lady, come and dance.
Away with your old wizened husband!
Throw off your stingy lord with his knotted money purse!

This was close to the truth of many households, yet many a maiden and young wife joined them in the streets, inspiring knowing looks from neighbors.

Another sang:

A man only lives when he lives joyfully
To live another way is not to be alive.

The freedom of the songs contrasted with Francis's days in the shop, which were fettered despite the promise of his privileged future. Much was expected of him and all the townspeople knew it. One day when a simple man came across Francis in the street, he removed his cloak and spread it on the ground before him. "Here is young Francis," he would cry. "He will accomplish great things and be honored by all the world!"

Given that Francis would later abandon the merchants' trade several times, it is safe to assume that he was often bored and that he contemplated other ways of life. Sitting in the shop he stared at piles of fabric until the colors swirled into blood-red seas of battle, where in his mind Francis defeated the Saracen, slashing at them with his trusty sword, freed the True Cross, or rode with Charlemagne against the Infidel in Spain. One day his imagination inspired him to create a costume that was half coarse burlap sacking and half madder-red brocade. When he wore it in the streets, laughing people called out insults to him and his tailor but he did not care. The adolescent Francis was eager for immediate action, and he would find it by terrorizing his betters, the nobles who continued to hold the merchants in their sway.

3

Fighting Man

IN THE FOUR MONTHS between September 1197 and January 1198 two great thrones in the Christian world fell vacant. One was that of the Holy Roman Emperor in Aachen, the other of the Pope in Rome. These voids created seismic shifts that convulsed the worlds of Francis, then in his fifteenth year, and Clare, age four. Henry VI, the Holy Roman Emperor, King of Germany and of Sicily, died in September 1197 in Sicily at age thirty-one, officially from malaria but possibly from poison. Since his son and heir, the future Frederick II, was only two years old ambitious nobles, including the boy's uncles, divided the imperial territories among themselves and fragmented the empire.

At the Vatican, on January 8, 1198, the very day that the aged Pope Celestine III died, Lothar of Sengi, reputedly his nephew, was elected his successor at the age of thirty-seven. Taking the name Innocent III, he would turn himself into one of the most ambitious and influential popes in history. Innocent III began his reign by announcing that he was far more than the representative of Saint Peter on earth, as all previous popes had done. He was the representative of Christ, the Son of God, the second person of the Trinity. "We are the successor of the Prince of the Apostles, but we are not his vicar, nor the vicar of any man or Apostle, but the Vicar of Christ himself," he said.

He also claimed dominion over large swaths of the Italian peninsula from the area of Ravenna to the Roman region, what the church called the Papal States or the Republic of Peter. It asserted that in the fourth century the Emperor Constantine had given this territory to the popes and that Pippin the Short had expanded it in the eighth. Innocent spent the first summer of his papacy, from July to October 1198, in the so-called papal towns, successfully undermining the authority of the nobles that the late Emperor Henry had installed. Duke Conrad of Urslingen, who governed several cities in Umbria, left Assisi in an attempt to ingratiate himself with the new and influential pope. He departed the hulking fortress called Roccia Maggiore, or The Major Rock, that Frankish invaders had erected on the mountain outside Assisi's walls two centuries earlier, and rode away to meet the pope in Narni. There Conrad yielded Umbrian fortifications, including the citadel of Assisi. However, the people of Assisi seized their chance as soon as Conrad decamped. They stormed Conrad's rock, destroyed it, and ended the rule of the nobility in Assisi.

Empowered, the Assisians went on to attack castles outside Assisi in a reign of destruction that sixteen-year-old Francis must have taken part in. The castle of Bassano, where Francis's father paid tolls near one of his properties, was also destroyed. The nobles who remained in town, including Clare's family, were not spared. The chronicler Arnaldo Fortini noted, "Judging from the lists of ruined houses that have come down to us in the records, it must have been a fierce no-holds-barred battle." Four-year-old Clare was surely terrified.

The pope was not pleased that the newly loyal Conrad and his vassals had been routed and that that the people of Assisi had deprived him of a major fortification. Innocent showed favor to their rival Perugia, where the Assisi nobles took refuge. He spent two weeks of September 1198 there and put that city under his protection. Assisi's

Bishop Guido's first allegiance was to the pope, so he excommunicated the leaders of the commune, which deprived them of the sacraments, including communion, proper burial, and marriage ceremonies. But Guido was also loyal to his city. After a brief time, the excommunicated persons told Guido that they had visited Innocent III in Perugia and had received his blessing. Whether he was truly gullible or simply willing to be fooled, Guido rescinded their excommunication just before he received a communication from the pope warning him not to believe the word of the Assisians unless they carried a papal letter verifying their claims.

Meanwhile the commune, with Francis probably among them, erected its own gate at the ruined site where the Rock had stood. Through it they gained free passage to roadways without payment to the nobles. In Perugia, the injured lords prepared to return to Assisi to exact revenge. Over the next two years the commune of Assisi joined with Gubbio and other cities to combat them.

In November 1202, these allies poured into Assisi, many of them knights on horses. Women, children, and men cheered from their open windows as archers, foot soldiers, and knights covered in steel filed by. The clang of their swords and shields was the rumble of a machine of war. Dogs barked in excitement, not knowing whether to chase these invaders from their turf or join them in the hunt.

In Francis's time the only requirements to become a knight were to have armor, a horse, and some training. Communes demanded calvary service of those who could afford it. Merchants, who had acquired wealth that rivaled that of the nobles, were able to buy into knighthood and thus gain social advancement for themselves and their families. These "new people" became armed knights of their communes in north and central Italy. Only later in the thirteenth century, and largely as a way to curb the roving violence of the warrior class, did knighthood throughout Europe become based on heredity and generations of lineage.

The warriors from Assisi and their allies pledged themselves to defeat Perugia before Assisi's chief consul. Attired in his red and blue robes and conical hat, he then strode to the *carroccio,* the official four-wheeled chariot of Assisi, in the center of the plaza and rang its bell to summon citizens to prepare for the battle to come. Such carriages, actually rolling platforms, had been features of the Italian city-states and their war-making for nearly two centuries. They carried the city's standard, an altar where a priest said Mass before battle, and trumpeters to call the men to prayer, attack, or in the worst case, retreat. These wagons were hauled into the middle of the fray to serve as a space for tending to the wounded and allowing soldiers to regroup.

By this point the Bernadone family prepared for a siege, filling casks with water and laying up stores of grain and salted meats so they could hold out if things went wrong and Assisi was overwhelmed. Francis said his prayers and donned his armor, a shirt of mail that reached his knees and a bowl-shaped helmet that came to a slight point and featured a metal strip that came down over his nose. This armor would in fact save his life not because of the protection it offered, but because it signaled that he was one of Assisi's wealthier combatants.

As church bells tolled, the forces of Assisi marched out though the gate. Nearly all men under the age of seventy were obliged to serve. Foot soldiers, under the banners of their neighborhoods, wore the everyday garb of their occupations as tanners or bakers, most with no more than quilted fabric to shield them. The city government supplied them with swords and pikes. Civic pride bound them together and made for comradeship, but they were also subject to strict laws that imposed fines on those who did not fight and gave the city the right to set fire to any home that gave shelter to a deserter. Others marched behind the banners of their guilds—the merchants, the shoemakers, the butchers, and tax collectors. After them came the archers and finally the knights, including Francis. Then four white bulls drew the chariot bearing the banner of Saint Rufino, the city's patron saint. Singing hymns to the glory of God, they marched through spent, brown autumn fields, past poplar trees, and crossed the Tiber River at the point where it narrowed to a shallow gravelly stream. In the early afternoon, with the enemy waiting on the plain below, the soldiers arranged themselves on the Collestrada hill. Then the archers climbed to their places atop the castle on that hill near the lepers' hospital. Although the foot soldiers were the least protected, they led the charge. Knights on horses followed. Francis was among those slashing and thrusting their swords, nearly trampling some of their own men. All were soon trapped in the clot of fighting, unable to go either forward or back. They were pulled, shoved, and slashed where they stood, knelt, or lay.

The battle overwhelmed the lepers' hospital. Hacked and broken bodies covered the field. Hands and feet were strewn about like leaves, entrails burst from gutted men, and eyes were carved from their sockets. Assisian forces were overwhelmed and their prized chariot, the embodiment of their city, was split in two.

Francis himself was captured. The Perugians handled him roughly, but seeing that he was a person of wealth who would attract a ransom, they tired of their sport, pulled him to his feet, tied his hands, and shoved him along a path toward their city. During the Middle Ages, men taken as prisoners of war were usually knights, because the lower orders were so ill-equipped that they died in battle or afterwards were killed outright because their relatives were too poor to pay for their return home.

Along with other Assisian survivors, Francis was marched through Perugia's massive gate as the victorious Perugians jeered and pelted them with offal and excrement. They were shoved together into a fetid prison and heard its door slam shut. A torch in the underground passageway would have been their only light. It hardly mattered whether they could see or not, with all their success turned to defeat, ruin, and death. Their cowering ill-prepared nobles whose fortresses they had stormed two years before had triumphed with the help of a trained army from an enemy city blessed by the pope.

In the following days Francis, who as a boy ate nothing that did not please him, was given whatever scraps would keep him alive until he was ransomed. Murky water was available for those with thirst too great to bear. Their straw was changed only when guards could no longer bear the stench. The captives' skin grew scaly and raw with dryness. Their cuts and scratches swelled with pus over the weeks as the men shat, pissed, vomited, and wept. In this desolation, according to his early biographers, Francis found peace. The concerns of a merchant, the cost of linen or its quality, had no place here, nor did rumors of floods that would wipe out flax crops or drown wool-producing sheep. He announced to his companions that they were all free. When the others shunned the prisoner who injured one of the group, Francis urged them to forgive him, as he himself had done. The suffering ones would hear none of it, however, and called him a fool. His reported amiability cannot be the full story of Francis's experience here because he emerged from it seriously weakened in spirit and in body. His ebullient old self was shattered.

With Assisi less than a day away from Perugia, negotiations for his release should have begun immediately. While many scholars have said that Francis was imprisoned for a year, it is unlikely. Precise dating of many events in Francis's life is challenging, but the wounded, maltreated prisoners for whom Perugia intended to fetch ransoms would not have survived that long. Once Peter Bernadone knew that his son was alive, he would surely have been willing to pay any price for his return. It likely that after no more than six weeks his father delivered a purse sagging with ransom money to the Perugians. Imagine Francis carried outdoors where, for the first time since the battle, he saw daylight and a sky so blue it might have been the Virgin Mary's cloak. Shutting his eyes against the low December sun, he was placed in a cart lined with sacks of grain, covered in blankets, and carried home past the field of carnage. Imagine his weeping mother falling on her boy and mingling her tears with his own. Possibly what remained of his filthy clothes was cut from him and his body washed and his face shaved.

Francis's convalesce was slow. He had days of despondence when he could not leave his bed. Often he lacked the strength to talk or the interest to see anyone. Spring called him to life, yet he was unable to respond, as though his youth had faded. These afflictions opened his mind to new and unaccustomed thoughts.

In April, walking with a cane, he began to move about the house. Surely his father bustled with plans for all they might do in the shop when Francis was well, the cloth they would buy, the inventory they would sell. His old friends and fellow warriors must have visited him, and the mothers of the slain. Lamentation was common enough in Assisi in 1203, as was the thirst for vengeance. In January when townspeople heard that the prominent Assisi noble Marescotto di Bernardo Dodici had pledged to acquire a house in Perugia, they tore down his family home on Assisi's Saint Rufino plaza. But such destruction did not prosper the merchants. Five months later, in June 1203, Assisi's consuls decided to rebuild their city and reconcile its factions. They appointed three arbiters to decide how justice might be served. By November they issued a Peace Paper announcing that the commune would build new houses in the city for the nobles it had displaced and repair damage done to their homes, provided there were no alliances with those outside Assisi. All were to be pardoned for their offenses and vengeance was proscribed. However, neither side honored this. In subsequent years scant compensation was made. Matters dragged on, punctuated by occasional skirmishes, raids, and looting.

Despite his malaise, Francis planned to take up arms again. Evidently, he believed his life path was that of a soldier and that he had acquitted himself well at Collestrada. The Crusaders' capture of Constantinople on April 13, 1204 may have stirred his martial spirit especially since Assisi reconciled with the pope and on June 8, 1204 swore allegiance to him, providing new opportunities for war. Innocent III was now focusing on Sicily, which he saw as an essential staging ground for troops intending to recover Jerusalem from the Infidel. For this he planned to rely on a new hero by the name of Walter of Brienne.

With a force of only sixty knights, on October 22, 1201, a year before Francis battled at Collestrada, Walter had defeated the king of Naples and the imperial German forces that had ruled southern Italy in a series of battles. The grateful pope made him ruler of Apulia and Campania, which he had conquered. Walter also captured the imagination of young men on the Italian peninsula who were eager for glory, riches, and a fight. They saw his triumph as an inspiring contrast to the blundering of the Fourth Crusade, which had detoured from its path to the Holy Land and attacked the Christian city of Zara on the Dalmatian coast in mid-November 1202. After Walter reluctantly and belatedly agreed to the pope's demands to capture Sicily, he called for fighting men.

A nobleman of Assisi, perhaps someone Francis had fought beside at Collestrada, decided to join Walter and fight not just for his cause, but for a share of booty and fame. Learning of this, Francis decided to go as well. Francis prepared himself for this new role of knight errant, a life that would suit his restlessness, add to his family's status, and leave his brother Angelo to carry on Bernadone business interests.

Francis was so extravagant in his purchase of armor that he outshone this nobleman. Wearing it, and carrying a wooden lance of oak or fir, he seemed a knight like any other. Possibly he felt like one as well until the day he was on horseback and chanced upon a man he knew to be a seasoned warrior. This person was walking along the road because he had lost, through defeat in battle or other misfortune, his horse and his regalia. Francis, feeling he was a pretender in comparison to this man, dismounted and gave his knightly trappings

to one he thought had more right to wear them. Francis then procured new armor, possibly through the largess of his long-suffering
father or from his own purse. Assisi law obliged the commune to
award forty fiorini of gold to a citizen who "through their prowess"
was named a knight.

Once again fitted for battle, Francis felt his confidence of old as
he awaited his day of departure. But one night he had an unsettling
dream. In it he saw his house, which was usually filled with textiles,
filled with lustrous coats of mail, bucklers, armor, and an array of
weapons. Amazed, Francis asked "Who is all this for?" His guide
told him they were all for him and for his knights.Medieval people, including popes and emperors, set great store by what came to
them in dreams. Bible stories shaped their world view and in them
God had spoken to man. Through them he had tested and rewarded
Solomon, and sent an angel to tell Joseph to keep Mary as his wife.
But medievals also recognized that the devil could come to them by
night, and so such messages had to be weighed carefully. Francis,
who believed that he was to do great things, had no such reticence.
He took his disembodied visitor at this word. He awoke certain that
he would become great and prosperous, possibly someone of the stature of Walter of Brienne himself, and yet he found he was not happy.

In later years when his closest companions recounted this story,
they revealed that even centuries before Freud people had a sense that
a person's mindset effected their dreams. His friends observed that
his generous gift of his armor to the penniless knight had inspired
the dream: "We think that this magnanimity played no small part in
bringing out the vision."

Unable and unwilling to admit his turmoil to his family or friends,
for possibly the first time in his life Francis turned to God. Until
now he had shown no signs of piety. The divine being was as real as
the sky to medievals, but Francis to this point seems to have given
Him as little thought as he gave to the air. What he knew came from

Gospel and Bible stories presented at Mass, from what the priests and his parents instilled, and from the huge painted crucifixes bearing the Redeemer of the World. As for specific prayers, he knew the Our Father, the Hail Mary, and the Nicene Creed. These were so universal that in the Middle Ages recipes would have such instructions as "boil for the time of saying six Our Fathers."

Thomas of Celano, whose primary task was to proclaim Francis's holiness, reported no virtue in him, except a kind manner, until he was almost twenty-five. Although Francis undoubtedly attended Sunday Mass, Thomas finds nothing godly in his early conduct while noting, in fairness, that he had been a kind youth, adaptable and friendly, even though his good humor made him look foolish. For this reason, Thomas said, people liked him.

Now Francis felt the need to pray privately, but he found solitude unbearable. He invited his closest friend, a man whose name is unrecorded, to accompany him to the countryside. He said that he had found a treasure in a cave and he asked his friend to be a lookout for bandits while he retrieved it. But Francis kept the chaos in his soul to himself. He did not confide that he was in misery, that he was uncertain of his way, and that he was conflicted over muddying the smooth path that seemed ordained for him.

Francis entered a grotto and prayed for direction as he contemplated his sins, perhaps reliving scenes of combat and the slaughter of his comrades on the city streets or the field of Collestrada. Whatever Francis experienced in the cave, when he emerged into the light, his friend found him to be so exhausted and under such a strain that he was nearly unrecognizable. As a contemporary related, it was as if one person had entered the cave and another had come out. His friend could only suspect that Francis had wanted that missing treasure very much.

Francis resumed work in the shop on the merchants' forum, but he still dreamed of escape, of adventure, and of danger to drive misery and frustration from his mind. If Francis no longer found satisfaction in the person he had always been, he was disturbed by the person he was becoming—holy, pious, removed from the world. Whatever outward respect he had paid such persons in the past, they were in fact the opposite of what he and his friends truly admired. In those days a hunchbacked woman crawled through the streets of Assisi, hideous, piteous and repellent to all. She haunted his thoughts as he feared he would end up like her.

Surely his struggles affected his work, made him neglectful and prone to error in calculating profit and loss and in promises made to customers. If Francis were honest with himself, he knew he was making mistakes, and failing hurt one who usually flourished and was admired either for his own efforts or for his status in the world. He announced he was planning new great things, but for now he was not going to Apulia to take up arms again.

As it turned out, this was a wise decision. Things went badly for his intended liege lord. On the night of June 14, 1205, around the time that Francis decided not to join him, Walter was encamped in Sarno on the Amalfi coast outside a German fortress, apparently without reliable security. The German Dipold of Acerra with some of his men crept up to Walter's tent, cut its ropes, and collapsed the structure upon him. They then stabbed and hacked him to death. In aborting his journey to Walter, Francis had avoided defeat and possible death. However, his return to the family home cannot have been without embarrassment or gossip. Some must have thought that the Francis who had fought honorably at Collestrada was now something of a coward. He himself was bewildered by his impulsive actions and his disinterest in pleasures that had given him joy before.

———

Francis did leave Assisi on a pilgrimage to Rome in the company of a few of his fellow merchants, probably staying with other merchants who joined them along the way. They could have reached Rome after about a week's travel, mingling with the cavalcade of medieval humanity: traders with carts of goods, jongleurs with monkeys, ladies and their retinues of knights, and shepherds with flocks that crowded travelers off the road. There were also the wandering dispossessed, some with withered limbs, others with the vacant grin of the feebleminded.

Descending the road from Monte Mario on the northwest, he caught sight of the imposing towers and massive palaces of the city that even in the days of Augustus Caesar was called Eternal. From afar, the bridges and ruins, the marble churches and monuments, were all shining in golds and creams, pinks and ochers in the crisp, cool air.

In the early thirteenth century, Rome was a city of popes, wealthy families fighting each other for ascendancy, and the lower orders that existed by serving all warring factions. Like Assisi, Rome had a commune. Its members had just erected a new Senate building on Capitoline Hill. From that point in the center of Rome it battled for dominance with the pope who sat in the Lateran Palace on the city's southeastern wall. Professional beggars outnumbered tradesmen. Whereas Lombard and Tuscan cities were flourishing through inland commerce, and Venice, Genoa, and Pisa had maritime trade, Rome relied on the aura of past glory. It was as if the animating spirit of the once-mighty city had shriveled so that only a footprint remained where a giant had stood. Householders and servants laundered clothes and linens outside their doors and cooked on open fires in the street, singeing the air with the smell of burnt fat layered on the aroma of decaying garbage and animal dung.

It was obvious that in the past a higher order of man had built the Parthenon, the Colosseum, the now-ruined baths, and the triumphal arches. These wonders were as much a part of daily Rome as the Cathedral of Saint Rufino was to Assisi. Perhaps these monuments were too familiar, because they were often plundered for materials.

A practical builder thought nothing of throwing an ancient statue or pediment into his lime kiln. Others were more appreciative. One stone cutter found a statue of a Roman general in a stream, cleaned off the mud and silt, polished it and set it in the middle of his workroom for inspiration.

Like other visitors, Francis would have had the chance to pace the width of the Parthenon and to attempt to throw a pebble to the top of the capital in the baths of Diocletian. Hot sulfur water baths were available, but those who found their stench too great allowed themselves to merely wash their hands. None of these wonders restored Francis to himself. Instead, he gave in to impulses that were decidedly odd for a young man on an out-of-town journey with friends.

At the tomb of Saint Peter, Francis had the opportunity to purchase blessed oils and holy water and light a lamp in honor of the apostle Peter, whom Christ chose to lead his followers. Standing in the flickering light, Francis became aware that the faithful had been stingy with their offerings. Enraged, he drew a fistful of coins from his purse and shot them through the grating, creating such a clatter, and showing such generosity, that when he turned his heel those around him stared at him in amazement. By tradition, the poor and disposed congregated at the bottom of the basilica steps seeking alms. He asked one of them to exchange his tunic for his own because he was curious to know what it would be like to be that man. Thus attired, he tried on the life of a mendicant by asking for alms, speaking in French as he would when he felt self-conscious, as if the language could shield him. But the experience, even the food he was given, gave him so much inexplicable joy that he would have joined them several more times if his shocked friends had not talked him out of it and pulled him away.

Once back at home he struggled to be what he had been before Collestrada—brave, energetic, carefree, ready for action—but he knew he was not the same as he went about old tasks. He could have been travelling to his father's property outside Assisi the notable day a leper appeared without warning on the road. There was no mistaking those with paralyzed muscles, unlidded eyes, and eroded noses. The body of a leper was such hellish terrain that even the church condemned them as bearers of evil. By law they carried clappers and bells to warn others of their approach, but if this man gave a warning Francis did not hear it. These ravaged people were Francis's greatest fear and the sight of them made him gag. If he came upon one, he turned his face and held his nose. This was not without reason, for not only were their faces putrefied, and their bodies reeking from their own rotting flesh and the encrusted rags they wore, they might spread their contagion wherever they went. Every new podestà, or mayor, had to search out and drive off any leper found living in Assisi. In the interim, townspeople were free to strike them down without any fear of punishment.

Based on the number of hospitals for lepers throughout Europe, medieval scholars believe that the disease might have been most widespread there during the twelfth and thirteenth centuries when Francis lived. Pope Alexander III was sufficiently concerned that he issued a decree at the Third Lateran Council in 1179 urging that they be separated from the populace and provided with separate chapels and cemeteries. In this the Vatican followed directives from Leviticus 13 and 14, which set forth laws on how to diagnose and treat the true sufferer, including by quarantine. Today modern medicine understands that leprosy, or Hansen's disease, is a chronic bacterial infection that incubates for as many as twenty years and is contagious only in its early stages and through prolonged contact.

But that day on the road, Francis stopped his horse. As he stared, the repulsive creature became magnetic. Francis dismounted and boldly strode toward what had previously terrified him. When the leper extended his arm asking for a coin, Francis brought the poisonous hand to his lips, as if in homage. Surrendering to his greatest horror Francis was in that moment set free.[†] It was as if he had plunged from a great height into a deep icy pool. In a sudden shock of revelation, he saw the power and force of all creation in the swirling energy of the hideous leper. In that man, whether he was real or a vision, he saw himself, destruction, salvation, and God.

Near his death, in his Testament, Francis would write that acceptance of the lepers was the decisive moment that led him to the service of God and man, "...I showed mercy to them. And when I left them what had seemed bitter to me was turned into sweetness of soul and body. And afterwards I delayed a little and left the world." That was Francis's turning point, but it was not sudden, as it had been for Saint Paul when he saw a blinding light. The return from Spoleto, the agonized prayer in caves, the casting off his tunic for a beggar's garb, all had been turnings as he staggered toward his destiny and relative peace. So elated was Francis by his encounter with the leper that a few days later he went to a house for lepers, probably the one run by the Assisi commune, Saint Lazarus of Arce, about two and a half miles south of the city walls. Leprosy was so widespread that nearly every town in Europe had at least one lazaretto, or isolated facility to care for them. Assisi had several and by some estimates there were as many as nineteen thousand on the continent. The establishments themselves were not unpleasant. Usually set on a hill, they consisted of multiple dwellings grouped around a chapel. Stands of trees sheltered them from the view of outsiders and so they had a safe world of their own. According to Fortini, the class distinctions of rich and poor, which were otherwise unbridgeable, vanished at Saint Lazarus, which was run by a chaplain who boarded there. If

---

† Some scholars doubt that Francis actually kissed the leper because this gesture occurs in the life stories of many saints, notably Martin of Tours. Hagiographers often included it to signal the outstanding holiness of their subjects. The act is, however, consistent with Francis's impulsive personality and with many of his later actions. Whatever the missing details might be, he said that his acceptance of lepers changed his life.

a person was found to be a leper, the commune consigned them here where they were given a grey tunic and veil. It is likely that revulsion, rage, and grief permeated the place. As Fortini imagined them, "their faces are as white as those of corpses, yet they still burn with all the desires of which life is cheating them." Into this atmosphere stepped Francis bearing a large sum of money, dividing it among the lepers and kissing each of their hands in turn.

His conflicts vanished. He wallowed in all that he had feared and he felt he had become whole. While he might not have recalled the delay as long, it was eventful and full of conflict because he was not yet ready to present himself as the man he had become.

Francis's friends elected him king of their revels, which may have been as much a tribute to his open-handed ways as to his sense of fun. But he now also took serious note of the needs of those whose poverty was its own kind of leprosy. He decided to help some of these by selling a bolt of valuable scarlet cloth that the Bernadones had acquired. Francis took it from the shop and sped to the market at Foligno a dozen miles from Assisi where he sold not only the cloth but his horse as well. Somehow he made his way home partly on foot, partly by catching rides on the carts of those who had sold their goods at the market. Less than a mile from Assisi he came to the tiny, dilapidated Church of Saint Damian, with its crumbling outbuildings that had centuries earlier been a Benedictine monastery. He decided to give the money to its priest.

The cleric, whose name was Peter, listened to the agitated young man, but he wanted none of his money. He was not persuaded when Francis fell to his knees and kissed his consecrated fingers that held the body of God at Mass. The priest knew Francis to be a reveler and a young man of sudden and reversible enthusiasms. He was afraid to accept this portion of the Bernadone fortune, even for the church, without consulting the young man's parents. But Francis would not be balked. The money was for God. He hurled the coins into the open window where some dropped clattering on the sill and the rest was deposited, as Francis intended, inside God's church.

Francis's early biographers wrote that God then spoke directly to Francis, telling him to repair the church and encouraging the idea that Francis would restore not just this tiny one, but the greater glory of the whole church. In fact, this supernatural drama, if it occurred, was less significant to Francis than his experience with the lepers. In summing up his life in his Testament, Francis did not mention God's speaking to him at Saint Damian at all.

The priest had not been wrong to fear Francis's father. Peter Bernadone had accepted, at least publicly, his son's giving away his costly armor almost as soon as he donned it, and the extra expense of his speedy purchase of a second set. He refused to believe that the family honor was stained when Francis aborted his mission to Apulia. That Francis's work had become unreliable was a problem, but it had been enough for Peter Bernadone that his son had survived the battle of Collestrada and the horrors of imprisonment. At least, it had been enough until now. He was alarmed that Francis had sold a costly piece of cloth and had given up his valued horse. He was dumbstruck that the youth felt free to give the proceeds away. Peter had indulged his erratic behavior, weighing it against his love of his son and the fact that there were times when Francis seemed stable, but the sale of the cloth and the loss of the horse were heavy weights that had tipped the scales.

Francis was not ready to deal with earthly consequences, nor at this point did he think they were particularly important. For a few days he hid in a pit, most likely the crypt of the Church of Saint Damian that could be reached only from inside the church by a set of smooth narrow steps hewn from rock. The space was about eight by twelve feet and had a seat hewn into its western wall, probably a remnant from its pre-Christian origins. He spent time sweeping the church and making small repairs, knowing that his father could not seize him on church property. According to Thomas of Celano's first biography, he hid also in a recess that he had prepared in a house, possibly the Bernadone country house in Stradetta, less than half a mile from this church, so that his whereabouts were both unknown and still within the familiar family orbit. Other early sources say he retreated to a cave. Possibly, he moved among these places.

Years later, Francis's closest companions would say that only one person in the Bernadone household knew of his hiding place. One is tempted to think that was his mother, yet surely she was under her husband's constant wary eye. More likely, a beloved servant with more freedom to come and go did not let his or her young master starve. After weeks of this existence of prayer and modified fasting, Francis found his courage and his resolve. He had chosen his path in life, which was not to be a merchant or a troubadour or a knight. He was to be a servant of outcasts and thus serve the Lord. Francis returned to Assisi, gaunt and slowed by his feral life. However confused and frightening the unraveling of Francis Bernadone may have been, townspeople knew that Peter had withdrawn his protection from his son. They sided with the father and they now degraded Francis by pelting him with showers of stone, mud, and invective.

News that his son had appeared sent Peter into frenzy. When he found him, he charged at the youth, pummeled him, and dragged him to the house where he had been raised and he chained him in a cellar room, much as he had been locked away in Perugia. While bitter family quarrels did not come under the commune's purview, its laws did allow him to imprison and beat his son for disobedience and for dissipating his assets. Coddling him and carrying out his every whim had not brought the boy to his senses. Harsh punishment was the only treatment yet untried.

Daily Peter threatened and beat him, expecting to drive sense into his son's scrambled head. Pica, who surely had also suffered from the behavior of her son, was more gentle, speaking to him, listening to him, and ultimately deciding that after months of anxiety and odd behavior, her son was choosing, at least for the moment, a life of prayer. When Peter left Assisi on business, Pica freed him. Francis set out for his cave, leaving his mother to face her husband, who exercised his right to beat the disobedient woman.

Peter was indisputably the head of the household, but Pica's inheritance from her first husband was the basis of the Bernadone fortune, according to Richard Trexler, and Francis would be heir to a share of it upon her death. Possibly she was in failing health, which made it imperative that Peter act before Pica could bestow any of her wealth or property on the erratic Francis or bequeath it to him to use for the church and for the good of her soul.

As a father Peter had been indulgent, but as a businessman he had to limit his risk. Francis had wasted money through high living and through almsgiving. Francis's largess could have been excusable as a sign of great family wealth, but now he was putting the source of their capital in jeopardy. At twenty-five he was of age. He was not a reliable steward of the family fortune, nor was he likely to become one, and the risk that he posed had to be curtailed.

Although Peter ultimately did receive the money Francis gained from the sale of the fabric, probably from the priest at Saint Damian, he did not let the matter end there. He asked the commune to void Francis's rights to the family fortune. However, since Francis was living in a church, he was considered to be an oblate, one living in the service of God, and thus civil law did not have authority over him. The commune said he must take the matter to Bishop Guido and so Peter did this.

Guido sent for Francis. Strong in mind, if no longer in body, Francis arrived at the bishop's palace in his dirty, ragged clothes. As townspeople caught sight of the mercurial merchant's son, now abased but formerly attired like nobility, the butcher set down his knife, the carpenter his hammer, and the servant her water jug.

Excitement mounted as word quickly spread. Barbers emerged from their shops, razors in hand. Matrons looked down from their windows and rival merchants shut their doors and headed off to see what would happen next to the young man who had become a disgrace and a fool.

The tribunal began at nine in the morning, the third hour of the day, on the bishop's plaza in front of the Cathedral of Saint Mary Major. Attired in a blue mantle and miter, Bishop Guido strode from his residence toward the steps of the cathedral and settled into the chair of his office, which had been placed under the arch of the main door. He took in the sight of the growing number of spectators, which included Francis's mother and brother Angelo. A ringing bell signaled the beginning of the proceedings, and the bishop called on Peter to state his grievance. Once he had his say, the bishop told Francis that it appeared that his father was in the right.

Chastened, indignant, and probably broken-hearted that his once-beloved father had taken so forceful a step despite the return of his money, Francis stripped himself bare, removing even the hair shirt he had purchased with earnings from his father, and placed the discarded garments in a pile. Naked before all who had assembled, his statement is recorded as, "Listen all of you and mark my words. Hitherto I have called Peter Bernadone my father; but because I am resolved to serve God I return to him the money on account of which he was so perturbed, and also the clothes I wore which are his; and from now on I will say 'Our Father who art in heaven,' and not Father Peter Bernardone."

The air was still, like the moment of quiet that follows a lightning strike. Peter, suffused with grief and anger, knew that Francis had placed himself beyond his father's power and beyond his help. He picked up the bundle and led Pica and Angelo home as the crowd stood stunned, with some moved to weeping. The bishop wrapped the shivering and naked Francis in his cloak, holding him and taking him under his protection. Francis had made his choice.

At the end of his life, he would say that the time between his discovery of the lepers and leaving the world was short, but in fact it was the process of several years. It began in the battle of Collestrata and his imprisonment in Perugia in 1202 when his sense of who he was cracked, leading him to surrender to the guidance of a dream. Waiting for answers, he sought to find his way through prayer, then people—jailers, outcasts, lepers—opened his door to God. If God chose Francis to be his messenger, he beckoned him through man.

$$\overline{4}$$

The Journey Begins

Francis had lost his place in Assisi, as well as his family home. He might have lived openly in one of the churches where he had hidden from his father, but he must have felt the need to make a break from his past because he headed north to the city of Gubbio through olive trees bleak in the purple night, crossing the bridge over the sparkling cold waters of the Tescio River. He traversed thick oak forests where animals had burrowed in for the winter and snow lay crusty and unspoiled. The cracking of brittle twigs was the only accompaniment to the songs of praise he sang in French. Alone and ragged, he was vulnerable. Robbers fell on him, but they were frustrated to find that he had nothing to steal. When he annoyed them by declaring that he was "the herald of a great king," they threw him into a snow-filled ditch.

He sought shelter at the Benedictine monastery of Saint Mary of Valfabbrica. It had been founded in the eighth century and had grown in wealth and power to the point that the monks had become warriors in order to protect their life and property. More recently they had fought with the Assisians at Collestrada and their defeat had greatly reduced their circumstances. The rule of Saint Benedict, Chapter 53, requires his followers to treat guests as if they were Christ himself and to give them special protection during their stay. Through the centuries, houses that followed this rule had saved many people during times of famine and pestilence. However, these particular monks did not take Francis in so much as they detained him as a servant. Willing to be of use, he remained with them a few days, sleeping by the kitchen hearth, living on nothing but broth, but happy to be out of the cold. His eager meekness incited the monks to grow so cruel that he was forced to leave. Whatever they did to him there, in the coming years they came to realize that the man who was revered throughout the Spoleto valley was the one they had memorably abused. The abbot then begged Francis to forgive him and his monks, which Francis did.

At length he reached Gubbio and his friend Frederick the Long Sword, the noble Count Spadalunga, who may have been one of his fellow captives in Perugia, who helped him. Gubbio, with a population of about fifty thousand, had wider streets and taller buildings than those in Assisi and was spread over the slopes of the steep Mount Ingino.

Over the course of the harsh winter, Francis settled into his new life, living with lepers, feeding them, and cleaning as best he could their moldering bodies and their sores. His place was with those who had no place, with those who served no purpose, and played no role, the people who were the discards of society. God's love became air and water to him. He knew that if people could give up sinning and fighting, the ways they hurt themselves and each other, and come to God, they would be filled with joy and peace just as he was, much of the time.

One can imagine that a man who had totally upended his life would have alternating moods, which when he was exhausted meant reevaluating the poor he was coming to know. Destitution does not make people pleasant. Francis had moments of contempt for their covetousness, their malice, their ugliness, their lice. When he was exhausted, they revealed themselves to be even greedier than the rich and far more interested in snatching a loaf of bread than in hearing the word of God. In some, misery had so congealed that they received the good things he did or gave with contempt, suspicion, and demands that he bring more. Francis was tempted to believe that what he was doing was folly and that he had made another mistake. He had survived the humiliation of aborting his service to Walter of Brienne, he could survive the humiliation of returning to the world. His father would welcome him as the prodigal son. His friends would mock him only for a while. He might never outlive the scene with Bishop Guido where he cast off all his clothes, but he could go back to the life he had been born to. He could sleep in a warm room, partake of delicious meals, marry and take a woman to his bed.

But those temptations did not win out. Dealing with people with whom he had nothing in common was no more tedious than doing nothing but bargaining over prices all day. The lepers revealed the insufficiency of his own old life because they were so utterly removed from it. They were without artifice or delusion. They could fool neither themselves nor others, as he seemed to have been trying to do through his imagination all his life, whether he was a merchant becoming a troubadour or an invalid pretending to be a knight. Surely in the lepers' ruined and bleeding faces, he saw the wounded of Collestrada. As he surrendered to the shelter of the leper hospice, he surrendered to God, God who was the bottom and purpose of the well into which he had fallen. If God, who in the person of Jesus, had demeaned himself to become poor, who was he, Francis, to disdain such a fate? He saw poverty and humility as one. To choose abasement was to abandon all that was pretense. It was to transcend the snares, sorrows, and failings of aspiration, of all that was demanded by a hostile world. He understood how humble Christ, the Son of God, must have made himself to veil his power and become human.

Yet if he was no longer the son of Bernadone, or a merchant, or a knight, he was still a son of Assisi and he needed his home. Had he been able to cut all earthly ties, as he proclaimed he had, he would have taken up residence in a city where he was unknown and where he could have avoided for months and years skirmishes with his past. Instead, in the spring of 1207 he returned to the streets of

Assisi where he confronted the people he knew, including his one-time social inferiors who seized the opportunity to belittle and insult him, and his former peers who expressed scorn as well as pity over his metamorphosis from dashing youth to humble servant of God. He forced himself to preach where he was known and went from door to door begging for food. He stood before the tower of the commune in full view of all. The "alms" he received—maggots, entrails, and discards from the medieval table—horrified him. The fastidious Francis forced himself to eat the slop and was dumbfounded that it did not kill him.

He completed repairs to the Church of Saint Damian and in the next three years moved on to restore the Church of Saint Peter of the Thorns, and then to Saint Mary of the Angels, called Portiuncula, or Little Portion, which belonged to the monks of Saint Benedict of Subasio. All three churches were well within three miles of Assisi and served rural people living outside city walls. He was frequently with lepers and often living in the wild with the dark night closing in upon him and the snap of a falling branch or a distant howl to tweak his nerves. He sheltered under pines and junipers, and in caves and hollows where rabbits and birds were his only friends. Living beside them, desperately lonely, he made their lives and their families his own. He understood the sparrows bringing twigs to their nests, much as he repaired church walls, the fox with her pups, the sprout fighting to burst through hard winter ground. He was one with God's creation.

But he was not one with the life of the town. One winter morning his brother chanced upon him, praying and shivering with cold. He was moved to goad a passerby, "Tell Francis to sell you a penny's worth of sweat." Francis answered with a smile. "Indeed, I will sell my sweat more dearly to my Lord." When Peter Bernadone crossed paths with his errant son, to cover his grief he swore at Francis. For a time an old man named Albert followed Francis. Francis asked Albert for a blessing every time Peter cursed him. Some consider him to be the unnamed first follower of Francis.

Francis leaned on Bishop Guido for guidance and comfort. Francis so valued this man, despite his temper and worldliness, that Francis throughout his life would see Guido in the priests of all ranks that he encountered. He never wished to see their failings or argue against them. He preferred to win them over through good will. "I want to love them, revere them and regard them as my lords," he said. Guido was unique in Assisi for recognizing in Francis a genuine penitent to whom the suffering of the crucified Savior was very real. Perhaps Guido was the man who found Francis walking alone on the road near Portiuncula in such an agony of sobs and grief that he seemed to be ill. Francis explained that he was crying over the suffering of the Lord. And he said that he should be in that state at all times because Christ's torments had been so great. With that, the man was moved to join in lamentations over the fate of the Savior whose suffering had ended twelve centuries before.

Francis typically dressed in a sort of hermit's garb, a greyish undyed tunic with a strip of leather tied tight around his middle. He carried a large stick as a staff and wore shoes on his feet. In Portiuncula at Mass on February 24, probably in the year 1208, the feast of the apostle Matthias who replaced Judas as an apostle, Francis heard the words of the Gospel in which Christ told his disciples to possess no gold, silver, or money of any kind; to carry nothing, not even a staff; and to preach the kingdom of God and penance. He felt that Christ had spoken to him directly. He pieced together a tunic with a cross-like shape, cast off his shoes, discarded his staff, and found a cord to use as a belt. Forever afterward he went forth to the world of Assisi, barefoot in a shabby garment, calling on people to atone for their sins. He adopted the oratorical style of the leaders of communes, beginning and closing with religious quotations and in the middle making his appeal in an emotional way, which to critics could seem like a rant. But he preached as one spreading good news, proclaiming and exhorting others to a more joyous life. In Francis's youth a man in Assisi greeted everyone by saying "Peace and All Good!" Francis took up this salutation as he went through the town.

Francis's zeal, his seeming certainty, intrigued other men. One joined him for a time but to Francis's disappointment, decided to return to the world. The noble Bernard, son of Quintavelle of Berardello, who had studied civil and canon law in Bologna, the preeminent university for legal studies at the time, was more cautious. Aware of the transformation of the merchant's son, and possibly inspired by his fearlessness, Bernard invited Francis to take shelter in his home on several occasions. Observing him praying through the night, rarely sleeping, and praising God and the Virgin Mary in his waking hours, Bernard grew convinced that the merchant's son had truly given himself to God. The lawyer decided to follow him and asked Francis what a person who had use of a noble's goods should do if he had no more need of them. Francis, who himself had had a problem with disposing of what turned out to be family property, said they had to find the answer. At that point Peter Cattani who, like Bernard, was a lawyer from Assisi, joined them. The next morning the three went to the Church of Saint Nicholas and sought God's guidance through a process known in the Middle Ages as *sortes biblicae*. They took the missal, or book of the mass, prayers and scripture, from its cupboard and asked God to tell them what they were to do. With that, they opened the book to a random page and found this admonition: "If you will be perfect, go, sell what you have and give it to the poor." (Mark 10:21) They closed the missal, then opened it again to read "Take nothing for your journey, neither staff, nor wallet, nor bread, nor money; neither have two tunics." (Luke 9:3) Closing and reopening it again for a final message, they read "If anyone wishes to come after me, let him deny himself, take up his cross and follow me." (Matthew 16:24)

Bernard divested himself of his share of his family's goods, distributed the proceeds to the poor, and made his lot with Francis, as did

Peter. Both then dressed themselves as Francis did, in a drab tunic tied with a knotted rope. Others followed. Besides Peter Cattani, there were Giles, Sabbatino, Morico, John of Capella, Philip the Tall, Barbaro, Bernard Viridante, and Angelo Tancredi, who may have been with Francis in the Perugia prison as well as being the nobleman who told him about Walter of Brienne. They lived in church outbuildings, in branch and mud huts they built in forests and fields, and abandoned shelters of various kinds depending upon the season, never travelling far from Assisi.

Francis, who had thought his destiny was to wander alone, was filled with happiness. He would pluck a stick from the ground, then lay it across his arm and draw it back and forth as if playing a vielle, an early fiddle, singing in French about the glory of the Lord. Then sometimes in the midst of his own happiness he would have a vision of the Savior's agony and he would dissolve into desolate tears.

He was often afraid that his companions would become overwhelmed by their rigorous life and abandon him. So he tried to spare them the shame and strain of begging. He would go out alone, but he was unable to obtain enough food for all of them. Rather than starve, the brothers insisted that they too must seek alms. Their experiences were intense, if not always spiritually transforming. They competed to see who proved to be the most effective beggar, an honor that was determined by seeing who brought back the greatest amount of food. That was not always an incentive. The patrician Bernard, on returning from his first day of alms-seeking, threw himself on the ground before Francis, abject with guilt and confessing that he had nothing to share because he had eaten every morsel as soon as he had it in his hands. Francis responded with tears of joy. Bernard, he said, had saved nothing for the future, which demonstrated his superior holiness. He was insistent that they trust the Lord. The brother who cooked was not allowed to soak vegetables overnight but had to wait until the end of morning prayers before touching the ingredients of

the day's meal. Sometimes they took the liberty of meeting immediate needs by digging turnips from the fields, taking care to keep
themselves well out of sight of the owners of the properties.

Hunger and cold were not the only trials. Ruffians delighted in
demeaning and tormenting these unworldly men, ripping the clothes
from their backs, pelting them with mud, even dragging one by the
back of his hood. Assisi's Bishop Guido was the one person who was
unfailingly kind. He is recorded as advising, to no avail, that Francis
be less austere in his way of life: "It seems to me that it is very hard
and difficult to possess nothing in the world," the bishop observed.
To which Francis replied that it was possessions that caused difficulty and that if they owned things they would have to protect them by
taking up weapons which would hinder them from loving God and
their neighbors.

Francis travelled through the villages around Assisi preaching
penance and carrying a broom so that he might sweep churches that
he found to be dirty. He called the priests of the area to meet with
him separately so he would not seem to be criticizing them when he
admonished them to keep their churches and altars and everything
that pertained to the sacrifice of the Mass clean for the glory of God.
Francis was able to deal with their rebukes, but his followers were
more susceptible to criticism. One became despondent when a priest
warned him to be careful not to become a hypocrite. Francis tried
to tell his brother that the priest had been wrong about him, but the
man insisted that he had to be a hypocrite because a priest was not
capable of lying.

Some of the men did penance by wearing hair shirts and iron
belts. Others exposed themselves to cold and refrained from all food
and drink. Mortification of the flesh to atone for sin or to appease
the gods was practiced in ancient Egypt and Syria. In the Christian
era through voluntary suffering and sacrifices, whether it was fasting
or self-flagellation, people participated in Jesus's sacrifice to redeem
the world from sin and to punish the body for its sins and vices. Such

practices did make Francis's men ill. The brothers' life was harsh and their flesh was human. They awoke one night to the moans of one who cried, "I am dying! Brothers, I am dying of hunger." Francis arose, had the table set, and began eating. He invited the others to join in, so that the starving brother should not be embarrassed by his need for food. As they sat in firelight eating crusts of bread and water in the middle of the night, Francis conceded that they had to keep up their strength, saying that depriving the body was as much a sin as stuffing it.

This he might have learned from his own rueful experience. Throughout his religious life, Francis would blame tribulations and temptations on the Devil and other evil denizens of Hell who knew how to taunt and vex him when he was most vulnerable, but his own mistreatment of himself and the ravages of semi-starvation were certainly responsible for much suffering. In a landmark study published in 1950, Ancel Keys and his colleagues at the University of Minnesota carefully observed three dozen healthy, young, psychologically normal males who agreed to reduce their food intake by half. On average, they lost a quarter of their weight and experienced pronounced physical, psychological, and social changes during their voluntary ordeal and well into the "renourishment," or recovery, phase of the study. They became preoccupied with food and found it increasingly difficult to concentrate on other activities. Their interest in sex waned. They dawdled over their own food and derived great pleasure from watching others eat or from just smelling food. Emotional distress was common and severe. A fifth of them deteriorated so markedly that they could barely function. Some grew elated, only to quickly fall into despair. Outbursts of anger were common and many began biting their nails or smoking to calm their nerves. Those who had once been fastidious became slovenly. Two had psychotic incidents. After two weeks of "refeeding," one man decided to rid himself of a few fingers. He jacked up his car and dropped it on his hand. Several days later he chopped the fingers off. For all that, the men overall experienced no loss of intellectual ability. The physical effects included stomach discomfort, decreased need for sleep, dizziness, headaches, hypersensitivity to light and noise, weakness, poor motor control, hair loss and visual and auditory disturbances. One can assume that Francis and his men were subject to many of these symptoms.

When they arrived in a town where they were not known, people saw dirty, ragtag men who seemed likely to steal what they could from market stalls and open doors. Those who knew them, like the people of Assisi, continued to regard them as ridiculous. Asked to share their own hard-earned bread, they refused to indulge what seemed to be the folly of men like Francis and Bernard who had thrown away privileged lives only to ask their social inferiors for sustenance. Francis was persuaded that these critics had a point and he decided that he and his men should offer their labor in exchange for food. Francis repaired walls and roofs while Giles made baskets. Others carried water, harvested olives and grapes, gathered wood, cleaned pots, swept workshops, mended shoes and sharpened knives according to their training and ability. Such servile work was reviled by all who did not have to do it. The sight of the one-time dandy spreading straw and shoveling dung persuaded many that Francis and his followers had undergone a true transformation into holy men. Others regarded them as fools and vented their anger and frustrations upon them, stripping them naked and beating and imprisoning them. Francis and his men bore all things courageously, mindful that Jesus said they were blessed when people insulted them because they served the Lord. They let only praise and thanksgiving come from their mouths.

Their devotions were fierce. Lest they fall asleep while praying, some held themselves upright by ropes, others weighed themselves down with irons while they lay prostrate, others tied wood around their waists. They lay naked on ice and beat themselves with thorny branches. If they were given a good meal, they ate it, but fasted afterward for days.

Whether it was because they had become too familiar with the ways of Assisi and needed fresh spiritual challenges, or because Francis was still a man who required change, soon after their number grew to eight he decided to send them out into the world. He intended his followers to be wanderers without fixed dwellings who often withdrew into prayerful seclusion but returned to the roadways and marketplaces to preach and serve as the poorest of God's poor, all the while dealing with the surprises God gave them. Francis sent them in pairs so that each had a companion and ally but the alms-seekers did not arrive in a new place in such numbers that they could be perceived as a threat.

Francis had learned early and painfully that two men could protect and support each other physically and spiritually and find work or beg for alms, but a larger group, however well meaning, was seldom welcome among strangers. He had also learned that God's love best expressed itself in each one's heart if he knew his role. In each pair, they were to take turns being "mother" and "son." The mother was to be responsible for material needs of finding food, choosing shelter, even planning the route, while the son was to focus on spiritual concerns and lead their prayers and preach the Gospel.

The day after Giles joined them, Francis set out with him for the Marches of Ancona traveling northwest over mountainous terrain. As they went, Francis sang out the praises of God in his enthusiastic but uncertain French. When they came to a church in whatever state of repair, or to a roadside cross, they recited a standard prayer: "We adore you, O Christ, and we bless you, because by your holy cross you have redeemed the world."

Francis told Giles that their movement would grow because they would invite everyone they encountered, in the manner of fishermen who cast large nets to make a large catch. Seeing how few in number they were, Giles doubted that Francis was right but kept this feeling to himself and was faithful to his leader. When they came across groups of people, even small ones, they wished "Peace and Good" to all. Francis would urge them to love one another and to do penance for their sins, whereupon Giles would add, "You must believe my brother Francis. The advice he is giving you is very good." Some of their hearers were welcoming, others thought them absurd, but most were more interested in Francis and Giles than the word of God. Where were they from? What order did they belong to? The two would then walk on in joy, heedless of the mockery they had inspired, conscious only of doing the work of the Lord.

Francis later went with Peter Cattani to Rieti and Giles and Bernard journeyed to Florence. In their travels the men preferred to stay with priests or lepers, but if they could not find such lodging, they sought out sympathetic people. When all else failed they took shelter in caves, crypts, or near outdoor ovens. In Florence one woman allowed Giles and Bernard to sleep on her covered porch near the warmth of a bread oven. This infuriated her skeptical husband until he learned that the two men had been seen in church and had refused to take alms that were meant for the true poor. At that point he invited them to move into the house with them. Francis also sent Bernard to Bologna where he had been a student. Seeing him endure insults, often from bullying children, a judge and law professor asked him who he was and why he had come to their city. Bernard drew from his tunic what he called the rule of Francis, the words they had received at the Church of Saint Nicholas. The judge pronounced it to be the highest form of religious life he had ever heard of and gave Bernard lodging in what is described as "a place where he could serve God in a suitable way."

People soon sought out Bernard to touch him and hear what he had to say, but he found such admiration troubling and possibly tempting. He returned to Francis and asked him to send others to Bologna to carry out the work so that he could return to his simple Gospel life. Francis then dispatched Bernard to go with Giles on the well-worn pilgrimage route to Compostela in northwestern Spain where the bones of Saint James the Great were said to lie. The power of this apostle, emanating from his relics, was credited with preserving northwest Iberia from conquest by Muslims from North Africa, known as the Moors, who had conquered most of the peninsula.

When people asked who the men were, where they were from, and what religious order they belonged to, they answered simply, "We are penitents and were born in Assisi."

For all that they might seem extreme, the men of Assisi walked a path that other groups were travelling, including some who had been driven to deny the church's teachings and be labeled heretics, a term that was derived from the Greek word for choice. At this time many lay people sought to live in the world as dedicated Christians taking their guidance directly from the Gospel of Christ. The Humiliati, or "the humble ones," was such a group. They originated in the area of Milan among wool workers. Rather than wander begging alms, these Italians adopted the life of manual laborers, staying in one place, owning property in common, and supporting themselves through the textile trade. Pope Lucius III condemned them as heretics along with Peter Waldo and his followers in 1184, but after study and discussions, Innocent III approved the three orders of Humiliati in 1201. The first was traditional and its members received the tonsure and had the status of clerics. They were allowed to build churches with the permission of the local bishop. They were cloistered but could return to the world at will. The second comprised men and women working in common but living in separate communities. The third and most numerous order consisted of lay people following trades and living with their families. They met on Sundays and preached sermons to one another although they actively and publicly supported the church.

A more problematic, and more widespread, movement was founded by Peter Waldo, a rich merchant of Lyon who became active around 1170, a decade before Francis's birth. He sold all his belongings and distributed them to the poor. Soon he gathered followers who practiced absolute poverty like the Apostles. These so-called

Waldensians read and distributed Scripture that was written in the people's native tongues. The women among them preached as well as the men, an innovation that Peter Waldo justified through Galatians 3:28: "There is neither Jew, nor Greek; there is neither slave nor freeman; there is neither male nor female. For you are all one in Christ Jesus."

Such original thinking horrified the church. In Lyon, the archbishop was scandalized to see that these Waldensians, simple laymen, were expounding on Holy Writ. In 1182 he forbad them to preach and by 1184 Pope Lucius III condemned them as heretics. Their response was to reject the Roman Catholic Church. They also declared that Christ was not truly present at the Mass since in their view the sacraments like the Eucharist were valid only if they were administered by someone in the state of grace, which most priests, in their experience, were not. Although the church said they were ignorant, the Waldensians established schools and taught the meaning of the Gospels and Epistles. Their sole prayer was the Lord's Prayer, because it came from Jesus. Waldensians could confess their sins to each other and be absolved. Faithful Catholics began to call them "the poor ones of God" and as they grew in influence these poor ones called the Church of Rome "the whore of Babylon." Throughout Europe, ordinary faithful Catholics were neither offended nor antagonistic toward these innovations. At that time even those who had been branded as heretics were allowed to go about their business and worship in their way in peace, a situation that concerned the church.

Around 1210, Francis, possibly under the guidance of Bishop Guido, felt that he and his handful of followers needed to be able to say that their work had the approval of Pope Innocent III himself. Carrying no money, travelling barefoot, they headed south along the mountainous spine of the Italian peninsula. After a journey of more than a hundred miles, usually on roadways edged with cypress trees and flat-topped stone pines, they reached Rome. The city was even more magnificent than when Francis had seen it four years before. Innocent III had fortified and improved the square three-story Lateran Palace, the residence for himself and succeeding popes. The palace Francis saw vanished in a remodeling in the 1290s, but we know that at its entrance Francis passed a mammoth sculpture of the emperor Constantine,[†] fourteen feet high, on horseback. Above him a tower loomed over this courtyard and soared five stories into the air. It was patrolled by archers, one of whom reportedly once shot his cross bow into a crowd of beggars by mistake.

On entering the Lateran Palace, Francis and his men passed gleaming mosaic scenes depicting the triumph of the papacy over German emperors, as well as a flock of early popes kneeling before the Blessed Virgin Mary. They may have passed some of the Lateran's great statuary, all from pagan days, such as a colossal head and hand of Constantine and the Thornpicker, a boy tending to his ailing foot, a vignette with meaning for those who had walked from Mount Subasio to Rome.

Bishop Guido from Assisi is recorded as being at the Lateran Palace and as being surprised to learn that Francis and his men had arrived. Impetuous as Francis could be, it seems unlikely that he could have decided to approach the pope without consulting the man who had consoled and protected him. Possibly Bishop Guido had in fact suggested or supported this trip to Rome, and then for strategic reasons had acted surprised, but more likely, this Guido was a new bishop who happened to have the same name as his predecessor. Nicolangelo D'Acunto has done research that indicates that there were three bishops Guido in Francis's lifetime. The last time the Guido of Francis's boyhood was mentioned was in a document dated October 11, 1208, months before Francis went to see the pope.

[†] The subject was later identified as Marcus Aurelius, but the idea that it was the emperor who brought Christianity to prominence saved it from being melted down.

Possibly Francis left for Rome after this Guido died and when he arrived, he discovered the new man who had been selected as bishop of Assisi. The Guido that Francis found, or "Guido II" as D'Acunto calls him, was immediately supportive of Francis. He introduced him to Cardinal John of Saint Paul, a member of the prestigious Colonna family of Rome, who became a monk and was later named head of the Benedictine abbey of Saint Paul Outside the Wall. He had served as a legate to the heretical Albigensians and he had experience working with other lay groups that had sought to follow the Gospels such as the Humiliati and Waldensians.

He urged the men of Assisi to join an existing order as he himself had done. Surely he recommended his order's rule of Saint Benedict, which had been written in the sixth century and was the template for how religious orders were to be organized, with set prayers and activities for every hour and week. Francis had seen it observed and abused during the miserable days he spent at a Benedictine abbey on the road to Gubbio. Chastity, obedience, and reverence were its hallmarks, as was strict regulation of work, devotion, and mealtimes, as were penalties for such transgressions as coming late to prayer or meals. On a fixed rotation, a brother was assigned to read aloud at every meal for a week and each monk was obliged to read from an edifying book at a fixed point during the day. Benedict also encouraged proper food, clothing, and sleep for his followers so that they would be fit in mind and body to serve God. But enclosure in a monastery with strict rules, ample food, and six to eight hours of sound sleep per day were not Francis's inclination, nor was it the direction that God had given Francis, Bernard, and Peter when they consulted the missal at the Church of Saint Nicholas. Francis countered all of the cardinal's reasonable suggestions so that at length the prelate agreed to take their request to the Pope.

Innocent III held a council three times a week during which he along with canon lawyers and a subgroup of his thirty or so cardinals deliberated and resolved cases put before them. Francis was probably not present when two prelates presented his request. While this first text has been lost, the testament that Francis wrote shortly before his death provides its essence: "When God gave me some brothers, there was no one to tell me what I should do; but the Most High himself made it clear to me that I must live the life of the Gospel. I had this written down briefly and simply and his holiness the Pope confirmed it for me."

Bernard of Quintavalle and Peter Cattani may have suggested formal language for the document, but Francis's rule was surely based on the guidance received through the missal at the Church of Saint Nicholas: "If you will be perfect, go, sell what you have and give it to the poor" (Mark 10:21). "Take nothing for your journey, neither staff, nor wallet, nor bread, nor money; neither have two tunics" (Luke 9:3). "If anyone wishes to come after me, let him deny himself, take up his cross and follow me" (Matthew 16:24).

The astute Bishop Guido and Cardinal John Saint Paul would have added a provision saying that the Lesser Brothers, as they would come to be known, would obey the Pope as loyal members of the church. To distinguish it from lay apostolic movements such as the Waldensians, they might have added Francis's respect for priests and his devotion to the sacrament of the Eucharist.

As for what Innocent III might have thought of movements like that of Francis, he had already seen snares in the kind of life that Francis and his men sought to follow. Some twenty-five years earlier, in his student days in May or June of 1187, he was a witness to the crisis of the Order of Grandmont in Limousin, France. When its founder Stephen of Muret died in 1124, the only rule he left his followers was that they must follow the Gospel. They did own a monastery, chapel, garden, and some beehives in the forest, but no other possessions. As their numbers grew, so did their problems. To allow the priests among them to pray, the lay brothers attended to the daily management of monastery. Outnumbering the priests by about seven to one, the laymen responded to whatever grievances they had by sometimes refusing to ring the bell to summon the clerics to meals. They thus began to effectively starve them and eventually they forced the prior to resign. He then departed with two hundred clerics and thirteen laymen who made their way to Rome to register complaints and request intervention. Innocent III, then Lothar of Segni, was in the church delegation at Grandmont that resolved the matter. Church authorities decided that to continue to exist, the Order of Grandmont must accept ownership of more possessions for its maintenance and install a cleric to correct abuses when they occurred. The prolonged episode remained in Innocent's mind as the prime example of the inherent dangers of the Gospel rule without additional regulations that protected orders and movements from falling into disputes, disarray, and eventually a break with Rome.

What Cardinal John of Saint Paul and Bishop Guido did not object to, the pontiff did not object to. At the next court meeting, held in the Mirror Hall of the Lateran Palace, Francis and his group were called in to receive the pontiff's approval and blessing. When Francis was ushered into his presence in 1210, Pope Innocent III was fifty years old and in the twelfth year of his papacy. He was an attractive man of medium height, distinguished not only by his aura of power but by his white skull cap, which marked him as separate and above the cardinals around him who wore red ones. Mosaic portraits indicate Innocent had thick brown hair, a long nose, large eyes and a mustache. Giotto, who painted his famous frescos sixty years after the pontiff's death, gave him a shaved and fleshy face. For Innocent III, the papacy was a family business during a long era when that office was controlled and exchanged among Italian clans who used it to increase their wealth and power. By one reckoning, he was the seventh of the thirteen popes that the Conti family would contribute to the church, along with forty cardinals and two anti-popes, men who claimed the title illegally. Two of his kinsmen, Popes Gregory IX and Alexander IV, would also impact the lives of Francis and Clare. He first burst on the world's stage in his thirties. Using his time productively when his family was out of papal favor, he wrote *On the Misery of the Human Condition*. This work includes the following admonition to mankind: "Observe the herbs and the trees. These produce flowers, leaves, and fruits and you produce lice. They offer oil, wine and balsam, you offer only spit, dung and urine." It was one of the great books of its age and was read throughout Europe for the next four centuries, influencing among others Montaigne and Chaucer. While Lothar promised that he would eventually write a positive tract about man's dignity, he never got around to that. At age thirty-seven he was elected pope.

The respect in which he was held was such that the cardinals of the church elected him pope when he was still a deacon, not yet a priest. Other deacons, notably Pope Saint Gregory the Great in 1073, had been catapulted to the papacy before they were ordained. But Lothar was victorious on what reportedly was the first secret ballot in Vatican history, on January 8, 1198, the very day that the old Pope Celestine III died at age ninety-one. Six weeks later, on February 21, Lothar was ordained, and then on the following day he was officially made bishop and pope. He took the name Innocent III (thus blotting out the memory of an anti-pope by that name) and at his consecration he signaled his sense of mission when he preached on Jeremiah 1:10: "I have set thee this day over the nations, and over kingdoms, to root up and to pull down, and to waste and to destroy, and to build and to plant."

Accounts in early biographies portray Innocent as asking Francis for reasons why he should receive approval. They also say that the pontiff conferred this only after he had a dream in which Francis propped up the Basilica of Saint John Lateran. These are probably apocryphal.† More likely, the men from Assisi were awed to silence. Innocent gave his approval and they became a recognized religious movement. For all the significance this meeting would have, not only in the lives of Francis and Clare, but in the history of the Western world, the approval he received followed earlier precedents and was not extraordinary.

Francis knelt before either Cardinal John of Saint Paul or Bishop Guido, who with a razor shaved away a bare circle of hair on the crown of his head and then of the others in turn. This tonsure of conversion marked Francis's entrance into religious life. As tonsured clerics they were required to recite the Liturgy of the Hours, or certain prayers at specified times every day, and to read, if they were literate, a breviary.

Burchard of Ursperg, a canon in a German abbey writing a chronicle some fifteen years later around 1231, observed that Francis and his men were given approval because they were a welcome contrast to the Humiliati and the Poor Men of Lyon, those two other bands that claimed to live like the apostles but who criticized priests for their sinful ways. Bernard said that while these groups wore mantles like those who belonged to religious orders, they were untonsured, and that the men and women in them walked together and stayed in the same houses, some of them reportedly the same bed.

Rejoicing, Francis and his men headed north for home, stopping only to pray at the tomb of Saint Peter. Francis felt they had achieved

---

† According to a story first published by Odo of Cheriton as early as 1219, after Innocent asked Francis why he should give him approval the Assisian replied that he and his followers were like the sons that a king had by a poor but beautiful woman. When the boys grew to manhood, they approached the king and were acknowledged and provided for. Innocent was at once reminded of his recent dream, in which the Basilica of Saint John Lateran, the official seat of the Bishop of Rome, the pope himself, was collapsing until a small insignificant man propped it up on his bent back. Thomas of Celano says in his second biography of Francis that this prompted Innocent to grant Francis his request. Giotto painted the scene in his famous frescos at the Basilica of Saint Francis in Assisi, but the story is identical to one told about Saint Dominic who founded the Order of Friars Preachers. It may have been misattributed to Francis.

an extraordinary blessing. He dreamed of himself walking down a road that led past a tree of unusual height, strength, and beauty. As he stood admiring the breadth of its trunk, its web of tapering branches, and the luxuriance of its leaves, Francis felt himself growing to so great a stature that he could touch the top of the splendid tree and pressing it, bent it before him to the ground.

Without water or bread, but with trust in the Lord, they headed north to Assisi on the Via Flaminia across land parched by the summer sun. One night near Otricoli, a city about forty-five miles north of Rome at the border of Umbria, after another day of hunger and thirst, their strength gave out in a barren spot where they could find nothing to forage. According to legend, they were saved from starvation when a stranger appeared, possibly a shepherd, and gave them bread. They rested there two weeks, possibly taking shelter in abandoned Roman tombs, taking nothing for the morrow but surely contemplating what was next.

5

The Happy Days

A CONDITION OF THE pope's approval of their movement was that Francis's men attach themselves to a church that would serve as their official home. Neither Bishop Guido nor the canons of the Cathedral of Saint Rufino had one to offer, so during the cold early months of 1210 they lived in an abandoned shanty by a meandering stream called Rivo Torto a half hour walk from Assisi. These quarters were so confining that Francis wrote the names of the brothers on the overhead beams so that each might have his own spot for private prayer or rest. Their obligations as tonsured clerics required them to recite and chant specific hourly prayers from matins at dawn to compline before bed. Those who were able to also read a breviary. Praying aloud, Masseo of Marignano droned on in a single tone like a cooing dove but Francis recited every syllable clearly. He amazed the others by remembering every prayer, verse, or text after he had read it once.

None were said to have complained about their circumstances, even when they had no bread and made do with turnips. They existed in a realm of their own, free of whatever unhappiness or strife they experienced before. As unable as each had been, inwardly or outwardly, to conform to the world, now he melded into a brotherhood with a single goal of living the Gospel. What one suffered, whether it was soaked skin in the rain or stiff fingers in the cold, they all suffered. Discomfort was erased by being greater than their one self. Theirs was the enthusiasm, the myopia, of first love but it was for their new life together. They persisted in this way until the day a man drove his donkey into their midst and seemed to take offense that they were claiming his animals' ramshackle shelter as their own.

At that point the Benedictine monks of Mount Subasio gave them the use of Saint Mary of the Angels, or Portiuncula, whose chapel Francis had repaired some three years earlier when he was still without companions. It was set on low ground, enveloped in fog when it was cold, and often damp. So thick with evergreen oaks was the forest that surrounded its clearing that pig keepers drove their herds there to feed on acorns. According to legend, Portiuncula was established in the fourth century by four holy men from Palestine who had visited Rome before building the hermitage there with a chapel and four huts. Francis had already restored its tiny stone church, which was about eighteen feet wide by forty-five feet long with an arched ceiling, a semicircular apse for the altar, and two arched doors, one in a side wall.

When he had first come upon it soon after he broke with his father, the one-story chapel was filled with rubble. He had carried away the unneeded stones on his back and restored its wooden pitched roof. Now near the church Francis and his men built a small shelter of tree and vine branches where they could sleep. They roofed it with dried rushes and daubed it with mud to keep out the wind and then they renovated as best they could the other buildings. They worked to revive the straggling grape and bean vines and fruit trees that remained from earlier long-abandoned cultivation. Francis took up residence in a small hut near a fig tree. To mark the boundaries of Portiuncula they dug a ditch around its perimeter and for further privacy they planted a hedge.

The men's bond with each other was protection against hostile forces from without and within, whether devils, hunger pangs, or leaking roofs. Francis fell in love with this place, as a devoted son loves his mother. He listened to its birdsong and inhaled the tang of pine when the air was hot. In late afternoon he watched wisps of inky clouds float across the pewter sky and saw the hilltops glow red as the sun bade them farewell for the night, only to rise again the next morning and light their day. The man who denied he had a home, who said he possessed nothing, held Portiuncula in his heart. He explained this reverence to his brothers by saying that he had received a revelation that Mary, the mother of Jesus, loved this church above all others.

He would say that this place with its branch and mud huts was to be the model of all dwellings of Lesser Brothers throughout the world, not just because of its simplicity, but because it was sanctified by the brothers' devotion, by their suffering and prayer, and by their readiness to avoid idleness by helping the poor with their labors in the fields. But Francis insisted that the Lesser Brothers did not own Saint Mary of the Angels, not by any means. To acknowledge that Portiuncula was only on loan to them, each year he lived, Francis sent his landlord, the Benedictine abbot, a tribute of a basket of fish. The monks in return thanked him with a jar of oil.

At regular intervals, after penance and contemplation at Portiuncula had reinvigorated him, Francis moved out into the world, not only up the slope of Mount Subasio to Assisi but to other cities, with a companion. When they passed a church they would pray, "We adore you, O Christ, and we bless you because by your holy cross you have redeemed the world." Sometimes when they entered city gates their unkempt appearances alarmed the residents. To show the unimportance of the conventional things of the world as much as to make use of what he had available, Francis mended his ashen tunic with bits of bark and plants. In cold weather the rich were particularly moved to give him clothes so that he might be better protected. He accepted these gratefully and passed them on to the first poor person who came their way. He and his companion brothers bid peace to all and called on them to love and fear

God and follow his commandments. It was an era, like many others that came after it, that believed it was living in the final days and that the great judgment approached. Surely Francis spoke of this but he won his listeners because he did not speak down to them or scold. In church, the priests veiled Jesus in the mysteries of the Latin Mass and dense Biblical passages that kept God hovering above the clouds. Francis, in the streets, spoke in the clear and direct Umbrian words they knew. He drew his direct, emotional style from the leaders of the commune, and he sometimes began by quoting from a popular ballad, which led him into a presention of the loving Jesus he had come to know, the Savior who had soothed his anguish and sacrificed himself for all mankind. Rather than accuse his hearers of their iniquities, Francis tapped into his own abiding sense of guilt and worthlessness. He spoke from his heart, acknowledging himself to be one who had sinned but who later found peace by changing his life. Above all, he preached what they did not hear in church. With joy he assured them that God loved them and that they should rely on his love. As if for the first time, people heard this. Jesus had said it, but this message from the pulpit had become obscured.

One time at Portiuncula when Francis was returning from prayer in the woods, Masseo approached him with a question that had been on his mind: "Why you?" He pointed out that Francis was not handsome, nor especially learned, nor a man of much importance, yet people were willing to hear what he said to say. "You want to know?" Francis repeated the question twice as if searching for an answer and then replied, "God has not seen anyone more vile or insufficient than I am. And so to do that wonderful work which He intends me to do, He chose me, for God has chosen the foolish things of the world to put to shame to the wise." Basically, Francis believed what Christendom believed, the teachings that had been set forth in the Nicene Creed of the fourth century. He believed in one God, a Holy Trinity of three persons. The Father had created all things that were seen and unseen. His Son Jesus came to earth and became a man born of the Virgin Mary to redeem humanity from sin. The Holy Spirit guided the Church. Francis believed in one holy Roman Catholic Church of the apostles. He believed that baptism freed man from the stain of Adam's original sin, that there was life after death, that Jesus rose in body from the dead, and that all would rise on Judgment Day. Most passionately of all, he believed that Jesus had died in agony on the cross in payment for man's sins, including those that Francis had himself committed. He felt that as a personal debt to be paid. The emphasis he placed on peace was something of a novelty for a Roman Catholic deacon at a time when the church was waging Crusades. It suggests that visions of his bloody combat against the nobles remained with him and that he valued the calm that his surrender to God had brought him.

Nonetheless, deep remorse over the sins he had committed, for which the Savior had suffered and died in agony, sometimes brought him near to despair. Then he was inclined to believe that his life was pointless and that he should abandon entirely the strange business of sleeping in holes like a fox and eating refuse like a dog. He never wholly trusted that he would not abandon the onerous life he had chosen for himself. Had he not attempted to be a merchant, then a knight? He had wanted to be a troubadour. Could the appeal of being a holy man fade as the others had? He wanted to drink wine, eat delicacies, have the pleasures of the flesh. When others honored his commitment, he said. "I can still have sons and daughters; do not praise me as being secure."

When carnal thoughts overwhelmed him, he countered them by throwing himself in icy water that formed in the ditch. Francis would be in agony until he felt God's grace bring him back from despondency. Then his heart would rise a greater distance than the depths into which it had fallen and Francis would be elated and would preach against the snare of hopelessness. Thomas of Celano quotes him as saying, "The devil rejoices most when he can snatch away spiritual joy from a servant of God. He carries dust so that he can throw it into even the tiniest hole of conscience."

He liked to refer to this as "Babylonian rust," drawing on an image from Ezekiel 24:6. Francis said that if a soul remained stupefied in sadness, "the Babylonian stuff will increase so that unless it was driven out by tears, it will generate an abiding rust in the heart." He told his brothers not to show themselves to be unhappy or upset either to each other or to strangers. "Examine your sins and weep and groan before God in your rooms," he told them. "Otherwise show yourselves to be joyful in the Lord."

This was another key to his success with people. Francis taught that the worship of God need not be a fearsome matter. His public self was always cheerful, particularly in comparison to many priests who affected a solemnity in public that belied their private lives. The church taught that life was a miserable prelude to the eternal happiness of heaven and that man must atone or go to hell. Francis instead urged the faithful to turn from sin, anger, and war so that they might better savor lives of love and the enormous joy of harmony with God. Unlike the heretical Cathars who stressed that the material world was the work of Satan, Francis took delight in the birds, trees, and flowers that God had created, and saw in them a sign of God's love, order, and plan.

Cathars, recognizing that the popular Francis was a friend to the Roman Catholic Church they so despised, sometimes assailed him. Once when Francis was in a city in Lombardy, one of them pointed out that the local priest lived with a woman. Learning that a priest in the crowd was the one in question, Francis fell in the dust at the prelate's feet and kissed the hands that held the Eucharist at Mass. "These hands have touched my sacred Lord," Francis said. "They are not able to lessen His power. This man might do bad things to himself, but he is good for me."

One priest in particular was touched by Francis's good will and equanimity, based as it was in the love that Jesus taught. Sylvester had met Francis in the early days of his conversion and soon thereafter had felt that Francis had cheated him when he purchased some of the paving stones that Francis sold when he was renovating Saint Damian. After Bernard of Quintavalle joined Francis and gave away his wealth to the poor, Sylvester felt that Francis should have given him the stones as a gift and he told Francis so. A smiling Francis then filled Sylvester's hands with money and the prelate departed a happy man. But over time he became preoccupied by Francis's generosity and good will. Sylvester mused that he was older than Francis and closer to leaving the world, but it was Francis who had in spirit already departed it and Francis who actually lived the Gospel message of love and renunciation that Sylvester only preached. One night in a dream the face of Francis appeared to the priest and from his mouth a golden cross emerged. It grew so tall that it touched the sky and so broad that its arms encircled both halves of the world. With no delay Sylvester joined Francis and his men at Portiuncula.

Not everyone was persuaded by Francis and his men, however, not even those who saw their merit, such as Boncampagno, a man from Signa, near Florence. A layman of proud and boisterous personality who taught rhetoric in Bologna, Boncampagno was as appalled as he was impressed by the followers of Francis. He was concerned that many were young and some were mere children and thus did not have sufficient judgment when they took up their arduous new life. He wrote, "Because of the frailty of their time of life, youth are inclined, as nature allows, to volatility and a lack of balance. These, indeed, have reached such a degree of foolishness that they wander about heedlessly through the cities, towns, and remote places, while enduring horrible and inhuman suffering which makes martyrs of them."

Some of the brothers did not so much sacrifice themselves as proceed through the world in their own unique fashion. Brother Juniper was eager to help a gravely ill brother at Portiuncula who said that he wished he could eat a pig's leg. Juniper went outside, found and seized one, then cut off its limb and cooked it. He rejoiced at the bounty of the Lord who had provided the pig so that he could comfort his brother. But then the swineherd appeared in their midst, swearing, cursing, and calling Juniper a madman. Francis rushed in, tried to take charge, apologized profusely and said they would do anything the owner wished to make amends. The man did not care. He was so angry that he heaped double curses on them all. He stalked off, leaving Francis concerned about the ill will he could stir up against the brothers. He tried to explain to Juniper that the man had good reason to be angry and he sent his mystified follower out to apologize several times. The swineherd rebuffed Juniper at first, but eventually he too was touched by the man's simplicity. Chastened, he roasted a pig and sent it to the brothers as a peace offering for having been so vile. Pleased with Juniper's patience in the face of difficulty, Francis said he wished he had a forest of junipers.

John the Simple became another enthusiastic follower. One day while he was plowing his family's field he heard that Francis was sweeping a church in Assisi and he quickly went to help him. Afterward, when the two were resting, John announced that he wanted to join the brothers. Francis said that all he had to do was to give away his belongings. John believed that his portion of the family property consisted of an ox that he used to plow their land, so he brought it to Francis. Meanwhile, his impoverished family, which included his much younger brothers, was in agony not only because he was leaving them but because he was taking away their means of income. Francis tried to explain that John's serving God would help their souls, but seeing their despair, he returned the animal.

Many people who did not want to overturn their lives completely asked Francis how they might become better people while still remaining in the world, many under the vows of marriage. According to Thomas Celano, Francis gave them guidance, but the wording of his instructions is unknown. Given that for Francis the words of the Gospel sufficed, and since they wanted to remain in their homes with their families, it might have simply consisted of the final of the three verses that Francis, Bernard, and Peter Cattani found when they consulted the missal at the Church of Saint Nicholas, one that called for self-sacrifice and obedience to Christ's teaching. Matthew 16:24 says, "If anyone wishes to come after me, let him deny himself, and take up his cross, and follow me." These followers included widows and unmarried women who might have joined a convent if they had had enough money to pay the required dowry, but after hearing Francis speak, or learning of the Beguines, they came together to live lives of prayer and mutual support in private houses. A notable number of the women of Greccio, a town that particularly welcomed Francis, joined in such an arrangement. Many took vows of virginity and adopted a religious habit. While some remained in their own homes, they led a common way of life by fasting, praying, and doing good works. They did not withdraw from the world as much as abandon its distractions, and they were guided by the Lesser Brothers. In later years a writer said of the people of Greccio, "Despite their youthful age and their great simplicity, they seemed to have been formed by holy religious women who had been in the service of Christ for a long time." Married people in this city and others committed themselves to lives of penance while remaining in their own homes. Some regard these untonsured lay followers as prefiguring the Third Order of Saint Francis. Nicholas IV, the first Franciscan pope, established the formal rule of the Third Order in 1289.

In the evening, after the Lesser Brothers staying in Greccio would sing the praises of the Lord, the townspeople, including nobles, servants, men, and women would come from their houses to join them in repeating over and over "Blessed be the Lord God." Even toddlers who could barely talk mumbled the words as best they could.

Clare took up her new life in Assisi in the spring of 1212. After fleeing the Offreduccio compound in the dark of night and taking shelter first with Benedictine nuns and then with Beguines at Panzo, Clare awoke one mid-April morning at Saint Damian with Pacifica and Agnes sleeping nearby. As roosters crowed in the distance, the glow of early dawn filled the narrow, arched window of the loft. She rose up from her mattress of vines, ready for prayers at first light. Agnes, née Catherine, and Pacifica also picked themselves up from the hard floor eager for their new life. Having traded their fine garments for the mottled grey homespun tunics typically worn by the poor women of Assisi, they pulled these over their heads, running their palms along the coarse woolen weave, pleased with the patches. Around their waists they tied ropes ending in three knots. Thus Clare began her first day at Saint Damian. Francis first saw the small seventh century monastery, named to honor a physician who was martyred with his brother Cosmas in the third century, when he was a young merchant and spiritual seeker. Then it consisted of a chapel, a room where the priest lived, and an underground chamber or crypt. With money Clare had given him and knowledge of construction he probably gained when the commune repaired the nobles' damaged homes, Francis had renovated the property along the lines of convents at the time. He took down the wall between the nave and the priest's room to enlarge the chapel. Then he removed the overhead beams, which allowed him to raise the height of the chapel by installing a pointed barrel ceiling. Above this he built a large sleeping loft. From the original floor of the crypt he removed the stone or terra cotta stone pavement.

In keeping with the construction of the time, the door to the loft was at least fifteen feet above the ground. Each night the women pulled up the wooden ladder and the entrance was shut and barred against intruders. Upstairs, Clare slept on a bed made of vines she had twisted and woven into a mattress that grew sharp and brittle as it dried. She used as her pillow a smooth rock from the river. By day in prayer Clare lay prostrate on the ground. She had no time or interest in simple conversation but "spoke the words of God" by reciting

Scripture. Thus she lost herself in the only power that was stronger than her family, the mighty and merciful God who had delivered her from them and placed Pacifica and Agnes by her side.

On Monday, Wednesday, and Friday Clare consumed no food and on the other days she ate so little that she became ill. Francis then ordered her to eat at least a half a roll of bread on three days of the week, and Bishop Guido repeated and reinforced this directive. Still, Pacifica grew anxious to the point of weeping when she observed the frail state that Clare's devotions had brought her to. Since giving the palm to Clare on Palm Sunday as a signal that all was prepared for her to join Francis's movement, Bishop Guido had been a source of strength and wisdom. But on July 30, 1212, barely three months after Clare left her family, he died after two years as bishop, which was a blow to everyone at both Saint Damian and Portiuncula.

At least two Lesser Brothers lived close to the women in branch-and-mud huts so that they might protect and support the women spiritually and physically. Clare's kinsman Rufino and Philip the Tall, who had accompanied Francis when he first met with Clare, are likely to have been the first two. Country people heard Mass at Saint Damian on Sundays, so Sylvester could have been present as well. It seems possible that soon after Clare, Pacifica, and Agnes settled in, Clare's mother Ortolana returned from the pilgrimage that Clare had urged on her and appeared at Saint Damian in an effort to come to terms with the girls' betrayal as well as with the beating that Agnes had suffered at the hands of her kinsmen. Ortolana also had news to bring them: Raniero, who had asked for Clare's hand, was now affianced to one of her cousins. Clare, Agnes, and Pacifica greeted her barefoot and dressed in the castoff clothes of poor women, with Clare also wearing a shirt of animal hair under her tunic. Surely they were as dirty as serfs, reddened by the sun, and bruised and scratched from their rough life.

What might Ortolana have said to Pacifica, with whom she had left Clare for safekeeping? Clare's youngest sister Beatrice is likely to have been placed under guard and as safe from the improbable lure of Saint Damian as she was ever likely to be. Let us assume that Ortolana brought the trio food, which they rejected, forcing the mother in subsequent weeks to send them table scraps and half-used bread—Clare rejected loaves that were fresh and untouched. After five months, in September, Clare's cherished childhood friend Benvenuta joined her from Perugia. Arrangements for the young woman's escape from home and travel from the enemy city were probably devised with the aid of one or two of the Lesser Brothers, for it is doubtful that Benvenuta's family would have approved her taking up residence with the outcasts of Assisi. However it happened, Clare was now the leader of a group of four.

Thus Saint Damian was firmly established as the second great center, after Portiuncula, of the Franciscan movement. Details of Clare's early days at Saint Damian are few, but we have an idea of what her labors entailed. The women themselves worked to overcome their physical limitations and plunged into tasks that servants had probably performed for them until they abandoned their family homes. Clare and her companions mended the brothers' garments, cutting patches from usable parts of discarded fabric then whip-stitching them over the holes and tears. In exchange, the brothers did heavy work as needed, including chopping wood and digging a garden where they could cultivate herbs, vegetables, grapes, and cereals like barley for bread.

Quite probably, out of true piety as well as a desire to prove herself worthy to Francis, Clare endured the hardships of mud, ice, and hunger. As Francis's follower, she served lepers at Saint Damian and at the nearby village for them, which included Saint Lazarus of Arce, the house that Francis had visited after kissing the leper in his path. Laypersons had long served in hospices and in 1212 a church council in Paris set down guidelines that dovetailed with what Clare had pledged to Francis. They could live among the sick if there was sufficient space, provided that they followed a rule that required them to renounce their property, live in chastity, promise obedience to their superior, and wear a religious habit rather than secular clothing. Clare did preach alongside Philip the Tall. One can infer that she was met with hostility, at least initially, because at the end of her life she recorded that she and her companions "did not shirk deprivation, poverty, hard work, vexations, or the ridicule or scorn of the world—rather we considered them as great delights." This moved Francis to swear to give the same care to the women of Saint Damian, whom he called the Poor Sisters, that he gave to his brothers. He wrote a "form of life," a few simple rules, for them but this document has been lost. Surely what she called the world's contempt for them might have taken the form of the derision of townspeople who could now safely berate noble women who had been born to a station so much higher than theirs, had lived on the tolls that noble families exacted from them, and had then been so reckless as to throw it all away to assume a religiosity that they were supposed to respect.

However the Assisians might have received her at first, her preaching inspired a few other well-born women to join her. As her own reputation and that of the community grew, people from Umbria turned to them for prayer and other forms of healing. Abandoned and orphaned female babies and toddlers were given to them to raise, and thus the laughter, cries, and incessant demands of children became part of their daily life.

The women of Saint Damian and the Lesser Brothers were ultimately able to avoid the kind of scandal that the Waldensians had created. Burchard of Ursperg, a German chronicler of the Middle Ages, wrote of the Waldensians: "They claimed to be leading the life of the Apostles: they refused all ownership, even a house to reside in, and they went about from city to town. But the Lord Pope took them to task for certain strange practices: they cut off the upper part of their shoes and walked around almost barefooted: they wore mantles like religious, but had their hair cut exactly like the laity; but the most reprehensible thing about them was that men and women travelled about together, lived together most of the time in the same house, and even sometimes, it was said, slept in the same bed. All these practices, they claimed, came from the Apostles themselves." Burchard wrote that in contrast to these, the Lesser Brothers had "renounced all eccentricities and all the excesses mentioned above." Women who wandered the world, even in groups, invited scorn and danger. Unlike the women of the Humilitari and Waldensian movements, who travelled with the men, Clare and her companions would remain in Assisi.

In time Clare would become a respected healer, but the one skill that she possessed at the outset of her life at Saint Damian was the craft of spinning, turning wool or plant fibers into threads and yarn. Idleness was abhorrent to Francis, who encouraged his followers to do whatever work they could so that they would not abuse the good nature of those who gave them support and alms. She obeyed him to the letter and embraced the life he had given her. That she was accomplished at spinning was noted during her canonization process and some linen threads that she produced, along with vestments she helped to make, are displayed among the few relics of her life. As a young woman working half a century before the invention of the spinning wheel, Clare sat on a stool with a rod or distaff holding flax fibers in the crook of her left arm. In her right hand she held a spindle about nine inches long with a weight, possibly of clay, at the bottom to steady it. Using her left-hand fingers to pull out the fibers from the distaff, with her right hand she drew, twisted, and spun the fibers into thread through a notch on the top of the spindle.

Cloth production would be the work of many companions with separate skills, possibly including the brothers, who may have been weavers and dyers when they had been in the world. Some wove Clare's threads into cloth that was sewed into vestments that were later embellished with embroidery. One example of this work on display today at the Basilica of Saint Clare is an alb with twenty patterns of stitches, including lozenges, crosses, squares, and a key motif along the hem. The pairs of stylized birds and animals may have been inspired by carvings found at the Romanesque Cathedral of Saint Rufino where a band of birds and mythical beasts surround the arched doorway.

The women of Saint Damian became known for producing corporals, tunics that priests wore while saying Mass. They placed these vestments in boxes and had them distributed, possibly by the brothers, to churches throughout Umbria. Theirs was a free offering. They did not sell them to the churches, but trusted that in giving what they could to the world they would receive what they needed to keep their community alive.

Clare's first summer at Saint Damian was a time of marvelous events. In 1212 the city renewed itself and began to salve the wounds and erase the scars of its rout of the nobles. The fountain near the bishop's palace was repaired so that its spring-fed waters flowed again as they had in Roman times. Clare's uncle Scipione, father of Rufino, made this possible when he donated a plot of land covered with olive trees that had once been a source of the fountain. Another landowner had to be paid restitution after he complained that the work on his property was done without his permission, but when the project was finally finished, these proud words were chiseled above it: "Bless the Lord, O fountains. Drink, sick one, and be healed." City consuls expected that the flowing water works would attract new residents and provide a product to sell beyond the city walls. In fact, for centuries afterward a tax on these waters was a major source of revenues.

The commune took over the ancient Roman temple to Minerva, goddess of wisdom. It had served as the abbey of Saint Donato on the merchants' forum, the home of some eight Benedictine monks. For various offenses the order had fallen into disfavor in the region. Seeking to regain good will and use its funds efficiently, it rented out the property to the commune for a term of one hundred years, with the expectation of renewing the agreement for at least a century after that. The temple/abbey became a mayoral residence and city hall where a magistrate rendered judgment on civil and criminal cases.

In July something yet more marvelous occurred. Saint Rufino, the martyred bishop who was city's patron, appeared to Francis's boyhood teacher Guido in a dream. This legendary figure of antiquity, whose dates are disputed, took the sleeper by the hand and led him to the cathedral that bore his name. They descended to its crypt, which was perennially soaked in stagnant water, and found that his bones were floating there. Guido had this dream two more times before he went to the canon. The canon went to the bishop who soon led a solemn procession of dignitaries to the spot. They excavated until a Roman sarcophagus carved with voluptuous figures of the goddess Selene and her lover the shepherd Endymion emerged from the muck. Inside were bones, which were presumably those of Saint Rufino. They were reburied in the crypt of the cathedral amid much ceremony and resulting miracles.

As this unfolded, young strangers arrived, sometimes in small parties, sometime in surges. The Children's Crusade, another spontaneous movement of the period, was flowing through Italy. Undoubtedly some of the ragtag army arriving from the north made its way to the streets and fields of Assisi. Sometime between Easter and Pentecost, when Clare was escaping her family and setting up her new life, groups of agricultural workers in northern Europe, including adults and adolescent boys and girls as well as children, possibly moved by the fervor of the Easter season, joined together in a mission to free the Holy Land from the Infidel. In several separate groups they followed a general route through the Rhine Valley, over the Alps and down into Italy.

They converged in Genoa where a youth from Cologne named Nicholas took command. From there they fanned out across the peninsula. Scholars disagree as to specific facts of the movement. Some believe it was a campaign of the poor people, few of whom were younger than fifteen. Some seven thousand are said to have reached

Genoa, whence some went to Marseilles and others to Venice where
they were boarded onto ships and sold as slaves in Arab markets in
the Holy Land. Still more went south through Umbria to Brindisi
in Italy's boot where a bishop prevented them from sailing. These
then returned home. Some accounts say Nicholas, the possible
inspiration for the story of the Pied Piper of Hamelin that would
be written sixty years later in 1284, died on the return journey to
Germany. Another possibility is that angry parents hanged his
father for giving birth to a son who had caused so much pain and
havoc. Other reports said that Nicholas reached the Holy Land and
fought at Acre and the siege of Damietta and eventually returned
home safely.

Whatever befell Nicholas, most chroniclers agree that he wore a
cross in the shape of a Greek Tau, the letter that Francis added to his
own signature. Whether it was a coincidence or not, in that summer
of 1212, Francis decided that like Nicholas he would travel to the
Holy Land. With a companion he embarked from Ancona, a port
on the low, sandy Italian western coast of the Adriatic Sea, but soon
pelting rain and obstinate wind forced his boat over more than one
hundred miles of angry waters to Slavonia on the rocky Dalmatian
coast. They found they had waited too late in the year for a sea voyage
to the Holy Land, and knew they would have to return home, but
Francis and his companion had no money for passage back to Italy.
Their solution was to slip on board a ship and stow away. Thomas of
Celano put this tale of Francis's impulsive misdeed in spiritual per-
spective and indicated that their passage was paid. He wrote that a
paying passenger protected the poor men when they were discovered
by telling the angry crew that he would share his own provisions
with the two stowaways and that they would pose no further trouble.
Then when another storm blew up causing further delays, the food
that had been reserved for the two holy scofflaws fed the whole ship
for the extended voyage.

The next year, 1213, Francis travelled with Bernard of Quintavalle to the shine of Saint James in northwestern Spain. Thomas of Celano suggests that his ultimate intention was to go to Morocco, a Muslim stronghold where he might try to win souls for Christ and even see its sultan. By now, there was no limit to his imagination of what the Lord could accomplish through him, and in his eagerness he sometimes raced ahead, leaving Bernard to scramble as best he could to keep up.

The time for such a trip had never been more propitious. During July 1212, Christian forces won a decisive battle against the Muslims in the Iberian Peninsula. Most of it was already in Christian hands, divided into the kingdoms of Castile, Leon, Aragon, Portugal, and Navarre. However, the extreme south bordering the Mediterranean continued to be under the rule of the Almohades dynasty, which was based in Morocco. Pope Innocent III, through the aid of bishops in Spain, persuaded the various monarchs to work together to vanquish them entirely. Under Alfonso VIII of Castile, with the crucial help of a local shepherd who knew the mountain passes, they defeated Mohammed-ben-Naser, known to Europeans as Miramamolin, the Sultan of Morocco, at Las Navas de Tolosa near the city of Jaén on July 16, 1212. About one hundred thousand Moors were killed, compared to an estimated two thousand Catholics. A jubilant Alfonso VIII sent the tent and standard of his defeated foe to Innocent III, along with a detailed report of the victory.

As a young man Francis's imagination had been captured by the story of Roland, a tale created a hundred years before Francis's birth, probably in Normandy by the poet Turold in 1095. It is possibly the greatest of the *chanson de geste*, a medieval genre that celebrates heroic characters and mighty, usually military, feats. *The Song of Roland* was inspired by what had in fact been a minor skirmish between Charlemagne's army and Basque forces in 778. The poet set aside historical facts and turned the defeat into a tale of inspiration.

Charlemagne was in his mid-thirties at the time of the real encounter, but the poet made him an old man with a flowing white mane of hair.

The story begins with a fabricated tale of betrayal by Charlemagne's brother-in-law against the fictitious Roland, Charlemagne's nephew, and his faithful friend Oliver. It celebrates the idea that the performance of feudal duty is a man's greatest deed and that he must sacrifice all else to this end. In the tale, Charlemagne stationed the brave and eager Roland at a mountain pass and ordered him to sound his horn if the Saracen attacked, but in his pride Roland delayed too long. One by one Charlemagne's dukes fell and his troops dwindled. Now Roland was ready to sound the horn. "Too late!" cried Oliver. "You have killed us with your pride!" Roland blew until his temples burst and salty blood poured through his throat. Still, Roland and Oliver were able to bow to each other before departing this life. When fierce Roland fell, the angel Gabriel himself raised his soul to Paradise where it was met by the heavenly host.

The Pass of Roncesvalles is the traditional site of the battle and the beginning of a route to the shrine of Saint James. Surely Francis walked the terrain where his hero Roland had fought and fallen. Whatever the path he took to get there, the journey home was arduous. A hostile host drove Francis and Bernard from their lodgings and an ailing Francis lost the power of speech for three days. As he recovered he told Bernard that he was so hungry he was ready to eat a bird. Before they took many more steps a horseman they had seen riding in the distance drew up to them and presented Francis with a fowl ready for the spit.

Sometime in these years, divine grace may have worked in his heart in another way. Francis, who urged his hearers to seek the forgiveness of God, may well have reconciled with his own father.[†] One small clue to this lies in his comment to the Bishop of Imola, a city

---

[†] Peter possibly died by 1215 because in that year Angelo is recorded in city archives as Agnelus Picae, or son of Pica.

about thirty miles southeast of Bologna. When Francis requested his permission to preach there, the bishop denied it, saying, "It is enough that I preach to the people." Francis meekly accepted the refusal, departed, but soon reappeared. "What do you want now, Brother?" the bishop asked. Francis answered, "If a father drives his son out of one door, he must come back in another." Could Francis have made such a statement if he had not done it himself? The bishop was so charmed that he told Francis that he and his men could preach in his city then and at any time in the future. In similar fashion, Francis who preached forgiveness to others may have made a way back to his father's heart. If the angry, disowned Francis cast his father from his heart, the penitent peace seeker surely thought better of it and invited Peter Bernadone to come back in.

PART II

6

The Pope's Daughters in Rome

IN THE CITY OF ROME lived a woman named Praxiteles who made her home in a dark narrow cell in the Aurelian Wall. There she spent her days in prayer and meditation, existing on whatever food or money passing pilgrims left as alms. For some forty years since her infancy, when she must have been abandoned but cared for by other women sheltering in the wall, she eked out her existence with a focused passion that burned away most human needs. Praxiteles was a legend, spoken about by visitors and their guides, palpable but unseen and praying in deepest shadow through the icy blasts of winter and the withering summer heat. Through it all she remained indifferent to the election and demise of at least three popes, and they were indifferent to her, until the coming of Pope Innocent III.

Innocent saw the pilgrims leaving food at the wall when he travelled the streets of Rome, going to his family compound in the Roman Forum or departing for the summer through the Flaminia Gate that led northward to the Papal States. The Aurelian Wall stretched for twelve miles around the city and had been constructed over a period of ten years late in the third century AD and refortified in the fifth to withstand barbarian invaders. About a dozen feet wide and more than twice as high, the bastion incorporated whole buildings along its path. Between those captured structures, the wall was built of bricks with a covered passageway that Roman soldiers had used on patrol. Now female recluses, many maimed or crippled by lives of deprivation or the violence of others, lived in the nooks of the section of the wall between the Lateran Palace where Innocent lived and the Stairs of Pilate. These were twenty-eight marble steps where Jesus was said to have walked and which Saint Helena, mother of Constantine the Great, had brought to Rome from Jerusalem in 326. Others besides Praxiteles had been deposited in the wall as unwanted babies and were cared for by sequestered women happy to have a child to raise for the service of God. Still other women took shelter there later in life, propelled to solitary prayer by painful tragedies and desperate situations. Through the goings and comings, Praxiteles remained.

Could there have been a greater contrast between the glory of Rome and the destitution of women without earthly ties? All his life in Rome, even from boyhood, Innocent III had been aware of the unmarried women throughout the city who lived supposedly religious lives. They were not all recluses. Some banded together in private houses and established their own devotional practices, as had the Beguines of Panzo near Assisi who had sheltered Clare. Others were nuns from orders that predated the coming of Saint Benedict, whose detailed regulation for every moment and aspect of monastic life had guided convents and monasteries in Christendom since the middle of the sixth century.

By custom, and without specific church sanction, the Roman nuns strolled through the streets and plazas in religious procession. They felt free to visit their relations and benefactors who provided just enough support to keep the ancient convents going without the need for a careful watch over deeds and finances. To Innocent's way of thinking, the diversity and haphazardness of these varied lifestyles invited dangers, temptations, laxity, and scandal in a city that was already rife with them. Rome, which in Jesus's time encompassed half a million people, had shrunk to about thirty-five thousand by the early thirteenth century. The city managed to retain the mystique of empire nonetheless, for it contained wonders of the pagan world, such as the Colosseum where early Christians were fed to lions, and the marvels of the Catholic ascendancy, such as the tomb of Saint Peter.

Practically speaking, at this time the Eternal City was reduced to being the administrative center for the pope and for a collection of competing noble families. Their power and bellicosity dated from the days of Charlemagne in the eighth century, although many claimed descent from ancient heroes including Aeneas, mythic founder of Rome. The families owned estates in the areas surrounding Rome, in the hills to the north, and in the Campagna region to the south by the Tyrrhenian Sea, but of course it was in Rome that they stamped their presence. They used the city like a game board to act out their squabbles and feuds, each in turn taking the upper hand and going so far as to install one of their brethren as head of the church, which through the centuries led to rival claimants and a number of anti-popes.

The common people of Rome relied on an economy that was based on pilgrimage and church administration. Both required food, lodgings, and other services that allowed tradesmen from cobblers to butchers and blacksmiths to support themselves in the messy business of life. The historian Richard Krautheimer said that medieval Rome was "covered with dirt, unpaved, impassable in rain and bad weather; flooded time and again by the Tiber; congested by beasts of burden and by porters carrying their loads; filled with obstacles from porches and stands to fences; and taken over all along by craftsmen at work in front of their shops or by housewives and maids doing their washing and cooking on the street."

By the time of Francis and Clare, Rome had been Christian for nearly nine hundred years. Constantine recognized Christianity as a legal religion through the Edict of Milan in 313 and had given the Lateran Palace to the leaders of the Roman Catholic Church, intending it to be the center of all their operations and the residence of their pope. The faithful, however, never embraced this place. They preferred sites that were infused with the history of their religion, such as the catacombs where the first Christians held Mass and, above all, Saint Peter's Basilica on the Vatican Hill across the Tiber, where the first pope had been martyred and his body entombed. Only in the fifteenth century, when the popes returned to Rome from Avignon, did they abandon the neglected Lateran and make the Vatican the administrative and spiritual center of the church.

As in everything else, Innocent III made his mark on Rome. Besides renovating the Lateran Palace, which had been the main residence of the popes since the fourth century, Innocent built the Holy Spirit Hospital and its hostel for pilgrims. The latter was to atone for his pride in building the Tower of Conti on his family compound in the Nerva section of the ancient Roman Forum. A massive structure somewhat taller than the Colosseum, the tower soared almost 200 feet and inspired one chronicler to say that it touched the clouds. In 1208, Innocent built a fortified three-story papal residence close to Saint Peter's Basilica that became the core of the Vatican Palace. It included office buildings, a bakery, wine cellar, kitchen, and housing for the staff, as well as a five-story tower. As for churches, Innocent III tended to renovate rather than build. One of these was the dilapidated Basilica of Saint Sixtus on the Appian Way near the ruins of the Baths of Caracalla, just within the walls of Rome. It was surrounded by streams, at least one of which was forceful enough to power a mill, and was so enormous that it contained three naves. He decided that this was the place where he would relocate all the religious women of Rome. His plan was to eliminate the side naves, halve the central one, and raise the floor to the center of the existing columns. Thus he would create a new and smaller church with a top floor that would house sixty women, all of whom were to take the vows of nuns.

Unification, centralization, and standardization were his goals for other groups as well. At the end of 1200, he tried to unite the three branches of the Humiliati religious group into one. Four months later, on April 19, 1201, he sought to merge the Cistercian and Augustinian orders of the city of Riga so that the relatively fine points of their separate orders would not confuse the pagans living in the surrounding Baltic lands. Innocent III had little success in these endeavors, which perhaps is why he chose to concentrate his efforts on behalf of women closer to home. The pope was the bishop of Rome, and as bishop of Rome he could mandate one rule, one garb, and one form of religious practice for women who insisted that they were loyal to the church. He decided to put them all in a cloister where they would be shut off from the world like recluses but live together in a group under the protection, guidance, and governance of the Roman Catholic Church. Only one group was exempt: the convent of Saint Agnes northeast of the city walls. This was the pilgrimage site of the grave of a Christian girl, Agnes, who in 305 AD was martyred after refusing to choose between worshiping the virgin goddess Minerva or being raped. All Christians knew her story, including Francis, who gave Agnes's name to Clare's sister Catherine after her own ordeal in Assisi.

Always strategic, Innocent III began his efforts with women who were already nuns living in small but actual convents that were scattered about the city. Most were in debt, though rich in land. In 1204, he took his first step by writing to the abbesses reminding them that they were in his special care and forbidding them to sell or transfer their assets unless he or his cardinal-vicar gave them written permission. He then focused on the nuns of Saint Mary in the Temple, who possessed an exceptional icon of the Virgin Mary that supposedly had been brought to Rome from Constantinople and was painted by the evangelist Luke (but has since been dated to around the eighth century after Christ). About thirty by fifteen inches in size, the icon depicts Mary with golden hands and a golden cross on her left shoulder. She is turned slightly, and gazes with concern at the onlooker. On holy days the nuns carried it through the city; but otherwise left it hanging in their chapel, where all the faithful were welcome to pray and to seek its miraculous intervention. Not only was Saint Mary in the Temple a magnet of devotion, it was practically adjacent to Saint Sixtus. Innocent intended that these nuns would relocate to Saint Sixtus with their famous icon and be an example and inducement to the other religious women.

Renovations at that basilica began in 1208. By 1213 Innocent had poured such extensive financial resources into it that he asked King John of England to make an annual contribution of 150 marks for the work. In return, Innocent agreed to support John as his vassal, which meant that the pope stood with him against the English barons and the Archbishop of Canterbury, Stephen Langton, who had been Innocent's fellow student in Paris. These men had drawn up the Magna Carta to limit the king's powers and had persuaded John to sign it, but Innocent III condemned and annulled the document, saying that the barons had forced the king to agree to it through force and fear.

Innocent decried the Magna Carta as a threat to kingship and to the church. In a letter, he told the English bishops that King John was entitled to respect as a Crusader. He accused them and Stephen Langton of being worse than Saracens, because in disrespecting John they disrespected the Crusades. In late November 1215 after John pressured the pope by reducing his contribution to the Crusades, Innocent III excommunicated the barons who had rebelled against their king.

The English Order of Sempringham was supposed to take control of the lives of the religious women of Rome, but they never took up the project, which was so far from their homeland. Finally Dominic Guzman, a Spaniard who had already proven his zeal for Roman Catholic orthodoxy and for establishing convents, was appointed to the task. He was born around 1170, some fourteen years before Francis, in Castile on the high plains of north-central Spain. Dominic gained a reputation as a reformer while still a young cleric in Osma. That city's bishop, Don Diego d'Azevedo, took Dominic with him on a mission to Denmark for Alfonso IX, the King of Castile in 1203. When their travels took them through the Languedoc region, Dominic and Diego were horrified to see that the Cathar heresy was rapidly gaining converts in Toulouse, a city of soft pink stone on the Garonne River in the northwestern foothills of the Pyrenees.

Cathars believed in the divinity of Christ and in his Gospel, but they took a dim view of creation. To them all that was physical, including the earth and the human body, was the evil work of the devil. Only the spiritual world was good, and it alone was the dominion of God. Since they regarded the flesh as bad, they denied that Christ had been human, forbade the eating of meat, and banned sexual intercourse. They believed that humans who indulged in these and did not repent were condemned to rebirth on earth again and again until they were reconciled with God. Cathars had sacraments that paralleled those of the Church, but their main religious rite was the *consolamentum*, a laying-on of hands that called down the Holy Spirit. This was done by one of their ministers, or *perfecti*, who lived by every tenet of Catharism. The rigor of their lives intimidated Roman Catholic priests and awed the Catholic faithful.

Believed to have been brought to the West from Bulgaria by merchants, Catharism took root among the Franks in the early eleventh century. By the time Dominic arrived, the counts of Foix and the entire family of the Catholic Bishop of Carcassonne had converted. The name Cathar was derived from the Greek word for "pure," but Cathars were also known as Albigensians, after one of the many places where they flourished. This was the dark-red brick city of Albi on the Tarn River, some fifty miles northeast of Toulouse.

Catharism spread rapidly throughout Italy and developed a strong base in Milan, which became a center for study of its theology. For the most part Cathars lived in peace with Roman Catholics and civil authorities, some of whom were converted because of the Cathars' exemplary lives.

Zoé Oldenbourg, a leading historian of the Albigensian Crusade, said that when Catholic priests spoke against Catharism, their hearers could hardly understand why they criticized it. She noted, "Between a world created by the Devil, which was merely tolerated by God (the Cathar doctrine) and a universe created by God but wholly corrupted and perverted by the Devil (the Catholic teaching), there might seem to be no great difference—not at least in practice." In sum, the church said that evil was due to human error, not to the nature of the world itself. The church condemned sin, not human existence.

In contrast to the Cathars, Francis celebrated the world created by God. He delighted in stones, worms, sparrows, and water as manifestations of God's love. All material creatures, including the wind and sun, were his brother or sister under the fatherhood of God. Francis surely met Cathars as he wandered throughout Italy, France, and Spain. He never preached against them as far as records show, nor did he attack their doctrines. Instead, he urged everyone to marvel in the glory of a world so marvelous that could never have come from the Evil One. The word "Cathar" or "heretic" never seemed to fall from his lips. Thomas of Celano wrote that when Francis entered a city the faithful rejoiced, while the heretics "slipped secretly away." He also said that when one heretic in Lombardy accused Francis of hypocrisy, the people made the wretch apologize. One of the miracles that Thomas attributes to Francis after his death was the freeing of a man falsely accused of being a heretic.

If Francis turned his other cheek, Dominic did not. In late 1204 he and Bishop Diego went to Rome to seek the pope's permission to convert unbelievers in distant lands. However, Innocent III did not grant their wish. He recognized them as men that he needed closer to home in his fight against the Cathars, which thus far had been unsuccessful. In the first year of his papacy Innocent III had relied on prelates from the Cistercian order. This relatively new order, founded almost exactly a century earlier in 1098, had a reputation for austerity, discipline, and moral reform.

However, even the Cistercians that the pope sent were prosperous, worldly, and disdainful compared to the simple Cathars, who were so admirably strict, hardworking, and devoted to the letter of the Gospels that they attracted the humble poor. Impoverished noble families in the Midi found them so commendable that they sent their daughters to the local Cathar convent to be educated. Innocent III dispatched Dominic and Diego to assist the ineffective Cistercians in Toulouse. By 1206 Dominic was preaching the Gospel barefoot in the streets throughout the region and debating with leading Cathars. One of them insisted, "The Roman church is not holy. It is the church of the devil. It is that Babylon that John, in the Apocalypse, calls the mother of fornication and abominations." Many Toulousois were inclined to agree.

Dominic's preaching against the heretics was largely unsuccessful and so he turned to threats. According to Stephen of Salagnac, a Dominican priest and historian writing a few decades after Dominic's death, Dominic told a crowd of Cathars at Prouille, France: "For several years now I have spoken words of peace to you. I have preached to you: I have besought you with tears. But as the common saying goes in Spain, 'Where a blessing fails, a good thick stick will succeed.' Now we shall rouse princes and prelates against you; and they, alas, will in their turn assemble whole nations and peoples, and a mighty number will perish by the sword. Towers will fall, and walls be razed to the ground, and you will all of you be reduced to servitude. Thus force will prevail where gentle persuasion has failed to do so."

Dominic's major achievement in his battle against Catharism was the establishment in 1206 of a Roman Catholic convent in Prouille for women who converted from heresy. It was so successful that he was put in charge of Saint Sixtus and he embarked on an outreach to the women of Rome. Dominic was, according to someone who saw him often at this time, a cheerful, happy man of medium height with a full head of reddish hair flecked with grey. His face was pleasing and his complexion ruddy, although his forehead seemed to shine. His hands were long and beautiful, and his voice powerful and resonant. On an almost daily basis Dominic, wearing the white tunic and black cloak that was the habit of his order, went to the Aurelian Wall to encourage the recluses, Praxiteles among them, that for their own good, whether or not they feared other people, or whether they had made specific and personal vows to remain in place, they had to move to Saint Sixtus.

Bringing the Eucharist and hearing confessions, he was said to have healed at least two recluses of serious physical afflictions. He found one named Lucy living behind the Church of Saint Anastasia and restored her arm, which was said to be nothing but an exposed bone. He healed the worm-infested breast of Bona, who lived in the Lateran Gate of the Aurelian Wall with her servant Jacobina.

Three cardinals assisted Dominic in his campaign: Nicholas of Tusculum, whose predecessor and namesake had persuaded King John to help fund Saint Sixtus; Stephen of Fossa Nova, who had overseen the finances for building projects such as this convent; and finally Hugolino, Cardinal-Bishop of Ostia, Innocent's kinsman and a man who would later shape the lives and affairs of Francis and Clare. One by one, each prelate went to the women, invoking the authority and wisdom of the church, insisting that they must come together in one cloister and be shut off from the dangers of the world.

At some point, Abbess Eugenia of the convent of Saint Mary in the Temple consented, but settling the house's debts and legal entanglements continued to impede their move to Saint Sixtus. The process stretched on for more than a year from the beginning of 1220. Friends and relatives of the nuns were against the plan, as were benefactors who were annoyed that the unknown Spaniard Dominic

Guzman and his men, called the Order of Preachers, were taking over the administration of all the Roman properties.

The matter was finally settled when the pope presented Abbess Eugenia with money to cover all the expenses of their move, including payment of outstanding debts. It was decided that on Ash Wednesday, February 24, 1221, Eugenia was to formally abdicate and surrender her office and its rights to Dominic at Saint Sixtus in the presence of the cardinals. On Ash Wednesday each year, the cardinals made a solemn procession from the Lateran to Saint Anastasia, where Cardinal-Bishop Hugolino anointed the foreheads of the faithful with ashes to remind them of their mortality. The group then proceeded to Saint Sabina for Mass.

The ceremonial pageantry, and the predictability of the event, was expected to obscure the fact that the women were being relocated. However, things took an unexpected turn according to one of the nuns, a teenage girl named Cecilia from the wealthy Caesarini family. As she told it in her reminiscences in old age, she stood among the nuns with Cardinal Stephen and Dominic at Saint Sixtus, awaiting the arrival of the procession, when a distraught man, screaming and pulling his hair, rode up. He told them that Cardinal Stephen's nephew Napoleon Orsini had fallen from his horse and was dead. Stephen collapsed.

Dominic quickly blessed Stephen with holy water and then hurried off to attend to the victim. He had the youth's crushed and torn body carried to a nearby house and then taken to Saint Sixtus where a Mass was said. At the consecration, the high point of the Mass when bread is turned into the body of Christ, Cecilia and the others were astonished to see Dominic levitate a foot off the ground. Wonders did not cease with that. After Mass, the cardinals and their retinues, along with all the nuns and Dominic, approached the young man's corpse. They watched as Dominic arranged its broken parts several times, levitated once again, and then commanded Napoleon Orsini to rise up in the name of the Lord Jesus Christ. As if waking from a slumber, the young man sat up and asked for something to eat. Cecilia recalled, "Then Blessed Dominic gave him food and drink and returned him in gay spirits to his uncle without even the slightest mark of injury. The young man had been dead from morning to three o'clock in the afternoon." More probably, the youth was concussed, but the event created a sensation that worked for Dominic's purposes.

On the first Sunday of Lent, four days after Dominic called the cardinal's nephew back to life, he received those nuns, recluses, and laywomen of Rome who had agreed to join the community of Saint Sixtus. Cecilia was the first to enter, accepting her new habit from him as he stood at the front door. She made her vows to him, followed by the abbess, all the nuns of Saint Mary in the Temple, and other religious and laywomen. After years of effort and much resistance, forty-four women had come to reside at Saint Sixtus. The next step was relocating their prized icon. Fearing that the people of Rome would oppose its removal from a site where they were welcome, church officials decided to move it by night. Dominic, the cardinals Nicholas and Stephen, and various others all barefoot and bearing lighted torches, carried the icon the short distance from the abandoned Saint Mary in the Temple to Saint Sixtus. Barefoot nuns prayed as the image was installed in a place of honor in their new church.

Notwithstanding the story of the cardinal's nephew restored to life, which surely spread through Rome, the nuns' friends and relatives were shocked to discover that Dominic had confined the women to Saint Sixtus and forbidden them to leave. A group of them appeared at Saint Sixtus and in the words of Cecilia, "They began to upbraid the abbess and nuns very severely for letting such a noble monastery (Saint Mary in the Temple) fall into disuse and for willingly putting themselves in the hands of that coarse and offensive nobody." Many of the nuns were persuaded that they had been wrong to move.

One morning after Mass, Dominic told them that he knew they had changed their minds and no longer wished to walk "on the Lord's highway." He called on those who still wished to stay at Saint Sixtus to repeat their vows to him. He was surely charismatic, because all of them, even those who had wavered, remained. Dominic then gathered up all the keys of the convent and assumed its full control. He appointed his lay brothers to guard it by day and night and to provide it with food and whatever else the women might need. Communication with the outside world was banned. The brothers were to prevent the nuns from speaking with their relatives or others.

Cecilia recalled in her recollections *The Miracles of Saint Dominic* that the founder liked to visit the convent at the end of the day after he had preached or heard confessions in the outside world. She said that in the evening he would have a conference with them, or give them a sermon, in the presence of other brothers. On one occasion, after he returned from a visit to Spain, he presented each of them with a spoon made of cypress wood.

Once he joined them at so late an hour that the nuns had retired for the night. Nonetheless, the brothers who guarded the door rang the bell that summoned them. Dominic wanted to share some good news. He told them that he had spent the day fishing and the Lord had rewarded him with a big fish: the only son of a prominent man of Rome had joined his Order of Preachers. After speaking for some time, he called for wine. The abbess told him they had only one cup, but Dominic was undeterred. He had the cellarer Brother Roger fill it to the brim. Then he blessed it, took a sip, and then passed it to his brothers, possibly six in number. They passed the cup around until each had had enough and then Dominic called a nun named Nubia to sip from it. She went to the cup with one of the other nuns and then they passed the cup along. Dominic kept encouraging "Drink up, my daughters," yet miraculously the cup remained full and not a drop was spilled, as if it were being constantly replenished.

When midnight approached, Dominic wanted to proceed to Saint Sabina, where his followers lived. It was a mile away, through dark streets and menacing corners. The brothers and nuns tried to dissuade him from venturing through Rome at so late an hour. Nonetheless, Dominic left with two brothers. Outside the door of Saint Sixtus a beautiful young man was waiting. Not only did this stranger escort them safely, he was able to move the bolt of the door of Saint Sabina. When the brothers of the house came down for matins prayers soon after, they were astonished to find Dominic amongst them unannounced. He told them that he had been guided by the angel of the Lord who had unlocked their door.

Dominic soon felt that the women at Saint Sixtus, coming from so many backgrounds, needed focused instruction in how to become one true community. In mid-April 1221, eight sisters from Prouille arrived at Saint Sixtus. He had sent them to help the mélange of one-time abbesses, recluses, and laywomen to adjust to each other and to their new way of life. Cecilia must have done so happily and well because in 1229 she herself would be sent from Rome to Bologna, to the new convent of Saint Agnes that had been established for all the diverse religious women of that city. There she instructed its inhabitants on the appropriate behavior that the religious women of Rome had been encouraged to learn.

For much of the time that this unfolded, Praxiteles lived in the Aurelian Wall, growing more anxious with each passing day. Before her was the prospect of leaving her life of solitude in the Lord for one where she would be pressed in among strange women and forced to follow strange ways. She agonized over breaking the vow she had made to God, even after one of the cardinals ordered her to accept the assistance of some religious women lest she die from abandonment or neglect. Praxiteles refused, yet the prelate persisted.

While she was still resisting, Francis heard of her plight during a stay in Rome, and he took the recluse under his protection. He gave her a tattered tunic such as his brothers wore and made her a member of his order. Thus, she was under his authority and not subject to Dominic or the cardinals. He probably did this around 1220, the year before the Convent of Saint Sixtus was finally established. Quite possibly the person who led him to Praxiteles was a young noblewoman named Jacqueline de Settesoli. Whenever or however they met, Jacqueline became his valued friend, as is well attested in early Franciscan records.

Descended from the Norman knights who had conquered Sicily, she was born around 1190, some six years after Francis and six before Clare. Her marriage to Gratian de Settesoli made her a member of the Settesoli branch of the Frangipani family that held extensive tracts of Rome, part of which were on the edge of the Palatine Hill near the end of the Circus Maximus. Within the huge walls, fortified by a tower, were a water mill, orchards, and vineyards. They also had a dwelling on the forum and possession of the Colosseum, which they reinforced and used as their stronghold. They owned lands in Campagna, Maritima, and Terracina. The Settesoli claimed descent from the third century emperor Septimius Severus, whose massive arch stood in the ancient forum by the Frangipani home. In fact, the family is unknown to history before the tenth century AD, when it built a fortress in Trastevere. It achieved the status of nobility in the eleventh century when one of its daughters married Baruch Pierleoni, a Jewish banker who converted to Christianity and took the name Benedictus Christian. The great eleventh century pope of reform, Hildebrand, or Pope Gregory VII, probably descended from this couple.

In his *History of the City of Rome*, Ferdinand Gregorovius underscored the general cruelty that prevailed in Jacqueline's era: "The Roman nobles of this age were a rude race, dwelling in ancient monuments, divided into parties, at lasting strife with both pope and emperor." He observed that the troubadour poets who were welcomed at refined courts in southern Italy and France were not known to have visited the manors of the crude Roman aristocracy, nor did the city's evocative ruins inspire their songs. Culture, taste, and artistry were not associated with the battling clans of Rome and their internecine plots. The Frangipani might have been the worst of them. They had no sense of law and accepted no pope who was not their kin. In 1204, to defend themselves against rival papal forces, the family had barricaded themselves in the Colosseum.

Their character was not congenial to Jacqueline. If she could have adapted, she would not have been the person to become friends with Francis. She first appears in official records in a May 13, 1217 transaction with a papal representative over the rights to the castle of Ninfa. Her statement begins, "I am that Jacqueline, wife of the late Gratian Frangipani, and guardian of John and Gratian, my sons." (*Ego quidem Iacoba, uxor quondam D. Gratiani Frangenspanem et tutrix Ioannis et Gratiani filorum meorum.*)

In this settlement she renounced all rights to the lands that her husband had claimed, and she paid two of the pope's nephews monies that they said they were owed. From this we know she had legal standing. In widowhood, aristocratic women of the Middle Ages attained full rights, including the right to return to their own family, but a desire to protect her small sons would have required Jacqueline to reside at the Settesoli home and remain unwed. A widow who remarried lost guardianship of her children. Even if she did not remarry, her husband's kinsmen would have some say in their upbringing, and it is likely that she wanted to minimize their influence.

Religion seems to have been her solace, although she surely lived in comfort. Francis, who ate what was given to him whether it was moldy bread or a succulent fish, was known to have especially appreciated the *mostacciolli* almond and honey cakes that she served. The wealthy in Rome at this time enjoyed the technological marvel of glass panes in their windows and the extravagance of linen hangings with painted motifs that brightened their interiors. Exotic animals were a fashion: nobles of the period were known to carry with them hawks, falcons, monkeys, and parrots. Dogs were constant companions, gnawing at bones, fouling floors where they would. Wolf cubs were also popular, at least until they matured into their wild natures.

Francis gave Jacqueline a lamb, possibly to comfort her after a particularly stressful incident, or more probably to find a good home for one he rescued. He so loved these animals that he cursed a sow that ate a newborn lamb at a Benedictine monastery he was visiting near Gubbio. The pig quickly sickened and endured three days of painful torment before dying, whereupon it dried up like wood so that not so much as a maggot would touch it. It and a large bird that ate the food of a smaller one, were rare animals that felt the full ire of Francis of Assisi. Another time when Francis found a lamb lost in a herd of goats, he persuaded a passing merchant to buy it from the goatherd who planned to kill it. Then he carried it with him for several days before depositing it with a community of women at Saint Severino. They later wove a tunic for Francis from its wool and had it presented to him at a gathering of his brothers. He was so delighted and amused that he hugged and kissed the garment created from his beloved lamb, and modeled it for his brothers with great joy.

Jacqueline was just as pleased with the lamb that he gave her. According to Saint Bonaventure, who possibly learned the story from Jacqueline herself, she and her pet were so in tune that if she slept late, it would nudge her and bleat to waken her so that she would have time to dress for Mass. The lamb accompanied her to church, remained by her side, and then saw her home again.

As for the recluse Praxiteles, Thomas of Celano wrote that the very calamity the cardinal had warned Praxiteles against did happen, but only after Francis's death. One day, seeking to retrieve some object, she climbed up to a cranny at the top of her cell only to fall to the ground, breaking her foot and her leg and dislocating her shoulder "totally from the joint." She lay on the floor in agony as night wore on, worried as much about being forced into the convent for her own good as she was about her physical well-being. She prayed to Francis, pointing out that since he had helped many that he did not know when he was alive, he should surely help her who had been his friend. She said, "As you can see, blessed father, I must either change my promised way of life or submit to a death sentence." Sobbing, she repeated this over and over until she had cried herself to sleep. Francis then appeared to her wearing white garments and said, "Arise, beloved daughter, arise and do not be afraid. Receive the sign of complete healing and keep your promise intact!" He then took her by the hand, helped her up, and vanished from sight. Thinking she was still moving through the vision, she went to the window and signaled a monk who was amazed to find her standing. In the light of his lamp, she realized she was awake and free of pain. The miracle that had saved her was written down, possibly to be given as evidence in Francis's canonization process.

Each age finds its own explanations for the miraculous, whether it is the intervention of a saint or the stories that fill a brain after a heavy blow. Possibly Praxiteles had not actually broken a bone or dislocated a shoulder, but the shock of the painful fall had made her think she had. After a deep sleep she awoke the next morning back to herself and mended. Praxiteles's exact fate will probably never be known for sure. There is one clue, however. A legal document listing the forty-eight "ladies or sisters" living with Clare in 1238 includes one named Praxeda. Medieval names are written with many linguistic and spelling variations, and certainly one name can be shared by many people. However, it could also be that Praxiteles the recluse was spirited out of Rome and taken to Assisi where with Clare she lived into old age, faithful to her vows amidst the respect and care of those who honored her, her path, and Francis.

$$\frac{7}{}$$

Consolidation of Power

N O REGION WAS more welcoming to Francis than the Marches, which stretch from the northeast border of Umbria eastward over bare mountain peaks to the beaches of the Adriatic coast. No people there were happier to see him than a community of women living in Colpersito outside the city of San Severino. These were the ones who took in the lamb he had rescued from slaughter, raised lovingly, sheared carefully, then spun yarn from its wool to weave into a tunic that they presented to Francis.

But however much joy they may have given to Francis, as he stood in their midst on a particular day around the year 1213, he saw that they could do nothing to lift the mood of another visitor. Illustrations of such persons have him wearing a long luxurious belted indigo coat. On his head a large soft cap fell forward over one shoulder. Near his hand, ready to be played at any moment, was a zither. He may have been named Guglielmo, or William, and born in Lisciano in the Marches hills to the south, but now living in the royal court at Palermo. While the cousin he was visiting had chosen to live a life of prayer and service, he had embarked on the grand life of a troubadour. His way with words and music was so dazzling that an emperor, either Henry IV or his son Frederick II, had named him "The King of Verses." Still, he was not happy.

Adulation and the comforts of court life were proving to be hollow, or perhaps he was grieving a loss, or feeling guilty over some misdeed. Whatever the cause, this impressive figure yearned for change. Looking at him, Francis, small, dark, and certainly shabby, saw the vision of the man he once would have liked to have been. The former merchant had expert knowledge of the cost of such beautiful raiment, both in money and in compromise. Francis surely told him of another kind of life that would bring him peace, yet the troubadour said he was not quite ready for it. He said that he would lead a better life eventually, possibly after he unburdened himself of his troubles, but Francis was in a hurry on his behalf. Having himself found peace in renouncing wealth and all worldly forms of gratification, including the thought of ever being a roving singer himself, Francis urged him to shake off the esteem that the world had given, along with his boisterous friends, and join the Lesser Brothers immediately. As this poet looked at the holy man, he saw two glittering swords appear and join over Francis, one extending from his head to his toes, the other from one hand to the other, in the sign of a cross. This vision showed him the way.

Thomas of Celano says the man announced, "What need is there for any more words? Let us turn to deeds! Take me away from people and give me back to the Great Emperor!" The next day, after this convert gave away his belongings, Francis gave him the tonsure and said that henceforth he would be known as Pacifico, for the tranquility that the Lord would bring to his life.

Of the variety of men who responded to the joy of Francis's public self, none had a more amazing history than Pacifico, but all manner of men were joining Francis for all manner of personal reasons besides the love of God, the certitude of Francis, and the fellowship of the brothers. There were disaffected knights like his old friend Angelo, penitent priests like Sylvester, the simple like Juniper, and refined seekers such as Bernard of Quintavalle. Whether they deliberated for months before taking their vows like Rufino, or joined on impulse like Pacifico, depended on their characters and how life had treated them. Records of the first dozen years of the Lesser

Brothers are lacking, as the great medieval and Franciscan scholar André Vauchez points out. Umbria offers most of what is available. From them we know that in 1213 the bishop of Gubbio, who was a Benedictine monk, allowed Francis and his men to settle in an abandoned church where a soldier named Benevenuto joined them and later took charge of a leper hospice. That same year Francis was also in Terni preaching from the top of an ancient column, in Foligno living with a family, and at Montefalco staying with "religious people." Based on stories of how frequently he drew followers in the early years, one could estimate that at this time there were a hundred Lesser Brothers in central Italy. With a group of this size Francis was a master of leadership and organization. He knew each of his followers personally and his plan of sending them out in pairs, of alternating periods of solitary prayer with work in the world, and of semi-annual assemblies where the brothers could be renewed and reminded of their common purpose, served the needs of each man and of the movement.

When happy, Francis was still moved to walk in dancing steps and draw a stick across his elbow as he serenaded God with phantom strings. Pacifico would be loath to ever take up his instrument again, and had probably given it away, just as he exchanged his fine garments for a poor man's tunic the hour he joined the Lesser Brothers. Imagine Pacifico humming praises to the Lord as he had once sung of willing maidens, and taking spiritual guidance not only from the Gospel, but from the legends of Roland and King Arthur that he and Francis knew so well. Pacifico was one of the brothers who reported having visions of Francis marked with God's favor. Once on the forehead of Francis, he saw the sign of the Tau, a Greek letter and symbol of Christ's cross that Francis frequently used, arrayed in varicolored circles like a peacock's glorious tail.

Devils apparently had an interest in Francis too and tempted him to succumb to lust. On these occasions, Francis would whip himself with the cord that he tied around his waist. Once when the whipping failed to distract Francis, he threw himself into a bank of snow even though his body was covered with black and blue welts. He then made seven large snowballs that he addressed as if they were his wife, two sons, two daughters, and a servant and a maid. He told himself to dress them quickly before they died from cold, but that if such responsibilities were too much trouble, he should simply serve the Lord. This drove off the devil in some confusion; but Francis later learned that one of the brothers had observed the drama. He told him to remain silent about it for as long as Francis lived.

Francis sought to pray alone in secluded places, but sometimes God called to him when he was with others. Then Francis would make a shelter of his cloak or his sleeve, pulling it over his face to commune with the Lord alone. Other times he would drop his head down into his breast for privacy, so quiet as to be inert. He praised, beseeched, and thanked God, depending on his need and feeling of the moment. His preferred form, based on what he told his brothers when they asked him how to pray, was to say a prayer he had learned in church, but with elaboration so it was not formulaic. His favorite seems to have begun something like this: "Our father, our creator, redeemer, consoler and savior, who are in heaven with the angels and the saints enlightening them to know, inflaming them to love, for you, Lord, are love."

He had a particular devotion to Mary the Mother of God, Michael the Archangel, and Saint John the Baptist. He prayed in a different manner when he was far from others deep in a forest or near a surging mountain stream. Then he convulsed in adoration, supplication, groaning, weeping. He would strike his breast with his fist and give voice as if talking to a judge, a father, a friend, or a lover. At times his prayer took hold of him and he was caught up as if becoming one with the Lord. Francis so focused on whatever he desperately sought—peace of mind, release from pain, forgiveness or a loving, forgiving heart—that it was as if he himself became his prayer. He was filled by what he sought instead of being depleted by its absence.

All the brothers saw marvels in the ways that the natural world reacted to Francis. He was travelling by boat to the brothers' dwelling in Rieti when a fisherman gave him a waterfowl. He cradled the bird then opened his hands to let it fly away, but the bird continued to nestle in his arms until he blessed it. A captured fish that he set free followed behind his boat, and rabbits that he was given to pet refused to return to the woods. He rescued doves that were on their way to market and made nests for them and their resulting families at Portiuncula. None of these animals left his presence until he released them with his blessing.[†] André Vauchez has noted that Francis had a special love for creatures associated with Christ, such as lambs, sheep, and fish. Humble larks that sing despite their hunger demonstrated to the eyes of Francis perfect joy. Migratory birds were like souls that travel far but manage to return to God. On the other hand, animals felt his wrath if they behaved like devils, such as the sow that ate a newborn lamb.

No vignette of Francis is more emblematic than his sermon to the birds. Some early sources say that at a time of doubt he asked Clare and Sylvester whether he should continue preaching or become a hermit and devote his life to prayer. Each advised him to preach. Elated, he immediately set forth through the Spoleto valley ready to spread the word of God. The first gathering he found was an assembly of pinkish doves, crows with blue-black feathers, and noisy black jackdaws with soft grey napes, all together in the early morning light, near the town of Bevagna, about twelve miles from Portiuncula. Francis was either divinely inspired or manic, most possibly a little of both, but when he ran toward these creatures, rather than scattering as he expected, they remained on the ground or settled in their perches as if they were waiting to hear from him.

[†] The early lives of Francis say nothing about his taming a wolf in Gubbio. The source of this famous story is unclear, although Saint Bonaventure does say in Chapter 8 of his *Major Legend of Saint Francis* that Francis called on the people of Greccio to repent if they wanted to save themselves from various disasters, including roving packs of wolves.

Taken aback, he preached as he had promised, telling them to praise the Lord for the feathers that covered them, the wings that gave them flight, and all that was necessary for them to live. They craned their necks, opened their wings, warbled, or merely gazed at him. He wondered why he had not had the idea of talking to them before, and he resolved that from then on he would preach not only to people but to all the birds and animals he encountered, whether they had feathers or fur, walked on legs or wiggled on the ground. Later in Alviano, some ten miles away, a flock of noisy swallows building their nests drowned out his words to people. He told the birds that they had spoken enough, that it was his time to speak, and that they should be silent until the word of the Lord had finished. The birds obeyed, amazing all who saw this and prompting them to declare that Francis was truly a man of God.

Far from this world of natural wonders, in Rome the earthly powers of Christendom were gathering. On November 11, 1215, in the eighteenth year of his papacy, Innocent III convened the Fourth Lateran Council, for which he had two purposes. It was intended not only to reform the church but also to spur a new crusade to recapture the Holy Land from the Saracens. It stands as the zenith of the late medieval papal power. Some four hundred bishops and cardinals, nine hundred abbots and priors, and seventy patriarchs and metropolitans from the Byzantine churches that had separated from Rome early in the eleventh century attended. So did representatives of the kings of France, England, Aragon, Hungary, Cyprus, Jerusalem, and the future Holy Roman Emperor Frederick II. The entire contingent added five thousand persons to a city that normally numbered thirty-five thousand.

Innocent III opened the council with a dawn mass at the Basilica of Saint John Lateran. There was such a crush of these worthy participants that several people were killed, including a bishop who suffocated. He alone was spared the vituperation of the pope who announced that the failings of the church, the corruption of its bishops, and the mediocrity of its priests had made the convocation necessary. Looking out over a sea of pointed bishops' miters, broad-brimmed red cardinals' hats, and the furs and multi-colored raiment of nobility and royalty, Innocent III charged that many bishops were devoid of spiritual training and pastoral concern and were so preoccupied with the pleasures of the flesh and aggression toward others that they were unfit to proclaim the word of God or to govern the faithful.

Those who had assembled had little to do but sit condemned because most of the council's work had already been done. Two and a half years earlier, in April 1213, Innocent announced plans for council in his papal bull *Vineam Domini*. He appointed committees that drew up seventy decrees for the full body to approve in the twenty days it sat in the magnificent Hall of Councils and the eleven chambers that radiated from it. Added to the Lateran Palace in the ninth century, the hall was covered with mosaics that celebrated the glory of the Roman Catholic Church. Several depicted apostles preaching to the gentiles. One showed Christ presenting keys to Pope Sylvester and a banner to the Emperor Constantine; another had Him giving a sign of authority to Pope Leo III and a standard to Charlemagne. The overall theme was that the pope was the channel through which Christ imparts authority to the emperor and other temporal powers.

That concept of worldly dominion led to the council's significant political pronouncements: it confirmed Frederick Hohenstaufen as the Holy Roman Emperor ruling over the West, and it condemned the Magna Carta of England as a threat to monarchy and to the church. It rejected a proposal from that country's Cardinal Robert Courson for compulsory relief for the poor of the world. In matters of faith, the rulings of the Fourth Lateran Council would hold for centuries. The one that was particularly meaningful to Francis was the doctrine of Transubstantiation, which meant that in the sacrament of the Eucharist, bread and wine were transformed into the actual body and blood of Christ, although the appearance of bread and wine remained.

Addressing the manner in which infidels could live in Christendom, the council banned Jews from holding public office. It also decreed that Jews and Muslims had to wear special dress of some sort, particularly in Paris, to identify themselves, notably since Christians had been having sexual relations with them, possibly in marriage. This indicates that these peoples may have been mingling so freely and peacefully with Christians as to become indistinguishable from them unless they were wearing special garb. This rule, or canon, apparently had lethal consequences because the pope later said that it need not be enforced if it endangered life. Another rule forbad clerics from participating in judgments by ordeal, meaning trial by water, fire, or oaths. The pope also issued a series of impactful decrees elaborating on preparations for the upcoming assault on the Holy Land to be known as the Fifth Crusade.

There is no proof that Francis attended the Fourth Lateran Council, but there were Lesser Brothers preaching in Rome. Around this time one of the curia's key administrators, a Brother Nicholas of the Cistercian Order who was close to the pope, resigned from his position to join Francis's movement. However, Innocent III declared Nicholas to be so essential to pressing church business that he recalled him to the Lateran Palace.

Francis originally believed that his work would be unaffected by the Fourth Lateran Council. It did decree that each religious order was to hold a general chapter of its abbots and priors—but not its monks—every three years. But Francis already had all his brothers return to Portiuncula each Pentecost and Michaelmas before they journeyed forth again. The Council's Canon 13 cast its shadow on him, however, by calling for a return to traditional monastic rules to avoid the confusion of too much diversity. It forbad the founding of new monasteries and said anyone who wanted to found one should join an existing order. Francis believed that since Innocent III had already approved his movement in 1212, it was not new but pre-existing and thus exempt.

What would prove to affect him and Clare more immediately was that the Fourth Lateran Council greatly diminished the power of bishops, a group that Innocent III held in low regard. They were stripped of authority over religious movements, including those that existed only in their dioceses. Instead, these would now come under the jurisdiction of the pope and his representatives.

The bishops of Assisi had been strong allies of Francis and Clare from their earliest days. All named Guido, the first presided over the public dispute between Francis and his father, the third and last of Francis's lifetime had helped Francis and his men navigate the procedures of the papal court on their first visit, going so far as to engage Cardinal John of Saint Paul, who became an important ally. As John came to know Francis and his brothers, he so praised them to his fellow cardinals that each of these princes of the church invited Lesser Brothers to live in their own households.

But John of Saint Paul had died before the Lateran Council opened, as indicated by the fact that his name is not on the list of attendees. By this time the behavior of Bishop Guido of Assisi had become a scandal. Surviving records show that he accused the clerics running one of the city's leper hospitals of stealing his wine and then had their supply carted back to his palace. When those clerics objected, he attacked them physically. His quarrels with the Benedictine monks over jurisdiction of churches and over rights to funeral offerings became so heated that the pope intervened and reprimanded the bishop for his greed. Finally, the canons of the Cathedral of Saint Rufino called in papal arbitrators who in August 1217 decided to allow Guido to receive no more than a third of the donations to the cathedral and half of the tithes that the canons had kept from him. The ruling also allowed the canons to be free to choose their own chaplains, provided that the bishop confirmed them. In short, Bishop Guido III had lost legal authority but he remained a prime inspiration for Francis's insistence that no matter how a priest might behave as a man, he was still consecrated to God with the power to change water and wine into Christ's body and blood, and as such he deserved honor and obedience.

However satisfied Innocent III may have been with the Council, a high-water mark of his power, on July 16, 1216, eight months after its conclusion, a shocking event in Perugia rocked the world. Innocent III died suddenly at the age of 56 after more than eighteen years on the papal throne.

The papal household was thrown into confusion and protocols and discipline were abandoned, as Jacques de Vitry, a prelate then in his mid-fifties, discovered when he reached Perugia. Jacques's clear-eyed accounts of what he saw in his travels and during the Crusades would make him a major chronicler of thirteenth century Christendom. At that point the priest was one of the most celebrated preachers in Europe and he had been summoned to the pope's summer residence to be consecrated as the Bishop of Acre.

Jacques learned that Innocent III was dead only on his arrival in Perugia. Even more shocking was the news that the late pope's body had been desecrated. In the night thieves had stripped the corpse of its vestments so that rather than lying in state, the remains of greatest pontiff of the Middle Ages lay exposed, naked, and decaying. "I saw with greatest faith how fleeting and empty is the deceitful glory of this world," Jacques later wrote in a letter to his friends in Liège.

This devout man was born to a noble family in Vitry, east of Paris, around 1160 and studied at the University of Paris with masters of preaching who sought to reform students and the clergy. At an Augustinian priory at Oignies in the diocese of Liège on the Meuse River he encountered a charismatic female religious leader named Marie who was the wife of Jean de Nivelles, one of his preaching masters. She had been born to a wealthy family around 1177 and married at age 14. She persuaded Jean to let her live in chastity and prayer. Lay women joined her and this group became one of the early Beguine communities. She attracted followers, including Fulk, the exiled bishop of Toulouse, who helped Dominic Guzman establish the Order of Preachers. Marie's faith, penance, and devotion to the Eucharist, her vibrant practice of religion, not to mention the ability of her followers to stand up to Fulk's probing questions as to whether or not she and her followers were heretics, impressed Jacques greatly. She was also impressed with him. Jacques preached so successfully in favor of the crusade against the Albigensians that Marie told him that he was the preacher she had prayed to God to send. Marie died on June 23, 1213, and two years later Jacques's fame was such that the clergy in Acre in the Holy Land asked Innocent III to appoint him as their bishop. Innocent agreed and summoned Jacques to Perugia to be consecrated.

Travelling south, Jacques reached the great city of Milan, which was encircled by a moat of canals and a round stone wall. He discovered that its spiritual defenses had been breached, however. Milan was filled with Albigensians happily going about their lives and living their ungodly faith. He was dumbstruck that the city's Catholics allowed these heretics to live among them in peace. He found that only the apostolic group known as Humiliati preached against them. Like Francis's movement, they were growing in number. They lived in one hundred fifty communities, many segregated by gender but still more living in their family homes.

When Jacques reached Perugia, his final destination, he found that nineteen cardinals and their retinues were pouring into the city to elect Innocent's successor. They appalled Jacques, who wrote: "After I had been at the Curia for a while, I encountered a great deal that was repugnant to me. They were so preoccupied with worldly affairs, with rulers and kingdoms, with lawsuits and litigation, that they hardly let anyone speak of spiritual things." They elected the new pope two days after the death of the old one.

About a fortnight after Jacques reached Perugia, he was conse-crated bishop of Acre on July 31, 1216. He liked Pope Honorius III, who was elderly and devout, a simple and humble man who had given all his goods to the poor. He also had the distinction of being kind. Jacques did not miss his opportunity to champion Marie of Oignies. He asked for and received permission for women in the dio-cese of Liège and throughout France and the empire to live together in community, which was the first papal approval of the Beguine movement and provided this concept with a toehold in the structure of the church.

Despite his disappointment in the curia, Jacques was encour-aged by what he saw of the Lesser Brothers and Sisters. He wrote to friends in Liège a few months later that they were his only consola-tion. They had been born rich but renounced everything for Christ and fled the world. They were held in high esteem by the pope and his court. He wrote, "They live according to the form of the primitive church of which it is written in Acts 3:32: 'The multitude of believers was of one heart and one soul...' They go into the cities and villag-es during the day, so that they convert others, giving themselves to active work; but they return to their hermitages or solitary places at night, employing themselves in contemplation. The women live near the cities in various hospices. They accept nothing but live from the work of their hands. In fact, they are very much offended and dis-turbed because they are honored by the clergy and laity more than they deserve."

After the Lateran Council, three hundred Lesser Brothers gath-ered for the general chapter meeting, which was hosted by the Benedictines at the Abbey of San Verecondo south of Gubbio, the very group that had so badly mistreated Francis after he fled Assisi. Chastened by the knowledge that they had abused a great holy man, they treated his followers to breads and dishes of barley, wheat, and millet, as well as fava and green beans and quince wine.

Whether or not Francis would have preferred to take no care for the future, as the Gospel admonished him, he had set guidelines for his followers from their earliest days together. They were to alternate between periods of private prayer and public preaching and to travel in pairs with one taking care of practical matters like shelter and the other devoted to spiritual work. Now because so many men were joining them from so many places he was unable to meet, much less guide, each brother personally. In a reflection of Matthew 23:37, where Jesus laments that he had wanted to gather together the children of Jerusalem as a hen collects her young, Francis had a dream of such a bird that was as dark and small as he was in comparison to other men. She was also like a tame dove and her legs and feet were covered in feathers. Multiple chicks surrounded her and pressed in close, all seeking her warm, protective wings, but there were too many for her to comfort. He recognized that he had the same dilemma as the little bird.

It may well have been after the Lateran Council that he wrote his often-cited brief form of life for Clare and the women of Saint Damian, which has been lost. At this time he did set forth his plan for his growing number of men. To establish a greater degree of structure, Francis divided the greater world into specific regions that he called provinces and he appointed a leader, or provincial minister, of each. He intended for half of the provinces to be on the Italian peninsula in towns south of Assisi. The rest were to be located elsewhere. Some sixty men were to go to Germany, and smaller groups were to travel to Lombardy, Venice, Hungary, Spain, and the Holy Land. Francis himself planned to lead a mission to France, which then comprised only the northern half of its current boundaries. Francis knew this region well from his days of attending the great fairs as a merchant and he spoke its language with joy. Yet given his earlier attempts to reach Muslim lands it is significant that as the pope prepared for the Fifth Crusade, Francis sent others to the

Levant to prepare the way for his later work there. Francis appointed as their leader a man named Elias, who may have been a public official in Assisi before joining the brothers. Whatever his background, Francis recognized him as an able administrator who was comfortable dealing with those with authority and power. For this mission that strength was as important as preaching.

At the chapter meeting Francis explained that he himself would visit France. He said that he had heard that the people there revered the Eucharist as he did, so possibly Jacques de Vitry had told him of the devotion of Marie of Oignies. Francis had long been troubled when he saw clerics who did not take proper care of altars and vessels containing the sacred host. He thought of sending the brothers through the world with pyxes, containers in which they might gather consecrated hosts that they rescued from such mistreatment. He was also concerned that priests were using any available bread for the sacrament and he thought of providing the brothers with presses for baking wafers for consecration. But he abandoned these ideas, possibly because of the Gospel command to carry nothing, neither purse nor sandals, in going out to preach.

He announced their missions to the world at Portiuncula on Pentecost in early May 1217. That meeting is considered to be the first general chapter of the Lesser Brothers. But in 1211 Francis had already established twice-yearly gatherings to be held at Pentecost in late spring and at the feast of Saint Michael at the end of September when they all returned to Portiuncula. May and September were favorable times for travel and whether the brothers had journeyed to the edges of Europe or remained on the Italian peninsula, they made their way home to Assisi.

When they gathered, they discussed how to follow the Gospel more perfectly and Francis spoke of the shortcomings they needed to correct in themselves and how they might praise the Lord with greater joy. He urged them to respect priests, going so far as to bow to those they met in the street or to kiss the hooves of their horses, because they were bringers of the sacraments, particularly of the Eucharist. The brothers were to honor the poor above all others, while respecting all persons and never criticizing anyone. He admonished them always to preach peace, which required first of all that they have it in their hearts.

He was so inspiring that a group of some thirty brothers decided to stay after the chapter meeting so that they might talk with Francis about the salvation of the soul. This presented Francis with a practical problem—how to feed their bodies. Townspeople had donated enough food to supply the expected throng for the set period. But providing an extra day of provisions to brothers who were listening to him rather than working in exchange for food posed a dilemma. He sent word to Clare requesting extra bread. Having three loaves for her community, she sent him two. To her gift he added the small store of provisions he already had on hand. Probably the people of Assisi donated as well because the brothers had food left over. But back at Saint Damian, Clare told her companion Cecilia to divide the loaf she had kept into fifty pieces, one for each of the women living there. Cecilia balked, saying that only the Lord's miracle of the five loaves and two fishes could get fifty portions from it. Still, Clare insisted she do it and somehow all were fed.

One who was particularly impressed by how the Lord met the needs of Francis's followers was Dominic Guzman. He stopped by one of their large meetings in the autumn of 1216 when he was travelling to Rome to have his own rule approved. Later he told his own men that they could live fearlessly without possessions because he had seen Francis and his brethren demonstrate it.

As the early years passed, many young noble women of Umbria, including two granddaughters of Clare's paternal uncle Hugolino, outraged their parents by joining Clare. Their families had suffered in the wars against the common people of Assisi. The women may have thought Clare's austere life was a refuge from discord, from mourning the bloody deaths of kinsmen, and a way to evade unwanted marriages. It was a chance to serve God and his creatures, as well.

Clare developed a reputation for curing the sick. When the women were ill, Clare made the sign of the cross above their heads, which alleviated many of their illnesses. Ailing townspeople who came to Saint Damian for help had similar relief, according to the records of Clare's canonization, and while the nature of the illnesses is seldom recorded, some believed her to work miracles. Clare had a beneficial effect on those who followed her. She strove to set an example and regarded herself as the servant of the others, covering them at night when it was cold, bringing them water when they needed it, taking on the least pleasant tasks like cleaning the stained mattresses of the sick. Once a carelessly moving foot she was washing hit Clare in the mouth, but she reacted by kissing the remorseful woman's sole. Clare cried over those who were afflicted in body or mind, but her greatest tears fell when she received Jesus Christ at Mass.

One time Saint Damian ran out of olive oil for the lamps and cooking. Clare told the Lesser Brother Bentevenga that she needed him to go begging for it. While he finished his other tasks, she prepared a jar for him to take, washing it and placing it near the entrance of Saint Damian where he could pick it up. When Bentevenga returned for it, soon after, he found that the pot was already full of oil. He grumbled that the women had been teasing him because although he searched the paths he could not catch sight of anyone who had come to fill it.

Cures by blessing aside, their living conditions fostered stomach and digestive problems, flu and viruses, and Clare, now in her twenties, herself began to weaken. On Sundays if there was wine for the table she would taste a little of it, but now it upset her system. Hunger inevitably led to dizziness, an altered consciousness akin to a spiritual state. Francis and Bishop Guido again intervened. They ordered her to eat every day, consuming at least an ounce and a half of bread. Francis further told her that she had to sleep on a sack filled with straw so that she might have a restorative night's rest.

In the early days Francis had chided the brothers when they were too harsh on themselves. Concerned that some went so far as to do penance by wearing armor and cinching iron belts around their waists, Francis forbad them to have anything on their bodies but a tunic. But now he saw that the brothers were growing lax. Perhaps Francis's growing popularity inspired men to join before they could consider what it meant to take up the burden of the Gospel lifestyle. Giles, who in the early days had doubted Francis's belief that their movement would grow, now warned him, "We are losing our true glory, since we receive glory from men."

Francis could be pitiless in enforcing poverty. When one brother heard that Francis was angry because he picked up an offering of money and tossed it on a windowsill at the Portiuncula chapel, he went to him to apologize. He offered to submit to a flogging for having touched money, but Francis had something else in mind. He ordered the cowering man to retrieve the coins from the windowsill with his mouth and, also with his mouth, deposit them on a pile of animal dung.

But in late summer 1217, when the dark green leaves began to fade and the days grew shorter, Francis turned his thoughts to France and placed himself on the familiar route north toward the Alps. He and his small party went two by two, walking in silence from dawn until terce, or about nine in the morning, praying silently and meditating as they inhaled the sharp smoky scent of resinous cypress trees and passed laborers harvesting grapes. Among the party was Pacifico, whose linguistic abilities would help them preach to the people in their languages. Finally, they reached Florence. With a population approaching fifty thousand, it was one of the largest cities in thirteenth century Europe and had become one of the wealthiest. Its prosperity was based on the textile trade but it was filled with skilled craftsmen in other fields including leather goods and jewelry. The Arno River that cut through Florence teemed with boats exporting the city's goods and powered the huge grinding wheels of the millers that lined its banks.

Around 1150, its commune expanded the city walls in a jagged circuit with twelve major gates around dense settlements that had grown up around the old walls. Since the church, the emperor, and local feudal lords all exerted near equal measure of control in times of controversy, the powers of Florence called in outsiders, including military leaders, to lead the city for the good of all. Still, the threat of violence was ever-present, as it was in all cities on the Italian peninsula, so the wealthiest families made their homes in ninety towers that surged heavenward as high as 150 feet. Each was pierced with narrow slits for windows and was topped by crenellated parapets. Recognizing that there was more strength in partnership than division, owners of adjacent properties joined together in Tower Societies so that they could control a section of the city.

Between priories and parishes, there were fifty churches in Florence. Francis intended to preach in many of them before moving on to France. But as was his custom when he entered a city, he first went to the bishop to introduce himself and seek permission. In September 1217, he headed to the tight northern sector of Florence where church power was concentrated. The Cathedral of Saint Repata with its sonorous bells was the center around which clustered the residence of the canons, the Baptistery of Saint John, the hospital of Saint John the Evangelist, the cathedral school, administrative buildings, the headquarters of confraternities devoted to prayer and charity, and the bishop's palace with a courtyard so imposing that even the emperor's envoys used it as a platform when making public announcements.

But before he obtained the permission to preach that he had expected, Francis collided with the realities of the church's growing interest in his movement in the person of the powerful Hugolino, Cardinal of Ostia and Velletri. Hugolino was one of the two papal arbitrators who had dealt with the case of Bishop Guido of Assisi and had reduced the income Guido received from tithes and donations. Hugolino had also worked with Dominic Guzman to persuade the religious women of Rome to abandon their separate religious lifestyles and to unite in one convent under Dominic's unifying guidance.

That Hugolino was one of the most influential men in the world had been revealed at the death of Innocent III in Perugia. The nineteen cardinals who hastily poured into that city, whom Jacques de Vitry described as being "like dumb dogs not able to bark," feared that an election would cause discord. They appointed Hugolino and Guido, Cardinal of Praeneste, to select the new pontiff, and on July 18, 1216, the day after Innocent's body was interred, the pair chose an elderly Roman, Cencio of Savelli, the Cardinal Priest of Saints John and Paul.

Cencio is depicted as having a long face, strong eyebrows, and a full beard that covered his jaw line to his earlobes. Under his papal crown, he was bald. Although somewhat retiring, he was versed in church administration and had tutored Frederick, the future Holy Roman Emperor. Perhaps best of all, besides the fact that he would surely not reign long, was that Cencio hailed from an aristocratic Roman family, which could win allies from among that city's factions that sought to dominate the church. Cencio was consecrated

Pope Honorius III in Perugia on July 24 and he soon appointed Hugolino as his representative in Tuscany, Lombardy, and in precincts that extended as far as Venice.

Hugolino's task was to be a peacemaker, but a peacemaker in the service of war. He was to arbitrate disputes between northern Italian cities so that their men and their treasure could be available to the upcoming Fifth Crusade rather than in battles with each other. When Francis arrived in Florence, Hugolino had just negotiated a settlement between Pisa and Genoa over their rival claims to Sardinia. Before he returned to Rome he began the process of acquiring land on which to build convents for the religious women of Florence, something he would complete the following year. Hugolino believed in order, which of course required and enabled control. Hierarchal order had served him very well and had placed him close to the pinnacle of the Roman Catholic Church.

He was born in either 1145 or the more likely 1170, making him either seventy-two or forty-seven when he sat down with Francis in Florence in 1217. Several posthumous frescos in Assisi depict him as tall and somewhat burly, although these portraits are not dependable as accurate likenesses. Hugolino was from the Conti family that dominated the papacy for much of his lifetime. Innocent III, who was probably a cousin, named him a cardinal deacon in 1198 and Cardinal Bishop of Ostia on August 30, 1206. He was one of four relatives that Innocent III raised to the College of Cardinals.

The stress of Hugolino's responsibilities might have been the source of what he acknowledged as his besetting sin—Hugolino had a temptation to blaspheme. Blasphemy, the sin of uttering a word of blame or criticism of God, was a shocking offense, but not a grave one if it was done through habit or if the sinner was trying to overcome this trait. In extreme cases, however, punishment was severe. The offender would be made to stand at the church door during the celebration of Mass for six Sundays and on the seventh he stood before the faithful barefoot with a rope around his neck.

In an attempt to correct himself, Hugolino wore not a rope but a finger that in life had been on the hand of the late Marie of Oignies. This withered digit, a relic, had been given to him by Jacques de Vitry, whom he likely met in Perugia when Innocent III died. To obtain the audience, Jacques sent the cardinal a weighty silver cup filled with nutmeg, a luxury that was said to freshen the breath and settle the stomach. Hugolino, who had a practice of refusing costly gifts, accepted only the spice, explaining that it was the fruit of the Orient, while the silver cup was the fruit of the city of Rome.

Once they met privately the two quickly developed a rapport because as their conversation continued, Hugolino unburdened his mind to Jacques and confessed his constant temptation to blaspheme. He said that the sin plagued him when he sat at the dinner table, when he tried to rest, and even in his dreams. Hugolino said that the only time he was free of it was when he was reviewing legal cases with his brother cardinals. Jacques proposed a solution. He told the cardinal of his dear and deeply spiritual friend Marie of Oignies who had died a few years before. He said that in her lifetime she had helped many blasphemers to conquer this very sin. Jacques was so impressed by her that he had written a book of her life that was filled with examples of such cures. He presented Hugolino with a copy in hopes that it would be of assistance.

Hugolino asked if Jacques had any of her relics—a piece of her clothing or a bit of her body—that might carry her power. Jacques obliged by presenting his treasured possession: the finger of Marie enclosed in a silver case. Jacques said that it had preserved him from dangers during sea travel, particularly from drowning in a flood in Lombardy, and had kept him safe when he visited the Holy Land. However Jacques might have felt about parting with this talisman, he did so. Thereafter, Hugolino kept this relic with him constantly, pressing it to his breast when he was tempted to misuse the name of the Lord.

Hugolino may well have received Francis in one of the less ostentatious rooms of the bishop's palace, a large space with heavy oak chairs and walls that were frescoed with faux drapery and Florentine coats of arms. When Francis told the prelate that he was on his way to France, Hugolino told him that was ill advised. The Lateran Council had discouraged new religious movements and Hugolino informed Francis that many of his brother cardinals were working now against the Lesser Brothers. He warned that their influence would be difficult to counter if Francis left the peninsula.

Francis replied that he would be ashamed to stay near home when only a few months earlier he had urged his brothers to travel to distant lands to preach. The cardinal asked if that had been wise. Had it been necessary to send them far away to die of hunger and other trials? Francis in turn inquired if the cardinal thought that the Lord intended the brothers to serve only the Italian peninsula. He said that they were to serve all the souls of the world whether they lived in lands of believers or of non-believers and that as long as they were faithful to their tasks, the Lord would serve them. Although Hugolino replied that Francis had spoken the truth, he forbade him to travel to France, which is the first recorded instance of the church constricting Francis's intentions. Obedient as always, Francis appointed Brother Pacifico to lead the group into France, and Francis returned to the Spoleto valley.

In the months that followed, Francis learned that Hugolino's concern about sending his men far afield was justified. Northern climates beyond the Alps were less benign than what they were used to. The harsh cold required more than branch huts or even caves to help them survive.

Preaching Christ to Christians was more difficult than it might have at first appeared, often because of language difficulties. The

brothers had relative ease overcoming the challenges of being understood on the Italian peninsula where each city and region had its own
dialect, but when they crossed the Alps their difficulties mounted. As
strangers ignorant of local languages, they invited misunderstandings
and hostility. Being willing to agree to anything won them a certain
amount of good will, but only for so long. In French lands, when
asked if they were Albigensians, they said "Oui," at which point they
were hauled before the Bishop of Paris and the city's learned masters.
They were able to prove they were loyal Catholics, yet their presence
broke local laws they were unaware of. Paris had banned wandering
preachers, especially those seeking alms, in 1213. A papal legate had
approved this, and the Council of Rouen extended the ban to the
entire territory the following year. Church prelates sought confirmation from the pope that the Lesser Brothers had his approval and
restricted their movements while they waited for an answer.

In Hungary men beat them with pikes and set dogs on them.
Unsure how they had provoked this hostility, the brothers decided
that the ruffians wanted their outer garments. The beatings did not
stop, even after the men peeled off all their layers of clothing, including their breeches. After being obliged to strip himself naked several
times, one particularly modest follower of Francis applied cow dung
and other loathsome repellents to his undergarment so that the dis-
gusted shepherds allowed him to keep it.

In Germany the brothers at first found that when they said "Ja,"
they were treated kindly, until their pleasant "Ja" caused them to be
stripped naked, jeered and taunted by a hostile crowd, and finally
thrown into a dungeon. Later they learned that they had said yes
when asked if they were heretics come to corrupt them as they had
corrupted Lombardy. Pronunciation was always a problem. When a
German named Hartmuth joined them, the Italians had to call him
Andreo Tadesco, or Andrew the German, because Hartmuth was
too difficult for them to say and he took his vows on that saint's feast
day, November 30.

Things went so hard for them in Germany, which had been Christian since the sixth century AD, that the Lesser Brothers decided that only those who were ready to face martyrdom should head toward the Rhine region and its fierce inhabitants.

Hearing these things, Francis became convinced that the approval and support of the all-powerful Roman Catholic Church was the best protection for his brothers as they went empty-handed into the world, denying themselves every comfort in following the steps of the crucified Christ.

8

Damietta

IN JUNE 1219, Francis of Assisi was thirty-seven years old. From the Atlantic coast of Spain to the Rhine, he had inspired hundreds of men and scores of women to follow him into a life of simple poverty based on the Gospels and to live in communities of Lesser Brothers and Poor Sisters. He had brought thousands more Christians to a deeper faith in Jesus Christ. Now he sought to bring the leader of the Muslim forces against Christendom, the sultan of Egypt himself, to the Savior. Not only would the sultan's soul be saved, so would the souls of his followers. Such an accomplishment would also return Jerusalem to Christian hands, which was the goal of the Crusades. Francis's task distracted him from the problems of dissention among his followers and from concerns over how the decrees of the Fourth Lateran Council might affect his movement.

Less than two years after Hugolino insisted that Francis had to remain on the Italian peninsula, Francis found that the cardinal's opposition had so faded that he allowed Francis to join the Crusaders' forces in Egypt in 1219 as a truce was ending. The forthcoming crusade would be the fifth that had been undertaken since 1095. The energies that surrounded it were such that the late Pope Innocent III saw the militant undertaking in apocalyptic terms. Believing himself to take the place of Christ on earth, at the conclusion of the Fourth Lateran Council he announced that on Judgment

Day he himself would judge those who refused to aid this cause as a wrathful God stood by. Innocent had marshaled all the resources at this command or within his influence to make the enterprise succeed. The moral reform he urged on Christendom, particularly the clergy, was in large part to appease God so that He would grant them victory. Innocent reasoned that the previous crusade had collapsed in failure because God was angry after Christian Crusaders attacked Christian Constantinople in 1204. After that misstep he took unilateral control of the strategy to secure Jerusalem rather than leave it to a collection of temporal rulers. He allocated church funds for much of it.

The Saracen, a name that derived from a plain in Arabia, were the great enemy from without that had conquered Spain and prompted the lords of Europe to set aside their differences, at least intermittently. They had seized Francis's imagination when he heard the Song of Roland, an epic poem that was the best-loved story in Europe and one that originated in the French *chansons de geste* in the prior century. One imagines that because the Saracens did not have Christ in their lives, Francis pitied them and dreamed of being God's means of converting them.

Two years earlier, at the general meeting of May 1217, possibly with plans for the coming Crusade already in his mind, Francis had sent Brother Elias to the Holy Land. Arnaldo Fortini, who studied the medieval records of Assisi, believes that before Elias joined Francis his name was Bonbarone and he was first consul of Assisi, and possibly a noble and widower. Brother Salimbene of Adam, a contemporary chronicler and critic of Elias, says that his father was from outside Assisi and that he had earned his living by sewing cushions and teaching children to read their psalters. Whatever his background, Elias had laid the groundwork for Francis by preaching and introducing Crusaders of all ranks to the Lesser Brothers for many months before Francis himself arrived. He was so effective in word and example that he inspired the renowned preacher Caesar of Speyer, who had been forced to flee German lands because he was too successful in persuading wealthy women to put away their jewelry and live simply as Jesus taught, to join them. Elias, Caesar, and other brothers would be awaiting Francis and able to advise him on the conditions he found and how to face them.

For the party that accompanied him on what he surely considered to be the most important mission of his life, Francis selected a handful of brothers including Peter Cattani, Leonard Gislerio, and one known as Illuminato. Leonard had been a noble of Assisi whose castle at Sasso Rosso had been destroyed by Francis and other merchants of the commune. One of his daughters had joined Clare's community, while his sons made a detailed claim against the commune for every inch of damage done. Possibly Francis in his youth had been among those assigned to repair the thirty-foot walls of their family home.

Given that Peter Cattani, whom Francis usually trusted to lead the brothers in his absence, and the able Elias would both be with him overseas, he appointed Brother Gregory of Naples to travel to the various communities while he was away to guide and encourage them as Francis would have done had he been home. Matthew of Narni was to remain at Portiuncula to watch over this beloved center and to receive new men into the movement. How Francis selected these men to assure continuity even as he undertook a potentially fatal journey is unknown, as is whether papal officials including Hugolino influenced his choice. Francis appointed Philip Longo, or Philip the Tall, who had accompanied Francis when he introduced Lady Clare to the idea of joining him, to watch over the women at Saint Damian.

With things thus arranged, Francis and his men trekked south to Rieti where they met with Pope Honorius III and Cardinal Hugolino and received a papal brief, a letter to introduce them to all the bishops and archbishops and other prelates they would encounter on their journey. Since the Fourth Lateran Council had condemned wandering preachers and subjected them to excommunication, Francis may have welcomed this particular document, known as *Cum dilecti,* dated June 11, 1219. In general, however, rather than have his followers present such credentials, he wanted them to behave with such humility and respect for all that their love alone would pave the way for them and testify to the truth of the joy of the message of the Gospels.

From Rieti they made their way northwest toward the coast through the pine-scented ravines of the Apennine mountains to the port city of Ancona on the Adriatic Sea, a journey of 150 miles on old Roman roads. There the sharp pine scents of land gave way to the briny odor of the sea. The waves splashing against the piers, the cries of gulls, the singing of sailors as they positioned their ropes, and the shouts of fishermen hauling silvery fish from their boats to nearby stalls filled their ears and must have quickened their anticipation.

The largest and best ships were for the use of the Crusaders as well as the merchants who were preparing to capture and control the rich goods of the Levant—its linens, dyes, spices, licorice, and produce—with the help of the Crusaders. Probably the Lesser Brothers found passage on a galley with oars that relied on sailors' strong backs to power the ship when the wind failed. Such crafts traveled from one port to the farthest one they could reach in a day. Francis refused to touch money and it is unlikely that a captain would have accepted the services of the scrawny Francis as even an apprentice oarsman, so one imagines that Francis either found a pious captain who would welcome the holy men as guests or that Hugolino had arranged their passage.

They most likely sailed down the Adriatic to Brindisi on the heel of Italy, which was the Crusaders' point of departure for Damietta. By late June 1219, Francis was on the Mediterranean bound for Egypt and the Crusades. Navigational devices for medieval sailors on that sea consisted of a compass card with a magnetized needle that pointed north and an hourglass to help them calculate the speed and distance traveled. They relied to a large extent on following familiar coastlines, so shipping routes hugged the shore. Francis probably traveled down the Dalmatian coast to the ports of the Greek Islands which offered fresh provisions.

At night sailors steered by the stars and judged their locations by lights from shore, while their own lanterns dappled the water with drops of light. By day Francis could probably see the crags and mountains on the land, observe the sailors adjusting rigging by tugging on ropes as if they were ringing cathedral bells. Birds often rode the masts to the Holy Land so that their twittering and cries joined the songs, laughter and cursing of sailors working their way along the wide expanse of waves. However cheerful he tried to be, Francis was probably not a good sea voyager. He was never hearty and he was frequently subject to stomach ailments on land. Probably he availed himself of the popular treatment for seasickness, an herb concoction of mashed minty pennyroyal and bitter wormwood mixed with oil and vinegar.

At the beginning of August 1219 Francis at last reached Damietta. In times of peace it was renowned for its white linen, known as dimity, as Francis could have learned at the fairs of Champagne. Situated in the fertile land at the juncture of two branches of the Nile, the city was shaded with date palms and its outskirts were lush with orange groves and fields of grain. Its position also provided a strategic advantage for trade between Europe and the Levant. To defend it, the Saracens encircled it with two high walls along the river, and three on the landward side that opened on a flat plain. These fortifications had twenty-two gates, one hundred and ten towers, and a large nav-igable moat. For good measure, the Saracens stretched iron chains across the waterway to thwart invading Christians, but the Crusaders broke through. The Saracens then sank their ships, thus blocking the harbor for the rest of the Christian fleet. Undeterred, the Crusaders cleared a disused channel and diverted the Nile. By the time Francis arrived, the Crusaders had surrounded Damietta entirely on land and were holding it under a blockade.

Because it had been well provisioned, the city was able to put up a fierce defense. When Christians stormed its walls, the besieged citizens poured deadly Greek fire down upon their heads. This lethal substance had been concocted by the Byzantines and held so close-ly as a secret weapon that its exact composition is still unknown. Mostly likely it was a mixture of liquid naphtha, petroleum, and sulphur held together by gum and set alight. Whatever it was, the Arabs were able to approximate the Greek original with consequenc-es horrific for the Crusaders.

On August 6, the Feast of the Transfiguration, the Christians filled the city's moat with sand and debris and brought up a war machine with a battering ram, but Damietta's defenders burned this too. Both sides were at an impasse, unable to gain a tactical advan-tage, although time was against the city as it used up its store of sup-plies. Francis was probably in the Crusader's camp when four Saracen spies, all at the point of death, were brought in. The Christians had hacked off their noses, their arms, their lips, and their ears as well as gouging out eyes, but stopped short of killing them. They had been apprehended when they attempted to swim the Nile carrying parchment and carrier pigeons with which to send messages about the enemy to the sultan. Another four of their comrades, mutilated in similar fashion, were displayed where the besieged citizens of Damietta could see them. By nightfall, the Muslims inside the city walls had found a Christian to maim in like fashion and sent him to the Crusaders.

Passion and frustration inflamed the Crusaders, who were already in disarray. All the great banners of Christendom had been planted on the shores of the Nile, flying over true and holy knights, as well as freebooters, adventurers, and cutthroats gathered for booty and remission of their sins. Merchants of Genoa, Pisa, and Venice, who had long traded with the Holy Land, jostled with priests and Knights Templars for profit and territory. Among the French were women in men's armor going into the thick of battle as well as some three hundred prostitutes who reportedly seduced some Muslims into renouncing their religion. Nicholas of Cologne, who had led a disastrous Children's Crusade down over the Italian peninsula five years before, was also said to be present. There is evidence that Sultan al-Malik al-Kamil purchased the members of the crusade at a slave market, allowed them to remain Christian, and used them as interpreters and teachers.

In Damietta, the Europeans met others from all corners of Christendom and discovered that they had as little in common with each other as they had with the Saracens. These men did not discuss the fine points of faith, yet the diversity of their Christian practices illuminates the gulfs between them. Nubians branded their children on their foreheads with a cross and believed, along with the Syrians and the Mesopotamians, that the Holy Spirit alone consecrated the Eucharist. The Georgians and the Greeks shared a divine service that differed from the Roman Mass. The Lebanese from the mountains followed the pope's doctrines, but those from the coast taught Christianity only to their sons and regarded women as the devil. The Syrians wrote in Greek but spoke Arabic. Russians had their own language, but followed the Greek Mass. Christians of the Near East, particularly the Copts of Egypt who claimed Mark the Evangelist as their founder, were comfortable with the Saracens, with whom they mingled freely in peacetime.

———— ❧ ————

The church's drive to send as many men as possible to aid in the Crusades inspired even those who were unfit to go to the Holy Land where they drained resources more than they added to them. Still more problematic was that the Crusaders' leadership was fracturing. John of Brienne, King of Jerusalem, led the military forces. At age 50, large and heavy, reputed to be as tall as Charlemagne, he was considered to be the bravest night in Christendom, yet before battle he shook like a leaf in the wind because he feared his soul was not prepared to meet God. He had acquired great influence through several marriages, largely because of the patronage of powerful men. Although he was the penniless younger son of a minor French count, King Phillip Augustus of France befriended him and betrothed him to Marie of Montferrat, the queen of Jerusalem. John had married her nine years before the siege of Damietta. She died while their daughter was an infant and he became regent of Jerusalem, which allowed him to act as its king. He then married the daughter of the king of Armenia, which gave him new allies. He arranged a five-year truce with the Saracens in July, 1212, and he used the time to persuade Innocent III to prepare for a crusade that would begin in 1217. As well as winning the Holy Land to Christ, this would benefit the kingdom John ruled.

Representing Pope Honorius III and speaking with his authority was Pelagius, Cardinal of Santa Lucia in Spain. He was emboldened by the prophecies of the ninth century heretical scholar Hanan, written in Arabic, which said that an army from the West led by a tall man with a lean face would conquer Damietta and possess Egypt.

The imposing, slender Pelagius believed himself to be that man and so without compunction he thwarted John's attempts to impose a consistent strategy. When the sultan made an offer of peace, John, the barons of the kingdom of Jerusalem, and crusaders from Germany wanted to accept it. However, Pelagius did not. Agreeing with him were the Knights Templars and a religious military order known as Hospitallers, who owed allegiance only to the pope, and the Italian merchants who wanted control of the trade routes to the Holy Land. They wanted access to the commercial opportunities of Damietta more than the capture of Jerusalem.

The Crusaders' good fortune was that Sultan al-Malik al-Kamil had difficulties on his own side. He had ascended to power some eighteen months earlier at the time when the Crusaders began to advance on Damietta. Before he could consolidate his rule there was a rebellion in his own army. He was able to put it down, but he was still testing the loyalty of his officers. Al-Kamil wanted to retain Damietta and to do this he was willing to give up Jerusalem, the alleged aim of the Crusaders, in exchange for their departure from Egypt. Pelagius rejected the proposal, saying the Crusaders would need the surrounding lands of the Trans-Jordan to protect the Holy City. Al-Kamil said he required this swatch of desert to assure the safe passage of caravans between Damascus and Cairo, so he offered instead the fortifications of Crac and Shawbak. Although John, French and Syrian leaders, and the Teutonic Knights were again agreeable, Pelagius, supported by the Italians, the Templars and the Hospitallers, again rejected the sultan's offer. He rested his decision largely on the expectation that Frederick, King of Germany and future Holy Roman Emperor, was about to land with fresh troops. This never happened because Frederick fell ill and turned back. Pelagius and a succession of popes would cast on him all blame for the failure of the Fifth Crusade.

During the time that Crusaders negotiated with the sultan, John of Brienne faced a revolt in his own ranks. Soon after his impatient soldiers mutilated the Saracen spies, they attacked Damietta. They propped ladders up against its walls and, having learned that water was useless against Greek fire, they used wine and vinegar to dowse the flames that rained down on them with every assault. To regain the semblance of control, John approved a hasty plan that divided his army into thirds. One would guard the camp, another would attack Damietta from the Nile, and the rest would attack the sultan's infantry by land.

When he heard of this scheme soon after his arrival, Francis thought it was disastrous. As a youth he had been among the Assisians who successfully stormed the nobles' stronghold outside Assisi, a venture that had taken weeks of careful planning and sub- terfuge. Francis had also been part of the city's futile battle against Perugia where he had seen his friends slaughtered. He saw no hope for the haphazard Crusaders to succeed even as he knew that no fighting was ever successful. As he walked through the camp, the moans of the wounded, the snarls of the warriors, and the mad fren- zied atmosphere of fear and heedlessness reverberated with his mem- ories of Collestrada. He wanted to warn them against going out to fight, but he hesitated.

Francis confided his quandary to his companion Illuminato. "If I speak, I shall be called a fool. And if I keep quiet, not having spoken out will be on my conscience." Illuminato reminded him that he had often been called a fool. "Follow your conscience!" he said. Francis then hastened before the soldiers, warned them against making an

attack, forbade them to do it as far as he was able, and finally predicted their defeat, but they laughed at him. Francis had a connection
to John that he might have used in an attempt to arrange a meeting. As a youth he had pledged his loyalty to John's brother, Walter
of Brienne, before heeding a dream telling him that he was not to
join that hero. Walter had been killed, but the feudal vow remained.
Whether or not Francis's warnings could have reached him, John
shared his assessment but he could not hold back the mob of fighting
men who were tired of digging trenches in the sand and wanted to
battle.

On August 29, 1219, the feast of Saint John the Baptist, the
attack began. Unable to watch, Francis prayed and sent Illuminato
out to observe. At first, Illuminato returned with encouraging news:
as soon as the sultan's troops saw the Christians, they folded their
tents and retreated from the field. The Christians were in pursuit as
Illuminato spoke. Francis considered the possibility that he had been
wrong. Illuminato then took up an observation post on a small dune.
Like the Crusaders' forces, the Muslim army was composed of men
from far reaches. Many were slaves captured from the sultan's enemies in Georgia, Armenia, Anatolia, and Byzantium, some of whom
had been given their freedom. Dark-skinned Arabs, Berbers, and
Sudanese were also in the group, as well as Bedouin tribesmen and
ghazis, "warriors for the faith," the fanatical bands who delighted in
suicide missions.

Illuminato saw the Saracens continue their retreat, going deeper
and deeper into the desert, separating themselves from their water
supplies. This unexpected carelessness seemed miraculous until they
stopped and pivoted. Now they faced the Crusaders, lined up for battle, but did not advance. While the Christian leaders consulted over
how to meet the enemy, their men stood in full metal armor in the
desert sun while the Saracens wore light chain mail. It dangled like
protective fabric from their conical hats with light arm pieces and

breastplates completing their equipment. Whereas the Christians relied on the force of their charges, the Muslims trusted in the use of crossbows that kept them far from the Crusaders' swords. The relentless sun beat upon the Christians' helmets, addling them with heat and light and making them desperate for water. When their ranks began to break, the sultan's forces attacked the knights of Cyprus on the right flank, but the Cypriots could offer only weak resistance. Illuminato told Francis that they and many others fled, while the Templars, German knights, and Hospitallers from France and Pisa fought off attackers and formed a wall against the enemy.

Illuminato's third and final report to Francis was dire, and confirmed all the doubts that Francis had about the Christians' plan. Crazed with heat, the Crusaders plunged their swords into hallucinations or dropped their arms and danced ecstatically in imagined rain. While the Saracens stood pat, Crusaders with presence of mind ran to the Nile for water. All in all, the Crusaders were said to have lost six thousand men to death or capture, out of some eight thousand who would have been on hand for this battle. Francis particularly grieved for the Spaniards who had come to the Holy Land with Pelagius. They fought the most impetuously and so had suffered the heaviest losses. A dense fog settled over the camp as reports of casualties arrived. Among the dead were fifty Knights Templar; thirty Germans; thirty-two Hospitallers; the chamberlain of the King of France and his son; the bishop of Belvaio and his brother John; and various counts from the Italian peninsula. Saracen troops went among the fallen hordes with swords and hacked off heads. The sultan sent sacks of these flayed trophies through all his provinces where they were displayed at the marketplaces where captured Christians were sold as slaves.

Many demoralized Crusaders began to decamp for home, including Roman barons, nobles from other Italian cities, and the bishop of Hungary. Word filtered back to those who remained that thousands of Britons returning home had been shipwrecked on the coast of Italy. They also heard that whole regions of Holland, whose soldiers set sail before the siege, had been washed away in floods. Francis and his companions wandered through the defeated camp offering what comfort they could, especially to the few Spaniards who survived.

Hoping that the Crusaders' defeat would make them more receptive to his offer of peace, al-Kamil called a truce and sent delegates to the Christian camp. Francis apparently seized this opportunity to seek out the sultan himself. Pelagius tried to dissuade him and said that no Christian should go forth to the infidel without a sword in hand, but Francis took only Illuminato. He may have been from the outskirts of Rieti, where in those days lived a Saracen who had converted to Christianity and left his people to travel with the Crusaders. Possibly Illuminato had learned some Arabic from him. Certainly the men who had arrived with Elias two years earlier would have been more fluent, but they might not have been at Damietta.

Al-Kamil was camped in Ashmun some twenty miles to the south. Under saffron banners as orange as the sun his force effectively barred the route that led south to Cairo and served as a staging area for reinforcements going north. Chanting "The Lord is my shepherd, I shall not want," Francis and Illuminato set forth to find the sultan. It was a paradox of Egypt that the dry country was flooded in summer despite the absence of rain. Not until the nineteenth century would the world know that the fertile fields of Egypt were enriched by runoff from heavy annual rains in Ethiopia, and that the river's source was Lake Victoria in Tanzania four thousand miles to the south.

That September 1219, the Nile did not reach its usual early flood stage and the land was parched. This only added to the devastation by war. Few people would venture out to risk confronting either of the warring sides. Certainly Francis on this march down the right bank saw crocodiles, long, scaly, ugly creatures that seemed to ooze from the muddy banks into the swollen Nile. The sight of two lambs grazing in the midst of all the desolation filled him with joy. He took it as a sign that God was guiding them, and he quoted Matthew 10:16 "Remember, I am sending you out to be like sheep among wolves."

Inevitably two of the sultan's men discovered them. One story is that they rained blows on Francis and Illuminato as the brothers cried out "Sultan!" "Sultan!" Another is that the Saracens arrested them. Al-Kamil had proclaimed that whoever brought him the head of a Christian would be rewarded with a gold piece from Byzantium but the truce had voided that promise, so the two brothers did not have a price on their heads. Most probably their captors decided that they could be ambassadors replying to the sultan's offer of peace, or at the very least, Christian deserters who wanted to renounce their faith and serve Allah. They led Francis and Illuminato into the sultan's camp.

Al-Kamil was a nephew of the mighty Saladin, the Kurdish prince born in Iraq who became vizier of Egypt and united Islam from the Nile to the Tigris. Saladin had driven the Second Crusade from every inch of Arab land, including Galilee and Jerusalem in 1188, when Francis was around five and al-Kamil a boy a few years older. Hoping to make peace with the leaders of the second Crusade, Saladin ceded land along the Palestinian-Syrian coast to Richard the Lion-Hearted of England. Then Saladin died suddenly in Damascus on March 4, 1193, at age 56, before he could enjoy the fruits of even tentative peace. A period of disorder followed during which his two sons ruled. Then Saladin's brother al-Adil took over, aided by his son al-Kamil. Damascus was the seat of their rule, but Egypt was starting to rival its importance. Together father and son rode into Cairo in July 1200. Al-Adil was proclaimed Sultan of Egypt and Syria and he named al-Kamil as his viceroy. Al-Adil concluded the peace treaty with John of Brienne, which lasted almost until his death in 1218, the year before Francis arrived in Damietta.

Al-Kamil succeeded his father and became the fifth ruler in the Ayyubid dynasty that Saladin had founded. He would prove to be a wise leader and was primarily interested in maintaining the land and cultivating its sugar cane and in keeping a tight hold on his purse during those interludes when peace allowed him to impose order.

A ruler such as he dressed in red and yellow satin embroidered with gold brocade and white fur. On his gold cap were golden clasps holding white bands embroidered with his titles. He wore a belt encrusted with rubies, pearls, and emeralds. In his hand he toyed with a saber with a hilt of gold. His closest advisers were arrayed in striped multi-colored robes, while those of lesser rank were resplendent in solid lustrous colors. Francis stood ragged and barefoot before them.

When a translator asked what his business was with the sultan, Francis announced he had come to save the ruler's soul. Seeing he was no emissary of peace, the Arab wise men advised their leader to execute Francis at once. The potentate, however, appreciated such boldness and good will, however insulting it might seem at first appearance. Al-Kamil had long been intrigued by Europeans, their languages and beliefs. When he was eleven years old, as part of peace negotiations after the Third Crusade, Richard the Lion-Hearted had knighted him in a quasi-religious ceremony at Acre on Palm Sunday, 1192. To learn more about Christians and their ways, he purchased a variety of them, from peasants to captured priests, at slave markets. These remnants of the Children's Crusade and other vanquished foes not only became his interpreters, secretaries, and teachers of his children, they included his personal physician and one of his scribes. Most were loyal to him and were allowed to practice their faith, unless they converted to Islam, as many did.

He frequently quoted a wistful verse that spoke of insight and resolve as much as it spoke of the tyranny of love: "Before you became the mistress of my heart, you never turned away from the sad and afflicted, and though you occupy a secure position in my heart, I still hope to prevail." This verse indicates that although the poet is disappointed, he loves her and hopes for change. Notwithstanding such sentiment, he had many wives and children. A Nubian slave girl was the mother of his eldest son and heir. Surely he regarded Francis as worthy of study and sport when time allowed. In the meantime, al-Kamil offered Francis the hospitality of his encampment. This exposed the Assisian to marvels, the first of which was medicine.

By now Francis was suffering from several ailments, which Muslim hospitality would have demanded that his hosts address. The beatings he had suffered through the years, most recently on the Nile, gave him pains and now he was having trouble with his eyes. Francis had long delighted in staring at the sun, which he regarded as the most marvelous of all God's creation. Its intensity on the open Mediterranean and in the searing desert, which he absorbed in wonder, had begun to impair his vision. In Egypt, he also contracted trachoma.

Arab physicians were far superior to those in Europe. Although anatomy was studied at medical schools in Padua and Bologna, European medicine relied on the discoveries of the ancient Greeks. Arabic medicine too was based on the ancient Greeks, notably Galen, but it had advanced further. By observing men torn open and bleeding during centuries of violent warfare, Muslim doctors learned human anatomy and a great deal about circulation of the blood, the function of the capillaries, and the action of cardiac valves and chambers.

In the tenth century, the surgeon Abbas al-Zahrawi of Moorish Spain had written on cauterizing wounds, proper extraction of arrows, oral hygiene, and the setting of bones. He used antiseptics, devised sutures from animal intestines, silk and wool, and designed surgical instruments. Like the Greeks, Muslim physicians believed that a healthy mind fostered a healthy body. They espoused the benefits of fresh air and personal cleanliness, of safe and beautiful surroundings. They encouraged moderation in eating and drinking, in work and in rest, a balance between wakefulness and slumber, and emotional harmony.

Certainly they believed in cleanliness. Al-Zahrawi wrote detailed instruction about fumigating clothes of parasites and annoying disease-bearing insects: "Put the garment inside an earthenware pot, close its opening and fumigate it with allochium and sandalwood until the garment is saturated with the incense. It is then ready for the patient to wear."

One can only wonder whether his hosts insisted that the ragged Francis submit himself to their ministrations. He had been elegant in his youth, finicky and demanding in his eating habits, painstaking in his dress. But for years he had lived on a diet of the vilest food and he was slovenly in appearance. He himself often tired of this life. "Do not always obey your superior," he snapped one morning when a Brother Stephen confronted him with the dry and insufficient breakfast he had ordered the day before rather than the egg that he had hoped would be forced on him. One imagines Francis now being compelled to bathe, doused with sandalwood oil to protect the nose of the sultan, and forced to eat dates, figs, and an array of succulent foods.

Saffron, nutmeg, cloves, licorice, rhubarb, aloe, cardamon— all the spices of the East—filled his lungs like a potion in the heat. Incense and perfume rose up from braziers and singed his nostrils. Not since the fairs of Troyes would he have experienced such heady fragrances. He saw up close the Saracens' armor of

Damascus steel, lightweight and superior to the best that Europe had to offer both for protection and the beauty of the undulating lines that decorated it.

Most intriguing of all would have been Saracen beliefs. Francis found, probably to his surprise, that far from hating Jesus, Muslims revered him and they believed in the virgin birth. They viewed his situation as like that of Adam, whom God had also created in a special way. The Quran said that while Jesus's enemies wanted to crucify him, God had saved him by putting his likeness on another man who was then subjected to that cruel death. However, Muslims rejected absolutely the idea that Jesus was God. There was no God but Allah Who was One. The idea that Christ was God was improper to them, as was the idea that God could be divided into the three-form Trinity. The Muslims that Francis encountered told him that they honored Jesus as God's messenger, as they did Moses, Aaron, and the other Hebrew prophets whose miracles were proof that Allah sent them. Who but Allah could cause Jesus to turn water into wine? Who but Allah could prompt Moses to bring water from a rock? Muslims accepted the scriptures of both the Jews and the Christians—the Old and New Testaments. They believed that after the creation of these great books God chose Muhammad as his final messenger, and sent the angel Gabriel to him to reveal the Quran, the bible of Islam that was the speech of God in written form. Muhammad was able to persuade, or subdue, the desert tribes of the Arabian Peninsula, many of whom were ready to accept the notion of one supreme God among the many they worshiped. By the time of Muhammad's death in 632 AD he was the leader of the peninsula and he was attracting followers in Syria and Iraq.

The Quran set forth a way for Muslims to deal with Jews and Christians who like Francis sought to convert them. Quran 29:43 reads "Say: We believe in that which has been revealed to us and revealed to you, and our God and your God is One, and to Him do we submit."

Francis's innate goodwill and courtesy probably inspired him to speak about the glory of Jesus, rather than belittle the prophet Muhammad. If he had disrespected Muhammad, they would have killed him.

Francis found in the sultan's camp religious monks similar to himself except that they worshiped Allah. Among the sultan's counselors was a holy man named Fakir al-Farisi, about ninety years old, who was one of the most celebrated Sufi masters of his time. Sufism, which tolerated other faiths, was the mystical strain of Islam that emerged in the hundred years following the death of Muhammad. The term means "man of wool" and dates from the ninth century when mystics wore the white coarse fabric as a sign of simplicity. As centuries passed, patched garments replaced the white ones, but the term Sufi remained.

Fakir is the Arab word for poor man. Fakirs were mendicants who sought sainthood by contemplation and mortification of the flesh. They ate and drank only enough to keep themselves alive and had no fixed abode. They went from village to village praising Allah and exhorting all to follow Him. They slept only a few hours, being totally detached from the goods of the world and dressing only enough to keep themselves decent. Like Francis, they neither studied nor disputed doctrines, but reached out to all men, no matter what their beliefs.

Fakir al-Farisi was from Persia where his teachers had included Ruzbehan, a mystic who had abandoned his life as a purveyor of food to seek religious knowledge. One of the stories about him that survives is that he was present at a gathering to honor a deceased holy man where he heard a song that went like this: *"For a long time I followed the path of love until the proofs of Truth appeared to me. I always testified that it was The One whom I was smitten with. Finally everything else left my Heart."*

Fakir-al Farisi was so struck by these words that he stood up, threw his turban on the ground and abandoned all decorum. He began to skip and whirl, transported by the perception that all loves are the love of God. He inspired everyone to join in this euphoria over a period of hours. The whirling of the dervishes, a term deriving from the Persian word for beggar, were an expression of Sufism.

Like Francis, Fakir al-Farisi taught the duty of repentance, self-discipline, renunciation, and other-worldliness. He welcomed the affliction of the self as a means to self-discipline. In the elderly al-Farisi, Francis would have found a Muslim version of himself. The indication that Francis was acquainted with Fakir al-Farisi, who was known to be at al-Kamil's court, comes from an inscription that was on the holy man's tomb: "He has many well-known virtues. And his experience with Malik al-Kamil, that is, the things that befell him owing to the Christian monk (*râhib*) are very well-known." No other Christian monk appeared at court, as far as records indicate, but there could have been many. Histories of the Coptic Christians of Egypt do not mention such a monk. Some early Franciscan works say that Francis threw himself into a fire and challenged fakirs to do the same to prove whose God was stronger, but the anecdote seems unlikely and inconsistent with Francis's character. Others have him accusing the sultan of blaspheming the name of Christ, which seems at best unlikely. One story that has been attributed to Illuminato, and is so clever that it deserves to be repeated if not totally trusted, portrays the sultan as testing Francis's wit.

Medieval people, Christians and Muslims alike, shared a love of subtle questions and clever responses. According to the story, the sultan had among his sumptuous possessions a magnificent carpet patterned with crossed lines. Calling for it to be spread on the ground before summoning Francis, he told his advisers, "If in coming toward me he walks on the crosses of the carpet, we will tell him he insults his Lord. If he refuses to walk on the carpet, I shall ask him why he disdains to approach me."

When Francis was ushered into the sultan's presence, it was reported, he eagerly traversed the length of the carpet and stood expectantly before his host. One imagines that the sultan was delighted to toy with his uncommon guest. "You Christians adore the cross as a special sign of your God," he observed. "Why then did you not fear to trample underfoot those crosses woven into the rug?" Looking down at his feet Francis discovered the motif. Calmly he replied: "Great Sultan, Our Lord was crucified along with thieves. To us he has given his cross. To you he has given the crosses of the brigands. These I do not hesitate to trample." The sultan was said to be delighted with this riposte. Certainly he showed Francis respect. When Francis departed, he declined the riches that al-Kamil pressed upon him, but accepted safe conduct and free admission to the holy places of Jerusalem that were normally open to pilgrims only after they paid a fee.[†]

Francis and Illuminato returned to Damietta under an escort of the sultan's guard. Francis told Pelagius and other astounded Christians that not only had he met the leader of the Saracen forces, but that this supposed cruel beast had been gracious. He had listened carefully to him for several days and finally broke bread with the brothers at a sumptuous meal before sending them back safely. While al-Malik al-Kamil had not converted to Christianity as Francis had hoped, the sultan did ask Francis to pray that God would reveal to him the most pleasing religion. Francis's deeds, his fervor, and this astonishing news excited the camp.

Before Lent of 1220 Jacques de Vitry wrote friends that several members of his party—his English clerk Colin, a Master Michael, and a Lord Matthew who had been expected to oversee the cathedral in Acre—had left him to join Francis and he was having trouble preventing several others, including a cantor, from doing the same. Writing only a few years after the event in his *History of the Orient*, Jacques wrote that he heard that at the sight of Francis, the sultan

---

† Relics at the Basilica of Saint Francis in Assisi include an ivory horn that the sultan reportedly gave to Francis. However, the first written record of it appears only in 1248 and the silver filigree embellishing it dates to just before that year, long after Francis left the Middle East.

became sweetness itself. However he expressed one reservation about Francis, saying that his practice of sending inexperienced young men out into the world two by two was a risky one. However, the men who left Jacques for Francis were not neophytes. At Damietta they had seen the worse of what man could do and they knew well what they were giving up.

Francis was in the Middle East long enough for many changes to be made among his followers back home. How he spent the many months from late September 1219 to sometime in the middle of 1220 is not known for sure, but there was enough time for him to give in to one undeniable temptation, the wish to visit the places where Jesus had walked, preached, and died. The sultan let him depart under the protection of what medieval European writers called "his finest knights." Conceivably they escorted him to Christian holy places far to the north with Francis bearing his token of safe conduct from the sultan permitting him to visit all the pilgrimage sites.† They probably followed a trade route at the time that led from Damietta a little more than 200 miles to Jerusalem through a populated region along the coast.

Enduring desert heat, sometimes parched for water, and possibly travelling at dawn and dusk to avoid the searing sun, he journeyed toward Jerusalem, the center of the Universe, the crown city of the Holy Land and of all who worshipped Christ. At this time the pope had indirectly banned Christian pilgrimage there. On July 23, 1217, Honorius III had issued a bull *Cum Carissimi Christo* that forbade them to enter Jerusalem because of the tolls they would have to pay to their arch-enemy, the sultan. Francis was surely aware of this

---

† Tradition says that Francis founded hospices and houses of brothers on Mount Zion, which was just beyond the walls of Jerusalem; at the Holy Sepulcher; and in Bethlehem and Nazareth. If so, the sultan would have allowed safe conduct for all of Francis's brothers. The Franciscans have been a presence in the Holy Land since the arrival of Elias in 1217. They were forced to flee to Cypress when the last Crusaders were routed in 1291 but they returned in 1333 when the sultan gave them legal possession of various sites and the right to use others.

proscription, yet he had free passage from al-Malik al-Kamil and so no payment would have been required of him. Visiting Jerusalem would allow him to walk the ground and follow the paths trod by his Master and Savior Jesus Christ. Pilgrims of his parents' generation had been to Jerusalem before its fall to the Infidel in 1187 when Francis was a toddler. They spoke of kneeling at the Sepulcher where Christ had been entombed and of walking the stony ground that Christ had taken to Calvary. Could Francis have resisted the opportunity to experience this for himself? Some scholars believe that he would not have disobeyed the pope's command, but the manuscript collection known as *The Chronicle of Ernoul* records that after Francis left Damietta he stayed for a time in Syria and from there returned to his homeland. Quite probably, Francis decided that it was the payment that was the problem, not the pilgrimage. He had seen the dangers brought on by the near-mania of too much fasting and renunciation. He was willing on occasion to indulge in treats such as special bread from the table of Jacqueline de Settesoli in Rome. To honor the giver, he consumed the gift with gratitude. Surely when Francis was so close to the actual places where his adored Lord had worked miracles and suffered on the cross, he would have abandoned any scruples, just as he had done when he stowed away in order to sail home after he aborted his first trip to Egypt.

If Francis did enter the Holy Land, he would have followed a well-travelled route. Medieval pilgrims began their climb toward the city, which was about three thousand feet above sea level, at the Gate of the Valley some dozen miles away. They prayed at a church built by the Crusaders on the site of a Roman fortress, passed Kiriath-Jearim where the Ark of the Covenant may have rested, and went on to Mountjoy, so-called because it was there that Crusaders fell to their knees at their first sight of the city. The rugged path led on past the birthplace of Jeremiah at Anathorth, the burial pace of Samuel, and to Ein Karem where Mary the Virgin visited her cousin Elizabeth. To the west they could see Emmaus, where the Lord appeared to his apostles after the resurrection. Although Titus, who would become the Roman emperor, razed to the ground the Jerusalem that Jesus knew in 70 AD, in the fourth century the Emperor Constantine reconstructed it based on legends and memories handed down by the Christian community. In the seventh century Arabs conquered it and in 1099 it was retaken by Christian forces that retained it for eighty-eight years until Saladin recaptured it in 1187.

In early 1220, Francis would have encountered a city of shallow moats, stone houses with flat roofs where people ate their meals, and mosques that had once been Christian churches. Commercial and administrative buildings bore witness to the influence of the Crusaders, who had introduced architectural elements from the West. This resulted in Arab structures with clustered pillars, groined roofs, and pointed ribbed arches, now all in the service of the Saracens.

Just a year before Francis's arrival, the Sultan Melek el-Mu'azzam ordered that most of Jerusalem's walls and towers be demolished so that if Crusaders ever recaptured it they would be unable to defend it. Christians had not been totally expelled, however. Saladin restored to the Eastern churches property that the Crusaders had seized from them and their members were allowed to observe their faith and maintain sites that were holy to Christendom. Armenian Catholics found the Arabs so preferable to Christians led by Rome that in 1190, three years after Saladin captured Jerusalem, they warned him of a pending attack by the Holy Roman Emperor Frederick Barbarossa. Frederick drowned en route and his army fractured so that it never reached the Holy Land in force.

In Francis's time a pilgrim walked from the Bethlehem Gate with the Tower of Daniel to his right and the market square to the east. He passed the Street of Judas's Arch where the traitorous disciple had hanged himself. Turning left on the street known as Via Dolorosa where Christ had carried his cross, he entered a pentagonal building with a flat lead roof and an open cupola that Christians knew as The Cathedral of the Holy Sepulcher. Medievals believed that it encompassed the places where Jesus was crucified, buried, and resurrected. In this view, which moderns find questionable, Calvary, the site of the Christ's crucifixion, was reachable by descending a long and winding stair in the southwest corner of the structure. In this crypt, Francis would have passed the tombs of the rulers of the vanquished Latin Kingdom to kneel at the Holy Sepulcher and to marvel at the stone that had rolled away before the risen Christ.

Another essential stop was the Dome of the Rock, believed in the Middle Ages to be the actual Temple of Solomon. Jews, who had been exiled from Jerusalem by the Crusaders and returned under Saladin, honored the stone as the place where Abraham prepared to sacrifice his son. Muslims revered it as the spot where Muhammad's horse leapt into the sky, taking him to heaven accompanied by the Archangel Gabriel. Christians believed that the rock sat above the cave where Christ defended the woman taken in adultery.

Bethlehem, where Jesus was born, was just a few miles away, as was Qasr al Yahud in the wilds of the Jordan Valley north of the Dead Sea and east of Jericho where John baptized Jesus. The terrain from Jerusalem to the Dead Sea changes swiftly. It passes from rolling hills though ravines and then to dry, arid, and rocky terrain before the land drops off to reveal the surface of the Dead Sea.

At some point in his journey Francis would have learned that the Crusaders, aided by the arrival of more than one hundred thousand reinforcements under the command of Savaric de Mauleon of Poitou, had recaptured Damietta on November 5, 1219, weeks after he left the area. This Christian victory decisively fractured its leadership. Pelagius, supported by the Italian forces, claimed that the city belonged to all of Western Christendom, whereas the military leader John of Brienne, who was now supported by the Templars and Hospitallers, had expected it to be his alone. Having lost face in the diplomatic battle, John departed to pursue other interests that may have included defending Acre from Muslim advances. Thus the sultan's defeated forces were able to regroup while the Christians fell out among themselves.

Francis himself must have achieved a measure of contentment. While he had not converted the sultan or advanced the cause of peace, he had knelt at Calvary and the Holy Sepulcher. Surely he would have seen Nazareth and the fertile plain leading to the stormy Sea of Galilee. By then he would have been twenty-five miles from Acre, the major port of departure for Europe. Like any weary traveler in a far-off land, he began to wonder what was going on back home.

Crusaders had the custom of turning to seers for news of loved ones. One of these clairvoyants had the reputation for being so accurate that she was known by the name Veredicta, or Truth Teller. According to the Franciscan brother Jordan of Giano, who wrote of the early days of the order, Francis consulted this woman and she gave him a disturbing report: "Return! Return!" she said. "Because of the absence of Francis, the Order is disturbed, torn asunder, and scattered!" Confirmation of her cheerless declaration followed quickly. A Lesser Brother named Stephen appeared unexpectedly, probably soon after Francis arrived in Acre. He was relieved to have found Francis, yet he was desperate to persuade him to return home immediately. He said that Gregory of Naples and Matthew of Narni were imposing strict dietary rules and that they had beaten those who dared to question them. At Saint Damian, Cardinal Hugolino was forcing the rules of the Benedictine order on Clare and her community. Only Francis could restore order. Stephen begged for forgiveness for leaving Italy without the permission of his superiors, yet just as quickly he denounced them.

Thus, Francis learned that not only had his order come undone, the curia was assuming his authority. Francis is recorded as saying,

"Until now the ulcer has been confined to the flesh and so there remained a hope of cure, but now it has penetrated to the bone and it will surely be incurable." As Francis mulled over this news he had Stephen read aloud the alien rules while he and Peter Cattani sat down to eat. They were being served meat, but by the new rule of Gregory of Naples it was a day of strict abstinence when it should be avoided. When Francis asked Peter what they should do under the circumstances, Peter said that he had the authority to decide the matter. Francis announced that they should follow the Gospels and eat what had been set before them. Then as soon as he could, Francis set sail for home and a confrontation with everything that he had sought to avoid.

PART III

9

In the Absence of Francis

FRANCIS OF ASSISI was dead. The terrible news was repeated in the roads of Umbria, in the marketplaces of the hill towns, and finally in huts and caves where the Lesser Brothers took shelter. Exactly how it had happened no one knew. He might have been killed by the Infidel or been undone by some well-intended blunder of his own. Word spread that after the Crusaders suffered an enormous defeat, Francis defied wise counsel and set out on foot to see the sultan with a single companion. If he had not been killed by the Infidel, he was surely their captive. Either way, Assisi would see him no more. Scoffers said that Francis, who had always placed his trust in the Lord, should perhaps have listened to knowledgeable leaders who urged prudence.

Cardinal Hugolino could only agree, despite the fact that he had allowed Francis to travel to the war in the Holy Land. Now with Francis unlikely to be alive, the cardinal assumed responsibility for his followers, a task that nicely aligned with his efforts to bring under control the contentious communities of women in Umbria and Tuscany. A group that he had never heard of, at Saint Damian near Assisi, had hampered his arrangements with the women of Monticelli outside Florence and the negotiations he had been working on when he met with Francis in September 1217.

On that fateful day when Francis was ushered into his presence in Florence, Hugolino was acquiring land for the new order of women

he was forming. His model was Saint Sixtus in Rome, the cloistered convent he had helped to create with Dominic Guzman and
two other cardinals. As had been the case there, women in central
Italy who claimed to dedicate their lives to God had taken it upon
themselves to create their own diverse ways of religious life. Such
innovations invited heresy and could not continue.

Hugolino had learned from missteps made with the unruly nuns
in Rome. This time he made sure that no other entities, particularly
local bishops, would be entitled to any revenues, tithes, or payments
from the convents he created. The papacy and not local bishops would
supervise the women. The cardinal himself would receive and manage all funds that would support them. The recent Lateran Council
decreed that the new orders were to follow the rules of an existing
one, so he patterned his after those of Saint Benedict. He called it
The Ladies of the Poor of the Valley of Spoleto and Tuscany. Under
Hugolino's paternal care, they were to be cloistered, shut away from
the world so that they could not encounter people and ideas that
could distract them from their professed dedication to God and a
life of prayer.

On August 27, 1218, Pope Honorius III had authorized this project in the document *Litterae tuae nobis*. It seemed that all arrangements were settled and that Hugolino had merged four undisciplined
communities into one under his sole direction. Then the women near
Florence reneged. Led by one named Avvengnente of the Albizzi
family who had donated her property as a dowry to establish the
house, they insisted that they were in fact under a prior agreement
to follow the way of life of the community of Saint Damian outside
Assisi. Reading this, the vexed Hugolino would have tugged at the
capsule that contained the withering finger of the late pious Marie of
Oignies and tried not to blaspheme.

Hugolino accommodated himself to the new situation. He united only three convents, those of Montelucce in Perugia, Holy Mary

outside Siena, and Holy Mary of Gattaiola in the diocese of Lucca. On July 27, 1219, he sent a letter to Monticelli saying that in addition to following the rule of Saint Benedict, they could also observe the practices of "the Ladies of Saint Mary of Saint Damian at Assisi." He did not mention his own Ladies of the Poor of the Valley of Spoleto and Tuscany by name, but it was not enough to mollify that uneasy community.

As summer faded and autumn began, they learned of troublesome developments in the other houses of the cardinal's new order. The women had welcomed the Lesser Brothers into their midst for years, but now a monk, usually a Cistercian assigned by Cardinal Hugolino, barred their admission and explained that he was in charge of regulating the women's dealings with outsiders, including the Lesser Brothers. They could no longer mingle with townspeople and instead of being able to wear any poor garment that was given to them, each was to dress in a long tunic, preferably covered by a sleeveless over-garment called a scapular. If they wished, they could add a hair shirt and a mantle, or cape, if the climate demanded it.

The Monticelli community decided to avoid further dealings with Hugolino and wrote to Pope Honorius III directly. They asked him for confirmation, possibly with the intention of presenting it to the cardinal if need arose, that they be allowed to continue to follow the model that Clare and her companions observed at Saint Damian. By the time the pontiff replied in a letter of December 9, 1219, Avvengnente was no longer in charge, or had at least declined the title of abbess. Thus he addressed his letter to "The Abbess," a title proper to the Benedictines and to Hugolino's order but one completely removed from the spirit of Francis. He affirmed that Monticelli could continue to observe a way of life patterned after Saint Damian but he also confirmed what Hugolino himself had said—that they must follow, in addition, the practices of Saint Benedict. Whether he knew it or not, it was not possible to follow both. However Hugolino may have reacted when he learned that Avvengnente had not trusted his word and the authority of the letter he had sent her on July 27, a document that a proud man would have written with bitterness of heart, subsequent developments proved that the cardinal was determined to bring the Florentine house into line. Since he was spending time near Saint Damian, he was able to learn more about the obscure community in Umbria that the Florentines followed, and he found that it was allied to Francis. In fact, its leader, the noble lady Clare, had sworn obedience to Francis directly. Thus Hugolino could settle the matter by informing Clare that since Francis had died, that vow was moot but they were not without a father. She and her followers would now join his order and live by its rules. He was satisfied that once they did so, Monticelli would follow his rules as well.

At the end of March 1220 with the earth muddy from the spring thaw and the trees beginning to bud, Hugolino left his palatial accommodations in Perugia, probably on horseback and escorted by knights, to make his journey over the narrow Tiber River and across the bumpy terrain below the city of Assisi to Saint Damian. Clare and her companions treated him with all the respect and ceremony that their poverty allowed. If the patched tunics and the dry bread they served him were the best they had, they were truly impoverished. The deprivation and hardship he found there, all in the service of Christ, stunned and shamed him. If this was the life the women wanted to follow, they needed his wise supervision. Adding to the significance of the occasion was that it was Holy Week, the time of commemorating Christ's horrific death on Good Friday and his glorious Resurrection on Easter Sunday.

He was dumbstruck that the women denied themselves every relief and comfort with great cheer. They lived in a loft reached by a ladder above a large chamber that was shrouded in darkness and aired only by slits in the walls. This was home to female lepers whom the holy women served. Besides the lepers, the community consisted of at least ten women including Clare, her blood sister Agnes, and Pacifica. Benvenuta, Clare's childhood friend from Perugia, had joined the initial trio the first autumn they were at Saint Damian. There were also Cristiana and Filippa, both from noble Assisi families who had also had grown up with Clare in Perugia. Cristiana had been in the Offreduccio house the night Clare escaped to join Francis and his movement. Filippa, whose father Leonard became a Lesser Brother with Francis, had been moved to join Clare after hearing her preach about the cruel sufferings of Christ. Cecilia was another woman who had been so inspired. There were also Clare's cousin Balvina, and Ginevra, the cousin of the Lesser Brother Angelo Tancredi. They had left their homes between 1212 and 1217, a period of increased strife in both Perugia, where civil war had broken out between its nobles and merchants, and in Assisi, which took advantage its rival's situation to lay claim to Nocera and the strategic city of Postignano.

The most recent addition to the community was a child named Agnes whose father was the podestà, or mayor, of Assisi. For whatever reason her parents had allowed such a young girl to take up this life, Agnes began as a daughter to the others and she would end it as an elder of a community forty years later. Less is known about a group of five women Francis had sent to Saint Damian. Clare agreed to accept four of them, but rejected the fifth, a noble woman of Assisi named Gasdia. Clare told Francis that Gasdia would not persevere in a life of poverty and that even if she could endure for as long as three years, she would ultimately return to the world. Francis, always convinced that a person could transform in an instant if they surrendered to God, wanted to take the eager noble woman at her word. He, and possibly others, pressured Clare to allow Gasdia to take up residence. Clare capitulated, but her good judgment was correct. Gasdia returned to the world after only six months.

When Hugolino appeared at her door, Clare was around twenty-five and still young enough for her body to withstand the rigors she imposed upon it. Clare herself spent much of each night lying face down on the floor awake and in prayer. When she did retire, she slept resting her head on a rock from the Tiber. Three days of the week she fasted totally. Other days, at the insistence of Francis, she ate at least half a roll of bread. She was a diffident leader, assigning tasks with great humility and preferring to do as much of the work herself as possible. She served the women of her community when they gathered for their meager meals, pouring them water and washing their feet. When any one of them was ill and soiled her mattress, Clare herself washed out the fouled bedding.

The women at Saint Damian lit no fires to thwart the spring chill unless the sickest among them required it. Bread that might have fed a single woman at one meal was instead a day's ration for several. They rose in the night to pray at the first canonical hour. They gave food and comfort to female lepers who resided in the large space below their dormitory. In daylight they met with townspeople who sought spiritual or medical aid. The cardinal saw for himself that the women were engaged with the world, grappling with its worst aspects, serving the needy, and following the extreme example of Francis. Always they were busy at something, whether it was gardening, mending, drawing water, spinning, cleaning, cooking, or praying. The women seemed to thrive on this life. However, Hugolino was aware of other communities where extreme living conditions led the members into sin and heresy, and he looked on Saint Damian with a wary eye.

However impractical Hugolino thought them to be, he must have found their spiritual practices to be sound. Aside from communal prayers, the women kept silent. Clare discouraged idle chat. They were chaste and respectful of priests. Nonetheless, Hugolino believed that it was fine to trust the Lord as long as one did not invite the Devil. Saint Damian's only concession to the reality of the danger of residing outside city walls was the presence of a few Lesser Brothers nearby, and the nightly removal of the ladder that provided access to their sleeping loft.

Philip the Tall watched over Clare's community. Only a few sentences about him have come down to posterity. The Latin descriptive "Longo" indicates he was slender and of exceptional height. A layman, he was perhaps the seventh man to join Francis's band. While he had not studied the scriptures formally as one training for the priesthood would have, he was greatly respected for his knowledge of the holy word and for his particular ability to explain it and make it relevant to daily life. Francis, Clare, and Philip the Tall had an exceptional and irreplaceable bond since Clare as a young noblewoman had met the two men in secret over the months when she was deciding to follow their way of life. Clare and Philip shared memories of their recklessness in the service of the Lord and a treasured sense of their great adventure, including its many vicissitudes, such as the beating Agnes received from her kinsmen, and Francis's indignation when he and his brothers were driven from a pig sty where they had taken shelter. Hugolino saw in Philip's bond with Clare and the women of Saint Damian something that the church could use to solve the vexing problem of who would oversee the daily life and needs of the various communities of his Ladies of the Poor of the Valley of Spoleto and Tuscany.

Other male orders did not want the task, but Hugolino had persuaded the reluctant Cistercians, whose organization and discipline he admired, to accept the women's care at least temporarily. This white-robed religious order had created the office of visitator, a man who travelled throughout the communities to promote spirituality, obedience, and their rules. The visitator to the women would also obtain earthly necessities such as food, clothing, and medicines while the women lived in prayer.

Now with Francis surely dead, Hugolino could assign this role to the Lesser Brothers. The Assisi men were loyal to the church and were known to defend priests, even the least worthy ones. In addition, the brothers had a history of working closely with various communities of women in the smaller cities of north central Italy, such as Saint Severino in the Marches, and they had the women's confidence. Francis's men had won the respect not only of the people of Assisi but of the cities where he had established his new order.

Philip the Tall was the exemplar of what he wanted in a visitator to the women. Hugolino witnessed for himself that Philip was able to preach more meaningful sermons than most priests. During that Holy Week he spoke of the Last Supper, which was Jesus's final meeting with his disciples, of the betrayal by Judas, and of Christ's painful march to Calgary and his horrific death. The cardinal also saw Philip willingly doing the humble work of chopping wood and tilling garden soil. The women of Saint Damian accepted Philip the Tall as their true brother. The difficult women at Monticelli who took Saint Damian as their model would surely approve of him as well. Like other Lesser Brothers, Philip had travelled through the Italian peninsula and was probably already known at Monticelli and at the convents in Siena, Perugia, and Lucca as well.

By the end of his visit to Saint Damian, Hugolino, Cardinal of Ostia, revealed his purpose. He told Clare that he was relieving her of all worldly distractions such as the care of lepers and that she and her companions would now be free to live a life of prayer and adoration of the Lord within the walls of Saint Damian, which they were never to leave, nor were outsiders to enter except for priests to say Mass and provide the sacraments. Now they were to be the Ladies of the Poor of the Valley of Spoleto and Tuscany, one of some nine communities in the territory that were under his guidance. They would pray at set times and fast in specified fashion under the rule of Saint Benedict. Furthermore, Hugolino was sending Philip the Tall away to assume the care of Monticelli. Hugolino might have pointed out that since it already followed the customs of Saint Damian, and had the pope's permission to be allowed to continue to do so, no one was better than Philip to keep that far off sister community strong in the ways of Saint Damian. A Cistercian named Ambrose would take Philip's place at Saint Damian and Clare was to be its abbess. The next step would have been for Clare and the others to profess the vows of their new order, but Clare declined, saying they lived under a vow to Francis who, despite their fears, might yet live. During another Holy Week only eight years earlier, she had sworn before God that she would follow Francis and thus she could obey no other. She knew what Hugolino was asking. She had lived briefly under the rules of Saint Benedict at the convent of Saint Paul of the Abbesses before Francis moved her, Pacifica, and Agnes to Saint Damian. If those rules had been right for her, she would have stayed there.

She was particularly unwilling to let go of Philip. She had always a deep need to keep her dearest ones by her side, even if it meant placing them in the harsh and unusual circumstances of Saint Damian. Certainly this might bring them closer to God, but in fact God could be served anywhere. Clare drew strength from the presence of Agnes and Pacifica, but she may also have been strengthened by the idea that if they were with her, she could keep them safe. She counted on Philip to look after them all.

He was a strong presence there, even though he surely also travelled and preached in the wider world. He is the brother most often mentioned in their early records and he spent more time there than Francis. He had accompanied Francis at his early secret meetings with Clare, but so did Bernard of Quintavalle. He was an accomplished preacher, as were Giles and others. Other Lesser Brothers were upset by Cardinal Hugolino's interference with the women's communities, but only Philip would be recorded as writing to the pope to obtain redress. Although he is one of the dozen or so brothers mentioned by name in the early biographies, he is never described as travelling with Francis, although most likely, he did. Finally, for all the glimpses the early documents gave of the bond and deep affection that the early brothers had for Clare, Philip was the brother Clare named in her appeals to Cardinal Hugolino. He was a strong, brave friend and he was an articulate advocate for the women, willing to stand up for them at Saint Damian and in the world beyond. Francis gave Clare her way of life and her authority, but it was Philip on whom she truly relied.

To no avail could a stunned and unwilling Clare point out that Philip was under a vow of obedience to Francis to be responsible solely for Saint Damian and that she and her women had been entrusted to Philip alone so that no other brother, particularly one outside Francis's movement, could be substituted.

Like a father standing fast in the face of a rebellious if beloved child, the cardinal was firm on one fact: Francis was dead. However grievous the news might be, however unwilling she might be, Clare had to accept that Francis had been martyred months earlier on the harsh sands of Egypt at the hands of the godless Saracen. Nothing had been heard of him after he departed the Crusaders' camp and headed to the tent of the sultan. In light of this new reality, the vows of the Lesser Brothers and Sisters to follow Francis had to be modified.

Under rules approved at the recent Lateran Council, the papacy had taken over responsibility for all religious life, including hers. As the pope's representative throughout north and central Italy, Hugolino said that he had direct responsibility for Saint Damian and he executed it. He told Clare that her community would follow the rule that Benedict had given to his sister Scholastica seven hundred years earlier, which would bring it into conformity with the rule of the recent Lateran Council. They would now take vows as Ladies of the Poor of the Valley of Spoleto and Tuscany and live enclosed within their walls with God.

Even as he hardened himself against Clare's tears, he believed that he was working for her own good, but Clare's piety and total dedication to the Lord still reproached him. His rule allowed nuns to have pillows of straw or hay, not the rock Clare rested on. Even though he was surely happy that a clean soft bed awaited him at the end of every trying day, and that he could wash his hands in water boiled with sage leaves before his meals, his creature comforts embarrassed him. He did not pity Clare as much as he pitied himself for being less than she must be in the eyes of God: less holy, less willing to sacrifice himself and endure physical discomfort.

He seemed to want to win her approval as well as her unquestioned obedience. In a letter he sent to her after his visit, the cardinal described himself as "a wretched and sinful man." He addressed Clare, who was half his age, as "the mother of his salvation" and said that the joy he experienced when they discussed the mystical union of Christ with the church had deserted him. He wrote, "I have always known and have considered myself to be a sinner, yet after having seen the sure sign of your merits and having witnessed the rigor of your way of life, I have learned with certainty that I have been weighed down with such a burden of sin and have so offended the Lord of the whole universe, that I am not worthy to be freed from earthly concerns and be associated with the company of the saved, unless your prayers and tears obtain for me pardon for my sins." The cardinal was declaring that only if she asked God to forgive him could he hope to be admitted to heaven.

Then came a change of subject and a bit of news: the pope would not be coming to Assisi, as had been suggested to Clare, but he himself planned to seize the first opportunity to return to them soon. He closed by sending greetings to "the virgin Agnes," and stating that she was his sister as well as Clare's. By the time they received this letter, the women of Saint Damian were beset by the sounds of hammers and shouting workmen. Their beloved home was being renovated according to the specifications that Hugolino had established for the nuns they did not wish to be. The lepers whom they had loved and served were dispersed. The dark chamber where they had lived was converted to a chapel, complete with a wall to separate the Abbess Clare and her nuns from the priest who celebrated Mass for them. Into this wall was cut a small window with an iron grille that was shrouded with a black linen cloth so that the women could not see inside the chapel. They could not look upon the priest, but they could hear his words as he said Mass.

Meanwhile, the Lesser Brothers were in turmoil. Not only was Francis gone, he had taken his usual deputy Peter Cattani with him to the Holy Land and left two relative strangers in charge. These were Gregory of Naples, who was to travel throughout the Italian Peninsula to oversee the brothers, and Matthew of Narni, who was to preside over Francis's beloved Portiuncula to guide men who wanted to join them. Francis probably trusted that church officials would make no further changes to the Lesser Brothers until those who led them, such as himself, Peter, and the increasingly influential Elias, returned to Portiuncula. In this, Francis was wrong. However they came to be appointed, Gregory and Matthew were not caretakers. They were quick to disregard Francis's principles, enforce new ones, and unleash months of disruption.

Francis envisioned his movement as one of laymen, but about five years before he left for the Holy Land, as early as 1214, an increasing number of priests began to join the Lesser Brothers. Outwardly those who had taken holy orders were indistinguishable from the others. They too wore patched tunics belted with a knotted cord, but they were better educated, more cerebral, and used to deference from those who had not taken Holy Orders. As priests they were required to read daily prayers. They were trained in the structure of the church and although they hoped to live a more deeply spiritual life by joining Francis, their outlook was different from that of brothers who had no learning or felt any need for it. Francis was convinced that the intellect was a snare. He was more interested in the formation of the heart than the head.

Francis himself had been required to read scripture on a daily basis since he had been made a deacon by Innocent III in 1209. He revered the word of God, but he believed that even those words were meaningless if reading them was a substitute for putting them into practice. Francis allowed the few ordained priests who joined the

Lesser Brothers to use missals while celebrating Mass. But before he left for the Holy Land he saw an increasing number of such books scattered throughout the huts at Portiuncula and he grew concerned. He feared that his brothers were reading the Gospel rather than living it.

The two men Francis left in charge modified not only Francis's rules but the spirit of his movement. They took upon themselves the task of bringing the Lesser Brothers into line with existing religious orders as the Lateran Council had mandated. Possibly they did this on the advice of Cardinal Hugolino; possibly they also heeded the wishes of other cardinals as well because Francis would describe this as a time of having "many popes."

At a gathering of all the brothers, probably in September 1219, Gregory and Matthew tightened the rules for days of fasting, an area where Francis was lenient because he knew that the brothers often had to accommodate themselves to the conditions they found as they travelled through the world. The two made fasting on Mondays and two other days obligatory and said that the brothers were to abstain from milk on Mondays and Saturdays. These modifications and distinctions were basically only a rearrangement of patterns approved by Francis, but they followed the rules of the Benedictine monks who spent their lives fixed in one place. Francis's itinerant brothers who acquired provisions chiefly through begging or in exchange for manual labor had taken Christ's words in Luke 10:8 as their guide: "And whatever town you enter, and they receive you, eat what is set before you." Sometimes they were forced to content themselves with slops or meager crusts. At other times they were served delicious meals. They were to accept whatever was given to them with equal gratitude, but now Francis's surrogates set aside the words of the Gospel for the strictures of the Order of Saint Benedict.

When Matthew or Gregory discovered a Lesser Brother who continued to follow Francis's guidelines about food, he imposed penances and punishments that were so severe that at least one prepared to leave the order. This was John Capella, an early companion of Francis who had travelled with him to Rome to obtain approval from Innocent III in 1212. Under Gregory and Matthew, he broke away to create a new religious order of lepers, and he petitioned Pope Honorius to approve it.

In another annulment of Francis's rules and philosophy, Gregory allowed and probably encouraged the brothers to establish permanent residences in various towns and cities, notably Bologna. Francis preferred his men to live in the outskirts. But not only was Bologna the crossroads of the Italian peninsula, its renowned university was the center for the study of canon law that guided church authorities. A decade earlier Bernard of Quintavalle had found it to be such a source of temptation that he fled the place.

Although Francis insisted that he wanted his followers to win approval through their good deeds rather than because of official credentials, the Fourth Lateran Council in its Canon 3 proscribed wandering preachers who lacked official sanction. Francis himself had accepted, and may have welcomed, a papal letter of introduction when he went to the Holy Land in June 1219, but the pope now did still more to smooth the brothers' way. On May 29, 1220, he addressed a letter *Pro dilectis* to all prelates, including bishops, archbishops, and abbots in France, in which he said that he had heard that some of them continued to reject the Lesser Brothers despite the papal letters that they carried showing that they were approved by the Holy See. "We want all of you to observe that we hold their Order to be among those approved by us, and that we regard the brothers of the Order as truly Catholic and devout men." He told them that he warned, exhorted, prescribed, and commanded the prelates to allow "the Order of the Lesser Brothers" to take up residence and to remain in their various jurisdictions.

Around the time of this letter Francis, alive but ailing, was aboard ship headed for home, his mind filled with Brother Stephen's dire report of changes in the order. He, Peter Cattani, Elias, Caesar of

Speyer, and other brothers departed the Holy Land, then sailed across the Mediterranean and up the eastern coast of the Adriatic Sea past Greece, surely stopping in the port cities of Durrës in modern Albania and in Ragusa, as Dubrovnik was then known. The clarity of the night sky, the stars burning bright, even the gulls flying close to the ship, were lost on Francis, who saw fog and clouds above at times that others said were clear. Something had happened to his eyes in the desert and his vision was beginning to dim.

Finally, after a voyage of weeks, during which Francis could only have brooded and prayed about unhappy developments at home, they landed in Venice. This fabled capital of the mighty Venetian Republic was bejeweled and festooned with the plunder of the Crusades. Four bronze horses that had been part of the booty of the sack of Byzantium in 1204 adorned its awe-inspiring Basilica of Saint Mark, imparting the air of Constantinople and the secrets and splendor of the East. Francis was too exhausted to preach to the people there or to take delight in the birds from far-off shores that landed in their plaza.

Sick with quartan fever, a type of malaria that is marked by convulsions and pains in the spleen and liver, and with trachoma, the source of his eye problems, he sent ahead others who could travel quickly. He asked Brother Leonard of Assisi, whose daughter was at Saint Damian, to accompany him on his own slow journey, and he was so debilitated that he had to ride part of the way on a donkey. The trip was so arduous that Leonard, who was of the noble class and was now following a merchant's son on foot, thought that he should be given a turn riding as well. Reading his thoughts, Francis acknowledged that the other was of a higher class and dismounted, to Leonard's horror and chagrin.

After a hundred miles south on ancient Roman roads through the rocky plains and wetlands of the Veneto, they reached Bologna. There to his dismay Francis learned of a building that was known as "the house of the brothers." Francis, who did not want his men to own books much less houses, was so enraged that he refused to go near the place. Instead, he took up residence with Dominic's followers, who two years earlier had been given the Church of Saint Nicholas in the heart of the university quarter. Abashed, Francis's repentant men persuaded him to stay with them, but then he learned that their house was filled with scholarly brothers studying at the University of Bologna. Gregory of Naples had directed Brother John of Schiacia, a doctor of law, to build the dwelling for them. Incensed, Francis commanded them all to abandon the place saying, "I want my brothers to pray more than to read." The occupants, including those who were sick in bed, promptly decamped.

By that point, word surely reached Portiuncula that not only was Francis alive, he was on his way to them. His early followers were elated, none more than Clare, who expected him to undo all that Hugolino had done. Surely the joy that greeted his arrival distracted Francis from his own physical and emotional misery, but he could not ignore the changes wrought by those he had trusted. Gregory of Naples and Matthew of Narni may well have told him that they had modified his rules under the direction of others who had decided that Francis was dead.

His mood was not lifted when he learned that the pope, believing Francis dead, had sent a bull *Cum secundum consilium* dated September 22, 1220, addressed to the "priors and custodians of the Lesser Brothers" and omitting his name. It imposed a year of probation on any man who wanted to join them. The title "prior" would have particularly upset him because Francis specifically banned it. He did not want any of his followers to seem to rank above the others.

Francis had rejected the idea of allowing men to try out living as Lesser Brothers before taking vows, although even sympathetic churchmen were concerned about the unsystematic ways of Francis's men. Jacques of Vitry, who had observed them in the Holy Land, wrote his friends that the order was dangerous because it dispatched unsupervised brothers, even those who were immature, untested, and unformed, in pairs throughout the world. Francis was known to welcome any man who came to him, trusting that God was working in his life and that the path of the Gospel was the best road for everyone, particularly those who recognized it. Paradoxically, women in Hugolino's order would have no testing period or novitiate, provided they were old enough to understand that they were agreeing to be locked behind closed walls for the rest of their lives. They were required to make their vows to the abbess within a few days of arrival.

The papacy was a mighty tree that in a deluge could either shelter Francis or attract a bolt of lightning to his head. The pope's letter of approval had surely been of use to Francis when he was in the Holy Land. But continued guidance threatened to transform his band of poor, wandering, penitent laymen into worldly priests and monks assigned to comfortable dwellings where they studied the fine points of arcane doctrine. Whatever joy he felt at being back at Portiuncula had to be short-lived.

Almost immediately, Francis was forced to confront another horrible calamity that had befallen his community. Francis, in sending five brothers to Morocco in May 1219, had sentenced them to slaughter. All had been beheaded in January 1220, two months before Hugolino visited Saint Damian, at a time when Francis was in the Holy Land. The quintet who had gone to Morocco were Berard, Peter, Accursion, Adiuto, and Ottone. Such was their zeal that when they reached Seville in Spain, they entered its Great Mosque on profane sandaled feet and loudly preached the Gospel. They were seized and imprisoned, then sent to Marrakech, the capital city of the Almohad caliphs. Through the influence of the brother of the king of Portugal, who was there leading a group of mercenaries, they were freed, but they persisted in their mission and preached openly. Officials decided that they were madmen and drove them from the city. Undeterred, the brothers returned to Marrakech.

Earlier they had been tolerated because they spoke only to praise Jesus, but now they spoke against Muhammad. Once they did that, they forfeited their lives. On January 16, 1220 they were beheaded for defaming the Prophet. Months later when their remains reached Portugal they were credited with working miracles.

While Francis may have believed that his martyred brothers were now with God and his angels, he and his followers were overcome when they learned of the grisly executions. Thirty years later, as old women, Clare's surviving companions would still weep when speaking of them. When Clare heard the news, she was in such anguish that she wanted to abandon Saint Damian and travel to Morocco to die for Christ as they had done. Since she did not travel far from Assisi in the relative freedom of her early days at Saint Damian, it is unlikely that she, a woman, could ever have ventured to Muslim lands to preach. Now under the rules Hugolino imposed, she could not venture beyond her doorway, so her bold notion has the air of a death wish.

Francis's indignation over the changes to his rule and the scholarly establishment in Bologna faded with his physical strength. In his late thirties, after a life of physical abuse compounded by his recent stay in desert heat and winds, he knew he was not physically the man he had been when he scaled The Rock in the commune's assault on the nobles' power. Emotionally, he was not that man either. For all the fervor of his preaching, Francis believed that the best way to persuade others of the rightness of the teachings of Jesus was by being humble and respecting the other. He heeded the Gospel message encapsulated in Matthew 5: 44-45: "Love your enemies, do good to those who hate you, and pray for those who persecute and calumniate you so that you may be children of your father in heaven." Francis wanted to undo Gregory and Matthew's directives, but he also wanted peace. While he was adamant that Innocent III had given the Lesser Brothers his approval, which qualified them as an order that existed prior to the Fourth Lateran Council, many in the curia disagreed, and many authoritative figures sent him advice. Francis realized, or was made to realize, that the Lesser Brothers needed an advocate at the pope's court. His model was Cardinal Leo Brancaleone, who had assumed that role in guiding a movement called the Poor Catholics led by Durand of Huesca away from heresy.

Francis travelled to Viterbo to consult with Pope Honorius III. According to Jordan of Giano, whose brief description is the most vivid record of the encounter, Francis did not approach the pontiff through his secretaries, but waited outside his door until he appeared. Then he greeted him, wishing him peace. Francis told Honorius that he knew the pope was too occupied by many burdens to oversee his order directly, but that instead of the "many popes" he had been given, he wanted one papal representative to guide him. He requested that this be the Cardinal of Ostia. And so it was done. Once Hugolino was officially in charge of the Lesser Brothers, he showed his benevolence by placating Francis.

The cardinal declined to approve John Capella's order of lepers and John apparently remained a Lesser Brother. He also voided the new rules about fasting that had caused such discord. As for the house in Bologna that the brothers inhabited, Hugolino publicly announced, possibly while preaching, that it belonged to him. The brothers did not own it, the cardinal insisted, they merely used it.

Exactly what Francis was able to do to improve Clare's situation is unclear. He had no desire for his brothers to have the care of women's convents and he made every effort to keep them free of this. He was willing to abandon the women who followed him to preserve the way of life of the men. However, Saint Damian was a special case. He had personally convinced Clare to leave her home and join his movement and since she had vowed obedience directly to him and to no other authority, Francis bore a particular responsibility for her community. He urged Clare to make some concessions, if not to Hugolino, then to the rules of the Lateran Council, and he more or less forced her to accept the role of abbess if not the title.

However, Philip, who had witnessed Francis's promises to Clare, may have taken an active part in trying to remove Hugolino from the life at Saint Damian. The insightful medieval and Clarist scholar Maria Pia Alberzoni believes that Philip himself sought from Pope Honorius III a letter that would restore Francis's way of life to it and the other communities and also recall the unwelcome Cistercian visitators from their midst. Jordan of Giano wrote, "Brother Philip, who was over-zealous for the Poor Ladies, contrary to the will of Blessed Francis who wanted to conquer all things through humility rather than by the force of legal judgments, sought letters from the Apostolic See. By these letters he wished to defend the Ladies and excommunicate their disturbers." Francis did avoid legal intervention but he would have sympathized with Philip's efforts to free Clare from confinement. Tradition and a possible misreading of the writings of Jordan of Giano have painted Philip as the one who offended Francis by betraying his intentions for Saint Damian. However, Alberzoni asks if the actions that Francis objected to might in fact have been those of Hugolino, not Philip. If Philip did reach the convent at Monticelli, he may have received guidance from these women who had extricated themselves from Hugolino's order by writing a letter to the pope.

However it happened, Hugolino relieved Philip the Tall of responsibility for the Ladies of the Poor of the Valley of Spoleto and Tuscany and returned him to Saint Damian. Francis neither ordered Clare to obey Hugolino nor freed her of him. Just as Honorius III had told Monticelli that they could follow the rules of both Saint Benedict and Saint Damian, so Hugolino now told Saint Damian they could observe both these very separate paths. Clare would be neither as free as she wished nor as confined as Hugolino planned.

The comity, the expression of mutual respect, that Francis had fostered in submitting to the authority and involvement of the church came at a cost. Through Hugolino, the papacy would now have a clearer hand in directing the future of the movement. Until now,

God had directed Francis. Now it would be Cardinal Hugolino, a development that apparently did not relieve his mind. To this was added his grief and guilt over the brothers who had died in Morocco. However willing Francis was to die for Christ himself, he continued to agonize over having sent the men to their deaths while he lived on in relative physical safety. Reflecting on their terrible end may well have brought back the horrors of the bloody slaughter he witnessed at Collestrada. He had serious doubts about what he was accomplishing. On one extreme, brothers who obeyed him, like those who went to Morocco, died in horrible circumstances. On the other, growing numbers were shirking the hard life that he and the Gospels advocated. He was upset to see that communities of women who had been friends and sister companions to the brothers, were being locked away and forced to live as cloistered nuns. In frustration Francis exclaimed, "The Lord has taken away our wives, and now the devil is providing us with sisters." The seed of his movement had flowered into an alien plant that he did not know how to cultivate.

10

Francis Obeys

As Francis struggled with his diminishing physical powers, as his sight dimmed and rest became essential, he was forced to confront the fact that at the very time he was at his weakest, his life's work was under attack. Having sought to follow the commands of God he was now obliged to follow the demands of human beings, albeit ones who led the church that he believed in. Cardinal Hugolino required him to write a detailed rule for his brothers to regulate every situation from patching tunics to fasting. And so, just as a merchant might turn from a great financial loss to plan for future profits, Francis decided to make a new beginning. Matthew 5:39 instructs "I say to you not to resist the evildoer; on the contrary, if someone strike thee on the right cheek, turn to him the other also; and if anyone would go to law with thee and take thy tunic, let him take thy cloak as well...." In turning his other cheek to those who had compromised his life's work, Francis decided to accept it as an opportunity for spiritual growth.

He recognized that leading the Lesser Brothers was now beyond his physical and emotional stamina and he decided to give it up. From the time when he had first attracted followers, he had been ambivalent about being in authority because it seemed inconsistent with the lowliness he preached. He saw the role of leader as the obligation to be the servant of each and all of them, but how could he serve the ones who wanted to own books and live secure in monasteries like cell-bound Benedictine monks? He did not wish to be an administrator, nor was his health up to that task. Instead he would be the guiding spirit and serve as the model of what a brother should be, all the while maintaining the life he wanted for himself. He would have as his personal companions only those who followed the commands of poverty that God gave him when he, Peter, and Bernard went to the Church of Saint Nicholas.

Francis believed this would benefit him, as he illustrated by telling a story in which the brothers, with love and affection, asked him to preach at one of their meetings. But then after hearing him, they decided that he was an illiterate boor. They booed and jeered and expelled him from their midst, rejecting his leadership. Francis said such callous treatment should be a cause for joy because, in contrast to the honor and respect they once had shown him, their repudiation would encourage a humility that would be good for his soul.

The brothers who arrived from various parts of Europe for the general meeting of September 1220 surely fell into discussions about Francis's return, his illness, his meeting with the sultan, the prospect of changes to the rules, and of course the brutal death of the martyrs in Morocco. If brothers learned that communities far from Assisi were enjoying study and satisfying meals, they found no slackening at Portiuncula where the ailing Francis was stressing the importance of poverty and self-denial.

Those who had known him in earlier years were probably concerned to find him frail and slowed by the ravages of quartan fever. Possibly his failing eyesight prevented him from recognizing some men until they were within arm's reach. New brothers who had joined the movement thinking that they would be spared from the excessive fervor of its strange founder began to ponder the unsettling effect of having him living in their midst.

When the time came for Francis to stand before the assembled group, he announced shocking news: "From now on I am dead to you." His infirmities were such that he was forced to hand over their care to another. "But see, here is Brother Peter Cattani, whom I and all of you shall obey." Many wept as he bowed down before Peter and promised to respect and follow him. Probably, Peter had served as their leader before. Citing the many stories that Thomas of Celano tells of Peter, the late medieval scholar Rosalind B. Brooke believes that is the case. When Francis travelled extensively, such as the time he travelled to Spain during his first failed attempt to reach the Holy Land with Bernard of Quintavalle, he probably left Peter in charge. Peter had proven through his prior capable stewardship to be the one to assume pastoral and practical care of the Lesser Brothers. He had the advantage of knowing exactly how Francis wanted things to be done and he was comfortable with the Lesser Brothers as a movement of laymen living as equals to the few priests among them. Peter had the support of the early followers and was one himself.

Besides having proved himself to be a true disciple of Francis, Peter also had a practical bent that was alien to Francis and that Francis was quick to overrule. For example, Peter was at his wit's end to find a way to feed all the brothers who flocked to Portiuncula for the meeting, and he thought it might be prudent to accept for the community a portion of the goods and resources of the novices before they distributed them to the poor. Francis declared that it would be better to gather up the many ornaments that adorned their altar to the Blessed Virgin and barter them for what the community needed. Francis assured him that the objects were expendable because someone would come along bringing yet more vessels and candlesticks to replace them.

Another time, the mother of two sons who had become Lesser Brothers found herself in such need that she asked Francis for alms. After Peter said that they had neither food nor money to give her, Francis told him to give her their New Testament, which was something of a treasure because it was the first that had been given to the

Order. Francis said that God would appreciate their helping the poor more than he would value their reading.

Francis asked Peter to appoint a guardian who would be his personal superior, but obedience remained a challenge for him. Meditation on this virtue inspired him to liken it to death. A man who was truly obedient was like a corpse, he said. "Place it where you will. You will see that it does not resist being moved, it does not murmur about its position, it does not cry out if it is allowed to lie there." Despite his best intentions, Francis made sure that his will prevailed as he tried to lead by example.

From the earliest days of his ministry, when one of his brothers cried out with hunger pains and he commanded the entire group to sit down to a meal, albeit a poor one of the meager rations they had on hand, Francis said that to deprive the body of what it needs was as much a sin as gluttony. Yet after he resigned and he was still weak with the lingering effects of quartan fever, he disdained any concession to his illness. He tried to sleep as he always had, on a tunic stretched over bare ground with a stone or a log for a pillow. After one of the brothers sewed a pelt of fox fur under his habit to protect his sensitive stomach and spleen, Francis insisted that he stitch fur on the outside as well so that everyone could see that he was indulging himself. Then he avoided wearing that tunic altogether.

As soon as he seemed to regain his strength, he decided that he had been self-indulgent during his convalescence. When winter settled in and the cold turned the brothers' breath to gentle clouds, Francis persuaded Peter that he had the strength to go to Assisi to preach a sermon in front of the Cathedral of Saint Rufino. Once he finished, he excused himself and asked the crowd to wait while he entered the cathedral. There he made Peter promise to do what he was about to ask. Stripping off his habit, he had Peter loop a rope around his neck and lead him naked through the streets to the stone in the forum where criminals were punished. The brothers, including one who refused to obey Francis's order to throw ashes in his face, were distraught as they led him to the forum where Francis, who was nearly convulsing in the cold wind, told the stunned townspeople: "You believe me to be a holy man. But I confess before God and you that during my illness I have eaten meat and stew flavored with meat."

Peter Cattani simply acquiesced to Francis's excesses and could not bring himself to curb them in any way, even when they nauseated him physically. Francis told Brother James the Simple, who lived at the leper hospice, to stop walking these poor afflicted "brothers in Christ" through Assisi and taking them into churches. Probably Francis hoped to spare them harm or insult, but he was soon mortified to have both criticized James and humiliated the leper who was with him. He set a punishment for himself, which he told the vicar general to approve. As Peter looked on in shock, Francis ate from same bowl as the leper, whose cracked and bleeding fingers oozed into the food that Francis put in his mouth.

In time Francis took up the unwelcome task that the church required of him, the writing of a rule that would be far more specific than Gospel commands and practices like travelling in twos and exchanging the role of preacher by personal choice. The model for this legislation was the rule of Saint Benedict that had governed monastic life for seven hundred years. However, monasticism was not what Francis had chosen. Monks were shut away from the world, usually in abbeys far from cities, while Francis intended his followers to be wanderers without fixed dwellings who often withdrew into prayerful seclusion but returned to the roadways and marketplaces to preach and serve as the poorest of God's poor, all the while dealing with the surprises God sent them.

In contrast, Benedict had structured a constricted world with written rules and regulations that were so clear and prescriptive that no individual monk, subject as he was to the weakness of human nature, would face any unique situation that required him to interpret the rule for himself. Seeking to avoid extreme self-sacrifice on the one hand, and self-indulgence on the other, Benedict allowed his followers to have sufficient food, drink, and rest so that they might pray and work for the greater glory of God. He intended his way to be reasonable and moderate. However, Francis wanted companions to be extremist fools for Christ and to be willing to undergo agonies that would atone for sin.

Francis surely found the Benedictine model daunting. It consisted of seventy-three chapters, nine of which set forth the duties of the abbot, thirteen delineated practices for prayer and worship, twenty-nine dealt with discipline, and twelve governed miscellaneous topics pertaining to monastic life. When Benedict wrote it, Christian monasticism had already been practiced for three hundred years. This austere form of life originated in Egypt when Christianity was banned and could only be practiced in the shadows. Pious men went off on their own to the desert to live a life of prayer, fasting, and celibacy. Then, in the fourth century, when Christianity became legal, some hermits joined together in communities that isolated themselves from the larger world, even as they continued to follow their own individual practices of prayer and penance.

In 529 AD, Benedict, who was born in Nursia near Spoleto, founded a community at Monte Cassino southeast of Rome. By 1000 his rule governed all monasteries in Western Christendom. He wrote it so that any individual could perfect himself and avoid spiritual errors. The guiding principle was total and unwavering obedience to the rule, to the teachings of Christ, and to the abbot in charge of each monastery. A Benedictine monk was also expected to be pious, wise, and humane. Some communities focused on learning and preserved early Christian and pagan writings. Their physical isolation allowed them to pray and study and protected them from the wars and plagues that ravaged human life. It also made them a refuge for weary travelers. Chapter 53 required guests to be treated as if they were Christ himself. This made hospitality an attribute of the order, something that had failed in the

Benedictine abbey outside Assisi where Francis sought refuge soon after he renounced his father.

Francis hoped to create a rule that would guide the spirit of his followers rather than structure their days. To help ground his rules in the authority of the teachings of Jesus, which he expected to be sufficient for the church, Francis turned to a learned brother who had joined the order in the Holy Land. Caesar was born in Speyer in the Palatine region of the southwestern German territories and had studied in Paris. Caesar himself was taken by Jesus's call to abandon the world to find peace of mind. He was so effective in preaching this idea that many prominent women in Speyer put away their fine clothes and jewels and began to live simply, to the horror of their husbands, who called for Caesar to be burned as a heretic. His teacher, Conrad of Speyer, rescued him by sending him back to the safety of Paris. Caesar soon travelled to the Holy Land where he heard Elias preach, found the Lesser Brothers to be kindred spirits, and quickly joined them. Francis met him there and included him in the party that returned to Umbria.

Francis and Caesar probably worked together at Portiuncula while Francis continued to convalesce. Francis intended to maintain his movement of peaceful brothers without power or hierarchy while also adapting it to the organizational demands of the church. With Caesar he produced a document that would permit the Lesser Brothers to continue in the way of poverty, penance, and preaching and also allow room for those who wanted to follow the extreme demands of the earliest days. It sought to discourage individual authority and to limit the terms of those in power. It stressed that those who served as leaders should see themselves as subordinate to others. The title "prior" was never to be used. All were minor, or lesser, brothers to each other and to the people in the world.

This rule from late 1220 was lost and can only be inferred from a later version, the so-called "Rule Without a Papal Seal" or *regula non bullata*. In its introduction, Francis said that it was the form of the life that Innocent III had approved for Francis and for all who would follow him. He was particularly succinct in two matters. The brothers could accept no money. They were to fast on Fridays and from the Feast of All Saints on November 1 to Christmas and then again from Epiphany in January until Easter, and not at other times. They were to follow the command of Luke 10:8 and eat what was put before them. As for books, Francis stipulated that brothers who were clerics could carry only those that they needed to fulfill their vows. Literate brothers could use a psalter, but those who could not read were forbidden to have them.

Respect for the enemy was not what the papacy required, but Francis instructed brothers who wanted to preach to unbelievers, such as the Saracens, to first obtain permission from their superiors and then go forth, showing deference to every creature so as to be an example of their Christian faith as they proclaimed the word of God. Any brother who sinned should be treated with love and compassion. Only fornication was so serious as to warrant expulsion without warning.

Francis stated that in the spirit of Jesus, who had called Judas his friend and gave himself up willingly to his executioners, the brothers were to regard those who caused them pain as their allies and to love them, because they brought them closer to Christ. This was Francis's approach when Hugolino contravened his will. He willingly endured the personal suffering the cardinal caused him for the love of God even as he grew less able to cope emotionally with how that prelate was moderating and reshaping the Lesser Brothers.

Francis's rule, the product of much thought and soul-searching, read more like loving counsel than a series of dictates. With Caesar's help, he authorized his directives by citing scripture rather than by employing the legalistic phrasing of canon law. He allowed room, in most cases, for men moving through changing conditions in the world to adapt to the needs of the moment, such as eating what was before them rather than worrying that meat was forbidden on a particular day of the week. However, in regard to women his rule was inflexible.

Saint Benedict did not spell out rules for chastity, but he implied them. Perhaps Francis had learned of sexual misconduct that might have occurred while he was in the Holy Land, ranging from unwelcome advances to actual physical violation. Above all, he wanted to prevent Hugolino from appointing brothers to oversee women's communities. For whatever reason, Chapter 12 of this rule expressed none of the mercy and love he showed in the rest of the document. He said that no matter where the brothers were, or where they went, they were obliged to avoid the sight or company of women when it was evil. One could infer that they were allowed to be in female company for purposes that were not sinful, but Francis said that he did not want any brother to speak to a woman alone except for those who were priests and could hear confessions, say Mass, or bring the Eucharist. Although Francis had invited Clare to make a vow of obedience to him eight years earlier, and had probably recently done the same for the Roman recluse Praxiteles, he now forbad his male followers to allow any woman to profess another such vow to them, although they might offer spiritual advice.

Probably, Francis's new rules had little effect on Saint Damian. Whatever Cardinal Hugolino had decreed in his absence, four Lesser Brothers, one serving as chaplain, lived in huts outside Saint Damian's walls. Clare in later life cited a written rule that Francis had given them, which has been lost. She quoted Francis saying these words: "Because it was God who inspired you to become daughters and handmaids of the most high supreme King and Father of heaven and to espouse yourselves to the Holy Spirit by choosing to live according to the perfections of the holy Gospel, I desire and promise you personally and in the name of my brothers that I will always have the same loving care and special solicitude for you as for them." Francis did not enforce Hugolino's idea that cloistered prayer was now Clare's only purpose. When a Brother Stephen was in the throes of mental illness, Francis sent him to Clare for healing. After she made the sign of the cross over the distressed man, he became so calm that he fell fast asleep in the chapel. When he awoke, she gave him something to eat and sent him back to Francis.

Francis himself, however, refused to visit her. The brothers asked how he could behave this way after all that they had shared and endured together. Francis insisted that he did still love the women at Saint Damian and he knew that it would be a great unkindness not to care for them after he had made them part of his movement, but he stayed away from them to set an example to the brothers.[†]

Philip the Tall, who wanted to help Clare and her community, returned and continued to serve at Saint Damian. However, when Francis learned that Philip had sent Brother Stephen, the one who had summoned Francis home from the Crusades, to a cloistered women's community at Bevagna under Hugolino's rule, he was furious. On the cold December day that Stephen related this to Francis and sought forgiveness, Francis commanded him to jump fully clothed into the nearby river and then made the wet and shivering Stephen walk two miles with him in that miserable state.

Francis had finished his work on the rule by late 1220, but harsh winter conditions and his still-delicate health meant it was months before he could take the document to Rome for papal approval. When he made that journey he received a fresh and unexpected blow. Around Ash Wednesday in March 1221, at the very time that

---

† Thomas of Celano records in his second biography that was published two decades after Francis's death that Francis wanted none of the brothers to volunteer to see or to help Clare and her community in any way. He intended that only unwilling and reluctant brothers, albeit ones who were spiritual and had long been in religious life, should be appointed to look after them. It was always important to him that the brothers not take up the administrative relationship that Cardinal Hugolino was eager to create. Francis himself did avoid seeing Clare in the months after he wrote the rule with Caesar of Speyer, yet it is more likely that Thomas was expressing what the brothers in 1247 wanted their relationship with women's communities to be and not what Francis intended in 1220. The primary argument for this is that Philip the Tall continued to serve at Saint Damian.

the breezes grew warmer and the brown earth sprouted with green shoots, Peter Cattani died, apparently without warning. The brothers had been preoccupied by Francis's health and now they were faced with an organizational crisis. It was suddenly clear that in drafting his rule with Caesar of Speyer, Francis had failed to address the mundane but essential matter of orderly succession in the event of the death or incapacity of the leader. When he received the news, Francis might well have already been on the road to Rome, where he was to meet with Cardinal Hugolino in preparation for seeing the pope. Wherever Francis was, Elias assumed charge of matters at Portiuncula.

Holy Week in mid-April found Francis at Greccio, a hill town close to Rieti about sixty miles south of Assisi. The brothers slept in cramped narrow caves overlooking the Velino River, but to celebrate the resurrection of the Lord, they prepared their common table with white linen and proper glassware. Their Easter meal, which they shared with needy visitors, was interrupted by a poor wanderer who stood at the door of their shelter wearing a battered hat and carrying a staff. He called out to them, begging for alms for the love of God. The brothers invited him to share their meal. After they gave him a plate of food, to their surprise he moved away from them, sat down alone, and placed his dish in the embers of the cooking fire. "Now I am sitting as a Lesser Brother should sit," he said.

This censorious visitor, who had borrowed the hat and staff of one of their guests, was Francis himself, who seldom joined them at mealtimes. They knew who he was when he told them that the decorated and carefully set table was not proper for poor men who begged from door to door. Their celebration of Easter fell to such ruin that at least some of the Lesser Brothers in Greccio saw Francis of Assisi not as a spiritual leader, but as a scold.

He was not totally without mercy in these days. When he was on the road, a sympathetic brother found a rabbit caught in a trap, released it and carried it to Francis. Francis asked the shaking creature, "Why did you allow yourself to be deceived like this?" When the brother placed it on the ground, rather than scampering away, it ran to Francis, who patted it softly as it lay quietly on his chest. When the rabbit seemed calm, Francis gathered it his hands and set it down, but the animal hopped up on him again, not once but several times. Finally, Francis told the brothers to carry it back to the woods. He wanted it to be free.

11

A Question of Rules

WINTER WEATHER persisted, pummeling Rome's stone structures with lashing rains and chilling winds. No matter how many logs might have fed them, fires cast inadequate warmth. Despite multiple layers of tunics and mantles, damp seeped into every change of robes. Francis arrived in this dreary Rome in spring 1221 to obtain papal approval for the rule he and Caesar of Speyer had crafted. With him was Angelo Tancredi, one of his earliest companions, a man of Assisi who had been imprisoned with him in Perugia and whom Francis described as "endowed with every courtesy and kindness." He had been in that early band that sought approval from Innocent III a decade earlier. At that time, they found shelter in a hospice for poor pilgrims in the Eternal City. Now they were honored guests in the palace of Cardinal Hugolino with its opulent hangings, soft carpets, and sweet smells of wood smoke, candle wax, and rushes. The two Lesser Brothers were offered every luxury, whether or not they accepted it, including hot water with rose leaves and bowls of bay leaves boiled in water to wash away the grime of poverty. At this time Hugolino was second in authority only to the pope. The previous November he had played a large and visible role at the coronation of Frederick Hohenstaufen, whom the Fourth Lateran Council had confirmed as Holy Roman Emperor. In exchange, the church expected Frederick to lead a crusade to finally and decisively recapture Jerusalem from the Infidel.

Hugolino gave lavish dinners for cardinals and knights while Francis stayed with him. The cardinal had just taken on the assignment of preaching the crusade to central and northern Italy, which made Francis, who had been at Damietta, an even more interesting guest. He had met with and been in the very camp of the Sultan al-Malik al-Kamil, the devil incarnate, whom they intended to drive from Jerusalem, but it is doubtful that Hugolino's friends wanted to hear what Francis had to say about the enemy's courtesy and refinement. At the cardinal's table Francis might also have heard talk that the Emperor Frederick II, rather than make good on his promise to lead a crusade, had been crisscrossing the Italian peninsula from Capua to Apulia. He was now in Sicily consolidating his power. He showed no sign of preparing to fight the Saracen.

The sumptuousness of Hugolino's dwelling and its atmosphere of bellicose power made Francis most uncomfortable. He had told his followers to eat what was presented to them, whether it was slop from an adversary or roast chicken from a wealthy friend. However, now that he was living in comfort, he took an action he might not have taken if he had been in better health or in a better frame of mind. After begging for alms on the teeming streets of Rome he returned one evening to distribute scraps of gnarly black bread to guests at Hugolino's well-appointed table. The recipients took them in good grace but after the dinner a chastened Hugolino called Francis to an inner room to ask how he could have chosen to embarrass him so. Francis insisted he had honored the cardinal by honoring a greater Lord who had chosen poverty when he might have been rich. Hugolino was said to have accepted this explanation kindly.

During this visit to Rome, he and Angelo would have spent time with Jacqueline de Settesoli, a daughter by marriage to the ferocious Frangipani family. At this point the clan's allegiance to the emperor was less problematic because they had reconciled with the church. They might well have been present at Saint Peter's Basilica when Pope Honorius III crowned him. Jacqueline was able to provide Francis with the best medical care in Rome, plus peace, quiet, and proper food, including delicious little cakes made of almonds and honey that later generations would call Frangipani bread. When Francis was happy, he allowed himself to follow the rule he had laid down for other brothers—he would eat what was set before him. Moreover, since he was sick, he was excused from his normal penitential diet. Thus he allowed himself such restorative treats.

Perhaps it was at this time that Jacqueline had a portrait made of him from life, standing indoors against a dark background, barefoot but wearing his hood. The folds of his tunic, which outline his leg and hip, are caught by a knotted cord. His pointed beard is well-trimmed. His nose is long and straight. His eyes seem lost in thought and he dabs a cloth to them, which is more likely to be a sign of his ailments rather than tears. The original painting, which could have provided much information on many subjects to modern scholars, was lost. What we know of it is from a much-retouched fourteenth century copy, with marks of the stigmata, that survives at Greccio.

Discussions over the rule that Francis had written, which was the purpose for his visit to the Eternal City, went less smoothly than reunions with friends. Hugolino, a trained lawyer who was well versed in the rules of Benedict and Augustine, could not approve of Francis's pastoral tone and his allowing the brothers to have so much discretion over their own behavior. He suggested that Francis specify the hours when certain prayers should be said. Hugolino could not have failed to point out that Francis's document had made no provision for the sudden death of the minister general, an event that had just occurred. Hugolino told Francis that the rule had to be rewritten in language more in keeping with canon law. As their discussions continued, Francis could have stressed that many brothers did manual work in exchange for alms and might be working in the fields at the times when Hugolino would have them at prayer, that he wanted those who wished to live in strictest poverty to be able to do so, and that the mission of the Lesser Brothers, as approved by the late Pope Innocent III, was to do penance and to preach.

The cardinal might well have brought up the Ladies of the Poor of the Valley of Spoleto and Tuscany and asked Francis to incorporate their care into his rule. "My brother, let me entrust these ladies to you," Hugolino urged. Francis wanted no such arrangement. The Lord had called the Lesser Brothers to serve all mankind and not one particular group, be they women or even lepers. To particularize his mission would be to compromise it. Even as Francis managed to protect Clare from the full force of Hugolino's authority, he watched as other communities of women came under the cardinal's sway. In September 1222, Pope Honorius told the women at Siena, Gattaiola, and Saint Mary of Monte Lucio that although the church was insisting that they accept property, they could observe the rule of Saint Damian as well as that of Saint Benedict. Francis recognized that the cardinal was assuming control of those he called the Lesser Sisters. "That's right, father," Francis said, "in future they shall not be called Lesser Sisters, but Ladies, as you now recommend to me."

As his time with Francis continued, Hugolino, as protector of the Lesser Brothers, sought to formally acquaint the other cardinals with this unique individual, to win important friends for him, and possibly make the Lesser Brothers more welcome in the cardinals' territories. But he knew that Francis had to show himself to be worthy of their help. Hugolino was sufficiently concerned with the impression that the ragtag man of God would make that he composed a sermon for Francis in Latin, the language of the princes of the church. Francis spent miserable hours struggling to memorize it, yet when he stood before the cardinals, all of them seated before him in hooded robes of jeweled colors, the words vanished from his head like birds taking flight. Only empty branches remained where there had once been chatter. He could not recall so much as the main idea of what he was supposed to say. He stared at the cardinals, who returned his gaze, some sympathetically and others with amusement. When Francis preached in the streets, carefully prepared words sometimes deserted him and he had to confess that he had forgotten what he planned to say. Ordinary people loved him all the more for this. Now at the Lateran Palace, Francis simply told the cardinals that he was at a loss. He opened his psalter at random and found Psalm 43. His eyes fell on verse 16 "All the day long my shame is before me: and shame has covered my face." Abandoning the pretense of speaking Latin, in his native tongue he told them that the clergy, whether deacons like himself, priests, or cardinals, were the face of the church, and that they must keep that countenance beautiful and clear, for a blemish on what was beautiful was more obvious than a mark on a surface that was marred. He said that when that face showed distain, arrogance, greed, or sinful desires it disfigured the church, and veiled its light from the people. He was caught up not in the majesty of the place where he spoke but with the glory of God who spoke through him. Francis's simplicity, his clear statement of what they knew to be true, and his gentle call for them to evaluate themselves, touched the hearts of those who were willing to hear him. As he spoke, Francis's feet began to move as if he were dancing. As Thomas of Celano noted: "...he spoke the truth boldly, so that even the most learned men, men enjoying renown and dignity, wondered at his words and were struck with wholesome fear in his presence." The message of Francis was irrefutable, and those who felt he had insulted them dared not acknowledge that fact.

Icy gales continued to buffet the city as his meetings with Hugolino concluded, forestalling a return journey north to incorporate as many of the cardinal's suggestions as he could. Francis accepted the invitation of the highly respected Cardinal Leo Brancaleone to remain in Rome and refresh his spirit as his guest. Leo Brancaleone had been a cardinal for twenty years, a man so able that in 1204 Pope Innocent III had sent him on important diplomatic missions to Hungary and Bulgaria. Now one of his tasks was to serve as protector to mendicants who were known as Poor Catholics, who had been Waldensians led by Durand of Huesca until Dominic Guzman converted them around 1208. The approved mission of The Poor Catholics was to bring heretics, including Albigensians, back to the fold of Saint Peter.

Leo had an affinity for those who served the poor and he himself provided food to a certain number of the needy every day at his mansion close to the Lateran Palace. He promised Francis that he would be treated as one of these poor rather than as an honored guest and that he could reside in a secluded wing where he could pray undisturbed. Angelo told Francis of a tower he had seen on the property that comprised part of the city wall. It had nine unused rooms where they might sequester themselves as if they were staying in a hermitage. Francis could devote himself to prayer there night and day while Angelo could leave food outside Francis's door without bothering him. After inspecting the arrangements for himself, Francis accepted Leo's offer.

But once he found himself free of human distractions, Francis was battered by supernatural ones. The first night he called out to Angelo from some distance away, "Devils have beaten me. I am afraid to stay alone." Both men remained alert and awake while Francis shivered as if in a fever. He wondered aloud how the Lord could have allowed devils to hurt him. He reasoned that the devils were God's policemen. Just as a mayor sends out the police to find and correct those who flout a city's laws, so the Lord had allowed the devils to pummel him. But for what reason? To give Francis a lesson? He had confessed all his sins, done penance, and been forgiven.

He reviewed his acceptance of the cardinal's generous offer, which he had accepted without guilt because his weakened body needed rest and healing. He thought of his brothers living in huts, dining on scraps, and being beaten on the roads of the world. What might they think when they heard that he, Francis, had been staying in a luxurious palace? Surely that would make the deprivations they had chosen harder to bear. They would resent his hypocrisy. Before dawn he decided that the devils had beaten an important message into him: he should not have taken refuge in the cardinal's glorious dwelling. He and Angelo left the tower and bade the cardinal farewell. Pursued by devils, led by angels, Francis departed Rome for the last time and headed north to Rieti and the hermitage of Fonte Colombo, nestled deep in the woods of oak and holly.

The two men had not been very long on the road when it began to rain. Because of his infirmities, Francis travelled on horseback, led by the faithful Angelo. In earlier years he had cautioned his brothers to remember that sleep, food, and shelter were necessary even for those who chose a life of poverty. Brother Body might be able to bear any discomfort, but it had to be cared for in time of illness, he said. But now as he travelled from Rome, he showed himself no mercy. At the hours when he as a deacon was required to say specific prayers, he slid his frail and ailing body from the back of the horse and he stood in the mud while praying in the downpour.

By Pentecost 1221 at the end of May, Francis reached Portiuncula, where Peter Cattani had been laid to rest. Francis's early biographers often record his lamentations over the suffering of the crucified Christ, but say nothing about his grief over the deaths of loved ones, except for those martyred in Morocco. Still, he must have felt intensely the loss of Peter on whom he had so relied. Along with Francis, the brothers were arriving for the special general meeting that was to formally present a successor to Peter Cattani.[†] None doubted that would be Elias, who was not only adept at dealing with worldly affairs but who also had a personal magnetism that enabled him to know what others wanted to hear. Francis once said that the perfect brother would have the qualities of several of his followers. Among these were Bernard for his perfect faith and love of poverty,

---

[†] Francis called both Peter and Elias minister general, but church officials and the brothers referred to them as vicars general, vicar meaning "one who stands in the place of." The church would continue to treat Francis as the leader of the Lesser Brothers for as long as he lived.

Rufino for his virtuous constant prayer, Angelo for his courtesy and kindness, and a young priest named Leo for his simplicity and purity. Little is known of Leo's origins, but his character and abilities were such that he would become essential to Francis. None of these ideal brothers emerged as a leader, however. Bernard, who had had a successful legal career, probably had the innate ability but he had firmly rejected the world after the temptation of the adulation he received during his early stay in Bologna. For a time until 1219, he was the provincial minister of Spain, but after that he returned to being a simple brother.

Francis knew that a strong hand was needed, a man who might be less likely to preach poverty to the cardinals than he was able to parry their demands. That man was Elias, who was born in the environs of Assisi around the same time as Francis, but was probably socially inferior to the merchant's son. After he joined Francis, he did not lose his ability to successfully deal with the world and the worldly. One imagines that when begging, rather than touch the hearts of those from whom he was seeking alms, he appealed to how giving alms could benefit them. When he was among the brothers, he was one of them, praying their prayers and doing penance. When he was with the prosperous, he connected with them as one who respected their achievements and knew how to rise in the world. Given his ability to assume various roles and responsibilities before all manner of people, Francis had entrusted him to lead the small mission of brothers that went to the Levant in 1216. Elias established relationships with the important nobles and churchmen who gathered there and he prepared the way for Francis's arrival, despite being out of contact with Francis for several years. A copy of a portrait made during Elias's lifetime shows him to be short and lean with dark hair and a trim beard. Although not yet elected, he surely assumed charge of Portiuncula after Peter's death and he was making arrangements for the gathering when Francis returned from Rome.

The general chapter meetings were normally intended to be joyous celebrations of fraternal love and renewal, but this one was charged with death, that of Peter first of all, the solemn event that had brought them together, but secondly still with the deaths of the brothers in Morocco that had both horrified all who heard the news and somehow roused them.

Brother Jordan of Giano said that three thousand brothers and novices gathered, sleeping in huts constructed of tree limbs and branches on the fields around Portiuncula. Over the course of the week-long gathering the brothers took their meals from twenty-three tables set and spaced around the field. People of the area provided them with bread, wine, and other nourishment and were so generous that the group lingered an extra two days to consume all that had been provided. This was a stark contrast to the meeting nine months earlier when an ill-prepared Francis turned Clare to provide them with bread. It also indicates that the capable Elias had solicited the people's support. Some members of other orders attended, including the Cistercians and Dominic's Order of Preachers. The ranking prelate was Cardinal Ranieri Capocci, whom the pope had named rector of the region, and who may have been a member of the Cistercian order. After a bishop, possibly Guido of Assisi, said the first Mass, Francis preached on the theme from Psalm 143, a prayer for deliverance from enemies and an acknowledgement of the frailty of man. He called on his brothers to be patient and to live as guides to others. He also gave a sermon to the lay people who stood on the periphery, many of them bringing food. Clare and others from Saint Damian may have been among them so that they might see their brothers returning from distant cities and to hear again the words of their beloved Francis.

As expected, Elias officially became the new vicar general and presided over the meeting. Francis, still physically weak, sat himself at Elias's feet in a show of submission, but when he wished to add a point, he pulled at Elias's tunic. Elias would then bend down, listen to Francis's guidance, and stand up to convey it to the crowd. At the close of the chapter, Elias reacted to a final tug and rose up to announce that Francis, whom he called "The Brother," wanted them again to preach in German lands, where their earlier visits had gone badly. Francis described the Germans as pious people. He reminded the brothers that they had seen them carrying large staffs and wearing heavy boots, sweating heavily as they trudged the roadways on pilgrimages to the shrines of the Italian peninsula. He said that because the brothers who had gone before had been badly treated, he would not order any of them to take on this mission, but those who were willing to go should gather together in a group. Nearly one hundred assembled, saying that they were ready to travel to German cities and preach to their fierce inhabitants.

One who had no intention of doing this was Jordan of Giano, a man a decade or so younger than Francis who had joined the Lesser Brothers two years earlier, just before Francis left for the Holy Land. Jordan's story offers insight into the interactions of the brothers and the human frailties they tried to manage. By his own admission, Jordan feared martyrdom, something that the bellicose Germans seemed likely to inflict. He also feared for his faith because he worried that if he preached to heretics, they might answer him with ideas that would lure him from the one true religion. Jordan viewed those who would volunteer as dead men. Throughout the days of the chapter meeting, he had seen the brothers gather around those who had known the martyrs of Morocco. He tried to hear what the five had been like in life and to learn how they had come to be so brave. Some accounts, which included praise for Francis, were written down and brought to Francis for approval, but he was appalled. He said they were too celebratory and that he himself deserved nothing but criticism. He forbad the stories to be read to the brothers, saying. "Let each glory in his own suffering and not in that of another."

Nonetheless, Jordan decided that in years to come he would like to be able to tell similar tales of the men who were bound for Germany and certain death. He approached one of them, a cheerful deacon from Monte Gargano in Apulia. This friendly man gave his name as Palmerius and enthusiastically told Jordan that he must come along with them to adventures on the other side of the Alps. When Jordan begged off, saying that he had only intended to introduce himself, Palmerius convinced him to sit down, at least for a moment, and meet the other volunteers. They all insisted that Jordan join them and they would not hear otherwise. Caesar of Speyer was appointed to head the mission to his homeland, but when he was asked to intervene he was unsure that he should force the trip on Jordan. He referred the matter to Elias. Elias told Jordan that he must simply make a decision. Even so, Jordan continued to hesitate. He weighed his own safety against the call of Palmerius and continued to be unable to figure out what might be the will of God. Finally, Jordan approached a brother who had been stripped naked by rambunctious natives in Hungary. This survivor of abuse advised Jordan to ask Elias to tell him to do one thing or the other. Elias, possibly out of patience, promptly ordered Jordan to go to Germany where, as it turned out, he spent many happy, productive years.

Francis's main task was now to rewrite his rule in a form that the church would approve. Although Hugolino told him it would be a relatively simple matter, he struggled with it from 1221 to 1223. As early as the summer of 1221, Francis withdrew to the heavily forested Rainerio Mountain seventy miles south of Portiuncula, close to Rieti. According to tradition, his favorite spot among the dense oak trees was a sunlit waterfall that cascaded from an overhead cliff. He called it Fonte Columbo, or Fountain of the Doves, and he took refuge near it in the deep recesses of a jagged rock. There he sought God's guidance, and he took care to be able to convey it to his fellow man.

He took as his companions Bonizo of Bologna, a former canon lawyer who could phrase the rule in a way that the curia would accept, and Leo, the young priest who served as Francis's confessor and secretary. Leo was able to say Mass and take down the words that Francis dictated to him, including letters to clerics and to leaders of the growing number of communities of Lesser Brothers throughout Europe. Leo wrote down in Latin what Francis dictated in his native tongue, a necessary linguistic skill for scribes in the Middle Ages. He was probably from Assisi, but nothing is known of his appearance and little of his background. Francis called him "Little Brother Sheep of God" because of his simplicity and gentleness, but he had the eye of an eagle and the heart of a lion.

After Francis's return from the Holy Land, when his health curtailed his travels and his name was better known, he preached through letters he dictated, including one he wrote to all the rulers of Christendom, whether they presided over a city or a wide territory. He gave them the familiar admonitions to remember the approach of death and the power of the Eucharist, but he also introduced a new thought, one derived from his days in Egypt and Syria. He urged them to summon their people each night to give praise and thanksgiving to God. Muslims did this in the *adhans*, or calls to prayer that he had heard in their lands, although he did not mention their influence.

Leo's work on these letters is invisible, but the man himself materializes like a beam of sunlight in the early writings about Francis. He is present at the key moments of Francis's life, proving to be Clare's staunch friend, and fearlessly upholding his will in the face of changes after his death. As a new priest saying his first Masses, he would pause to meditate on the grace and consolations that came to his mind. Francis urged him to abandon this practice and to act as other priests did at the altar lest the Devil tempt him through pride. Francis said he was concerned that the minds of those hearing a drawn-out Mass might wander into judgment of him and decide that he was showing off or abusing their time. After the Mass, he suggested, Leo could go to his cell for private devotions and reflection.

Francis, Leo, Bonizo, and possibly an unknown fourth companion, would have lived by the instruction that Francis wrote for hermitages around this time. He said each community should consist of not more than four brothers and be like the sisters Mary and Martha in the Gospel of Luke. Mary listened as Jesus spoke while Martha served him food. Some brothers were to be Marys, living apart from the others in separate cells and keeping silent. They were to arise at sunrise and spend the day in prayer, except midmorning when they could ask for food, which they could not take to their cells. Marthas were to keep outsiders away, except for the brother who was in charge of the nearest community of Lesser Brothers. In keeping with Francis's ideal that they were all were to be flexible and non-hierarchical, the Marthas and Marys were to exchange roles according to what was best for the moment.

Each day Francis, who took the role of a Mary, retired to his cave to call on the Lord to tell him how the brothers were to live. He was mindful of the guidance that he, Peter Cattani, and Bernard of Quintavalle had received at the Church of Saint Nicholas in the dead of night, as well as his movement's transformative and somewhat confounding growth. He was also aware of the desires and surely well-meant intentions of Cardinal Hugolino. How was he to balance what God demanded of him and his followers against the insistent directions of the Roman Curia? Christ would help him find the way. When Francis felt that he understood what the Lord wished to be done on a certain point, he would emerge to reveal the Lord's dictation. Bonizo then did his best to phrase this in alignment with Saint Benedict's rule. Leo then set these sentences down on scrolls of thick, glossy grey paper, called "cloth parchment" because it was made of linen rags that were processed, pressed, and polished with a stone. Later the formal document would be copied on vellum, parchment made of animal skins.

Francis intended to permanently undo most of the changes wrought while he was in the Levant, but many of the newer brothers had welcomed improved food and ownership of their precious books. It was clear to them that the church had rejected the rule that Francis had produced with Caesar of Speyer and that he was revising it, so they were emboldened to express their concerns to their provincial ministers. These then went to Elias to ask him to intervene before Francis codified practices that would make their lives unbearable. By now, Elias had felt the stings of the founder's rebukes, which might have involved his displeasure over the preparations for the chapter meeting and Elias's own ideas about how the rule could be modified. Elias told the dissidents that he would not go to Francis, saying that the brothers could seek Francis out on their own. However, they eventually persuaded Elias that he had to lead. He guided the group to the spot near the waterfall where he knew Francis would be. Rather than call out to Francis, he exclaimed, "Praise the Lord!" On emerging from his cave and discovering a delegation, Francis reminded Elias that he had asked for solitude. "What do these brothers want?"

Elias explained that they were ministers who wanted the rule to be one they could live by. They felt that the Lord had bestowed on Francis a uniquely strong spirit for deprivation that they lacked. Furthermore, they had declared they would refuse to follow a harsh rule. According to an account that was certainly a later embellishment, Francis raised his eyes to heaven and said, "Didn't I tell you that they wouldn't believe you?" With that, the voice of Christ boomed out that he had made the rule, not Francis. The Lord said he wanted it to be followed without gloss and that those who did not like it could leave the order. Surely this was what Francis heard thundering in his ear, and he conveyed the directive to the rebellious brothers, who quickly departed.

When Francis, Bonizo, and Leo returned to Portiuncula, Leo entrusted Elias with the new rule, but later when Francis called for it, Elias reported that he had mislaid it. Francis's great effort and the will of the Lord had seemingly come to naught, but Francis did not hold the minister responsible. He believed that the loss of the scrolls was not Elias's doing but was the work of the devil, who was trying to thwart the Lesser Brothers. Determined that Satan would not prevail, Francis returned to Fonte Colombo with Leo to recreate the rule to the best of his recollection with the guidance of the Lord.

In addition to his struggles with the rule, Francis had to grapple with two disturbing developments. On August 6, 1221, three months after Elias became minister general, Dominic Guzman died in Bologna. Dominic too had lost heart in the face of the curia's demands about how he was to run his order. He attempted to resign in 1220 at a chapter meeting. "I am slack and useless," he said, "so put me out of office," but the Order of Preachers insisted that he continue. Cardinal Hugolino said his funeral Mass.

A few weeks later, on August 30, 1221, two years and a day after Francis warned against a coming battle, the Muslims decisively defeated the Christians at Damietta. Their Fifth Crusade had collapsed in complete and irreversible failure. Under the terms of defeat, the Crusaders had to evacuate the city and all places they had conquered in Egypt. The Saracen would return the part of the True Cross they had captured. While these agreements were underway, hostages were exchanged to guarantee compliance. Al-Kamil sent his son and nephew to the Crusaders and King John moved into the sultan's tent. When al-Kamil learned that the vanquished Christian soldiers were starving, he sent them food and gave them safe conduct for the passage home. His mercy stunned the Europeans. An appendix to the narrative of Oliver of Paderborn, a participant and chronicler of the Fifth Crusade, had this observation: "Those whose parents, sons and daughters, brothers and sisters we killed with various tortures, whose property we scattered or whom we cast naked from their dwellings, refreshed us with their own food as we were dying of hunger, although we were in their dominion and power. And so, with great sorrow and mourning we left the port of Damietta, and according to our different nations, we separated to our everlasting disgrace."

In this time of spiritual turmoil, many continued to esteem Francis as a wise leader. One indication was a letter one minister wrote to Francis. He was concerned for his own soul because he was finding it difficult to love God, especially in the face of challenges posed by a certain brother in his care who kept falling into the same sin. Francis wrote that whoever vexed him, even if he did him physical violence, was a heaven-sent opportunity for the minister to strengthen his soul. He must love that person and even if he sinned a thousand times, he should love him and forgive him if that is what the sinner wanted. He promised that the rule he would present at the chapter meeting at Pentecost would speak more on mortal sin. At that meeting Francis, who at that point was enjoying recovered health, found much that vexed him and much that he had to forgive.

When Francis returned to Portiuncula for the General Chapter of 1222, he found to his horror a new, commodious, if hastily constructed, house of stone that seemed to be as comfortable as any he might find in the region. Elias, a fine manager who remembered Peter's struggles when they ran out of food the year before, may have suggested that the commune build a dormitory so that townspeople would not be disturbed by visiting brothers wandering the roads and streets seeking food and shelter. Whether he initiated it or not, Elias had allowed the useful structure to be erected in a beloved place where Francis wanted to see only the straw-covered huts and protective wall of branches that the brothers had constructed when they took up residence eight years earlier.

Francis's health had improved to the extent that in his outrage he clambered to its roof with the help of a few others and they began to rip off tiles and slates and throw them to the ground. The brothers below who were dodging the debris cried out that Francis must come down before he fell, and they warned him to take care for the sake of others, but Francis was louder than they. He demanded that they all help him to dismantle this affront to their vows and to Lady Poverty. A knight from Assisi intervened by telling Francis that the house belonged to the commune, which had built it. Francis allowed himself to appear mollified and was helped down from the damaged roof.

The structure remained at Portiuncula for the rest of Francis's life and beyond. Possibly it stood until the middle of the sixteenth century when Pope Pius V encased the once-lowly Portiuncula in a vast basilica that accommodated the crowds of pilgrims that flocked to it. In 1832, an earthquake damaged the grand edifice while sparing the simple stone structures that had sheltered Francis in his lifetime. A little over a century later, in the late 1960s, the foundation of the commune's building emerged like a haunting during excavations on the deteriorating basilica.

Cardinal Hugolino arrived on horseback for the meeting with a large retinue of knights and clerics and was greeted with a joyous welcome. He dismounted and walked with the brothers to the tiny chapel. When he was with the brothers he often dressed as they did, going barefoot in a rough belted tunic. As he moved among them, he noted not the new building but the miserable beds, which seemed more fit for animals than humans. Most brothers slept on beds of spiky twigs. It was written of this meeting, "He who had a few half-torn rags over some straw considered that he had a wedding bed." He seemed to think the nests of twigs and stones reflected not so much the brothers' sacrifices as the state of his own soul. "See, here the brothers sleep," he told his entourage with tears so bitter that his friends too began to weep. "What shall become of us, miserable as we are?" he asked. "We make use of superfluous things."

In Francis Hugolino could sometimes see the living authority of the words of Christ, the words that left Hugolino's mouth by rote when he said mass or read his breviary. His mind was too preoccupied to ponder the command to turn the other cheek, to do good to those who hurt him, or to allow the little children to come to him. Francis lived the words and showed their wondrous, terrifying, upending power, and the horrible cost of their truth. But in thinking of how he could be of use to the church, Hugolino regarded Francis as if he were an uncut sapphire: the finest of gems, something precious that needed a master jeweler to facet and polish it to reveal the glory of a sky-colored heaven. Left as he was found, Francis was rough, misplaced, and a great deal of trouble.

A major task of the meeting was to discuss what was expected to be the final form of the rule for the Lesser Brothers. Visually they were united in their frayed tunics, but in fact the men were divided into several factions. Some of the scholarly among them expressed concerns to the cardinal about Francis's method in writing his rule. These men had studied scripture, canon law, and the rules and teachings not only of Benedict of Nursia but of Bernard of Clairvaux who had reenergized Benedict's rule after his followers grew lax. Furthermore, they were knowledgeable about the rule of Saint Augustine, which allowed communal property and was for an order that was primarily clerical. This was the one that Dominic's followers had adopted. The bookmen complained that they had offered to give Francis counsel for more than two years, but he had rejected them and the knowledge they could impart, particularly about following the rules of existing orders. Unwilling to be schooled, Francis had isolated himself and had insisted that all his followers follow the extreme practices to which he had subjected himself, extremes that had destroyed his health. These dissidents asked the cardinal to order Francis to hear and heed their words.

At the same time, other brothers went directly to Francis himself to report that some bishops had refused them permission to preach, which prevented them from doing good works for the people of God. They asked Francis to obtain a statement from the pope that would command bishops throughout Europe to allow the Lesser Brothers to speak and to hear the people's confessions wherever they wished.

Francis was stunned. He faulted them for their misunderstanding of what he had been telling them through the years. He said that they should win the bishops over by their humility and deference, not by papal command. Francis admonished, "When they see the holy life that you lead and the respect that you show them, the bishops themselves will ask you to preach and convert the people. This is better than the privileges you clamor for that will lead you into pride." Francis was not concerned about their right to hear confessions. He said that if they converted sinners, the penitents would find confessors on their own. Francis said that the only privilege he sought was from the Lord: to convert the world by living a holy life, not by talking about it. Much had changed since the fateful day when a brother fell to the ground and ate dung to punish himself for quarreling with another and thereby changed the life of the troubled young nobleman Rufino of Assisi, cousin of the Lady Clare. Rufino stood with those who wanted no change from the early days of poverty and simple prayer.

Cardinal Hugolino made his own preference clear. When he suggested that Francis meet with the learned brothers because they had much to teach him, Francis took the prelate by the hand and led him before the assembly. Hundreds stood rapt looking at the two men, one radiating the power of the papacy, the other a slight and ravaged man covered in a shabby habit cinched by a rope. But it was Francis's words that rang out: "My brothers, God called me to walk in humility and showed me the way of simplicity. I do not want to hear any mention of the rule of Saint Augustine, of Saint Bernard, or of Saint Benedict. The Lord has told me that he wanted to make a new fool of me in the world, and God does not want to lead us by any other knowledge than that."

He had a warning for them: God would use their learning to confound them. Francis knew that because he understood the Lord's resources. "He has policemen to punish you, and I put my trust in Him." The cardinal was stunned into silence, as were the brothers.

Some recognized that their lives would become more miserable because Francis was retaining his insistence on poverty and his distrust of books. Others were shocked because Francis had come close to calling down a curse.

That Francis remained the guiding force of the brothers is demonstrated by the fact that he wrote to the ministers and custodians of Lesser Brothers throughout the world and sent the letters forth in the care of the brothers who had gathered at the meeting. At the conclusion of the general meeting of 1222, he wrote to the minister and brothers in France where Gregory of Naples would succeed Pacifico as leader the following year. He entrusted this letter with Brother Martin, whose own brother was one of the civil guards who saved the house the commune erected from Francis's wrath.

Martin, who spent much of his life in England and could have been on his way there at the time, reported that Francis wrote while sitting in the rain, which seemed not to touch him. Martin spoke of marvelous events surrounding Francis. One of the brothers fell into a well but emerged unscathed after Francis said urgent prayers in the chapel. Francis had a presentiment that a widespread earthquake would topple the church in Brescia and he dispatched a warning to that effect in faulty Latin. The following Christmas a quake collapsed a church there on one of the brothers who was rescued unhurt from under a pile of fallen masonry.

Whenever he was able, Francis travelled through the Italian peninsula where people were eager to see and hear him. Those who had once thought him a fool for renouncing the prosperous life of a merchant now regarded him as saintly, not only because they knew his reputation but because they experienced his power for themselves. Bishops who had once tried to drive him from their precincts now welcomed him. Francis had won them over through the very behavior that he recommended to the brothers. In every city he entered, he introduced himself to the bishop with humility and respect. Although his fame was growing to the point that church bells rang and people greeted him waving olive branches, he approached the bishops with the deference of a supplicant.

The respect in which he was held was clear in Bologna on the Feast of the Assumption in mid-August 1222. All ranks and orders, whether they were nobles, scholars, merchants, or peasants, assembled in the public square to hear Francis speak on a topic that was announced as "Angels, Men, and Demons." In fact, however, he spoke of the duty to end hatred and bring about peace. He spoke concisely about sin and good, punishment and glory, and above all, he sought to help his listeners.

A young cleric named Thomas from the city of Split on the Dalmatian coast was there. In his writings, which would become the major source for the history of medieval Croatia, Thomas included an account of that day in Bologna. He reported that as untutored as Francis was, he spoke with such crystal clarity that he inspired profound admiration among the scholars of the university. Thomas did not quote Francis, but he was captured by Francis's effect. "He was wearing a ragged habit; his whole person seemed insignificant; he did not have an attractive face. But God conferred so much power on his words that they brought back peace in many a noble family torn apart until then by old, cruel, and furious hatreds even to the point of assassinations." Two students from noble families in Ancona, Pellegrino from the town of Falerone, and Riccerio from Muccia, told him they wanted to leave the world and join his movement. Others sought to touch him or, better yet, tear a piece from his clothing to keep as a talisman to protect them from harm.

As the months passed, Francis reflected on the ways that his movement of men was being compromised and he recognized that his intentions were followed in only one place—at Saint Damian. By custom, four Lesser Brothers, including a chaplain and two laymen, lived in nearby huts and could offer assistance when needed. Since all indications are that these men were faithful to Francis's original way of life, the quartet at one time or another included Giles,

Sylvester, Angelo, Bernard of Quintavalle, Rufino, and Philip the
Tall. He sometimes stayed with them, but he refused to visit Clare.
Whether it was to set an example of following the new rules, or a
sign of his dread of facing her after he allowed Hugolino's interference, Francis refused to preach to the women. Elias, unlike Peter
Cattani, was willing to use his authority. He ordered Francis to
bring them God's word.

Surely Francis's heart pounded and his steps were slow as he made
his way along the short path that he had once trod easily, assured of a
welcome and a friendly reception. He entered the door to the structure that he had renovated with his own hands and stood under the
beams that supported the loft that all those years ago he knew would
be filled with female followers. He heard the footfalls of the women
entering the chapel with Clare in their midst, all happy to see him.
He said nothing but called for ashes. Clare watched as he dipped his
hand into the pot and sprinkled the cinders in a circle around himself, then poured the remainder on top of his head. He stood silently
and then recited Psalm 50, the fourth penitential psalm, which was
the confession of David after he had sinned:

> Be merciful to me, O God, according to your great mercy.
> And, according to the plentitude of your compassion, wipe out
>   my iniquity.
> Wash me once again from my iniquity, and cleanse me from
>   my sin.
> For I know my iniquity, and my sin is ever before me. Against
>   you only have I sinned, and I have done evil before your eyes.
> And so, you are justified in your words, and you will prevail
>   when you give judgment.
> For behold, I was conceived in iniquities, and in sinfulness did
>   my mother conceive me.
> For behold, you have loved truth. The obscure and hidden
>   things of your wisdom, you have manifested to me…

He had nothing else to say. He departed Saint Damian, leaving only silence. Clare and her companions began to weep. Many shook with sobs. Francis had declared himself to be as powerless as he was ashamed and he was leaving them on their own.

———

Francis took Leo with him to Rome for final approval of the rewritten rule and possibly Bonizo as well, although that was not recorded. Certainly Francis first presented it to Hugolino for evaluation. The cardinal would later say that he had assisted in its preparation and in obtaining its confirmation, but after Francis's outburst at the general meeting, if the cardinal objected to the substance of what he found or if he puzzled over the suitability of Francis's occasional use of the first person (such as "*I* strictly forbid all the brothers to accept money in any form…" or "*I* advise and admonish….") versus the more magisterial "It is forbidden"), he deferred those matters to the pope. Perhaps even this keen jurist did not have the heart to argue further with a man whose patience was at an end. Possibly Hugolino had grown more tolerant, knowing that time would bring other opportunities to improve the ailing Francis's rule and to revisit the challenge posed by the women at Saint Damian.

Known as The Rule of 1223, the document was more temperate and streamlined than what Francis had produced two years earlier. Instead of twenty-three chapters, there were a dozen, and the biblical quotations were omitted. Its Latin was flawless, a sign of ecclesiastical editing. It referenced hierarchical duties and it was clear on how those entering the order were to be treated during their probation. It did away with the obligation to do manual work, but praised it, saying that some brothers did this as a grace. Brothers were never allowed to receive money, but they could make use of any other payment that was necessary for their needs and those of others. All were to beg with honor and confidence, and the illiterate were permitted to remain unlettered. A short section was devoted to preaching. Francis was against verbosity. He told his brothers that for the benefit of their hearers, their words should be brief because the Lord, when he was on earth, was succinct.

Although in his 1221 rule Francis had commanded brothers to be respectful toward the Saracens when preaching to them and had tacitly recognized their humanity, this rule said merely that those who wanted to convert them had to obtain permission from their provincial ministers. Roman Catholic prelates, who were preparing another attack on the Muslim-held Holy Land after their earlier rout, were not prepared to be generous in this matter. Brothers who committed mortal sin were not to be judged but were to be referred to ministers and priests. Whereas Francis's 1221 rule prohibited evil doings with women, this one forbad them to enter convents, which would have included those in Hugolino's order, without church approval. Fornication was not mentioned.

As for Francis's intention to protect the brothers who wanted to follow his will to the letter and live a life that was harsher than the order allowed, Pope Honorius said he was concerned that this rule required the ministers to permit the brothers to do as they thought best. The pope feared that this passage might allow them too much latitude. He told Francis that this provision opened the way to error and division because those who sought exceptions to the rule might not be grounded in virtue and truth.

Francis did not agree. He insisted that Christ had put those words in the rule and they could not be changed. Honorius explained that he only wished to amend the letter of the rule to preclude the possibility of brothers breaking it under the guise of following it. He modified Francis's tenth chapter to say that those who felt they could not observe the rule spiritually should seek an exemption from their ministers, who were obliged to serve them. The pontiff then gave his approval, offering a bit of doublespeak in his preface. Honorius wrote that he undertook to approve it because Francis and his brothers wanted him to confirm and sanction their rule, which had already been approved by Pope Innocent III. Francis would have preferred that prior approval be accepted without further elaboration, but the church wanted a rule that was detailed and inclusive of topics Innocent III had not reviewed, such as preaching to the Saracens, dealings with women, and the requirement that new brothers undergo a year of novitiate before taking their vows.

Pope Honorius III put his seal to the document on November 29, 1223 with his guarantee that it would stand for all time. Francis had bowed to the authority of the church by writing a formal rule that went far beyond the Gospel texts that were given to him at the Church of Saint Nicholas, had constricted the brothers' dealings with communities of women, and relaxed his rule that able brothers perform physical labor. Thus, he had bowed to the good intentions of the church, however unwelcome its demands had been.

With the rule approved, Francis headed north to Greccio. On the day he arrived, his friend, a noble named John, came to see him and gave him a pillow that Francis, because of on-going eye pain and insomnia, agreed to use. That night, when he stood in prayer in the tiny cell, his knees buckled. His head and body began to tremble and he was unable to walk. He thought of a time when he had eaten bread made with a grain that turned out to be poisonous, but then he discerned that the source of his maladies was Satan, who had taken up residence in that soft, tempting pillow. He called to one of the brothers and tossed it at him, telling him the devil was in it and had been attacking his head.

The brother picked it up, put it on his left shoulder, and pinned it with his right hand. Then he too felt the devil's force and horror so filled him that his arms and legs were frozen. Francis shouted until the man came to himself and was able to throw the pillow aside. He rushed to Francis who told him that it was a lesson in how the devil worked. "He cannot harm my soul because of the grace of God, so he attacks my body. He wants to snuff out the enthusiasm and joy that are truly in my heart so that I will give in and complain." Francis continued to be determined to live in joy, although joy was now like a ruby that he had to mine from rock.

When Francis accepted the beguiling pillow, he asked John to find a manger where they might represent, complete with an ox and an ass, the birth of the Savior. Francis felt his heart expand with good will in the season of peace, a time of celebration. He wanted to honor the birth of Christ in poverty and impart the wonder of this miracle into the hearts of those present. Nativity scenes with living figures of Mary, Joseph, and the Christ Child, as well as shepherds and Wise Men, had been part of a few Christmas celebrations for several centuries. A crèche stood near the main altar from which Pope Gregory VII was kidnapped in 1075 while he said Mass at Rome's Church of Saint Mary Major. There had been abuses of the sacred scene through the years. In 1207 Innocent III sent a letter to an archbishop of Poland telling him to curb the clerics' custom of including ghosts and other bizarre figures in celebrations of the Nativity of Christ. Creating a new religious practice was frowned upon in Francis's era. Saint Bonaventure would later take pains to explain that Francis's manger was not an innovation because the pope had given him permission for it on Nov. 29, 1223.†

For all that, in late December, with the frosty air tinged with the sharp tang of pine needles, Francis transformed Greccio into the new Bethlehem. Townspeople and the Lesser Brothers gathered by lantern and torchlight for the midnight High Mass on Christmas Eve. Francis set aside his tattered tunic to don the vestments of a deacon. He pulled on the alb, or long white vestment that Clare and her community stitched for Umbrian churches. Over this he placed a patterned woolen robe called the dalmanic. Then he draped the stole, the scarf of clerical authority, over his left shoulder. Finally,

---

† Francis is often falsely called the creator of the Nativity crèche. It is true that it became part of the celebration of Christmas because his Lesser Brothers carried it to the world. His commemoration was in the tradition of the liturgical play.

he pulled over his head a chasuble, a richly decorated gown that was like a poncho, and stood near the altar. A priest said the Mass, but Francis sang the words of the Gospel, the story of Caesar Augustus decreeing a census of the whole world and Mary and Joseph travelling to Bethlehem to register there. Because there was no room at any inn, she brought forth her son in a manger where shepherds and angels attended him.

Caught up in the scene, Francis pronounced the word Bethlehem like the baa-baa-ing of a sheep, drawing out his vowels and licking his lips as he savored the mention of Jesus's holy name. As he did so, one man had a vision of a child lying lifeless on the straw until Francis woke him. The townspeople went home filled with joy, most carrying away bits of hay from the manger that they later said worked miracles. It was recorded that when sick livestock ate it, they recovered, as did some humans, including women in the throes of difficult labor. In a contrast to the austerity that Francis had demanded of the Greccio brothers some eight months earlier at Easter, Francis said that if he could ask one thing of Emperor Frederick, it would be that everyone would have an abundance of food on Christmas Day.

But as 1224 unfolded and the new rule was disseminated, Francis continued to fret about it. In the nearly three years of life that remained to him he would continue to mull over its neglect of so much that was important while it specified more than was necessary. When he grew too ill to shave himself, he told the companions who cut his tonsure, the circular bald spot cut into the hair to mark a cleric, to keep it small like those of the lay brothers rather than creating a large one that marked the ordained. He wished that this practice could be inserted into the rule but because the pope had already approved it, it was too late.

12

A Song Ends

IN 1224, the forty-third year of his life, a frail Francis of Assisi travelled painfully through the mountainous terrain of Umbria and Tuscany, resting at various hermitages, accompanied always by at least one of the few men that he trusted most. The tight circle of early companions who were faithful to him included Angelo Tancredi who was known for modesty and good judgment, the robust John of Lauds and, most necessary of all, Leo. The humble, much-loved Juniper was also with them, partly to cook their meals, partly so that they could keep their eyes on him. His intentions were pure, his actions bizarre. He had walked into the city of Viterbo naked, except for his underpants which he wore on his head. Still, he was ever ready to work and disregard insults. He carried an awl so he could mend shoes and a stove because sometimes people would drive him out of their presence and into lonely places where he would have to cook for himself.

Now because of his declining health, Francis travelled by horse or donkey. He rode as far as he or the animal was able, or until he reached the home of a generous supporter who could lend him a fresh animal. One of the holy man's companions would then feed and water the beast that Francis had exhausted and return it to its owner. People along the way tried to reach Francis, or tear a swatch from his clothing, certain that he and whatever touched him had the power to heal. On one occasion men from a village near Arezzo were inconsolable when they discovered that the brother leading a borrowed animal back to its owner was not Francis. They regarded the holy man as the only hope for a woman who was in danger of death from an agonizing labor. The best the Lesser Brother could do was to give them the reins that Francis had held in his hands. The men hurried home and placed this gift on the suffering woman, who felt the calming, healing power of Francis flow through her so that she finally and safely gave birth.

People of the Middle Ages were considered old in their early forties, but while the average life span was about thirty-five years, those who survived childbirth, battle, and accidents lived into their eighties. Francis had no such expectations. He knew that his body was failing. He experienced fever, chills, and dropsy, a general swelling that was probably related to his damaged liver and spleen. Probably he suffered from some form of leprosy, such as tuberculoid. His eyes were a particular problem. Francis stumbled about even in rooms he knew well and bumped into doorways instead of passing through them. His vision of the world around him had grown cloudy and dim, but in memory he held one sight sharper than ever—that of a blind man led through Assisi by a little dog.

Francis observed that his closest companions had aged with the passage of years under the strain of poverty, but they still had more vigor than he. John of Lauds, who in his prime had been the strongest of men, could still lift Francis up on a donkey's back. The others could support him over rocky paths when he was unable to walk on his own. Francis, who had long recognized the need to give special consideration to ailing brothers, worried that caring for him taxed the strength of his companions, distracted them from prayer, and interfered with the daily life of their community. He told them that although he would not be able to repay them for their help, the Lord would find a way. As for himself, he who was devoted to the suffering of Christ experienced his own afflictions as a means to atone for his sins and to strengthen himself spiritually. He took consolation in what he had accomplished, observing near the close of his life: "Father, all those whom you have given me in the world were yours and you have given them to me. The words that you gave me, I have given to them; they have accepted them and known in truth that I have come from you and they have believed that you have sent me."

The occasional periods of improved health that Francis enjoyed were his signals to fast and do extreme penance, wearing nothing warmer than his tunic in bitter cold or flagellating himself when he had strength. He made sure that others see these mortifications and that he far surpassed what could reasonably be expected of a penitent, hoping that he would inspire the Lesser Brothers to follow his example and exceed the bare minimum practices that the new, church-approved, rule for the order required.

Predictably, his overt exertion caused relapses. Olive oil upset his stomach, so he ate vegetables cooked especially for him in pork fat. Francis occasionally showed his body extra mercy and indulged it in the simple ways that were left to give it joy. One night he asked for parsley. The cook, who was one of the brothers who now openly viewed Francis as a nuisance, declined to fulfill this humble request. He said that he had picked all the parsley from the garden earlier in the day and that he would not be able to find any more in the dark. Francis told him to bring whatever herbs he first laid his hands upon. The brothers who loved Francis examined this bunch and found sprigs of healthy, tender parsley that Francis ate with relish, savoring the sharp aroma and the freshness that filled his mouth. Satisfied, Francis then reminded his companions that his words had power and that they should obey him as soon as he spoke: "Do not say that something is impossible."

Francis openly confessed that he was eating special food. He told his companions that he wanted always to live as if he were being watched. "Since they consider me to be a saint," he told them, "I would be a hypocrite if I did not live the life of a saint." His stomach and spleen troubled him most in the extreme cold of winter, so

Francis agreed to the comfort of having a fox pelt on his lap. "My conscience is concerned about the care of my body because it is afraid I will take such good care of it while I am sick that I shall expect delicacies after I am well," he said, "not that my body can delight in anything after being worn down for so long by illness, or that I have any taste left to satisfy."

Once when Francis was walking through Assisi followed by a crowd, a poor woman asked him for alms. He promptly pulled the cloak from his shoulders and handed it to her. He then told his admirers, "Doing this makes me proud of myself." He was unwilling to accept more praise than he felt he deserved.

During these closing years of his life, he worried over the future of his life's work. It had been modified by the requirements of the Lateran Council, by his submission to the will of bishops and cardinals, and by changes that others had made when he was in the Holy Land. Francis had intended for all of it to be much more simple. He was concerned that what the church demanded of them now undermined God's will for his movement. Educated priests were taking control of the order away from lay brothers and the new men were more interested in study than in prayer. Francis's followers, so-called, were now living in comfortable houses rather than taking shelter in mud and branch huts, and the pope was ordering bishops throughout the Italian peninsula to give the Lesser Brothers preference over the local clergy.

Many men were drawn to Francis's movement because of its growing prestige. The Lesser Brothers numbered three or four thousand at this time. Newcomers saw the beauty of living a life with few creature comforts but they were unwilling to live a life of degradation. They could point to the effects of such a course on Francis, who stumbled among them on the arm of one of his favored companions, both of them wearing rags. In the experience of these men, Francis either isolated himself by praying alone in his cell or joined the larger community only to chide and scold.

Indeed, Francis did sometimes seem to be demented. Whenever he discovered any written religious material lying about, he would make sure it was put out of harm's way so that it would not be damaged or disrespected, even inadvertently, because it could contain the name of God. When he was in the Holy Land he had seen Muslims take similar care in reverence for Allah.

One day as Francis was reverently gathering stray ragged sheets, a brother pointed out that he was picking up papers in which there was no mention of God. How could there be, the brother asked, when they were written by a pagan author? Probably the pagan in question was Aristotle, whom the learned brothers were studying for his systematic approach to knowledge and his convincing means of argument. Francis replied that care must still be taken because some of the letters could be combined into the name of God. He added, in an insight that could have ended the controversy that raged for years in Paris as to whether or not Christians should read Aristotle, that whatever good there might be on the pages did not come from the pagans or from any other human beings, but from God. Francis was equally scrupulous about his own dictation. If he corrected himself, or if his transcriber made an error, Francis would not allow a letter to be scraped from the parchment because it was potentially a component of the name of God.

But just as there were those who considered Francis to be an irrelevant artifact of an earlier day, so there were other new brothers who admired and honored him and were unable to accept that he was against their possessing and reading their beloved books. This doubt gnawed at them as much as near-starvation had plagued his early alms-begging companions. One of them was Anthony who had originally been a member of the order of Saint Augustine and a canon at the cathedral of Coimbra a hundred miles north of Lisbon. At age twenty-five in 1220 he saw carried through the streets the bodies of the three Lesser Brothers martyred in Morocco. The young priest, born Fernando Martins de Bulhões, was so moved that he joined

Francis's movement so that he too could seek martyrdom, but his health soon declined and he was forced to remain in Europe. When brothers asked him to teach them theology, Anthony sought approval from Francis, which he granted in a letter: "I am pleased that you teach sacred theology to the brothers provided that, as is contained in the Rule, you do not extinguish the Spirit of prayer and devotion during study of this kind."[†]

Another novice, whose name is lost to history, received permission from his immediate superior to own a psalter, but he sought to have the approval of Francis as well. Francis did not respond directly. Instead, he recalled the glorious deeds of his personal, tragic, and fictional, heroes Roland and Oliver. "They became honored by fighting and dying for a cause," he said. "Others want to receive honor by merely telling the story of what they did." Francis regarded the action of humbling oneself for the glory of God and encouraging the salvation of man to be preferable to reading a book, even of Scripture. He said that sacrifice for the Lord transformed the spirit, whereas kneeling in prayer might do no more than please one's own mind.

Nonetheless, this novice continued to want that psalter as much as he wanted Francis's approval. When he found Francis warming himself by a fire, he sat down and brought up the matter again. Francis, knowing that a possession of any kind leads to a desire for more, told him that the next thing he would want was a breviary, and then a chair where he might sit so he could ask someone to bring his book to him. Francis grew so exasperated that in his frustration he picked up some ashes and rubbed them into his head.

Still, the man persisted. Months later they were both were at Portiuncula, Francis's most beloved spot on earth. The novice again

---

[†] Anthony became an outstanding preacher, a miracle worker, and one of the most renowned saints of the church. He is known as Anthony of Padua, for the city where he died in 1231 at the age of 36. He is the beloved patron of finding lost objects because Anthony is said to have successfully invoked God's help in regaining a treasured psalter that had been stolen from him.

queried Francis as he was heading toward the cell where he slept. Francis told him to do as his minister had told him and walked on alone. After a few minutes of reflection Francis turned and called out, "Wait for me, brother! Come back with me to the place where I told you to do as your minister said." When they reached that spot, Francis fell to his knees and begged for pardon. Francis said that he had made a mistake. He told him that whoever wished to be a Lesser Brother should have only as little as the rule allowed. From that point forward, his answer was the same to anyone who asked about books: "A person is only as learned as his actions show, and a religious is only as good a preacher as his actions show."

Sometimes outsiders understood Francis's wisdom better than his own men. When he was in Siena, a doctor of theology who was a follower of Dominic Guzman called on him. He asked Francis to tell him the best method to convert sinners and heretics, specifically in the light of the guidance of Ezekiel 3:18 in which the Lord says that he will hold his preacher accountable if he does not warn a wicked man of his wickedness. Francis tried to beg off, saying that he was uneducated and that someone else would be more qualified to explain it to him. However, this master replied that he had already heard many commentaries from the learned. What he wanted now was Francis's insights. Francis answered that in his understanding, the verse meant that the holiness that emanated from one truly devoted to God was not in his preaching but in the example of his righteous life. The humble theologian returned to his colleagues telling them that their learning crawled on the ground compared to the soaring eagle that was Francis's life and knowledge.

Francis sometimes tried to accommodate himself to the changes in his order rather than defy the situation that he had allowed to take place. Perhaps his moods depended upon the degree of pain that Brother Body inflicted. When he decided that his trials were a good thing, he reviewed each aggravation, whether it was his stumbling feet, his cloudy vision, a brother lying on a well-made mattress, or hammering on new small buildings being constructed at Portiuncula. All these were like rungs in a ladder that he could climb upward. As he stepped on each and overcame the temptation to anger or despair, he rose higher with a strengthened soul that brought him closer to God. Francis decided then that it was dangerous to lead others, especially at this time when wickedness had grown so greatly and increased so abundantly; and he insisted that it was better to be ruled. He would sometimes say, "Let us begin, brothers, to serve the Lord God, for up to now we have made little or no progress."

All his ideas for improvement involved the Lesser Brothers returning to their early days. He wanted to serve the lepers again and to retire to remote places where God might speak to him directly. As if knowing that he had to savor every bit of life, he expressed reverence for everything around him. He protected oil lamps and candles, not wishing to extinguish their brightness. When his cell caught fire, he carried to safety the fur pelt that had kept him warm and then felt guilty because he had thought only of his comfort and had deprived Brother Fire of a morsel to consume. He stepped respectfully on stones, forbad his brothers to cut down whole trees, and ordered that a place in the vegetable garden be devoted to growing flowers that had no purpose but to beautify. He rescued worms from the road lest they be crushed, and he had honey and wine set out for the bees so they could maintain their strength in the cold. He treasured water as well and he washed his hands carefully so that drops would not splash to the ground where they might be stepped upon.

When his body was weakest, his anger burst forth. Once he sprang up from his sickbed with the cry, "Who are these who have snatched my order and that of my brothers out of my hands? If I go to the general chapter meeting, I will show them what my will is!" He then disavowed changes that the church was making, including recent interventions that gave his movement special status as the pope's favored ones. Beginning in 1222, Pope Honorius III went beyond his earlier orders that bishops had to allow the Lesser Brothers to live and preach in their districts. He gave the brothers the new privilege of having their own churches where they could celebrate Mass over the objections of the local bishop, even in cities that had defied the pope and been excommunicated. In such places the sacraments were not supposed to be administered, but the pope in a letter of March 22, 1222, said that the Lesser Brothers—and not local priests—could celebrate the rites of the church there in low voices behind closed doors. In December 1224, he gave them the privilege of carrying portable altars, again so that they could say Mass without involving the assistance of the local bishop. In October 1225, the pope granted the Lesser Brothers who preached to Muslims in Morocco and Spain the right to absolve heretics and persons who had been excommunicated. With these actions he prioritized the brothers who were priests over those who were laymen and he established them as a cadre that could set aside disgraced clerics. In March 1226, the pope allowed them to carry money, which Francis strictly forbade before all else. Perhaps it was at this time and in response to the pope's interventions that Francis wrote what has been called his "Letter to the Entire Order" to stress what he expected of his followers. First, he called on them all, lay and ordained, to follow God's commands and to venerate the Eucharist. He implored the priests to celebrate the Mass with purity, reverence, devotion, and dignity, and to venerate holy written words and the altar as sacred things. When they gathered in community, he wanted one priest to say the Mass for all of them rather than have each of them say his own separate Mass because the Lord was one and undivided. He confessed that he himself had not always observed the rule, or said his prayers as prescribed, but he wanted them to observe the rule exactly and to say their offices with devotion and not with the intention of impressing others. Francis told them that as far as he was concerned, those who did not observe these practices were neither Catholics nor brothers. By April 1226, Francis knew that contrary to his wishes, Cardinal

Hugolino had made Brother Pacifico responsible for the care of the women in his order. It is uncertain, however, that this Pacifico is the former troubadour.

Another blow came when Francis learned that Clare, only thirty years of age, was confined to her bed. She had fasted away the reserves of her youth and most likely succumbed to a constellation of maladies brought on by malnutrition. Rickets caused skeletal defects like bowed legs, curved spine, pelvic deformities, fragile bones, and painful, weak muscles that would have made it difficult for her to stand. Scurvy, which was common across Europe in late winter when fresh food was hard to come by, manifested as bruising throughout the body, loss of hair, poor healing of wounds, bleeding gums, and loose teeth.

Whatever her symptoms, when Francis heard that she was at the point of death he insisted that he be taken to her without delay. Perhaps it was at this time, early spring 1225, when he was en route to Saint Damian, that a countryman in the fields saw Lesser Brothers travelling the road, one slumped forward riding a donkey, another leading him. He abandoned his plow and ran up to ask the ailing rider if he was Francis and Francis acknowledged that he was. The man urged him, "Try to be as good as all men say you are, for many put their trust in you. I beg you not to ever be anything other than what we expect you to be." Francis slid from the animal's back, dropped to the ground and kissed his feet.

At Saint Damian the women greeted him with joy, reverence, and tears. To some, his long-sought arrival may have confirmed that Clare really was passing from this life. Even those who remained in the cloister peering through a parted curtain over the iron-grilled window saw that Francis's own decline had been precipitous, as evidenced by his haggard face and blighted eyes that turned from the light. Here at last, however, he was surrounded by those who loved him, not only Clare's community but also brothers who were loyal to him.

What Francis and Clare said to each other is unrecorded. Because she was so ill, Clare was set apart from the others so that she could rest and receive care while the regular life of the community continued. Francis, finding her lying on a plank of wood, ordered that a sack of straw be found for her mattress. Her voice was weak, almost unearthly, but the vision he held was of the younger, fair, and vital woman whom he had persuaded to serve repugnant lepers and to preach to scoffers on the streets of Assisi. Now the lepers were banished and Clare was dying, deprived of the world that Francis had opened to her when she swore obedience to him after fleeing her family in the dead of night.

When he had last seen her about a year earlier, he had let a psalm of repentance speak for him. Whether he now tried to explain to her, or to himself, that he had tried to save the Lesser Brothers by abandoning his female followers, and whether or not he asked directly for her forgiveness, surely she forgave him and claimed there was nothing to forgive. Francis had managed to undo the worst of what the cardinal had dictated for her life. Philip had returned, the brothers could visit them, and they were not entirely shut off from the world.

His emotions may have overwhelmed what was left of his strength because soon his eyes failed and light became unbearable. He would remain for more than fifty days in a hut prepared for him a few yards outside Clare's window. Rather than die, Clare was restored to life, if not to total health. She saw that he too needed care and she sat up and called for scissors and thread, then snipped nineteen swatches from the hem and back of her own cape and neatly sewed them on the cowl and in other shabby spots of Francis's tunic.[†] Possibly it was she who stitched a special new hood that dropped well down over his sensitive eyes to block out painful light.

---

† Renowned textile conservator Mechtild Flury-Lemberg believes that Clare mended his tunic after his death because the seams were not worn. I attribute the lack of wear to his relative immobility and to the probability that the brothers set aside this special garment to add to the collection of mementos they would treasure after his death. At this point, Francis frequently exchanged tunics with others.

As he lay in gloom, animals, which were usually a joy to Francis, became his tormentors. Mice overran his tiny shelter of branches by night and day, squeaking and burrowing, swarming his table, depriving him of peace at the moment when his spirit had finally found solace among friends. He believed that his misery was punishment for his sins and he asked God for strength to endure them. Then one night he heard a voice tell him to be joyful and at peace as if he were already in heaven. Illumination dispelled his agony.

The next morning, he decided to compose a song of praise. He sat and thought until he came up with the first line, "Most High, all-powerful, Good Lord God" and the rest of it began to flow, filled with a rhythm of the long vowel sounds of the Umbrian dialect. Meditating on the sun that brought the splendor of the day, and the fire that pierced the darkness of night, he both celebrated the world and bade farewell to it. Now he could behold it only in memory. He began to dictate, probably to Leo, what became known as *The Canticle of the Sun* or *The Canticle of the Creatures*:

> Most High, all-powerful, Good Lord God, to Thee belong
>   praise, glory, honor and all blessing.
> Praised be my Lord God, with all His creatures, and especially
>   our brother the Sun, who brings us the day
> And who brings us the light: fair is he, and he shines with a
>   very great splendor. Oh Lord, he signifies us to Thee!
> Praised be my Lord for our sister the Moon, and for the stars,
>   which He has set clear and lovely in the heaven.
> Praised be my Lord for our brother the Wind, and for air and
>   clouds, calms and all weather, by which Thou uphold life
>   and all creatures.
> Praised be my Lord for our sister Water, who is very serviceable
>   to us, and humble and precious and clean.

Praised be my Lord for our brother Fire, through whom Thou
gives us Light in the darkness; and he is bright and pleasant and very mighty and strong.

Praised be my Lord for our mother the Earth, which doth
sustain us and keep us, and bring forth diverse fruits and
flowers of many colors, and grass.

(Translation based on that of Matthew Arnold)

In this great hymn, of which Francis was so proud, he celebrates
the Creator. His own life's work had been about abnegation and penance in the shadow of Christ's excruciating sacrifice. Now as Francis
was bidding earthly life farewell, he hailed what had given him joy
and never disappointed him: the sun, moon, stars, clouds, the fire
that had warmed him and lit his way, and the earth that had sustained him, all the creation of God the Father, and all above the
confines of doctrine, humanity, and dispute.

He had his companions sing his laudation with him over and over
again as he grew more enamored with it, and his friends more weary. As the days passed and he sang and enjoyed his own *Canticle of
the Sun*, the humble Francis developed the single-mindedness of a
proud author, albeit one at the service of God. He displayed the love
of performance that had made him the master of revels in his youth.
Francis announced that to make known *The Canticle of the Sun* he
would send Pacifico, who had been a great troubadour, into the world
with one of the finest preachers from among the Lesser Brothers.
Pacifico would sing it, then there would be a homily. At the end, the
two would invite everyone to join in Francis's song, after which the
preacher would conclude by saying: "We are the jongleurs of God,
and the only reward we want is to see you lead a truly penitent life."
Francis, who had once thrown away a cup that he had fashioned from

clay because he took too much pride in it, was now ablaze with vanity in the service of the Lord. In fact, his judgment was correct and his pride was justified, for *The Canticle of the Sun* is regarded as one of the earliest poems in Italian literature. Every day that remained to him on earth he sang or heard it as an antidote to his own suffering and he asked everyone around him to fill the air with it.[†]

As he lay outside Clare's window, the civil conflict that was always near the surface in Assisi flared again, this time in reaction to internal disputes in the neighboring city of Perugia. Bishop Guido excommunicated the mayor, his former friend Oportulo de Bernardo, whose adolescent daughter Agnes was a member of Clare's community. Oportulo responded by forbidding townspeople to conduct business with Guido. Francis believed that his song had the power to restore peace. He added a strophe for the occasion:

> Praised be my Lord for all those who pardon one another for
> love's sake, and bear weakness and tribulation.
> Blessed are they who endure in peace, for Thou, Oh Most
> High, will give them a crown.

At Francis's request, all the parties assembled in Guido's courtyard. A Lesser Brother announced that Francis, in the midst of his sufferings, had composed a hymn praising God. As they listened to the brothers sing the celebration of the great universe that they shared under God, the mayor clasped his hands and dissolved into tears, sobbing that he forgave the bishop, who was his superior. He said that was ready to forgive anyone, even if they killed his son or his brother, and he threw himself at the bishop's feet. Guido then confessed that although he was supposed to be humble, he was in

---

[†] Francis has been credited, famously but erroneously, with the internationally more famous "Peace Prayer" that asks God for acceptance of things that cannot be changed. In fact, it first appeared in a 1912 French publication *La Clochette*. The author is unknown.

fact a man who was too quick to anger, and he asked the mayor's pardon. The two embraced bringing harmony to Assisi while Francis remained in his hut at Saint Damian, undoubtedly singing his song, which soon inspired him to create a new one.

He intended it to console Clare and her confined women and to honor those who did the exhausting work of caring for the sick, including Clare and himself. His *Canticle of Exhortation* went like this:

> Listen, little poor ones called by the Lord who have come
>   together from many parts and provinces.
> Live always in truth, that you may die in obedience.
> Do not look at the life without, for that of the Spirit is better.
> I beg you out of great love, to use with discernment the alms
>   the Lord gives you.
> Those weighed down by sickness and the others wearied
>   because of them, all of you: bear it in peace.
> For you will sell this fatigue at a very high price and each one
>   will be crowned queen in heaven with the Virgin Mary.

This would be a parting gift, but not this only one. Francis decided to make clear his intentions for Saint Damian to protect them from those who would steer them from the life they had chosen together. He wrote a last will for them that said: "I, little brother Francis, wish to live according to the life and poverty of our most high Lord Jesus Christ and his most holy Mother and to persevere in this to the last. And I beseech you, my Ladies, and I exhort you to live always in this most holy life and poverty. Keep close watch over yourselves so that you never abandon it through the teaching or advice of anyone."

Elias now insisted that he had to go to Rieti to have his eyes treated. Francis had long trusted not only Elias's administrative skills but also his devotion to the Lesser Brothers and to the Gospel. Aside from those who travelled with him and saw to his personal needs, Elias was the brother whose guidance Francis trusted most.

Spring was far enough advanced, and Francis had gathered sufficient strength, so that he could no longer postpone the journey. The
brothers tied the new blindfold of linen and soft wool over his eyes
and sewed it to the edges of the new large hood the women gave
him so as to better block out painful light. They hoisted him up over
a donkey's back as the weeping women of Saint Damian took their
turns at a window to bid him farewell. There was no better way to
see him off than to sing his new songs as he departed but this would
not be a consolation to any of them. Clare, making clumsy steps, was
helped back to her bed of straw. She and Francis, as they undoubtedly
suspected, would not meet again in life.

Francis rode some fifty miles south through mountains thick with
oak and spiny holly shrubs toward Rieti. This city on the Velino
River located in the very middle of the Italian peninsula in the Lazio
region was a center for the treatment of eye ailments. The ailing man's
journey was as painful emotionally for those who loved him as it was
physically debilitating for Francis himself. Perhaps it was at this time
at the cliff-side hermitage at Greccio that the falcon that typically
awakened him in the middle of night for prayer changed its habits.
In earlier years, if Francis was slow to rise, the bird awakened him
with its low insistent call and rustled in its nest until Francis was on
his knees, but when Francis was ill, it let him sleep until light broke.

At the hermitage of Fonte Colombo four miles southwest of
Rieti, a leading physician came to examine him. A man of his
profession would have dressed in a red gown trimmed in squirrel fur, felt Francis's pulse, and presented a large glass flask for
Francis to fill with urine. Then, holding the sample to the light, he
would have checked its cloudiness and consistency. He observed
the alarming build-up of other fluids in Francis's body, particularly
in one of his eyes. The physician said he would have to treat this by
searing the cheek near Francis's worst eye with a hot iron up to the
eyebrow. Francis asked that this course of action be delayed until
Elias arrived because the minister general had said he wanted to be

present for any serious procedure and to see that Francis was cared for properly.

Elias, however, delayed too long. Francis was persuaded to allow the cauterization to proceed. A fire was lit and piled with logs until it grew into a roaring blaze hot enough to make the medical instrument, an iron rod, glow to a dull red. Francis entered the warm treatment room with his companions and sat down, determined to be serene in the face of pain. But when he saw the fire rise, heard it gnaw and consume the logs and crackle with sparks, panic rose in his breast. Fire had been his friend and his companion, comforting him in cold, warning off menacing beasts during his nights in many forests. Had he not told his brothers to show mercy toward the fire when it was burning his leg? He addressed it as a beloved ally: "Brother Fire, the Lord made you noble and useful among all creation. Be gentle to me in this hour because I have always loved you and will always do so for the love of the Lord who made you. I ask our common Creator to restrain your heat so that I may be able to endure it." And with that, he blessed the flames.

The brothers had to flee the room because they could not bear to witness Francis's pain. Hopefully he was given *spongia soporifica*, the anesthesia that had recently been introduced to Europe. It was a solution of dissolved opium, mandrake, and hemlock juice soaked into a sponge and held under the patient's nose in the hope of rendering him unconscious. Whether that balm was given to Francis or not, and whether it sedated him in any measure, when the hot metal seared his cheek, only the doctor who was with him witnessed it. Afterward, his returning companions found Francis relaxed and possibly giddy with relief that the ordeal was finally over. "Cowards!" he said. "Men of little faith! Why did you run away?" He told them that he had felt no pain, not even the heat of the fire, and he said that if the doctor had not burned enough, he was welcome to start again. The physician said that he had seen stronger men unable to tolerate such a searing but that Francis had not so much as twitched.

Nevertheless, this treatment did Francis no good. His eye problems continued, aggravated by a bad burn that invited infection.

Throughout his stay in Rieti many sought his help. Francis comforted those in spiritual distress, but by prearrangement with his companions when he wanted to avoid a visitor, he would recite Psalm 118:11 "Thy words have I hidden in my heart, that I may not sin against thee." Then the brothers would gently lead away the unwelcome intruder. People now wearied and disappointed Francis, who was so drained by his emotional and physical afflictions that he could not and would not overcome his growing distrust. He could no longer pour himself out to others or ignore signs that they did not mean him well. He learned that many persons who professed to agree with him in private actually held contrary beliefs. He knew that some praised him to his face but mocked him after they left his side. Some took credit for actions that belonged to others. Francis felt he was losing the ability to discern between those who walked in truth and those who could not be trusted.

Francis could not effect a cure for himself, but he continued to be revered as a miracle worker. One of the brothers who was plagued by a temptation asked the companions to give him Francis's nail clippings because he believed that these tiny pieces of the holy man might give him strength to conquer it. Although Francis had ordered that such things be discarded, when he heard of the man's plight, he told one of his companions to find a scissors and trim his nails. The brother received these parings with gratitude and said he was freed of his woe.

The nearby village of Saint Eli had been stricken with cattle-plague, or the disease rinderpest, which was killing scores of cows and oxen. This viral affliction of hoofed animals could wipe out entire herds in a two-week span and, as scientists would discover in the twenty-first century, had by 1100 AD been transmitted to humans in the form of measles. One villager had a vision that to save his animals, he had to obtain some of the water in which Francis washed his hands. Francis's companions must have been well aware of the devastation of cattle-plague because they not only gave this supplicant what he asked for but something else as well. They persuaded the unknowing Francis to wash his feet and they added this water to the gift. The man returned home and sprinkled the liquid on his ailing oxen who were said to recover quickly. Their lesions healed, their fever departed, and they were able to move and graze once again.

Francis was grateful for his doctor's daily visits and told the guardian, the Lesser Brother in charge of the community, to offer him something delicious to eat. To Francis's annoyance, the guardian replied that he was too embarrassed to invite him to share a meal because the hermitage was so poor and their pantry so meager. The physician, who had declined earlier invitations, broke the tension by replying that to him their poverty would be a delicacy. Thus, the brothers and their guest sat down to share a few cups of wine, some loaves of bread, and vegetables from their garden. A knock at the door interrupted them. They found at the entrance a woman bearing a basket filled with fresh bread, fish, lobster pies, honey, and grapes, all sent by a noblewoman who lived some seven miles away. The brothers were astonished, but not the doctor. He told them, "Neither you nor any of us who live in the world understand as we should the sanctity of this man."

On another day this same physician mentioned to Francis that he was paying for the treatment and support of a poor woman. Francis decided that the brothers should help her too. The guardian had lent Francis his own cloak to make him more presentable when he met with important people in Rieti. Francis decided that the woman must have this item. "Brother Guardian, we must give back what belongs to another," Francis announced. But the guardian explained that the garment was his. Rather than state that the brothers had no possessions of their own, Francis simply asked him to be courteous, at which point the man acquiesced. Francis then asked a sympathetic layman to take her the cloak, along with twelve loaves of bread.

The woman was unable to believe that something so wonderful could happen to her, or that she could possess something so fine, and she accused Francis's emissary of trying to make a fool of her, but finally she accepted the gifts. Later that night, fearing that she would be robbed, she fled Rieti and returned to her home. But Francis had not finished with her yet. Francis told the guardian to pay for the woman's treatment. Around this time, against the expressed wishes of Francis, Pope Honorius III decreed that the Lesser Brothers could carry money. Francis made every effort to disburse the material abundance that he found the Lesser Brothers gathering to themselves, whether it was baskets of fish, wheelbarrows filled with grapes, luxurious new tunics, or coins.

For a portion of Francis's time in the area of Rieti, the papal court, including Cardinal Hugolino, was in the city and the pope consecrated its new cathedral dedicated to the Virgin Mary. When Francis moved to the home of a poor priest near the church of Saint Fabian three miles north of the city gates, the cardinals began to visit the humble dwelling, which they reached by cutting through the priest's vineyard. The ripe grapes begged to be tasted and the rustic setting encouraged the august prelates to take siestas under the olive trees in the open air. The strain of such lofty visitors, and the damage they caused, proved to be too much for Francis's host. He grumbled that he would not be able to produce any wine that year because the cardinals had pillaged the vines. He lamented that even in ordinary years he had only enough grapes for his own small needs.

Francis told him not to despair or burden others with his complaints. He said that humans could do nothing about this, but that the Lord could undo the harm. "How many loads of wine does your vineyard produce each year?" Francis asked. "Thirteen," was the reply. Displaying the self-assurance of a merchant negotiating for a bolt of cloth, as well as the confidence of a man of prayer, Francis prophesied that God would give the priest twenty loads of grapes that year. He said that if there were any less, Francis himself would make up the difference. The holy man did not have to settle the bet. At harvest time the vineyard that the cardinals had desolated produced the predicted twenty loads of grapes, an increase over normal years of some sixty-five percent.

Pacifico arrived after Francis moved to the home of a Teobaldo Saracino, who may have been a physician. The former troubadour had renounced the worldly joy of his music and its lusty connotations when he joined Francis. But Francis now asked him to take up this instrument again to sing his song. Surely Pacifico still longed for it as a thirsty man longs for drink, but he was afraid to indulge his great temptation. He tried to talk his way out of Francis's request. Francis acknowledged that zithers were used to promote vanity and desire, but he said that that the two of them had an opportunity to change that, to turn them to the glory of God and the comfort of souls. Francis told him to obtain one through some respectable man so they could set *The Canticle of the Sun* to a worthy melody.

Pacifico insisted that the people of Rieti knew of his past and he was afraid that they would be shocked and disappointed to hear that he was returning to his old calling. Francis, a former merchant who would not have considered selling cloth to raise funds for the poor, finally accepted Pacifico's refusal.

The next night around midnight, as Francis lay sleepless, he heard a melody more exquisite than any he had heard before. Someone nearby was playing the zither. Francis listened enthralled for an hour until the music faded as quickly as it had begun. At daybreak, Francis told Pacifico with some reproach, "When I asked you, you refused my request, but the Lord who comforts his friends when they are suffering consoled me." He declared that the Lord himself had played the zither for him, since Pacifico would not. The brothers believed this and considered it a great miracle, but who knows who

God might have used as his instrument? Perhaps Pacifico took up the zither again in the dead of night unseen by all but God.

Largely at the insistence of Cardinal Hugolino, Francis continued to undergo various eye treatments. Boiled herbal solutions were wrapped around his head, his veins were cut, salves were applied to his eyes. He grew worse. At Fonte Colombo, doctors pierced each of his ears with a red-hot iron. This failed to provide relief. Then pain filled Francis's stomach and liver and he began vomiting and spitting blood. Certain that he was at the brink of death, he called Brother Benedict of Piratro, a priest who often said Mass for him, to write down his last wishes. These were that the brothers love each other always, be true to Lady Poverty, and be faithful to the church. Elias was called to his side from "a distant place" and Francis rallied, possibly because Elias's presence calmed his fears. One goal remained to Francis: to die at Portiuncula.

Both Elias and Francis were aware that Francis could give up his spirit at any time on the journey home. This prompted Elias, with or without Francis's knowledge, to plan a route that skirted the major cities. The fear was that a commune would claim Francis's body for itself and use it to attract wealthy pilgrims like weighted dice in a golden cup. Thus, the itinerary took longer and was more rigorous than a direct one would have been for the feeble Francis, but it included trustworthy rest stops such as leper houses where they would be secluded and safe.

While staying with the brothers at Le Celle near Cortona, Francis rallied in body and spirit and was able to console a poor widower whose wife had left him with grieving little children. To the horror of the brothers, who had gone to some pains to find a new mantle for Francis, he gave the garment to the needy man, saying it was a gift on the condition that he not give it to anyone unless he received a goodly sum for it. Such energy did not last when he was travelling. Francis was often too weak to sit erect on his donkey. Instead, he lay lifelessly slung over the animal's neck and was insensible when admirers rushed up to touch him or rip a patch from his tunic. He would sometimes awaken and ask when they would reach a certain place only to learn that they had left it hours before. Eventually they arrived at Bagnara, north of Nocera.

He was forced to remain there, only ten miles from Portiuncula, for many days because of swelling in his feet and legs. This rest was interrupted by the arrival of knights from Assisi. Word had reached them that Francis was relatively close and its commune wanted to be sure that he died among them. They put Francis on the move again. At the poor village of Satriano, Francis, Elias, and the brothers with them moved to a private home while the knights scoured the town for food to buy. No one was willing to sell them anything, and so they asked Francis to share his alms. Francis refused. He told them that they had made the mistake of trusting money rather than God. He sent them back out: "Offer them God's love instead and ask for alms," he told them. They did as he told them and were given freely the food that earlier they had been unable to purchase.

When the solemn party reached Assisi, Francis was too exhausted to continue on to Portiuncula. Bishop Guido was away on a pilgrimage to the shrine of Saint Michael on Mount Gargano in the south, but the shivering Francis was put to bed in his palace wearing a fur vest over his rough tunic to combat his racking chills. Even in his precarious state, he called for the singing of *The Canticle of the Sun*. He told the brothers that it would praise God and delight the townspeople who were keeping vigil with him outside the bishop's palace. Elias cautioned that while he personally was comforted by Francis's joy in the song, Francis should be more serious in the face of death, particularly for the sake of the people. Francis disagreed. Two years earlier, Elias had told him that he had seen in a vision that Francis had only two years to live. Francis said that since that time he had meditated on his demise so that he now rejoiced in it. Francis insisted that everyone have the pleasure of his canticle. Awaiting his fate covered by a vest of animal pelts and a patched burlap tunic topped by a soft fur cap over his aching forehead, Francis was able to joke, prob-ably with Giles, a beloved brother of tart wit and profound insight, about the way that Assisi would soon venerate his lifeless body. Giles teased, "You're wearing sackcloth now, but many canopies and silk draperies will hang over you someday." "You're right," said Francis. "That's how it will be."

Knowing that their time with Francis was growing short, some brothers sought his guidance to carry them to the end of their lives. Roger, who had abandoned his studies to join Francis after hearing him speak at Bologna, asked how Francis's intentions for the order had changed. Roger was especially interested to know which books clerics like himself might keep, given that they were not personal possessions but that they belonged to the order. Francis no longer dissembled. He told Roger that if his brothers had listened to him, they would have nothing but a habit, a cord, and underwear.

A doctor who arrived from Arezzo insisted that Francis would recover, but Francis knew better and he insisted on hearing the truth. The physician then acknowledged that he would die within weeks. Francis immediately prepared to go to Portiuncula where he wished to be buried. He called the brothers to his bed and placed his right hand on the nearest head. Learning that he touched Elias, Francis smiled said that was who he wanted. He blessed him and thanked him for taking on his burdens and responsibility for the brothers. He said that in blessing Elias, he blessed them all. He told them to remain strong and to persevere in what they had begun, for they were going to face challenges. He himself was leaving them and going to the Lord.

In secrecy the brothers carried him on a stretcher through Assisi's Moiano gate by the bishop's palace and down the mountainside. When they reached the crossroad that turned away from the city and toward Portiuncula, Francis asked to be set down on the ground facing Assisi. He knew that he would never return to the place of his birth where he had learned to use the abacus, to say his prayers, to defy his father, and to renounce his wealth. Only in memory could he see the thick defensive walls and the outlines of the houses whose residents he knew, or the bell towers of the churches where he had prayed and preached. But he raised himself as best he could and called God's blessings down upon it. He asked Christ to continue to love Assisi and he asked that it always be a home to those who knew how to love and glorify God's name. Then he told his brothers to carry him on to Portiuncula.

One imagines the silent, sorrowful brothers lined up along the foot path inside Portiuncula as bearers brought Francis's litter through the entrance in the hedge. They settled him in their sturdiest building that was the least open to the autumn chill. Once more Francis rallied and found himself with unexpected strength. He seized on this turnabout to dictate a final testament that was suffused with his original principles and the concerns he had expressed in recent months. While he said it was not to be considered another rule, through it he sought to undo the last years of alterations and nullifications of his will. Francis expected that all would heed it.

Francis began this document by saying that the Lord had called him to a life of penance through lepers and that he loved them, the churches, and all Roman Catholic priests, whose sins, if any, did not interest him. He said that the Lord had given him followers and had told him what to do with them. This was to live the Gospel. Francis said that he had written this down and the late Pope Innocent III had approved it. Thus, he made clear that recent papal decrees were counter to his wishes and even contrary to the rule that Innocent III had approved. He was not so bold as to tell the curia not to give orders to the Lesser Brothers. But he was adamant that his followers should not seek out the possessions, assignments, favors, or advantages that the church was pressing upon them. Francis did so in clear language: "I strictly forbid the brothers wherever they may be to petition the Roman curia, either personally or through an intermediary, for a papal brief, whether it concerns a church or any other place, or even in order to preach, or because they are being persecuted." He added, "If they are not welcome somewhere, they should flee to another country where they can lead a life of penance with God's blessing." He commanded his followers to obey their guardians and to recite their prayers according to the rule. Those who could not should be handed over to Cardinal Hugolino, the protector of the order. He forbad additions, deletions, and attempts at interpretation of this, his final statement. Francis stressed that the document was clear and required only simple understanding. On all who observed it, he called down blessings. With that work done, he relapsed.

When one of the brothers, possibly Angelo or Rufino, brought the terrible news that Francis was dying to Clare, she dissolved in a fit of weeping and could not be consoled. Her health was again so precarious that she had expected to die before he did, leaving Francis to protect Saint Damian. In what would be her final words to him, she sent the brother back with the message that the thought of not seeing him again left her desolate. Francis did not want her in that state. He replied with a letter of blessing, absolving her of guilt for any violation of his orders or wishes. He promised that she and the others at Saint Damian would see him again, and he told the brothers to be faithful to his promise to her. Then he urged Leo and Angelo to stop weeping, and to joyfully sing *The Canticle of the Sun* instead. Francis added new and final verses:

Praised be my Lord for Sister Death, from which no man
    escapes.
Woe to him who dies in mortal sin.
Blessed are those who die in Thy most holy will,
    for the second death shall have no power to do them harm.
Praise ye and bless the Lord, and give thanks to Him and serve
    Him with great humility.

Finally, he sent for Jacqueline de Settesoli. Francis told his brothers to let her know that she should hurry. He asked that she bring
wax for candles, the almond and honey cakes he liked, and a length
of the grey fabric worn by Cistercian brothers for his shroud. The
brothers were arranging to send a fast courier to Rome a hundred
miles away when they were interrupted by the neighing of horses
and the shouts of men at arms. They found Jacqueline herself with a
large party at their entrance. She told them that a voice had told her
to rush to Portiuncula where Francis lay dying, and she presented the
very items he had asked for, as well as incense for funeral preparations. Her one surviving son John, who was now a consul in Rome,
accompanied her, along with a number of servants and horsemen.
The Lesser Brothers, mindful that women were forbidden to enter
the dwelling, left her standing in the road by the ditch that circled
Portiuncula until Francis told them that she was not under the ban
because she was Brother Jacqueline. Her presence revived his spirits
and some of his energy, although he could tolerate no more than a
few bites of her cake. She was on the verge of sending most of her
party back to Rome while she stayed with him, but Francis stopped
her. He told her that he would die on the coming Saturday so she
would need her entourage the next day for her journey home.

The vigil continued, with Francis's closest companions taking turns sitting beside him. At Elias's request, Francis said he
absolved the brothers of their faults, as far as he was able. Feeling
life slip away, he told them to remove his clothes and place him
naked on the bare earth. He crossed his left hand to his right side
and lay there as the brothers wept and waited. Time passed. Elias,
as his guardian, understood that Francis wanted to leave the earth
as a man who had surrendered everything, but hours or days could
remain to Francis and Elias wanted him to be comfortable. As his
guardian who must be obeyed, Elias told him to accept as a loan
underclothes, a tunic, and a hood and he forbad him to give them
to anyone else.

The brothers put these on Francis and moved him to a bed. He asked for bread and gave them each a piece of it. He told the doctor who attended him that death for him would be the gate to life, and he called for a reading of John 13 in which Jesus, naked except for a towel, washes his disciples' feet and with this example tells them to humbly serve others. At times Francis recited Psalm 141, David's prayer when he was fearful and hiding in a cave: "Deliver me from my persecutors; for they are stronger than I. Bring my soul out of prison, that I may praise thy name: the just wait for me, until thou reward me."

On Sunday, October 4, 1226, one hour after sunset, in his forty-fourth year, after much struggle Francis passed from this life. Elias allowed the weeping Jacqueline to hold his lifeless body in her arms as word was sent to those outside and bells began to toll. Clare heard them at Saint Damian and knowing what they meant, shed bitter tears.

As the day faded, watchmen guarding Portiuncula were amazed to see larks gather in the sky. These birds loved only light and avoided twilight, but they circled the house where Francis died, making a great noise of joy and lament.

Francis had wanted to be laid to rest in the ground of his beloved Portiuncula. During his long days awaiting death, he had planned his embalming and interment, seeking wax, incense, and cloth for his shroud from Jacqueline, stipulated that there be a procession to Saint Damian so that Clare might see his body, and instructed them on what they were to do in the moments after his death. He told the brothers to lay his corpse out naked on the ground as he had been two days earlier and leave his body there for the length of time required to walk a mile at leisure. Church and civic leaders, however, overruled his cherished wishes once he was safely dead. The morning after he died, a procession of Assisians arrived singing hymns, sounding trumpets, and bearing olive branches and torches.

They claimed his corpse and carried it away, stopping only at Saint Damian. Inside the women's dwelling, the cloth was drawn back from the iron grille that opened into the chapel and Francis's coffin was brought in. His body was covered with the ash-colored cloth Jacqueline brought. Her embroidered linen veil had been placed over his face. This was removed so that Clare saw the visage of the man who had changed her life. He had been her hope and her despair and she had willingly forgiven him. She beheld how he had been shrunken by illness, malnutrition, and death, his temple burned and his ears pierced in a failed attempt to save his sight. A brother who was close to her, possibly Leo or Elias, lifted his dead hand to the window and she placed her lips upon it in a gesture of homage and farewell. Weeping, she ceded her place to the other women, including Agnes and Pacifica who had been with him from the beginning, and all of whom Clare had taught to see him as their truest guide.[†] Finding no consolation anywhere, she and the other women abandoned themselves to mourning. In the medieval custom of female *pianto*, they grew frenzied in their lamentations and wailed, "To whom do you leave us who are so desolate? What do you bid us do, shut up in this prison, us whom you will never again visit as you used to?"

The dead Francis gave no answer. Five months later, the problematic Hugolino was elected pope and Clare's true battles began. She knew that her future was not to be what had Francis promised her, but it would certainly not be the one that Hugolino had planned.

---

† Details vary as to whether Francis's corpse was borne on a stretcher or coffin, or was displayed at Saint Damian for a minute or an hour. This author chose a stretcher because it would be easier to carry and an hour seems the more likely, particularly if, as some surmise, the brothers answered the women's *pianto* mourning cries with the male *lamento*.

PART IV

$$\overline{13}$$

Discoveries

NEVER WAS AN absence more palpable. The grieving Lesser Brothers beheld the withered body of the man who had led them and surveyed the dead flesh that stretched over the angles of his bones. Decades of fasting and years of sickness showed in the scars and fissures on his papery skin, scabless sores that never had a hope of healing, and nicks and cuts on feet that had resisted the comfort of soft shoes. Slowly, however, something marvelous happened. On Francis's corpse, along with the ravages of self-mortification and disease, the men discerned marks that were like those of the crucified Christ—nail heads on his palms, wounds on his feet, a lesion over his ribs so like the lance wound that a soldier had inflicted on the dead Christ. As the brothers pointed out these wonders to each other, and said that his skin, usually so dark, had now become white and soft, this revelation eased their grief. Elias said that he had suspected that Francis bore Christ's wounds and he had confirmed it one day when he and Francis exchanged tunics.

In hindsight the brothers felt they should have known this all along. Rufino said that once when Francis was suffering an itch, he rubbed the spot. It was where a lance wound might have been. Francis had been so upset that he called on God to forgive Rufino. Another recalled confronting Francis about a persistent stain on the right side of his tunic and asking, possibly to make him admit to how much he suffered, whose blood it could be. Peevish, Francis had cut him short, pointed to his eye and demanded, "Ask what this is if you do not know that it is an eye." Nonetheless, at least one young man thought they were mistaken. The son of Jacqueline de Settesoli, who had accompanied his mother to Francis's deathbed, believed that the wounds he was seeing were simply the afflictions of disease and the mistreatment that Francis had inflicted on himself.

But the brothers recognized, in things that had seemed inconsequential before, more indications that Francis had kept a divine secret. He had always covered his hands, had washed his fingers but never his palms, had extended only his sleeve when admirers begged to kiss his hand. He must have been hiding the nail marks! Of course there had been many hints: had he not padded the tops of his feet with fur to protect them from his rough scratchy socks? Did he not grow irritable when the brothers examined him too closely? Now they understood that he had not wanted them to know of the special favor with which Christ had marked him.

It fell to Elias to announce Francis's death, but in his letter to the brothers scattered far and wide he was also able to console them by saying that before he died Francis had blessed them all and forgiven every failing. To this Elias added marvelous and unexpected news: God had singled Francis out above all other men. He had marked Francis's body with the signs of Christ's crucifixion as surely as if he had been on the cross itself.

In Rome Pope Gregory IX, the former Cardinal Hugolino, doubted that this could possibly be true, but when the Bishop of Assisi heard of these wounds, he was reminded of the strange experience he had had on one visit to Portiuncula. He had stopped by Francis's cell and knocked, as was his custom. Then he started to enter, but at his first glimpse of Francis praying, the bishop began to shake. His legs stiffened and he could not speak. He was blown back to the ground some distance away. Surely that occurred because he would have seen something of Christ's wounds and he was not worthy to see them, or because God wanted Francis's secret kept.

—⟨∞⟩—

Francis might not have been the first stigmatic. A Benedictine hermit named Dominic Loricatus who lived near La Verna in the middle of the eleventh century was said to have had the marks, and so was Saint Paul. Setting aside divine intervention, modern science and psychology offer explanations for the phenomenon. Two twentieth century Franciscans holding medical degrees say that Francis's wounds as they are described could also be understood as being secondary infections from leprosy. Scripture does not record the exact location of Christ's wounds, such as whether his hands were nailed to the cross through his palms or through his wrists. Compounding the mystery is that in the Greek in which the New Testament was written, the word for hand denotes an appendage that includes the wrist, palm, and fingers, so the nails are as likely to have been hammered into Christ's wrists as his hands. Artists have had the license to depict the marks as they wish.

In the centuries since Francis's lifetime, many people have been recorded as bearing the stigmata. Most, but not all, have wounds in the middle of the palms, while some had bleeding wrists. Some lesions are slits, others holes. Of twenty-eight stigmatics in the nineteenth century, twenty-two had the appearance of a lance wound on their left sides. Six had it on their right. Through the centuries, stigmatics have shared several traits, including a heightened awareness of Christ's suffering and close identity with earlier stigmatics. Their wounds have first materialized on a holy day and at a time of extreme personal stress. Many have had altered states of mind, such as trances, numbness, paralysis, blindness, or loss of hearing, and they have been able to enter into altered states of reality. Significantly, their individual marks have conformed to those on their favorite crucifix. Francis fits all of these criteria. He identified with Christ, and according to Saint Bonaventure, received his wounds on September 14, 1224, the feast of the Crucified Christ, when he was experiencing great anxiety about the direction of his movement as well as going blind.

The details of Francis's stigmata varied from the beginning. Among the earliest biographies there are discrepancies about his wounds, the manner in which they occurred, and when Francis received them. Jordan of Giano wrote that Elias sent the letter announcing Francis's death and stigmata, but he did not quote from it. A copy of this letter, purporting to have been written by Elias to Gregory of Naples, was discovered in Belgium in 1620, four hundred years after Francis died. The author who published it, William Spoelberch, never claimed to have seen the original thirteenth century text that was written in Elias's hand. As the scholar André Vauchez notes, this letter is "authentic in its substance," but it "has come down to us only in a late version, bristling with textural difficulties." For example, in Spoelberch letter, Elias commands each priest to say three Masses, each cleric to pray from the psalter, and the lay brothers to say five Our Fathers for the soul of the dead Francis. This is a prescription that otherwise does not appear in the Order until 1260, thirty-four years after Francis's death.

There is also the issue of timing. In this letter, Elias said that shortly before his death Francis was marked with perforations that were as black as nails, but after he expired, Francis's flesh whitened and he was more handsome than ever he had been in life. In contrast, Thomas of Celano in his first life of Francis said these marks were not holes but were brownish fibrous growths made of Francis's own flesh. Although Elias said that the marks appeared shortly before Francis's death, Thomas said that Francis had received them two years earlier at La Verna. Accounts vary as to whether a six-winged angel, or seraph, appeared to Francis or if it was Christ himself.

If the Spoelberch letter is not genuine, then no letter written by Elias has come down to us. Thomas's physical description of the stigmata is the only one that exists and there is nothing else to compare it to. In his first biography Thomas wrote two separate accounts of

Francis receiving the stigmata. In Chapter Three, it takes place at La Verna when an angel appears. Francis has "a vision of God," in which a winged man stands above him looking like a seraph with his hands spread out and his feet joined. Like Christ at Calvary, the angel was affixed to a cross. Francis was filled with wonder and was happy to see that the beautiful seraph looked at him with kindness. However, he was pained to see that the vision suffered greatly from his crucifixion. As Francis pondered with some alarm the meaning of all this, the nail heads began to appear on the tops of his hands and his feet. They were bent and pounded back, just as they had appeared on the angel. Then Francis felt his right side open with a bleeding wound that would continue to ooze until the end of his life.

Later, in Chapter Nine, when Thomas writes of Francis's body being laid out for the brothers to see, his description changes. He then follows the hagiographic pattern of many accounts of the lives of the saints, including those who lived before Francis, in which the flesh of the newly dead become beautiful and firm. Thomas writes that after his death, Francis's corpse became as white and supple as a fresh white rose, and that the marks appeared on the body as if occurring for the first time. The brothers saw on his right side a long cut reminiscent of the lance wound the Roman soldier inflicted on Christ. In the middle of his hands and feet the brothers discerned not holes but nails as black as iron formed of Francis's flesh. In Thomas's words, they looked "just as little black stones do when they are set in a white pavement."

Some forty years after their discovery of the stigmata, Leo wrote a brief account of how it had happened. He said that two years before his death Francis had gone to La Verna to fast and pray from the feast of the Assumption in mid-August to the feast of Saint Michael on September 30. In this wild mountainous setting where boulders heave up through staggered trees, Francis had seen an angel and been marked with Christ's wounds. Later to thank God for this gift he wrote the praises of the Lord in black ink on a piece of goatskin parchment that had been ripped from a small book. These praises cited thirty attributes of God, including patience, beauty, meekness, strength, and refuge of mankind. Some scholars find these reminiscent of the Muslim "Ninety-Nine Most Beautiful Names of God."

Leo also wrote that at La Verna he was troubled by a temptation not of the flesh but of the mind and spirit. He had said nothing about this, but Francis saw that something was amiss and called for parchment and ink. In wide-spaced letters he wrote from memory in Latin the Lord's blessing for Aaron in Numbers 6:24-26 "May the Lord bless thee, and keep thee. May he show his face to thee and have mercy on thee." Below this he added "May God Bless You Leo" and drew a Tau above and through Leo's name, as if to provide an umbrella of protection. The Tau seemed to rise out of a curious drawing that Leo described as a head.[†] Francis told Leo to carry it with him for the rest of his life to protect him from spiritual and physical harm. In his old age, on this same parchment in red cinnabar ink, Leo wrote his account of the seraph, probably so that it would never be lost. However, it is unclear whether Leo saw the stigmata when he was with Francis at La Verna or if he later, after the stigmata was accepted as fact, decided that the marks must have happened there.

Jacques Dalarun, a medieval and Franciscan scholar, notes that the known facts are that before his death, at an uncertain time and place, five wounds resembling those of Christ crucified appeared on Francis's body. Few companions saw them in his lifetime, but they were revealed to all after his passing. The reports about them are speculative. According to Dalarun, in writing about the stigmata, Thomas of Celano tried to create a narrative allegory that was then taken literally. Supporting this idea is that in his second biography

---

[†] Michael F. Cusato believes it to be the turbaned head of al-Malik al-Kamil touching the sandy shores of Damietta and suggests that Francis at that time was troubled by news that the emperor was preparing forces to finally make good on his promise to lead a crusade. A close-up of the drawing suggests that it could be a face with beard stubble. See Cusato's *The Stigmata of Francis of Assisi*, pp. 58-60.

of Francis, disseminated in 1247 about twenty years after the first, Thomas presented the brothers' accounts of how Francis hid the marks, but in a separate later chapter he wrote that when Francis was at the point of death, he asked to be placed naked on the ground in full view of the grieving, weeping brothers, who did not take any note of special wounds. Thomas made no mention of the wounds of Christ in the vivid scene.

Francis himself had said nothing of it in his lifetime, not even when he wrote his last testament to repudiate and cast off the interference of the church. The power he claimed in making this defiance was that God had told him directly that he and his followers should live in strict and evangelical poverty. How much stronger would have been his authority if he had announced that God had marked him with the wounds of his only son.

Scholars and the faithful can continue to debate questions about the stigmata of Francis of Assisi, whether it was a psychosomatic manifestation of Francis's love for the crucified Savior, a medical condition that resembled Christ's wounds, divine visitation, or something he had inflicted on himself in a pious act of self-flagellation. Jacques de Vitry praised the holy woman Marie of Oignies for doing just that, for cutting hunks of her flesh from her body and hiding them in the ground, after which she had the vision of a seraph.

Petrarch, the great Italian poet and humanist, wrote his understanding of the phenomenon to his friend Thomas of Garbo in 1366: "Surely the stigmata of Francis had their origin in the fact that he embraced the death of Christ in so constant and powerful a meditation that, when in his mind he had for a long time transferred it on to himself and seemed to himself attached to the cross with his Lord, at last his pious thought transferred the true image of the thing from his mind onto his body." The contemporary world would call this a psychosomatic condition.

Whatever the facts of Francis's stigmata, whether it was a phenomenon of group persuasion or divine intercession, reports of it transformed Francis into something more than an ordinary mortal. As word spread, the church was able to portray him as one that God had chosen for a singular, super-human role, which meant that no one, including prelates, could be expected to make the extreme choices that he had made. Thus, his service to the poor and afflicted was no more of a model than his following the literal message of the Gospel had been. The brothers discovered that the tortured man who had sat among them in recent years was not the isolated crank they thought they knew. Instead, he was a special being guarding a divine secret, racked by special pains that he shared only with Christ. Thus, the movement that Francis had founded achieved special significance, which the church was ready to put to use.

The commune of Assisi entombed Francis's body at the Church of Saint George where he had learned his lessons as a boy. They placed it in an ancient coffin of local travertine stone that had been fashioned in Roman times as a sarcophagus, but more recently had been used as a drinking trough for animals, a typical history for such objects. So that pilgrims might glimpse the body without approaching too closely, the coffin was placed in an iron cage with a closely latticed iron top. Inside, the head of Francis, who had disdained pillows, rested on a pink Assisi stone.

Winter followed quickly and aggravated the deep sense of loss at snow-bound Portiuncula and Saint Damian. At Greccio, the memory of the Christmas manger that Francis had created could only have brought as much sorrow as joy. Then, the coming of spring brought news that was startling if not entirely unexpected. Just as Francis had predicted, Cardinal Hugolino had become the pope. Honorius III had died in Rome on March 18, 1227, and the cardinals quickly elected Hugolino to succeed him.

Pope Honorius III had been forbearing and slow to act. Not so the newly elected Hugolino, who took the name Gregory IX. This impatient man, prone to such anger that he blasphemed, was determined not only to bend the Holy Roman Emperor Frederick II to his will but to renew the church by means of its laws. He pledged himself to eradicate heresy and to impose order on unapproved forms of religious life, such as the communities of pious women known as Beguines and lay religious movements.

The Humilitari were the first to feel his efforts. Gregory instructed Henry de Settala, the archbishop of Milan, to see that members of this movement, which had been approved by Pope Innocent III, dress in approved garb and live together in communities or join the Benedictines or another existing order. His lack of success with this group, which was loosely organized and without a strong hierarchy to enforce the pope's dictums, may have prompted Gregory to refocus on the orders founded by Francis and Dominic.

In the matter of renewing the church, Gregory IX decided to use the Lesser Brothers, notably the educated ones, and the reputation of Francis of Assisi as his instruments for reform. The Lesser Brothers had grown dramatically throughout Europe to number some thirty to thirty-five hundred men divided among more than a thousand small hermitages in a dozen provinces, half of them beyond the Italian peninsula. Since Francis himself had been less active publicly since his return from the Holy Land, he was known beyond the Alps through the work of his followers who roamed the world with their knotted rope belts and brown tunics.

The order was increasingly becoming an educated one. To elevate its stature, Gregory IX was determined to make Francis one of the most revered saints in the Roman Catholic liturgy. He himself had been personally touched by the man he called a friend and he tried to emulate him, going so far as to invite lepers to live in the Lateran

Palace. Sometimes he would humble himself by putting on a worn tunic and visiting monasteries and churches in the company of the Lesser Brothers. He was so incognito that at hospices when he tried to wash the feet of the poor, some shooed him away and called for other brothers who did a better job of it.

———— ∞ ————

In the spring of 1227, Elias was busy preparing for the general chapter that would elect a minister general who would truly lead the order now that Francis was gone. He had reason to expect that person to be himself. He attempted to bring peace to the competing factions of the Lesser Brothers by ruling with an iron hand. Even before Francis died, he allowed the church to improve the brothers' living conditions. When those living in Valenciennes protested against moving from a hospital on the outskirts to a palace that was given to them in the center of the city, Elias wrote them that the pope had approved their relocation and that Countess Joanna, who had donated the house, had contacted him personally. He ordered them to move to the villa with humble gratitude. Despite that, he believed that the brothers should honor the life of poverty that Francis extolled and that laymen like himself should continue to play significant roles in the order even though the number of priests was growing among them.

Under the rule of 1223, the meeting to elect the minister general was called for Pentecost 1227 and it was limited to sixty-five Lesser Brothers who were ministers of the provinces and the custodians, sometimes called guardians, of the individual communities. Although Elias opened the meeting, he did not close it. Instead, something shocking happened: he was voted out. John Parenti, the minister of the province of Spain, was elected to take his place. John, who had succeeded Bernard of Quintavalle as minister of Spain in 1219, was originally from Carmignano, a dozen miles west of Florence, and he had been a doctor of laws at the University of Bologna before joining the Lesser Brothers. After he became a judge, John looked out his office window one day and saw a farmer having difficulty herding his pigs. He gained control only after commanding the animals: "Enter your sty just as surely as lawyers and judges will go to hell." John took that rebuke of his profession as a sign. Soon afterward he entered Francis's movement along with his son and he became a leader.

Because he was highly educated, he was acceptable to the new men who did not want to answer to a layman like Elias. Yet John was himself a layman, which might have mollified those who clung to Francis's original call to poverty, simplicity, preaching, manual labor, alms-seeking, and disdain for learning. Moreover, Francis had praised the Spanish province after he heard a report of the pious and faithful lives the brothers there were leading. He called on the Lord to bless them generously and to bestow a special gift on all who followed their good example. There might have been an additional, more fundamental, reason for Elias's unseating. Francis had schooled the early brothers that in order to preserve humility, leadership positions should not be permanent.

At the time of John Parenti's election, the papacy of Cardinal Hugolino, now Pope Gregory IX, began on a high note. In the summer of 1227, his first in Saint Peter's chair, he saw Emperor Frederick II at last undertake the Crusade that he had promised in 1220. Frederick departed from Brindisi at the heel of the Italian peninsula but he became ill en route under summer heat so extreme that it killed hundreds of his knights. The ailing emperor was forced to return home, prompting his forty thousand troops in Egypt to return as well. Thus, once again, the campaign to recapture Jerusalem had collapsed and the pope was thwarted.

Gregory IX, on the verge of apoplexy, surely clutching the finger of Marie of Oignies lest he curse God himself, excommunicated Frederick on September 29, 1227. The emperor expressed his reaction in a letter to Henry III of England: "...the Church of Rome is like a leech; she calls herself my mother and nurse, while all her acts have been those of a stepmother. The whole world pays tribute to the avarice of Rome. Her Legates travel through all lands, with full powers of ban and interdict and excommunication, not to sow the seed of the Word of God, but to extort money, to reap what they have not sown...The primitive church, founded on poverty and simplicity, brought forth numberless Saints: she rested on no foundation but that which had been laid by our Lord Jesus Christ. The Romans are now rolling in wealth; what wonder that the walls of the church are undermined to the base and threaten utter ruin."

Scholars question whether the cosmopolitan Frederick was a committed Christian, but he was not one to put up with excommunication. He retaliated. While Gregory IX sat in isolated splendor at the Lateran Palace, the emperor purchased the land surrounding him from the most powerful families of Rome, including the Frangipani, at their asking prices and immediately returned the property to them to as fiefs. Allowing them to both sell their property at a profit and keep it made the emperor popular with the powerful. It also stirred up such antagonism against the papacy that on Holy Thursday 1228, three days before Easter, Gregory IX was forced to flee the Eternal City. He stopped at Rieti, then Spoleto, and finally settled in Perugia. He began thinking of Assisi, which was now synonymous with Francis, as a possible new residence for the papacy, a center of power that would link the church to the poor holy man while sheltering the papacy from the rapacious families of Rome.

When the pope visited Assisi in May 1228, the townspeople and the Lesser Brothers welcomed him with joy and enthusiasm. One imagines him passing by the old western gate, the typical entrance from Perugia, which would have taken him and his entourage through dark narrow streets. Instead he would travel through the eastern gate of Saint George with its huge plaza where the faithful could have seen him and cheered him on. Gregory IX proceeded to

Francis's tomb at the Church of Saint George, where he broke down in tears. Soon he set in motion the process of making Francis of Assisi, the merchant's son, a saint of the Roman Catholic Church, a status that would mean that his soul had entered heaven where he dwelled with God. It would also increase the prestige of the Lesser Brothers and underscore their legitimacy. In the history of formal papal canonization, which began in the tenth century, the church had never acted with such speed. The celebrated Thomas Beckett, who was murdered in the Cathedral of Canterbury in late 1170 after he defied his king to support the church, was not declared a saint until 1173. More significantly, the canonization process for Dominic Guzman, who had died five years before Francis, in 1221, did not begin until 1233, a dozen years after his death. This despite his many services to the church from fighting the Albigensian heresy to gathering the religious women in Rome into one dwelling under a single rule.

The transcripts and records of the process of Francis's canonization have been lost, but it is known that in May and June 1228, a papal consistory heard the testimony of those who had known him in life and those who had seen and experienced miracles that he had performed after his soul left the earth. These tended to mirror those that Christ himself had performed—the lame walking, the blind seeing, and devils being driven out. This did not complete the process of canonization, but it was enough for Gregory to call for Thomas of Celano to write a biography of Francis to make him known to the world and to begin preparations for a special church to house Francis's body. He appointed Elias to manage its construction. When Simone Puzarelli, in the presence of Bishop Guido and six witnesses, donated land just outside the city's western walls on the slope of Mount Subasio, Elias accepted it on behalf of the papacy on March 30, 1228. But money was needed. A month later, from Rieti on April 29, 1228, Gregory IX issued a bull *Recolentes qualiter* offering indulgences, or the removal of all sins from the souls of those who would contribute funds. In this way, a sinner could buy their way out of punishment in purgatory or hell. Since professional architects as such did not then exist, Gregory IX and probably Elias outlined a design for the structure.[†] On July 16, 1228, Gregory IX, adorned in pontifical vestments glittering with gold and gems and flanked by bejeweled weeping cardinals and bishops in purest white, stood outside the Church of Saint George to declare in his bull *Mira circa nos* that Francis was a saint. He decreed that October 4, the date on which Francis's soul reached heaven, would be his feast day. Significantly, however, he did not mention the stigmata. At that point Gregory remained dubious and would not lend it credence.

Those assembled to hear this included John of Brienne, who fought at Damietta, various counts and princes, and the people of Assisi in their finest clothing. They turned the streets to rivers of green with leafy olive and oak branches that they held aloft. Gregory's proclamation compared Francis to Old Testament figures including Abraham, Jacob, and Samson, saying he had slain thousands of Philistines simply by preaching in simple words. He said that Francis had made a holocaust of his own flesh and that he had taken heaven by force. The metaphors he chose were violent, as if to include the man of peace in the august company of martyrs who had been slain for their faith. The air filled with hymns and the strains of various organs as pope, cardinals, and people joined in singing. Gregory then descended from his throne and by the lower steps of the Church of Saint George entered the sanctuary where Francis's body lay and he kissed his tomb. Giles's prediction that Francis's ill-clad moldering

---

[†] Art historian Gregory Paul Caicco notes that guild masons would execute the details of construction as they worked on the site. See his *Ethics and Poetics: The Architectural Vision of St. Francis of Assisi*, pp. 171–173. According to the sixteenth century painter and biographer Giorgio Vasari, Elias engaged a renowned architect from German lands, Jacopo Tedesco, whom Florentines would later rename Jacopo Lapo, to plan the church. German art scholar Henry Thode at the end of the nineteenth century discounted this idea completely and posited that Vasari invented Jacopo.

body would be glorified had come true. The next day Gregory IX and his retinue travelled to the western end of Assisi, to the rocky promontory known as The Hill of Hell, a one-time place of execution like Calvary, where he laid the cornerstone for the enormous complex of church, papal apartments, workshops, and more than one hundred fifty brothers' cells that the papacy was building to honor its devoted servant, Francis.

Throughout this period, the Holy Roman Emperor Frederick was endeavoring to make good, in his own way, on his promise to lead a Crusade capture the Holy Land for good and all. At the time of Francis's canonization, in June 1228, Frederick again set sail for the Holy Land, embarking from Brindisi at the heel of the Italian peninsula. His trip was productive. Rather than fight al-Malik al-Kamil, he negotiated with this sultan, whom Francis had charmed, to obtain Jerusalem, Bethlehem, and Nazareth for a period of at least ten years and ten months, the maximum time Islamic law allowed for a truce with non-Muslims. Frederick had achieved possession of Jerusalem, the goal of the Crusades, and he had done so without bloodshed. In exchange, the sultan gained Frederick's support against his enemies, including Christians, for that period. Frederick crowned himself King of Jerusalem in the Church of the Holy Sepulcher on March 18, 1229, after entering the city along the route that Jesus the Messiah had taken when he entered the city in triumph.

The pope was not happy with this peaceful, bloodless solution. Frederick had led an imperial rather than a papal crusade and, being excommunicated, he had set forth without the blessing of Gregory himself. Gregory had wanted Jerusalem conquered for all time and the Muslims obliterated. Instead, Gregory was mired in a stalemate, unable to take overt action for another ten years, if he lived that long. Since the emperor had dislodged him from Rome, Gregory was forced to base himself in the Umbrian cities of Rieti and Perugia. Whatever else that cost him, it enabled him to keep a close eye on Assisi and to involve himself in the construction of the church, the friary, the papal suites, and the problem of Clare and Saint Damian.

Even though Francis was dead, Clare continued to resist the idea that her community had to follow the norms of his Ladies of the Poor of the Valley of Spoleto and Tuscany. With the pope living in Umbria, members of his court had the opportunity to see and report that the women of Saint Damian strayed out of their purported cloister and lived much as they always had, serving lepers where they found them, and counseling townspeople in physical or spiritual distress.

At this time Clare defied the pope, as in her younger days she had defied her parents. Her anguish and her desperate efforts to stave off the cloister are reflected in a desire she expressed to go to Morocco and be martyred like the brothers. Her misery can be inferred from a letter that Gregory wrote her shortly before he canonized Francis. He said that the right thing was for the women to take delight in God, their Heavenly Spouse, and in nothing else. He wrote, "We certainly hope and have confidence that, if you focus on God, what now seems bitter will become wholesome and sweet for you." He urged them to forget how they had lived in the past and to look to the future.

Gregory IX probably visited Clare in mid-August 1228 when he left his residence in Perugia to spend a few days in Assisi. Not only was this a few weeks after Francis's canonization, it was also soon after the death on July 30 of Clare's great friend and supporter Bishop Guido. The pope may well have had the opportunity to meet Clare's mother, who entered the community in these years, probably after she was widowed. Clare's youngest sister Beatrice would join them a year later in 1229. Taking stock of the singular path their lives had taken, Ortulana frequently told the women about Clare as a little girl and all the signs that signaled that she was destined to devote her life to God, such as the way she had counted out prayers with little pebbles. Clare, who discouraged unnecessary conversation, might well have been uncomfortable with this. One can never know if she was impatient with her beloved mother, but certainly the world outside

Saint Damian had taken note of Clare and the sanctity that gave her powers for good. When a little boy living in Perugia developed a film over one of his eyes, his parents brought him to Clare. She had him close his eyes, placed her fingers gently on the afflicted one, then touched the other and made the sign of the cross over his head. She then told the parents to take the boy to Ortulana, who also blessed the child. When he opened his eyes, they were clear and unclouded. Ortulana announced that Clare had cured him while Clare attributed the apparent miracle to her mother. At other times by making the sign of the cross, Clare relieved various Damianites of a persistent breath-stopping cough and a longstanding underarm fistula.

Agnes, the daughter of Assisi's mayor, believed that God had singled Clare out for special graces. Just after one Easter when Brother Philip was preaching, she saw a three-year-old boy materialize by Clare and listen to the sermon. Suspecting it was the Christ Child, she prayed not to be deceived and then she heard the words of Matthew 18:20 "I am in their midst." Clare stood enveloped in light and a sweet fragrance permeated the room. Another time Agnes saw Clare surrounded by a sparkling red aura and she heard the words "The Holy Spirit will come upon you."

A possibly apocryphal story in *The Little Flowers of Saint Francis* has it that during a papal visit, Clare asked Pope Gregory to bless some loaves of bread that had come fresh from their oven. Gregory replied that it was Clare who should bless them, but she said that she would deserve to be rebuked if she, "a vile little woman," should presume to do such a thing in the presence of the vicar of Christ. He said that since he commanded her to do it, no one could blame her. Clare then drew her hand over the loaves, whereupon a cross appeared cut neatly into each loaf. Some morsels were eaten and some preserved because of the miracle. When the pope departed, he took a portion of the wondrous bread with him.

Clare gave him bread, but not his dearest wish: her consent to have Saint Damian join his order, which would impart the prestige of Francis to his effort and also encourage the other straggling women to agree. Perhaps Gregory felt pity for Clare, or wanted her respect so much that he did not force her to obey him. But it is equally likely that this great jurist knew that a vow she made against her will would not have had legal force. He remained confident of his eventual success. Gathering all the religious women of Rome in a single convent had taken seventeen years. He had worked for only a decade to establish a unified order in Tuscany and the Spoleto valley.

By April 1226, even before Francis died, Gregory had appointed a Brother Pacifico, who was probably that same Pacifico who had been Francis's close companion, as visitator of his ladies. Then in December 1227, in his bull *Quoties cordis*, Gregory assigned the task of looking after these communities, which he now called The Poor Cloistered Nuns, to the entire order of Lesser Brothers. This did not placate Clare. She had long known that the Lesser Brothers were deviating from Francis's wishes, but she intended Saint Damian always to be faithful to his principles. She remained adamant that she would not accept property and that the women would continue to live in poverty just as Francis had wished. Gregory IX, in contrast, mandated that his nuns have reliable income.

Soon after he became pope, Gregory IX had appointed his kinsman and aide Raynaldo of Jenne, a man then in his mid-forties, to succeed him as cardinal of Ostia and protector of the Lesser Brothers and of religious women. He had been beside the former Cardinal Hugolino in all his dealings, and Francis had been so ingratiating as to call him "Prior." On August 18, 1228, Raynaldo wrote a letter to twenty-four women's communities and placed Saint Damian before the others, all of whom had incorporated the Virgin Mary into their names, a practice that Gregory IX encouraged. He announced that Pacifico had asked to be relieved of the duties of being their guardian, duties that he found to be "unbearable." Philip the Tall, whom he described as "our very dear friend" and one who had "suffered many hardships and vicissitudes for them," was now their visitator.

This is what Gregory IX wanted to achieve when he first visited Saint Damian as Cardinal Hugolino eight years before, but possibly this was a compromise Gregory made with Clare, so that someone she trusted was guiding the women's order. He made a greater concession still—he would allow Saint Damian to continue to live in poverty.

On September 17, 1228 while Gregory was still residing in Perugia, he sent Clare a letter *Sicut manifestum* stating in language that would seem to be airtight that he was giving Saint Damian the "Privilege of Poverty." The bull stated "...we confirm with our apostolic authority, as you requested, your proposal of most high poverty granting you by the authority of these present that no one can force you to accept possessions. Therefore, let no one be permitted to tamper with this document of our concession or dare to oppose it with rash temerity. If anyone shall presume to attempt this, let him know that he will incur the wrath of Almighty God and His blessed apostles, Peter and Paul." [†]

Clare carefully tended and preserved this parchment document, which safeguarded her right to forego property, all her life. She had achieved something significant, but the cost of it was that she agreed to join his order and live as a nun. The doors of Saint Damian closed to outsiders, although not as firmly as the pope expected. Within them Clare began a struggle that would last a decade. The pope sent Clare and her community the letter saying that since they had chosen to enclose themselves he was confident that what might now seem bitter and rough would become sweet and smooth. However, as far as surviving records indicate, Gregory IX himself never returned to Saint Damian after this visit, although he was often in Assisi. Years earlier he had written Clare saying that her goodness and sacrifice

---

[†] Werner Maleczek has offered convincing proof that a document that had long been attributed to Pope Innocent III granting Clare and her community the privilege of poverty around 1215 was a forgery created in an Umbrian convent in the mid-1400s.

made him feel that he could never enter heaven unless she vouched for him before God, but now it seems he recognized that her goodness encompassed a strength that he did not find edifying.

For all that, the women of Saint Damian were now under the direct control of the Roman Catholic Church, as were the fractious women outside Florence who had insisted on following Clare. They were now under Gregory's rule. They were nuns subject to most of what Clare had experienced and rejected when she took refuge at the Benedictine convent Saint Paul of the Abbesses after joining Francis. They were never to leave their enclosure, unless they were sent to a place in service of the order. Those who could read were to read the psalms at prescribed times, others could recite the Lord's Prayer. Clare as leader was to be called abbess. All were to keep silent, and if a religious or secular person wished to meet with a member of the community, she had to be notified. If she gave permission, then the woman who was receiving the visitor had to be accompanied by two others. Days of fasting were scheduled, subject to changes depending on the availability of fresh vegetables and fruit. During Lent they should fast on bread and water four days of the week. They were to sleep on planks of wood that the abbess could allow to be covered with straw or cloth. Prelates who had permission to enter, even cardinals, had to be accompanied by one or two appropriate companions. The new rule provided the women with two tunics and a mantle in addition to a hair shirt. At the discretion of the abbess, this could be amended. One imagines Clare did not permit new and better garments to be procured.

These rules required yet more reconstruction to the physical Saint Damian. The sound of the hammer and the pungent smell of raw wood invaded the place. Its main wooden door was reinforced with iron bars that could be unlocked only for reasons stipulated in the rule. Stalls where the women might kneel and pray were added to the room to the right of the chapel. Since they were not allowed to see a priest, they were not allowed to see the celebration of the mass. Still, they could hear it and later, after the priest departed, they could see and adore the consecrated host, the apparent wafer of bread that had been transformed into Christ's body, encased in the monstrance, a vessel that displayed it.

While Clare's life grew smaller, the monument to Francis grew apace. It was to consist of two churches, one on top of the other, a feat of engineering. They would combine the Gothic and Romanesque styles, which was not uncommon at the time. The upper church, more narrow and airy, was closer to the Gothic spirit and was intended to serve as the pope's chapel when he was in residence. Its main embellishment would be a gift from Gregory IX, a crucifix covered in precious stones that contained a relic of the True Cross. Constructing the Romanesque, low, dark, and rounded lower church, which would house Francis's body, was Elias's immediate task and he had to do it with relative speed. That somewhat squat structure was designed not only to support the upper building but to contain one of the most treasured relics of the Roman Catholic Church.

By now Elias was in his forties and suffering from ill health, possibly gout. This made travel difficult, so for the most part he remained in Assisi. Whereas Francis in the last painful years of his life had traveled on a donkey and berated himself for indulging in such luxury, Elias rode on horseback even when he had to go no farther from Portiuncula than Assisi. He had a staff of servants in colorful uniforms and reclined upon a couch before a comfortable fire. Perhaps these affectations began as a concession to his ailments, and as a means to put wealthy donors at ease, but it became his normal way of doing things. Bernard of Quintavalle once tried to show him the error of his ways by interrupting Elias while he ate, separate and apart from his brothers, and forcing the uncomfortable man to share with him his sumptuous and inappropriate meal.

As he worked to secure donations to fund the complex, far from wearing the most tattered tunic he could find, as Francis routinely had, Elias donned one that was less likely to offend the donors he cultivated. He was never so humble as to diminish or rebuke the importance of the great ones whose help he needed to further the Lesser Brothers and the work of the church.

To attract contributions from those unable to make large donations, Elias set up a collection box made of marble on the so-called Hill of Hell, just outside the west gates of Assisi, where the church was going up. As far as it is known, Francis's followers did not object to the construction of a fine church to honor him and to glorify God, but the collection box and the elaborate friary did outrage Francis's closest companions, especially Leo. They traveled a few miles to the west to consult with Giles, who was living in Monteripido northwest of Perugia. Giles took stock of the news they brought and said that the small marble collection box for contributions from the poor was itself an offense against the wishes of Francis, not to mention the expensive structure of the same material being erected in his name. He counseled Leo that if he valued his life as he knew it, he should remain silent. If, on the other hand, he was willing to endure the rage and vituperation of Elias, he should take action. Whether Leo decided instantly what he would do, or whether he worked out a course of action while walking back to Portiuncula, when he reached Assisi, Leo smashed the box, an action that would have required a great deal of sustained and determined force. The defiance did enrage Elias, who as he built the church complex was trying to please the pope, the commune, benefactors, and those brothers who wanted to live a life of strict poverty along the lines Francis intended, as well as those of educated priests and scholars who were changing the work of the order day by day.

On April 19, 1229 Gregory sent a bull to John Parenti taking the edifice under his protection as the property, not of the poverty-loving Lesser Brothers, but of the Holy See. After touring it, Giles was said to have asked the brothers where they housed their wives. He said they were breaking their vow of poverty, why not chastity as well? Francis's beloved, humble Portiuncula, which he had intended to be a model for his brothers for all time, was now eclipsed.

By the end of the thirteenth century, the Church of Saint Francis would be decorated with works attributed to Cimabue and Giotto, whose faithfulness to nature and narrative power ushered in the Renaissance. Compared to the mud and branch huts that Francis had favored, the brothers lived in a celestial palace that encouraged rumors that dark activities such as divination and alchemy took place there. Perhaps they did. Honored churchmen such as the English Lesser Brother Roger Bacon and the Dominican Thomas Aquinas would later write treatises on alchemy, the secret experimentation that led to the science of chemistry.

By the eve of Pentecost on May 25, 1230 the lower church was ready to receive Francis's body. Some two thousand Lesser Brothers, about two-thirds of the total number, assembled for the final entombment and to learn the results of the general chapter meeting that would follow it. They arrived from various corners of the world and their words and demeanor made clear how the movement had changed. Those who conversed in Latin, English, French, and German were as prevalent as those who spoke Italian dialects. Many carried books. The priests among them, now a majority, brought portable altars so they could say Mass anywhere, including in the fields and under the olive trees surrounding Portiuncula. If they knew that Francis wanted no more than one Mass said for all present each day, they ignored his wishes and each said his own.

Gregory IX remained in Rome. He was once again welcome there and was reconciling with the emperor. He sent three nuncios to Assisi to represent him, along with a bejeweled gold reliquary containing the promised splinter of the True Cross, golden-threaded vestments, and various precious vessels for the altar. His message to the assembly announced that Francis, now in heaven, was performing miracles and had restored a dead man to life. The pope promised more indulgences to those who would continue to provide money to support construction of the complex.

At the appointed hour, Francis's closed coffin was solemnly removed from the Church of Saint George and placed on a cart. To the sounds of trumpets and other instruments, horses drew it westward through city streets. Several thousand people, some from distant lands, packed inside the city's walls and narrow angled passageways while others spilled into outlying fields and roads. They wanted to see the cortege, to glimpse Francis's body, and perhaps to be healed by it. Quickly, however the event spiraled out of control. The jostling crowd swarmed over the coffin. According to papal documents, Francis's relics were somehow "profaned," but in fact, Francis body was not in the coffin. It had been moved secretly three days before.

Nevertheless, Elias and officials of the commune took hold of the empty coffin and barred all people, including the close companions of Francis, from entering the lower church. Once they were inside, as those outside shouted and howled, they slammed the heavy bars in place to lock them out, depriving the Lesser Brothers and the townspeople of the conclusion of the service, miraculous cures, and entry into a church where they felt they belonged. What was supposed to have been a hallowed, transcendent experience had become first a riot, then a secret ceremony that excluded Francis's dearest companions, all the other brothers, and even the minister general.

Possibly Elias, who had long grappled with the competing concerns and changing demands of multiple interested parties, had decided that the best way to honor whatever he could of Francis's wishes was to let him be interred clandestinely, to assure that his body would rest whole and in peace. In making his plans for the lower church, Elias had included a vaulted chamber twelve feet square carved into the rock foundation below the high altar of the lower church. Probably this had always been the intended place for Francis's tomb, but since a robbery attempt seemed likely at some future date, the cavity was made impregnable. One clue that the secrecy was a last-minute decision is that just before the translation of the body, the brothers Sanguonio and Tommaso di Uffreduccio discovered that one of their travertine walls had been vandalized and large slabs removed. Later they learned that this was done as part of the construction of the church, but it would be nearly a decade, until May 27, 1239, before Elias formally admitted responsibility for the missing slabs and agreed to compensate them for their loss.

On the day they interred Francis in secret, Elias and trusted men from the commune began their work by the light of hanging lamps. They placed Francis's coffin in the protective cage of latticed iron bars from the Church of Saint George in the cavity under the main altar, with his head to the south. Then they lowered a great travertine stone on top of that to close out forever their view of what remained of Francis. Workmen drove additional iron bars into the side walls and set another stone set upon that.

The general chapter meeting immediately followed the melee of Francis's final entombment. Many brothers had come for the translation and they wanted to go to the meeting. John Parenti, however, forbad this. By the rule of 1223, now only provincial ministers and custodians were allowed to attend. Furious, those who supported Elias carried him from his cell to the room where the leaders of the various provinces had assembled to reelect John Parenti. Insisting that Elias should be at the important meeting, they broke down the door and attempted to place him in John's seat. John quelled the uprising by stripping himself naked and giving up his office, which so stunned the brothers that order was restored and John was quickly reelected. He soon disbanded the unhappy faction by dispatching Elias's proponents to separate provinces. Elias himself withdrew to

Cortona where he did penance and let his hair and beard grow long and shabby as a sign of his remorse. He no longer had the responsibility for completing the new church. In his place John Parenti appointed Picardus Morico and Philip of Campello to oversee its funding.

For all that, Elias seemed to remain in the good graces of Gregory IX despite many complaints. Gregory IX weighed accounts from the cardinals who had been present, from Elias himself and probably from others as well. A few weeks later he issued a bull *Speravimus hactenus* in which he placed responsibility for the melee on the civil authorities of Assisi and he condemned them for it. He spared Elias himself by name, but for a time he took away the administration of the new church from the Lesser Brothers and put it under the authority of the bishops of Perugia and Spoleto. Eight weeks earlier, he had proclaimed that this church would be the "head and mother" of the order, but now he revoked the Lesser Brothers' authority over it and forbad them to live or hold a general chapter there.

14

Into the Light

By this time, Thomas of Celano's *Life of Saint Francis* was teaching the faithful in many places about the life and glory of the new saint, a man subservient to the church and enveloped in the mysteries of God. The books came from the scriptorium attached to the new burial church. Here a scribe made two copies of the manuscript, which his fellow scribes duplicated, and on and on until every church, friary, and bishop's palace in Europe received one. Their contents were read to more of the faithful as increasing numbers of books appeared. Each was some fifteen inches high by ten inches wide, made of vellum or parchment pages that had been cleaned, bleached and polished smooth, then folded in half and bound together by stitching. Typically each page presented two columns of forty-one lines of text, with initial letters and section headings that were written in a uniform hand. Francis, who would have abhorred the existence of such a book, might have taken consolation in the fact that the vellum used in this prodigious effort was of such poor quality that its product appeared to be as spare and simple as the subject himself.

Elias was Thomas's primary source for the work, which indicates that however Elias may have courted the wealthy in his task of building Francis's church, he remained true to Francis's insistence that poverty was the essential way of life. Elias had inspired Thomas to fall in love with Francis and thus with those who knew him best.

In standing up for the simplicity and humility that Francis had preached, he rebuked those who seemed to flaunt these virtues. He praised the women's protector Philip the Tall, who had apparently been subject to criticism because Thomas compared Philip's detractors to scholars in the temple of Jerusalem who had belittled the apostles Peter and John. Thomas also singled out Giles for having knowledge that could not be gained by scholarly study: "...giving us examples of perfect obedience, manual labor, solitary life, and holy contemplation." He mentioned Rufino and Bernard of Quintavalle in passing but there was nothing of Leo, who had served Francis closely, possibly because Elias remained angry with him. Most significantly of all, in glorifying Francis, Thomas also ushered on to the world's stage Clare of Saint Damian. Thomas spoke of the dozens of women there, of their silence that had made it difficult for some to speak, of their piety and love of God. He said that they lived in such high poverty that their food and clothing left them in extreme need.

Thomas bestowed the former Cardinal Hugolino with as much credit as Francis for their existence. He wrote that Pope Gregory IX had given the ladies their "wondrous life and their glorious institutions" when he was bishop of Ostia, but it was Clare who lived this exemplary life. Where Francis was known, she was known. Thomas's life connected Clare to Francis and the Lesser Brothers. Those whom Gregory wanted to know about the life of Francis now also knew about Clare.

———✠———

Those Lesser Brothers who had considered the founder of their order to be an ill-tempered recluse discovered a new Francis in Thomas's book, as an account by Brother Jordan of Giano attests. Thomas of Celano gave Jordan some locks of Francis's hair and a few tunics that he had briefly worn to take to Germany. By then, in 1230, Jordan had spent nine happy years there and his return journey took many weeks. Jordan and his companions made their way up the western coast of the Adriatic and up through the Alps, staying in the Lesser Brothers' huts, the houses of lepers, or occasional refuges in towns. When Jordan reached Wurzburg, a straight line north of Assisi as the crow flies but seven hundred miles on land, he sent word ahead to various communities that the brothers could gather to meet him in Eisenach, about a hundred miles to the north of Wurzberg.

When Jordan arrived at the brothers' dwelling in Eisenach, the porter slammed the door in his face. He stood in some confusion until two brothers advised him to enter through the chapel. When those doors opened, Jordan stepped into the warmth of the interior and found himself to be revered. The entire community met him, walking two by two, carrying crosses and palm branches, and chanting, "This is he who loves the brothers." Jordan had been away from them for some time, but he still found this welcome to be excessive. He could not persuade them to stop. As incense filled the chapel they continued to sing and to take in the sight of him with awe.

Slowly, Jordan understood the meaning of the brothers' celebration. They had heard what he was bringing and were spellbound not by him but by the relics of Francis. Jordan carried the treasures slowly and respectfully to the altar while the brothers knelt in veneration. At that moment, and for the first time, Jordan understood that the Assisian had been far more than the peevish invalid whom he had ignored. Thomas's account of Francis's life and the marks of Christ that he bore had taken hold as the true meaning of Francis of Assisi.

But questions remained about how the brothers were to live. In Italy, some were upset by the requirement to obtain official permission every time they wanted to visit women that they had worked and prayed beside for years. Others wanted no part of them. Clare's supporters particularly wanted to know if the pope's rules affected Saint Damian, which they regarded as a special case. The brothers were also divided over Francis's last testament, in which the dying man repudiated changes that the church had made to the poverty and simplicity of the order's early days.

Some would have preferred that no questions be asked so that they might do as they wished. John Parenti did not feel free to render guidance on his own, and so he led a delegation of provincial ministers to appeal to Gregory IX, who was then in Agnagi. This hill town forty miles southeast of Rome was the stronghold of the Conti, his family and that of his kinsmen popes, the late Innocent III and the future Alexander IV. Besides John Parenti, the group was multi-national and educated. It included Anthony of Padua, a future saint; Haymo of Faversham, a scholarly Englishman teaching in Paris who had joined the order on Good Friday 1224; as well as Brother Leo of Parengo, a future Bishop of Milan; Gerald of Modena; Gerald Ruscinol, a papal penitentiary in charge of administering indulgences; and Peter of Bescia. None of Francis's closest and earliest followers, including Elias, was included.

In late September 1230, in time for the chapter meeting at Michaelmas, the pope announced his decisions. In the bull *Quo elongati* he declared that without the consent of the Lesser Brothers and their ministers, no change to their rule of life could be made. He acknowledged that Francis's last wishes were certainly heart-felt, but said his last testament did not bind them. So it was that although Francis, like his hero Roland, ultimately took decisive action, he had blown his trumpet too late.

In his bull the pope made a distinction between having money and using it. He told the brothers to select one of their benefactors or lay friends to buy and manage necessary goods on their behalf, a practice that led to such misunderstandings and abuses that fifteen years later, in 1245, a successor to Gregory IX had to grant Franciscan leaders the use of money.

Gregory also said that the trained theologians among the brothers did not need the permission of a provincial minister to preach. Their education rendered them qualified unless a provincial minister decided otherwise. In addition, he said that only provincial ministers and one custodian from each province would have the right to participate in future chapter meetings, capping at twenty-six the number of men who would elect a minister general.

In his closing paragraph, which was for Clare the most explosive, Gregory IX addressed the brothers' concerns about his 1227 bull *Quoties cordis*, in which he entrusted them with the care of nuns. The pope took note of the eleventh provision of the rule of 1223 that said that the brothers could not enter the convents of the nuns without the permission of the Apostolic See, meaning the pope himself or those he designated. He said that when Francis was alive the brothers had believed that referred only to "The Poor Enclosed Nuns," and they believed that they were free to visit other women. Now he would clarify: this rule applied to all convents. They could not enter any of them without expressed papal permission. Although he did not mention the convent that lay below Assisi by name, he most definitely included Saint Damian in the ban, and thus he ended the special relationship Clare had had with the brothers.

Quo elongati would have more effect on the Lesser Brothers than any ruling made by Francis in his lifetime. With these pronouncements and his absorption of Saint Damian into his women's order, the former Cardinal Hugolino had established his own preferences as the rule for Francis's followers, whether they were male or female. He had voided Clare's connection not only with the brothers but with Francis himself. At least he thought he had.

John Parenti most likely sent one or two brothers through the Umbrian autumn to inform Clare that henceforth Cistercians, and not Francis's men, would provide Saint Damian with spiritual and material support. They would bring the bread, olives, fruit, and

vegetables on which the community of Saint Damian was to subsist. On hearing this, Clare's response was immediate. The messengers may have been men she was close to, they may have been
her foes, but whoever they were, she threw them out and declared
that henceforth no male of any order would be admitted within her
walls unless he was a Lesser Brother. She proclaimed, "Let him
take away all the brothers since he has taken away those who give
us the food that is vital."

By this she meant preaching infused with the spirit of Francis,
a celebration of the life of poverty and strict adherence to the
teachings of Christ in the Gospel. Whether she banished the men
with a sigh, as her official biography would record, or with a hiss, it
had the effect of a slamming door and a screaming slap. Clare and
her community were now for all purposes on a hunger strike that
could lead to death. Even more significantly, she had barred those
who could say Mass or provide the Eucharist. Her will was such
that she would sacrifice not only her body but, in the eyes of the
church, compromise her immortal soul. Undoubtedly disconcerted,
the messengers returned to Portiuncula and conveyed her reply.

John Parenti had been married and lived with his wife, but
unlike his predecessors as superiors of the order and those brothers who had been closest to Francis, he had not worked side by
side with women. Once again, he appealed to Gregory IX and
awaited further orders. The pope was no more willing to make a
decision than John Parenti had been. For the second time Clare
had defied him, the vicar of Christ, the first being her refusal to
accept property to support Saint Damian. Now this woman had
evicted all clerics and placed herself in what amounted to a state
of excommunication. Brother Angelo Clareno, who drew on oral
tradition in writing of the Lesser Brothers' tribulations a century
after Francis's death, said that Gregory IX had in fact at one time
excommunicated her.

Whether or not the anger-prone Gregory IX was ever driven to such extreme action, he avoided further responsibility now. He gave the minister general direct control of Saint Damian to handle as he thought prudent. Thus, Gregory IX again united Clare and her community to the Lesser Brothers under the authority of the minister general, however reluctant he might have been to give her a command. She had outmaneuvered the pope again.

Still, her life followed a pattern. Each day after terce at nine in the morning, the Damianites took up their manual work: spinning, embroidery, baking, cooking, gardening, or other tasks. At least one of them looked after the orphaned, unwanted, or abandoned girls in their care, sharing their joys, teaching the Our Father, drying their tears. Aside from these little ones, who might choose to go or stay at age twelve, silence prevailed, except for the prayers. Hour faded into hour, terce into sext when the sun was at its peak, then nones at three. The days merged into each other except for Sunday, when through the grille in the cloister wall the women heard the priest at the altar saying Mass.

In appearance, Clare seemed to be the least among them, wearing the required coarse garb with the greatest number of patches, and a much-mended black veil. She had given up her hair shirt as Francis had insisted, and she slept on straw rather than on a wooden plank. When she was well enough to be out of her bed, she sat to the side of the work room spinning yarn on her distaff while the others passed silently around her, preparing to hoe the garden, knead the dough, or scrub the scullery floor. They watched her as closely as she allowed them, because care of her was now one of the community's most important tasks. She remained a guiding spirit who could soothe anger, jealousy, and discouragement among the women, having in earlier years experienced all these emotions passionately herself.

Clare's amusement was the cats that resided at Saint Damian. Once when she was bedridden, she wanted a certain towel, but she was alone in her corner and the others were too far away to hear her ask for it. To Clare's amazement, one of the convent cats began to pull it toward her and as it struggled, she asked why it was getting the towel dirty. With that the animal started to roll it with greater success.

As it turned out, the promise that Gregory IX had made to her when he first tried to lock her behind convent walls was coming true: what had been bitter was becoming sweet. Weakened legs rather than the pope's direction now kept her inside Saint Damian, but this set her mind more firmly than ever before the throne of God. Here she found delight. Although she preferred the Lesser Brothers, the Cistercian visitors that Gregory had intermittently imposed on her brought new sources of God's message that she developed for herself and her community. This included in particular the Song of Songs, or Canticles, the book of the Old Testament attributed to King Solomon. It is written as love poetry that Jews and Christians, notably the dynamic Cistercian Bernard of Clairvaux, experienced as an allegory of God's love for Israel, the church, the Mother of God, or the human soul. It is a rare selection of scripture in which the female is accorded as much importance as the male. It seemed particularly suited to nuns who saw themselves as the human brides of a divine bridegroom. Clare particularly quoted a verse that occurs in the second and eight chapters: "His left hand is under my head and his right hand shall embrace me." In the protection of her Heavenly Spouse she found strength and confidence that helped her to cope with the Holy Father, the pope.

Nonetheless, immobility did sometimes frustrate and sadden her, although she tried to appear serene. At dawn one Christmas when all the others had gone downstairs for prayers, she felt dejected about being unable to walk and join in on such a special holy day. Soon she heard music, the brothers chanting the psalms, the blending of their voices, and the individual strains of the lutes and ringing bells. As she listened, the newborn Jesus appeared lying on his bed of straw. Later when the women returned to her, she told them that the Lord had not left her alone as they had. He had taken her to hear all the joyous Christmas celebrations at the Church of Saint Francis.[†]

For some years, perhaps since 1221, under the rule of Cardinal Hugolino, some in the community had the role of "serving sisters." The one thing that is certain about them is that they performed tasks outside the convent walls. Whether they also did all manual work, such as preparing food and sweeping floors within the walls of Saint Damian while others had the spiritual tasks of praying, is unknown but that idea would have been anathema to both Francis and Clare. Nonetheless, Hugolino included the status in his rule.

Probably, to be a serving sister at Saint Damian was to have a time-limited assignment to conduct some business for the community rather than to be part of a permanent caste. Under the rule of Saint Benedict, which was the model for Cardinal Hugolino's order, nuns took one-week turns doing menial tasks and waiting on others. Moreover, serving sisters had to be old enough to have sound judgment and they needed to be sufficiently healthy and strong to undertake a journey into the world, even if only for a day.

It was a point of pride for Clare that early on the women did not avoid hard work, vexations, or the shame and contempt of the world, and that Francis had rejoiced in this, so it is unlikely that Clare would deprive anyone in her community of the chance to serve. The existence of the serving sisters who went into Assisi and its environs, and the rule stipulating that one member of the community

---

† On February 17, 1958, Pope Pius XII declared Clare the patron saint of television in honor of this event. His other candidate had been the Archangel Gabriel because, much as television carried the nightly news, Gabriel brought word to the Virgin Mary that she would conceive and bear a Son. However, Clare won out because she experienced a "miraculous broadcast" when she had the experience of the Mass that she was unable to attend in person.

be constantly monitoring the door, indicates that enclosure at Saint Damian continued to be fairly open.

Serving sisters engaged with life. When Clare sent them out on a task, she told them to praise God when they saw the expansive trees, the glorious flowers, and verdant bushes. She told them always to praise God for all things, and to praise God in all the people they passed and animals they met. Cloistered by ill health, she must have missed seeing these sights for herself.

———❧———

In 1232, John Parenti resigned as minister general. Elias had by then spent five years as a simple Lesser Brother, albeit one who was in charge of building an enormous church, and he was again elected minister general. Despite the rule that only provincial ministers and custodians were allowed to vote for a successor, at the 1232 meeting in Rieti, the ordinary Lesser Brothers—especially those from the Italian peninsula who supported Elias—made their wishes known. Elias warned them that he was unworthy of the honor. He said that because of his poor health he would not strictly observe the rule. He would have to eat good food to keep his strength up, and when he travelled he would ride a horse. Possibly aware that he had no one to guide him spiritually as Francis had, he stated clearly that he would not be able to set a strict example for them.

Again in turmoil, the brothers referred the matter to Gregory IX, who perhaps welcomed the prospect of a minister general who was capable of settling complicated matters. He approved the election of Elias. Thus Elias was put in charge not only of those who wanted him to be minister general, but of the leaders of the various provinces and communities who objected to him. John Parenti, who may have triggered the untimely election by announcing his resignation two years before his full term ended, retired to Sardinia, where he stayed for the remaining ten years or so of his life.

During the time that Elias was out of office he had won back the hearts of the lay brothers. He had also mended his frayed relationships with Leo and Giles. For all that Elias was still willing to foster the growth of the order in the ways that the church encouraged, he wanted all the brothers to believe in the emotional and spiritual benefits of the life of poverty that Francis had espoused. Above all, he wanted newcomers to love and revere Francis as those who had lived with him at Rivo Torto had done.

Several new accounts of Francis's life were circulating in the early 1230s. One was not totally reverential. This was *The Versified Life of Saint Francis* by Henri d'Avranches, a poet born in Normandy around 1180, who had won favor at the English court. By 1228 he was with Gregory IX at the Lateran Palace. There he became known as "the poet of courtroom debate" because he was able to summarize points of canon law in verse. Henri's verses were cited in legal deliberations, including one that selected the Archbishop of Canterbury. Gregory enlisted Henri in his effort to solidify Francis's stature as an important saint, and commissioned Henri to put Thomas of Celano's life of Francis to verse. The poet felt free to digress, going so far as to describe Francis as greater than Alexander the Great or Caesar, but also to mock the naïveté of Francis's good will and trust in others. Henri could not have dared to be so bold, nor would these thoughts have been circulated, if the pope had not shared that sentiment, which was held by many in the curia.

Another author, Julian of Speyer, chapel master and director of young brothers in Paris, composed hymns and chants in honor of Francis and a brief biography based on Thomas's work. These were included in the office, or daily prayers, of the priests in the order. With learned brothers in every community reciting Henri's verses and reading Julian's text, Thomas's foundational portrait was being eclipsed. Elias wanted a life of Francis to foster Francis's devotion to poverty, simplicity, and joy in a new work that the brothers could carry with them and reread frequently. He called on Thomas of Celano to abridge his volume into nine parts or readings. This was reproduced for each brother in 122 bound parchment folios without a cover. The copy that was discovered in 2014 was, in the words of Jacques Dalarun who helped bring it to light, "crumpled, stiff, weather-beaten and stained...the image of Franciscan simplicity and poverty."

Church politics affected Thomas's narrative. He omitted the story of Bishop Guido's covering the naked Francis with his mantle after Francis rejected his father, possibly to sidestep the issue of whether the Lesser Brothers should be submissive to local authority. He did not mention the encounter with the leper that in his last testament Francis described as the turning point of his life and which Thomas had featured in his first work. The care of lepers was no longer a focus of the Lesser Brothers.

More significantly, given that Elias fought to maintain the importance of lay brothers like himself, Thomas emphasized that in the golden early days when Francis had only a dozen followers, their number included only a few priests and was a brotherhood of lay men. The book indicates that Elias was now generous to his onetime foes. Thomas wrote that John Parenti never transgressed an iota in his observance of the rule or of evangelical perfection. Most telling of all, in a sign that Elias and Leo had reconciled, Thomas included Leo by name and described him and Angelo Tancredi as "who among all were most dear" to Francis. The "holy conduct and magnificent life" of the "poor ladies of Saint Damian" are mentioned only briefly, with the explanation that only a future work and additional time could do them justice.

That these brothers were again at peace with one another as Francis had wished surely heartened Clare, but her joy at Elias's return to authority had to be greater still. She might defy the pope, but she was loyal to her friends. From the time when Francis appointed him to lead the brothers, Elias had been steadfast in his support of her, even to the point of forcing Francis to visit Saint Damian despite his rules that discouraged contact with women. Quite possibly during his time out of office Elias had found ways to support and encourage the women's communities in Umbria, notably Spello, Foligno, and Perugia. He was not only Clare's friend and defender; he was a partner in planning for the good of Saint Damian and all women who wanted to follow Francis. Elias was determined to nourish Francis's ideals, including the emphasis on poverty, the predominance of laymen, and the connection to women's communities, even as he followed Gregory's wish that the order grow in new ways that would renew the church.

However, Saint Damian continued to be reconstructed. Gregory's rules required more rooms, additional walls, and a stronger lock on the door. There were also to be a more substantial hearth, a refectory where the nuns could take their meals, and individual small cells where each woman could sleep. When they all lived in one dormitory and Clare lay awake in her ceaseless prayers, she could hear the others breathing. Their separate inhalations united into one in common spirit. Each cough, snore, and footstep was as identifiable as a face. Now each one lay alone and apart, and such isolation may have felt like separation from God. Renovations were so extensive that the commune of Assisi was persuaded to contribute money for them.

Possibly because of this disruptive remodeling, Clare sent many of her companions to other houses, either with the pope's approval or his total lack of knowledge. She dispatched capable women who were committed to her and her ideals and whose very being was a testament to the life of poverty, service, and engagement that Francis had given them. Installing women from Saint Damian in his new convents may have lent credibility to the idea that the order founded by the former Cardinal Hugolino had its origin in the sainted Francis, but Clare's capable delegates had little experience with the new rule. They had no guidance to offer other than that of Francis and Clare. A document written by Gerald, the bishop of Trent on Sept. 8, 1229 provides evidence that convents of Poor Ladies in Assisi, Perugia, and Siena were allowed to reject endowments for their support. Quite possibly other communities did so without formal permission.

Clare sent Balvina di Martino to Arezzo; another Balvina to Spello; Benedetta to Siena and later to Spello; and Lucia of Rome, who at that time was probably an adolescent under the guidance of another companion, to establish a community at Cortona, where Elias had done his penance. At great personal cost Clare assigned her sister Agnes to one of the other convents, probably Monteluce in Perugia. Either would probably have preferred the physical agony of having a limb torn away to the emotional torments each endured at their separation. In an undated letter written while the pain of parting was still fresh, Agnes wrote "...I am almost unable to speak because I have been physically removed from you and my other sisters with whom I had hoped to live and die in this world. The distress has a beginning, but it knows no end. It never seems to lessen, it always gets worse... I believed that we who have one and the same flesh and blood would be buried in the same grave. But I see I have been deceived."

Turning to brighter news, she wrote that she had found harmony in the community and no factions, which surprised her, and that the women wished to follow Clare's precepts. In the final passage, Agnes affirmed that the pope had agreed to their position on the ownership of property. They would not be required to accept it. Gregory IX had granted them the privilege of poverty June 16, 1229.

Agnes closed by asking Clare to have Elias visit her more often because he brought her consolation. This request underscores that the two were in frequent and happy contact. Each was one of Francis's closest and most valued followers and thus members of a group that had been shunted aside after Francis's death. If nothing else, as a man who could understand varying points of view and make people feel he was addressing their needs, Elias would have been sympathetic to Clare's concerns and sought a way to resolve them.

But unknown to them, a new partner in fidelity to poverty was emerging some three hundred miles to the east. In 1234, the Bohemian princess Agnes had with great pomp and ceremony joined the Poor Ladies of Saint Damian, lending it honor and prestige. Now in Prague, she was the abbess of Gregory's newest convent, and was reading Thomas's first life of Francis. In it she discovered Clare. Her surprise at this remarkable life would have consequences that would shake and vex the papacy.

Only a year earlier, the Lesser Brothers had arrived in Prague. It was a city divided into two spheres by the Moldau River. On its high western bank, the castle of the ruling Premysild dynasty encompassed, besides tapestried living quarters, a cathedral, a basilica, and a church. Across the Judith Bridge, a feat of engineering in stone, the commercial area thrived with merchants of many nations and growing numbers of German settlers who were introducing new methods of construction and their language. Here King Otakar I gave the brothers the Saint James Monastery for their residence.

Agnes was the youngest daughter of Otakar and his second queen, Constance of Hungary. From her birth in 1211, just before Clare joined Francis, she had been a pawn in the game of strategic royal alliances. Her father was an imperial elector and an adept politician who used the rivalry of the various claimants to the title of Holy Roman Empire to his advantage. He achieved the status of king with the right of his sons to succeed him and he launched Bohemia's golden age. Otakar entrusted Agnes to Premonstratentian nuns, whose good will he valued because they owned extensive farmlands. When Agnes was nine, around 1220, he betrothed her to the son of the Holy Roman Emperor Frederick II, and she was sent to join the boy, the future German King Henry VII, who was her age, at the court of Duke Leopold of Austria. That betrothal was aborted when

Henry married Leopold's own daughter instead. With that, Agnes's father wanted to affiance her to Henry III of England, the son of King John, who had been forced to sign the Magna Carta. By this time Agnes was in late adolescence and the widowed Holy Roman Emperor Frederick II himself sought her hand.

As an eastern European of Slavic descent, she might have had dark blonde hair, milk-white skin, wide almond-shaped eyes, and a firm jaw strengthened by her growing will. She wanted no part of this imperial marriage and she appealed to Gregory IX to obtain a release from the engagement so that she could devote her life to God. The pope was only too happy to deprive his enemy Frederick of an important alliance with the rulers of Bohemia and he complied. Adopting a diplomatic and philosophical stance, Frederick declared that he would be offended had his rival been anyone but God. He married instead Isabella of England, sister of Henry III, and installed her in his harem along with women from Arab lands who were guarded by eunuchs from Africa.

Agnes found the simple ways of the Lesser Brothers so appealing that she endowed three buildings for their use. One was a hospital, another a dwelling for the brothers working there, and the third was a convent for the women's order that Gregory IX had founded but was now attributing to Francis and calling the Poor Ladies of San Damian. On June 11, 1234, Agnes and seven other noblewomen entered this convent. They followed its rules with devotion until Agnes discovered Clare and her community in the biography of Francis. Thomas of Celano wrote that Francis himself had inspired her to leave her own noble family, and that she was "the most precious and the firmest stone" of the order of Poor Ladies. Thomas said that humility and mutual charity reigned in her community of more than forty women. Agnes learned that some had spoken aloud so seldom that their tongues and throats could barely make a sound. They had barely enough food and clothing to meet their most minimal needs. Thomas wrote that Pope Gregory, when he had been Bishop of Ostia, had given his form of life to Clare's community. But if this was true, if Saint Damian and Prague were in the same order, how could the women of the Prague convent be living a more comfortable life, with each possessing two tunics and living on revenues from the hospital that Agnes had founded?

Agnes could also have confirmed with the Lesser Brothers in Prague that Clare's way of life was quite different and more rigorous than the one that the pope had presented to her. She decided that if Clare was so exemplary, Agnes and her community should follow her. With the help of sympathetic Lesser Brothers, Agnes may have opened communications with Clare directly in a lost letter. But however Clare, supposedly sealed away from the world in her cloister, learned that Agnes had established a community that intended to follow Francis, she took decisive action. In the summer of 1234, soon after Agnes took her vows, she sent the Bohemian princess a letter of welcome to the path of poverty and humility. She introduced herself not as the abbess, but as the servant of the enclosed women. She saluted Agnes as the daughter of the king of Bohemia and as one who had chosen the Lord above all others, including the "illustrious" emperor.

Her entire letter was a hymn to poverty. In saying that renunciation of material goods fostered strength, she drew on an often-cited image from Saint Jerome of a naked combatant: "You also know that one who is clothed cannot fight another who is naked, because she is more quickly thrown who gives her adversary a chance to get hold of her." She counseled steadfastness in serving the Lord without the distractions and corruption of the material world, and she closed by urging Agnes to pray for her and for the women at Saint Damian.

Clare's words were phrased in accomplished Latin and her style was fluid and more literary than that of Francis. Given that Clare "had never studied letters," according to one of her companions, she had not learned to read and write, and Francis's distrust of study would have discouraged her from taking it up. While she would have known words and phrases of Latin from the Mass, she probably dictated her letter to someone who had the ability to translate it into Latin. Such near-simultaneous translation was expected of scribes in the Middle Ages. The style was also consistent throughout her four letters to Agnes that have been discovered, which indicates that one trusted person served as her secretary for this important correspondence from 1234 to 1253, much as Leo had assisted Francis in his letters in the last years of his life.

Along with her letter Clare bestowed treasured gifts. These included a scarf that Francis had wrapped around his head, a bowl from which he ate, and a drinking glass that had touched his lips. That Clare surrendered these items, probable souvenirs of Francis's final stay with her, indicates the degree to which she honored Agnes and how far she was willing to go to gain her good will. Clare did not mention Francis by name, but given that she stressed the importance of poverty, she may also have included a copy of the form of life that Francis had written for Clare's community on his final visit to them. Clare sent these materials northward in the hands of faithful Lesser Brothers who were journeying that way, possibly making their return trip to Prague.

By this point Gregory IX was spending time in his papal residence in Assisi, possibly musing on the ways his reign was vexed. In the days of Innocent III and Honorius III, the pope was the ultimate arbiter of every legal issue whether it directly affected the church or not. As Cardinal Hugolino, Gregory IX had helped both of them centralize power. This control of every episcopal office meant that huge sums of money flowed to popes and cardinals and their families grew in wealth and status. But now the power of the papacy was counterbalanced by Frederick II, who was not only the Holy Roman Emperor ruling over German territories but through his mother was also heir to Sicily and the southern end of the Italian peninsula.

Frederick routed Gregory from Rome in early summer 1234, just a few months before Gregory issued the Decretals, his most enduring accomplishment, the codification of authoritative decisions in canon law. Compiled on his orders by his chaplain and confessor, the Spanish Dominican brother Raymond of Penyafort, this collection remained in use for nearly seven hundred years, until just after World War I. The significance of the Decretals is such that when the US Capitol Building was remodeled in 1950, a marble relief portrait of Gregory IX was one of twenty-three installed over the gallery doors of the House of Representatives to commemorate lawgivers. This same honor was awarded to Innocent III in recognition of their preserving "the remnant of Roman law during the Dark Ages."

Codifying law was easier than controlling people, including women. The more Gregory learned of Saint Damian, either from his retinue or the Lesser Brothers, the more he felt uneasy over the future of those living in poverty. The Lesser Brothers were not the only male religious order that had scant interest in supporting their sisters in Christ. In 1228, the Cistercians and Dominicans had passed legislation in which they rejected assuming responsibility for nuns, although individual members could accept limited assignments to help them. Gregory was convinced that the women would need regular income generated from land if they were to survive in relative stability.

He was also concerned that Saint Damian was welcoming visitors. A few weeks before Christmas 1234, while he was staying in Perugia, Gregory IX felt it necessary to remind Clare that he alone controlled who could enter her door. He sent her a letter saying that unless he had given his expressed permission, no one could call upon her, a sign that she was having communications of which he did not approve. But Clare may have been acting within the framework of his orders, for he had handed the care of Saint Damian to the minister general in 1230. The minister general was now Clare's friend Elias who may have allowed her to have visitors, including himself and those who were travelling throughout the world, including Prague.

Agnes of Prague was also vexing Gregory IX. In May 1235 the pope denied her request to forego the support she received from the Hospital of Saint Francis. In his letter *Cum relicta saeculi* he said that while he admired her desire for her community to follow the poor Christ as poor women, the arrangements they had already made continued to be in effect. He pointed out that Agnes herself had constructed the hospital on church land and it would forever belong to her convent. The two entities were effectively one and her convent would continue to share in the revenue from the hospital. A few months later, on July 25, he wrote insisting that Agnes had to use the gifts her mother and brother had given her.

The pope may have felt that he had gained the good will of Agnes of Prague because he had recently canonized her cousin Elizabeth of Hungary, which bestowed great honor on her family, but Agnes remained firm. Raised as the princess of Bohemia, she did not accept rebuffs. Instead, she sought Clare's advice about how to proceed.

Clare's counsel, again sent by letter, was tactical as well as spiritually supportive to keep Agnes strong and help her persevere in her fight for poverty, even in the face of the revenues and gifts that were being thrust upon her. She opened with the fervent wish that Agnes always live a life of the highest poverty, which she called the "one necessary thing," a phrase from Luke 10:42 where Jesus told Martha, who was busy serving food, that her sister Mary, who was listening to him, had chosen to do the one thing that was required. Clare also drew on Romans 14:13 and Psalm 49, as well as Francis's insistence that the things of the world are dust. Probably by dictating to a scribe, she gave her guidance that can be read as poetry:

"What you hold, may you hold,
What you do, may you do and never abandon.
But with swift pace, light step, unswerving feet,
    so that even your steps stir up no dust,

May you go forward
    securely, joyfully and swiftly
on the path of prudent happiness,
    not believing anything,
    not agreeing with anything
    that would dissuade you from this resolution
    or that would place a stumbling block for you on the way,
so that you may offer your vows to the Most High
    in the pursuit of that perfection
    to which the Spirit of the Lord has called you."

Furthermore, Clare told her to follow the guidance of Elias, whom she called "their venerable father," a title she had previously reserved to Francis. She urged Agnes to rely on him above all others. Clare's admonition can only be interpreted as urging her to disobey the pope: "If anyone would tell you otherwise or suggest something that would delay your perfection, or seem contrary to your divine vocation, even though you must respect him, do not follow his advice. But as a poor virgin, embrace the poor Christ."

Agnes followed through by using her status as the sister of a monarch whose help Gregory sought for an upcoming crusade. This brother, King Wenceslas, appealed to the pope on her behalf in a letter of February 2, 1237 that opened with an acknowledgment of the pope's past benevolence combined with a frank reminder of the influence he himself could wield. He said he was encouraged to write by the pope's earlier kindnesses to his sister as much as by the extensive temporal power he himself enjoyed through his kingdom, family, in-laws, and friends. He said that he would be at Gregory's service if he agreed to Agnes's request.

The pope, who now realized that Agnes did not keep herself cloistered from her brother, quickly agreed to her wishes. He capitulated in one of several letters he wrote in April 1237 from Viterbo that may have been delivered in a single packet. Gregory IX told her that the church had accepted the gift of her convent's land and that the hospital was now under his protection. He had entrusted it to the newly formed order Crusaders of the Red Star, who followed the rule of Saint Augustine. He soon wrote again with further clarification, allowing her to renounce the revenues of the hospital and effectively granting her the privilege of poverty. He also gave Agnes special permission to peer out from her interior cloister window five times per year to look upon the priest as he said Mass.

Rather than appease her, this encouraged Agnes to seek more changes to Gregory's rule. She wanted to more closely follow the actual practice at Saint Damian. Agnes sent Clare a letter, now lost, apprising Clare of the pope's concessions and asking her to send Francis's specific rules about fasting.

Clare rejoiced at Agnes's great progress. But in her response, she confessed that Agnes's success made Clare feel that she had been lacking in her own attempts. "In an awe-inspiring and unexpected way, you have brought to ruin the subtleties of our crafty enemy, the pride that destroys human nature, and the vanity that infatuates human hearts." Agnes might have expressed regrets over something because even in the midst of her enthusiasm Clare, using phrasing from Hebrews 1:3 and 2 Corinthians 3:18, urged her not to let bitterness or sadness overcome her: "Set your mind before the mirror of eternity. Set your soul in the brilliance of glory. Set your heart in the figure of the divine substance! And transform your entire being into the image of the Godhead Itself through contemplation." This is the message she would have proclaimed to the wider world if she had been allowed to preach, and it reveals the limitless refuge she found in God.

Clare's use of the popular spiritual image of the mirror, of which Bernard of Clairvaux was particularly fond, offered a way to picture the state of one's soul and improve it. Clare invited Agnes not just to praise God but to be caught up in him and to follow in the footsteps of the Mother of the Son of God, especially in poverty and humility, so that she could carry Christ in her soul as Mary had carried him in her body.

As for the practical matter of fasting, Clare offered Francis's plan for Monday through Sunday, Easter week, and Christmas. He had given the women, who were settled in one place, more precise rules about food than he had the brothers. But in a sign that she regretted the damage she had done to her own health, Clare cautioned Agnes to be prudent in her devotions. Over what was probably a period of months, Agnes then combined the rules that Clare presented with selections from the one that Gregory IX had given her into a new rule for Prague. She sent this document to the pope for his approval in the hands of the prior of the Hospital of Saint Francis, the very hospital she had successfully asked to be severed from.

When Gregory read it, he focused, possibly for the first time, on what Agnes was presenting to him and the larger implications of her request became clear to him. Gregory responded with a crescendo of emotions in a packet of letters written in May 1238 from the Lateran Palace. First, on May 5, he allowed her to change her rules of fasting because she lived in a cold climate. In a second letter dated May 9, he claimed inaccurately that Francis had instituted three orders—Francis had established one, to which he admitted both men and women—and he implored Agnes to give him her devotion. He urged her to spend her time in praise of God and, by inference, not in designing other rules. His manner seemed weary, wounded, and almost pleading, but then two days later in his third letter, his tone completely changed. He seemed to have taken time to question Agnes's messenger, the prior of Saint Francis Hospital. He surely asked who Agnes had met with, which Lesser Brothers had been to Prague, and whom this prior had spoken with in Assisi. By the time Gregory IX wrote this third letter he knew that Clare had been advising Agnes to act contrary to his wishes, and was disobeying him, and that Elias had been a willing party acting against him to revive and encourage Francis's wholly inappropriate form of life for women. That Agnes's messenger could have held the title "prior," a term Francis strictly forbad because he said that all his followers were minor, meaning lesser, shows how Francis's wishes had been brushed aside.

It was clear that Agnes had composed her own rule, a rejection of his own, using documents that he regarded as illicit, including a copy of Francis's written rule for Saint Damian. She could have obtained this only from Clare, who must have dispatched it to Prague, although she was supposed to have withdrawn from the world. He took note that Clare considered Elias's advice to be more valuable than his own and that she was still living by Francis's guidance, despite the fact that she had taken a vow to live by the rules of his order in exchange for the privilege of living in poverty. Besides interfering with his plans to establish safe, secure convents for women, Clare was meddling in his dealings with the royal house of Bohemia. Gregory IX had enough. He commanded Agnes to accept his rule and be done with the matter.

He wrote Agnes that she should accept his authority with a devout heart and follow it with zeal, especially since her purpose was to serve God. He supported this idea by belittling Clare. He told Agnes that the guidance that Francis had given to Clare was pap, a milk drink, rather than solid food. Clare, Gregory wrote, had agreed to set aside Francis's "formula." Her community now followed the same rule required of all the women in the order. To do other than to follow the one rule he gave the women to unite them would invite dissention. He said that anyone who suggested doing anything else lacked sufficient knowledge. What was important, he told Agnes, was to please God, to be acceptable to him as pope, and to benefit her community. She must diligently observe his rule because the one that Francis had created no longer existed. With a note of sarcasm he said, "It is not observed by the oft-mentioned Clare, her sisters, or by others." Unasked, he absolved Agnes from any promise to follow the rule of Francis, and he closed by telling her that if in future she wanted to relax any the burden of his rule, he would consent. By implication, she was not to make his rule more arduous.

At this same time, he grew so concerned over the "destitution" of the women living near Perugia at Monteluce that he offered an indulgence of forty days, or a reduction of forty days from the time they would spend suffering in purgatory before they were worthy to enter heaven, to anyone who would contribute money to their support. Thus he rescinded their privilege of poverty that had so pleased Clare's sister Agnes. He may have attempted to bring Clare into line as well by bestowing property on Saint Damian.

If he had ever trusted that the pious, respectful Clare would submit to his will, he should have known better by this point. He may well have tried to impose property on her because in 1238, through an agent, she transferred a building and land situated along the Tescio River from her community to the Church of Saint Rufino. Among the women listed on the document of sale was a Pacifica, who was probably Clare's companion from childhood, a Beatrix, who might have been her younger blood sister, and a Praxeda, who was possibly the recluse from Rome. A few months after receiving Gregory's letter rejecting the rule she had proposed, Agnes of Prague resigned as abbess of her convent. On December 18, 1238, as if to underscore his displeasure, Gregory rescinded any concession he had ever given to the Prague community on fasting. He said they must follow only the rule that he had originally approved for them. This letter closed as had his other directives: "It is not permitted for anyone to infringe upon this statement of our decrees or for anyone to oppose it with boldness. If anyone presumes to attempt this, let him know that he will incur the wrath of Almighty God and his Apostles, Peter and Paul."

The sequence and means through which "the oft-mentioned" Clare received news of all this is unknown. Letters and oral reports surely arrived through trusted brothers travelling the seven hundred miles between Prague and Assisi. Hearing the pope describe Francis's treasured rule as "a milk drink," may have inspired the vision that Clare related to her companions Filippa, Cecilia, and Balvina. In this dream state she was rushing up a staircase bringing a bowl of water to Francis, along with a towel so that he could dry his hands. When she reached him, Francis uncovered his breast and said, "Come, take and drink." After she finished sucking his nipple, he told her to drink again. What she tasted was sweet beyond description. His nipple remained between her lips until she put it in her palm. Holding it, she saw it was golden and so bright that she seemed to be looking in a mirror. Her allegiance to Francis was unchanged.

$$\overline{15}$$

Darkness Falls

T HE DEATH OF FRANCIS, however it grieved those who had loved
him, had less impact on his closest followers than events that
happened in Paris, a city he never visited, in the last decade of his life.
Francis had set aside his own desire to go to France in the autumn
of 1217 at the urging of Cardinal Hugolino who warned him to
stay close to home so he could deal with those in the curia who dis-
approved of his order. Francis complied with regret and appointed
Pacifico to lead a small party there. They travelled past ripened fields
where farmers were harvesting cereals and grapes until they reached
Vézelay where tradition says that a few brothers remained. Pacifico
and the rest continued on for one hundred forty miles to the western
bank of the Seine River and the town of Saint Denis. Filled with
wooden houses, markets, and workshops, Saint Denis was celebrated
for its fairs and festivals, but even more for its magnificent, massive,
light-filled cathedral with buttresses that flew down from exterior
walls to root the edifice to the earth. Completed seventy-five years
earlier by Abbot Suger, the cathedral of Saint Denis had become
the spiritual center of France and the model for the architects of the
Cathedrals of Notre Dame in Paris and Chartres.

The hospitable Benedictines gave the Lesser Brothers shelter in
a house behind the small Church of Saint Peter northeast of the
basilica. From there, Francis's men went out preaching and begging and eventually made their way south to the Île de la Cité and

the growing city of Paris. Its streets were little more than passages between buildings, many of which ended in culs-de-sac, others of which were crammed with tables set up by merchants to display their wares. There was too little open space to allow a preacher to gather much of a crowd, yet the earnest Lesser Brothers with their belts of knotted rope became a familiar presence on unpaved ground that was dusty when dry and otherwise muddy.

But if the people welcomed the brothers to France, its bishops did not. On June 11, 1219, while Francis was still in the Holy Land, Pope Honorius III had written a letter *Cum dilecti* to all prelates throughout the world saying that the Lesser Brothers were approved by the Roman Catholic Church and beseeching and commanding them to treat Francis's men kindly. However, many French bishops banned them from their dioceses. A year later, on May 29, 1220, the pope wrote a second letter, *Pro diletis*, to the French, reminding them of his previous missive and saying that he had received reliable reports that they were ignoring his wishes. He said that henceforth they were to welcome the Lesser Brothers, whom he pointedly referred to as an order, an indication that they did exist within the approved guidelines of the Fourth Lateran Council.

When Pacifico left Saint Denis in 1223 to be with the ailing Francis at Portiuncula, Gregory of Naples succeeded him. Paris had become the recognized center for the teaching of theology. Pope Innocent III himself had studied there under the master theologians Peter of Corbeil and Peter the Chanter. He looked to such scholars to preserve and disseminate the orthodox dogma of the Roman Catholic Church.

Although Francis created a movement of lay persons after he won approval from Innocent III, he welcomed priests like Leo and Sylvester. While such clerics were better educated than most people, they were not trained to debate the fine points of Saint Augustine's teaching, nor did they use logic to explain the love of God. Beginning as early as 1214, scholars, many of them ordained, joined the Lesser Brothers, including Thomas of Celano. However, Francis expected the scholar to abandon his study and logical arguments to take up the life of the poor Christ, just as he required a poor cobbler to set aside his trade.

Then when Francis journeyed to the Middle East and ceded control to Gregory of Naples, the sight of a Lesser Brother carrying or reading a book became more common. Gregory established the brothers' presence in two cities with great universities—in 1217 Bologna, which was known for the study of law, and six years later in Paris, which focused on the divine. Both were sites of intellectual ferment. To the relief of the papacy, which could trust only educated Lesser Brothers to preach to the faithful and serve as pastors, Francis's order grew through the addition of intellectual men who benefitted from the good will that the early brothers had earned while having an education that allowed them to expound on church teachings.

The intellectual framework of the new Lesser Brothers was scholasticism, a system that comprised learning, commentary, and disputation, and was everything that Francis was against. Learned brothers from the universities began to introduce it to Portiuncula when Francis was away in the Holy Land. Francis knew enough about this system to know he wanted no part of it—no commentary that was derived through conflict, logic, argument, or any eagerness to compare and challenge authority, or to uncover points of disagreement between learned texts. The command "Love one another" required no clarification and would only be weakened by discussion. His earliest followers knew this. Brother Giles once counseled a brother who wished to go to the University of Paris, "The height of knowledge is to fear and to love God. This is enough for you."

Master theologians of the university had no thought of setting aside their learning or their books. The most notable of these was the

Englishman Haymo of Faversham, a keen intellectual who was also recognized as a great penitent because everyone could see his hair shirt hanging around his knees. Moreover, he had so undermined his health by fasting and self-mortification that he was subject to debilitating chills. One night as he slept in Paris, he dreamed that he was back at Faversham, in his native Kent, praying before a crucifix when a cord descended from heaven, seized him and pulled him up to heaven. The next day in the street he saw a pair of Lesser Brothers with their knotted rope belts. Were these men to be his way to heaven? Was he meant to join this band of men?

He consulted with three other noted English masters, Bartholomew, Simon, and Simon of Sandwich, and persuaded them to ask the Lord while they were saying Mass to show them the surest route to their salvation. All received the message that the Lesser Brothers was the way. Even so, the masters sought guidance from Brother Jordan, the leader of Dominic's order, which was much closer to their own thinking because it consisted of ordained and educated priests. They had been in Paris since 1217 and were established at the university. Everywhere their order was becoming a rival to the Lesser Brothers. Hosts of scholars were joining them, and part of their appeal might have been that despite the vow of poverty, they were allowed to study at no expense while dedicating themselves to the glory of God. Certainly Haymo and his companions, as well as Brother Jordan, must have believed that the scholars would have a more congenial home with the Friars Preachers, but dreams like Haymo's carried great weight because they were viewed as the means through which God spoke to his people. After some reflection, Jordan told Haymo and his colleagues that he believed they were called to join the Lesser Brothers.

On Good Friday, April 12, 1224, at Saint Denis amidst great rejoicing, Gregory of Naples clothed the four Englishmen in the rough brown habits of the Lesser Brothers and received them into the movement of Francis of Assisi. Haymo then preached a sermon on Psalm 125 "...the Lord hath done great things for us: we are become joyful." Two days later, on Easter Sunday, Haymo asked and received permission to preach. His message so moved the people that for three days they flocked to him so that he might hear their confessions.

Haymo travelled from Paris to Portiuncula for the general chapter in May 1230. Thus he was present at the chaotic translation of Francis's remains. Haymo saw some things that pleased him, and others that did not. He was gratified that several Lesser Brothers were beginning to assume high offices in the church. The city of Assisi, which they had all but taken over, was a major pilgrimage site with the construction of the large Church of Saint Francis. Haymo was happy to see more brothers studying and fewer begging. Even if the friars did not own books, they still had use of them. Surely he took heart in seeing the house the commune had maintained at Portiuncula, which was still standing despite Francis's attempt to dismantle it stone by stone, and to see that the brothers were given decent if simple accommodations and rations of food.

But there were other things that concerned him, particularly the fact that uneducated laymen like Elias had at least as much influence, if not more, on the care of the order as the newer, well-educated men. He was encouraged when John Parenti, an educated layman, replaced Elias as Minister General. Parenti appointed Haymo to the delegation that asked Gregory IX to settle questions about the support of women's communities and whether or not the brothers were to honor Francis's last testament. But after John Parenti resigned, the brothers returned Elias to office in 1232. Civil leaders apparently agreed with their choice because they asked Elias to settle a dispute between the communes of Spoleto and Cerreto. But his main secular task was raising money to complete The Church of Saint Francis. The papacy had provided the initial funds and granted indulgences to all others who would contribute. Benefactors included Jacqueline de Settesoli, whose donations to the order over the years would be such that she herself would be allowed to be buried there. In 1232, to help meet additional costs of construction, the commune of Assisi forced its citizens to pay a tax on grain. Those who did not comply were banished. That same year Elias ordered the brothers to beg alms specifically for this project to venerate Francis. This culminated five years later in 1237 in his imposition of a high tax on each province to pay for the casting of five massive bronze bells. One who heard them pealing after they were installed described them as "filling the whole valley with their delightful harmonies."

Probably because of the state of his health, Elias did not travel farther from Assisi than Cortona forty-five miles to the northwest, but the pope wanted Lesser Brothers to act as his emissaries. Since Haymo had gained his confidence, Gregory IX sent him to Constantinople to end the schism between Rome and the Greek Orthodox Church. Like many others he failed, but he retained the good will of the pope. On his return to the Italian peninsula in 1234, the year Clare wrote her first letter to Agnes of Prague, Elias assigned him to teach theology to the brothers in Tours, which was then a backwater, where his influence would presumably be contained.

Another English scholar joined the Lesser Brothers in the person of Alexander of Hales. He was around fifty and renowned at the University of Paris when he joined them in 1236. After taking his vows, he taught his classes at the Franciscan monastery. Neither the university nor many of Francis's followers were happy with this arrangement. Nonetheless, every Franciscan province gained the right to send two learned brothers to Paris. Thus Francis's movement became known for its growing intellectualism and attracted those who wanted to study without paying onerous financial fees.

The year Alexander became a Lesser Brother, he visited Rome to attend the chapter meeting. He stopped in Assisi to introduce himself to Elias and to visit Francis's tomb and the new church that enfolded it. The scholastics called Alexander "Doctor Irrefragabilis," or "Impossible to Refute." He taught using Peter Lombard's twelfth century collection of the writings of the early church fathers rather than scripture itself, the first time that a book other than the Bible was used for theological study. Perhaps he drew on this when he gave Clare and the women of Saint Damian a spiritual talk.

Among his audience was Giles, who had no fear of speaking up, as even his superiors could learn to their detriment. He was known to declare that Paris, by which he meant intellectualism, was ruining the order. Whether Alexander ran on too long that day, or whether his theories seemed baffling and beside the point to an audience of people who lived through their hearts and not their brains, Giles decided to interrupt. "Stop, Master!" he cried from his seat. "I want to preach!" and so he did, briefly and with eloquence. He then invited Alexander to pick up where he had left off.

After the Irrefutable Doctor finished, Clare was profuse in her thanks, but not to Alexander. She was full of praise for Giles. Whether or not the Irrefutable Doctor understood her native Umbrian dialect, the Englishman must have discerned her preference for the unlettered layman. She did pay him one compliment, however. She commended him for shutting his mouth. It is written that she said, "This is what our most holy father Francis wanted, that a doctor of theology should have enough humility to be silent when a lay brother wished to speak in his stead."

Alexander's visit to Assisi, where he surely stayed in the new monastery that was still fresh with the smell of cured lumber and clean white plaster, gave him the opportunity to take the measure of Elias and find him wanting. He discussed his concerns, probably in Paris in 1236, with Brothers John of La Rochelle and Haymo of

Faversham, whom Elias had just passed over when appointing the provincial of England. Surely they wondered if God had called them to their ragtag order to guide it into better ways.

Starting around 1237, Elias himself grew reform-minded about the state of the brothers' souls. He sent visitators out to the provinces with the unwelcome and accusative message that the brothers must be faithful to the rule and be ready for their souls to meet the Lord. Mongol hordes were threatening Hungary and lands to the east, inspiring a heightened sense of coming apocalypse. Many were persuaded by the prophecies of Joachim of Fiore, a zealous Cistercian monk who before his death in 1202, prophesized that a new order would emerge in the last days to convert all pagans, Jews, and Greeks. Learned Lesser Brothers spread these ideas and Francis's men believed themselves to be the order that was foretold. The office of visitator, an innovation of the Cistercians, was not written into the Lesser Brothers' rule of 1223, and the men Elias sent were described as harsh, threatening, and vigilant lest anything be hidden from them. They felt free to dispatch brothers who disagreed with them or their methods to new communities. Resentment grew. Brothers from Saxony complained to Elias, who rebuffed them. They then went directly to the pope, as did delegations from England and France. Gregory IX, pointing out that they could not agree on exact charges, told them to meet a month before the chapter of May 1239 and come up with a plan for reforming the order. He soon sent the English Brother Arnulph, a priest who focused on the administration of the sacrament of penance, to help them organize themselves and set the stage for Elias's ouster.

Still, Elias seemed to continue to enjoy the confidence of Gregory IX. In early February 1238, before Gregory discovered Elias's collusion with Clare and Agnes of Prague, the pope sent him on a mission to the Emperor Frederick, who was in Cremora, two hundred miles northwest of Assisi. The emperor, determined to secure his rights in northern Italy, had defeated the Lombards on November 27, 1237 in the Battle of Cortenuova, but he could not hold on to his gains. The pope, seizing this moment when Frederick seemed weak, wanted the minister general to persuade him to end his military campaign. Elias, like other papal emissaries, failed. The pope excommunicated Frederick on March 20, 1239.

Two months later Gregory IX presided over the Lesser Brothers' general chapter meeting in Rome, attended by seven cardinals. Elias's opponents had organized themselves well. With Haymo as their chief spokesman and the Englishmen key among them, they accused him of living a lavish lifestyle, riding horses, and eating on golden dishes. They said that he was autocratic and did not travel to the various communities. The most significant charge was his cruel use of visitators. After Elias's supporters charged Haymo with lying, the pope rebuked them all for not behaving as religious men. Cardinal Raynaldo advised Elias to resign, which he refused to do. Gregory then dismissed him from office saying that the brothers seemed no longer to want him.

In his place the custodians and ministers elected Albert of Pisa, who was the first minister general to say mass for them. From that time forward, only clerics and not laymen could be elected to the offices of ministers or provincials, and they were to be men from the region rather than the Italians who had been favored. Albert appointed Haymo to succeed him as minister of England.

Elias withdrew to Cortona and, in a sign of how Francis's movement had fractured, as many as two-thirds of the brothers accompanied him. Surely these were mostly lay brothers, some as simple as Brother Juniper, who had come to feel unwelcome or lost under the growing control of the well-fed priests and scholars among them.

Elias continued to feel free to visit Clare and other enclosed women. For this, Gregory IX excommunicated him. On hearing this news, Giles threw himself upon the ground. "I want to get as low as possible," he said when asked why he was lying inert, "since Elias fell only because of his leap." "Let me lie," he often said afterwards, remaining a simple brother without responsibility for others. "If I do not rise, I cannot fall."

Elias took refuge with the emperor, possibly hoping to reconcile him with Gregory and succeed where he had failed before. In 1242 Frederick sent Elias, who once had been unable to travel far, to Cyprus and Constantinople. He may have had a dual mission: first, to foster peace between two rival Eastern emperors, and second, to heal the schism between the Greek and Roman churches. He achieved neither, but after Elias returned to Cortona in 1244 laden with relics, including a piece of the True Cross, its commune gave him and the Lesser Brothers land on which he built, with relative speed that drew on his past experience, a basilica with a double structure dedicated to Saint Francis. Albert of Pisa tried to make peace, but Elias had no interest in reconciliation. After Albert died in Rome on January 23, 1240 after only eight months in office, Haymo succeeded him. Elias, wearing a patched tunic and following Francis's rules, lived mostly as a hermit, as Francis himself often did.

Philip the Tall served as visitator to the Order of Saint Damian until 1246. That year, on a Sunday evening in July when Clare was well enough to walk, she was near the heavy door that locked her away from the world. Constructed according to Gregory's rules, it was of heavy wood, affixed with iron bars, and secured with a pair of locks with different keys. However, this defensive portal could not withstand the tampering of time. Succumbing to rot, the door separated from its hinges and fell on top of Clare, crushing her to the ground where she lay inert. Her companion cried out for help, and women came running to her side. Moaning and struggling, they finally succeeded in lifting the weight from her body. Clare looked up at them unfazed, took their hands, and rose to her feet as three Lesser Brothers labored to move the door out of the way. She brushed aside all concerns, saying that the door felt no heavier than a cloak. The open doorway showed the path to the city. Clare turned her back on it and walked inside.

The more the women of Saint Damian were forced to detach themselves from the world, the more they dwelled in the realm of spirit and saw increasing wonders. One night by making the sign of the cross over Amata, Clare cured her of a dozen years of suffering from dropsy, fever, and a distended stomach. Cristiana said that after having tried medicines, all ineffective, to cure her deafness, she went to Clare who touched the affected ear, at which point it began to clear so she could hear fully. In this manner Clare also cured a boy with a high fever who was the son of their agent for business matters. From Spoleto came a boy named Mattiolo who had pebble up his nose. No one had been able to dislodge it, but it fell to the ground when Clare blessed him. Perhaps a twenty-first century scientist could explain these events on a case by case basis but as it is, the explanation of Saint Augustine of Hippo will have to suffice. He said that miracles were not contrary to nature, only to what we know of nature.

———

On August 22, 1241, Gregory IX died in Rome, having effectively been a prisoner there for months as the forces of the emperor closed in. His passing effectively triggered a vacancy of twenty months in the papacy. Some religious women seized this interregnum as the opportunity to take control of their lives. Many, possibly inspired by the women Clare had sent to various convents, had already vexed him by belting themselves in knotted cords and walking barefoot in the streets, claiming that they belonged to the order of Saint Damian. Gregory tried to put a stop to this by writing bishops and archbishops that the only true members of the order were cloistered and could not be seen. He told the prelates to compel these impostors to put away their cords and habits. This was ineffective. Papal complaints about such women would continue for decades.

Once Gregory died, the nuns of Monteluce divested themselves of property that Gregory IX had forced upon them in 1237. When Pope Innocent IV was finally elected in June 1243, Agnes of Prague wrote him that her convent was finding it impossible to follow both the rule of Benedict and the form of life that Gregory had given them. Similar pleas came from communities on the Italian peninsula and from Barcelona and Salamanca in Spain, indicating that the women were managing to communicate with each other to mount a concerted resistance, possibly with the help of sympathetic Lesser Brothers. However, the new pontiff dashed their hopes. Born Sinibaldo Fieschi to a Genoese family that was influential in business and the church, Innocent IV was expert in canon law and had been a close associate of Gregory IX. In May 1244 he affirmed Gregory's directions and told the bishops to have the nuns reclaim the property they had renounced. A few years later in August, 1247 he tried to resolve matters by decreeing a new rule for the women himself.

Saying that he wished to restore the women's peace of mind, preclude the need for amendments, and answer their prayers, Innocent IV said that he would allow them to follow the rule of Francis. However, the "new" regulations he imposed, including enclosure, were the opposite of that. He relaxed fasting and otherwise attempted to include what he believed the women were actually doing, a difficult task since there was little uniformity. Finally, he put them under the direction of the Lesser Brothers, something that many men had been working to avoid. But his major mistake was tactical. He attempted to impose his rule without consulting Cardinal Raynaldo of Jenne, who continued in the role of protector of the women as well as the brothers. After a year of trying to placate the offended Raynaldo, Innocent IV announced that the nuns could chose to follow his own rule or the earlier one, and so his rule of 1247 was never formally implemented.

At this point Innocent IV was presiding over the church from Lyons. He so feared the growing power of the emperor in Rome that he had fled to France. On his way there he left the papal treasury for safekeeping with the Lesser Brothers in the secure lockbox Elias had constructed in the bell tower of the Church of Saint Francis. For six years Innocent IV lived in Lyons under the protection of King Louis IX. When he heard that Frederick had died in December 1250 at the age of 56, Innocent immediately prepared to return to Rome. While the papal residence in Rome was restored and renovated, he established his court in Perugia in early 1251. For the first time, having the pope nearby would come to favor Clare.

Cardinal Raynaldo had remained in Rome, but he joined Innocent in Perugia. In mid-September 1252, he visited Clare, bringing the Eucharist. She was believed to be on the brink of death, so much so that her blood sister Agnes had returned to share her final days. Raynaldo found that although Clare's health had deteriorated, her reputation had grown. Assisians believed she had saved their city and their lives.

In June, 1241, when imperial forces were marching down to Rome, soldiers under the command of Vitale d'Anversa encircled Assisi and prepared to attack. Clare summoned the women to her bedside, removed her veil, and covered her head with ashes. She then sprinkled ashes on every woman's head and told them to pray in the chapel for the deliverance of the city. As they did so, unknown to them, d'Anversa withdrew. Felice Accrocca suggests that Elias, who was then staying with the emperor, might have persuaded him to call off the siege, possibly after Clare got word to him. Whatever happened, Assisians believed that Clare had successfully interceded for them with the Lord.

The cardinal might also have heard of Clare's heroic deed that was supposed to remain secret in her lifetime. On a Friday in September 1240, the women of Saint Damian were shocked to find themselves face to face with Saracen soldiers dropping from their wall into their courtyard. The women screamed until their invaders were immobilized.

Hearing what the commotion was about, Clare fell forward on the floor, weeping and praying, "Lord, help these servants of yours because I cannot protect them. Defend the city of Assisi as well." At least one of her companions clearly heard a voice respond: "I will always defend you." She told them to carry her to the entrance of the refectory and to bring her the ciborium, the lidded goblet containing the Eucharist, the manifestation of the divine force that could save them all. She told them to have no fear because she would serve as a hostage. Then they carried her down to meet the Saracens.

If depictions in illustrated manuscripts of the period are to be believed, the intruders were dark and bearded, their heads wrapped in scarves or covered in pointed helmets, and they clutched daggers and scimitars. Whatever their intentions, Clare certainly expected the worst of them, but when she appeared, the men were possibly as taken aback as the women were. Before them was a lame woman close to fifty borne on a stretcher thrusting a small container at them. The Saracens departed at once, leaving the women surely as amazed as they were relieved.

One explanation for this strange occurrence is that they were soldiers of the emperor looking for Elias and mistook Saint Damian for Portiuncula. Another is that they were an advance party of scouts. Frederick had settled a large number of Saracens in the Sicilian town of Lucera and this party may have come from there. Although they seem to have meant no harm to the women, Clare's leadership and heroism were real. But if she had once repelled a party of marauding Saracens, now when she met with

Raynaldo she was in tears, overcome by the importance of what she asked of him.

For years she had treasured and kept safe the parchment on which was written the privilege of poverty that she had wrested from Gregory IX. But she knew that with Gregory gone others, such as a minister general or bishop, might challenge it. Wearing the nun's black veil and brown tunic, now shabby, that she had fought so hard to avoid, Clare asked Raynaldo to have Innocent IV confirm the privilege of poverty that Gregory IX had granted them. He agreed. From that moment, whether it was a deliberate act or not, Raynaldo, this kinsman of Gregory IX, became the instrument of undoing as best he could the rules that Gregory had imposed on Clare. Within a short period he gave his own approval of the privilege of poverty for Saint Damian itself and he persuaded Innocent IV to do the same. Clare had achieved her dearest wish. That gave her hope that she could achieve still more.

With Benedetta, who had unofficially taken over the duties of abbess, Leo, and possibly others, Clare discussed the development of a new rule for women who wanted to follow Francis and herself.[†] Now close to sixty, Clare had accepted the life of the cloister, but she hoped to foster a rich and loving life for women who dwelled within it.

In this "Form of Life for the Poor Sisters," returning to the name that Francis has given to their movement in its early days, she stated (despite credit that had been given to the late Gregory IX) that Francis had founded them. The document emphasized poverty and the

---

† Catherine M. Mooney has pointed out that no source contemporary to Clare stated that she herself had composed the form of life she so desperately wanted Innocent IV to approve. Only in the late nineteenth century did some scholars infer that Clare had done so. Subsequently, Clare has been described as the first woman to write a canonically-approved rule for religious women. More likely, her form of life, along with her final testament, were compiled from ideas she expressed verbally in her final months. See Mooney's *Clare of Assisi and the Thirteenth-Century Church*, pp. 161-196.

gospel of Jesus rather than enclosure and the rule of Saint Benedict. It was something of a patchwork, incorporating her commentary; some elements of the rule that Gregory as Cardinal Hugolino had given them, including the title abbess, which she did not apply to herself; and passages from the rule of Benedict. It said that only a Lesser Brother should serve as their visitator and she asked, as a favor, that their chaplain be from that order as well. Finally, she pledged that the community would be submissive to any cardinal protector the pope had appointed for the brothers. Cardinal Raynaldo again bowed to her wishes and approved this rule on September 16, 1252. However, both knew that she needed the pope's approval to make it binding.

Clare apparently sent a copy to Agnes of Prague. As far as is known, the two had not been in written communication for more than a dozen years. But it is likely that they had news of each other through the few but loyal friends who managed to visit them. In her final letter, Clare saluted Agnes as her favorite daughter and said that her delay in writing was due to the lack of messengers and the dangers of the roads, situations that could also refer to how the leadership of the Lesser Brothers had marginalized her since Elias's downfall. She praised the Brothers Amatus and Bonaugura whom she said conveyed her letter. Since these names mean "beloved" and "good wishes," she may have masked their true identities. Clare said nothing about sending a new rule, just as she had omitted mention of her gifts of Francis's scarf, bowl, and drinking glass from her first letter. Instead, her words were a loving farewell until they would meet before God.

As the months dragged on, the pope delayed in approving her rule. Clare told her companions that she hoped to place her lips upon the papal seal that confirmed it and then, on the following day, to die in peace. While she waited, she propped herself up in her bed, keeping busy with a task that had occupied her when she first came to Saint Damian: spinning thread on her distaff that the others wove and sewed into long tunics for priests to wear while saying mass. Some fifty sets of them were wrapped in silk or purple cloth and sent to churches in the surrounding area.

No accounts of these days indicate that John of Parma, the Minister General of the Lesser Brothers, came to call although he was popular with Francis's early followers and he encouraged poverty. Brother Niccolò, who was the bishop of Assisi and an adviser to the pope, did visit, as well as various cardinals. By now few in the curia would have known of her battles with the late Pope Gregory. No longer seen as a problem, Clare was revered as an aged holy woman and one of the last links to Francis, now dead nearly three decades, whose order was now a force in the world. Many who believed in the influential prophecies of the mystic and theologian Joachim of Fiore, saw Francis as "the other Christ," foretold to come in the last days. Of the brothers who went to Gregory IX nearly a quarter century earlier for clarification of their rule, Leo of Parengo was now Archbishop of Milan and Anthony of Padua had been canonized. Lesser Brothers were leading academics, many teaching the clergy in towns throughout the continent. At this point only men who could read and write were to be admitted to the order.

At the end of April 1253, Pope Innocent IV moved from Perugia to the papal apartments at Assisi. A month later, on May 24, 1253, he dedicated the Cathedral of Saint Rufino, and the double church that he was the first to call the Basilica of Saint Francis to signify its importance.

Now the pope visited Clare for the first time. He had found the Basilica of Saint Francis to be so plain that he ordered silk and gold embellishments to be added to it. What could he have thought of Saint Damian as he walked through its small dark chapel, which was as humble as a manger, and found Clare lying on a sack of straw? He did not grant approval of her rule that day, yet the encounter buoyed Clare. That evening she marveled that on that day she had received God in the Eucharist and had seen his representative on earth. She seemed to have made her peace with her life, with what she had tried to do, and with how, in many ways, she had failed. Her attention was on going to God. Whether or not she or Innocent made mention of the rule she desperately wanted approved is unknown. Perhaps she let the matter pass. In deciding what to do, the pontiff must have wondered whether his approval would foment discord with the brothers and with the other convents in the Order of Saint Damian. A secondary problem was its tone. Patched like the women's mantles, it was canonical in sections, conversational in others. As he continued to deliberate over the summer, Clare's condition worsened. Her sister Agnes would not be comforted and begged her not to leave her, but Clare told her that it was God's will and that he would console Agnes and take her to heaven not long after Clare.†

One Friday evening she began to murmur as if gathering courage. She urged her soul to depart her body in peace because the Holy Spirit, who had always guarded it, would guide it now. Filippa told one of the sisters with a keen memory to write down Clare's words on the Trinity. But Clare told them that they would remember them only as long as God permitted it. Over the course of seventeen days, starting in the last week of July, Clare ate nothing but she remained relatively strong. A Brother Raynado urged her to be patient. She told him in a strong clear voice that since she had come to know the grace of Jesus Christ through Francis, no pain had been a trouble, no penance a burden, and no weakness difficult.

---

† Agnes died the following November 16. Clare's other sister Beatrice is not mentioned as being at her deathbed, but she did testify before the papal commission that considered Clare for canonization. Beatrice died in 1260.

She asked Juniper, whose sometimes-bizarre behavior had by now earned him the nickname "Jester of the Lord," if he had any new messages from the Savior. He replied with words that were described to be "like burning sparks coming from the furnace of his fervent heart" and she was cheered. Feeling yet again that her end was near, she told the women to praise God and be true to poverty. As they struggled to remain calm and silent as Clare had taught them, Angelo Tancredi and Leo tried to comfort them. Angelo's presence was a sign of the tight binds among Francis's earliest and most devoted followers, no matter how the church or Lesser Brothers might view them. A few months before, on April 11, 1253, Angelo had been with Elias in Cortona when he died.†

The stamping of hooves and the neighing of horses transformed the mood from mournful to expectant. Papal messengers arrived with her new rule, now approved by the pope. Innocent IV had chosen to be compassionate. He did not admire Franciscan poverty, and he had less connection to Francis's movement than any recent pope, but Clare had touched his heart. After nearly a year's delay, knowing she was in her last hours, he granted her wish. However, he approved it for the inhabitants of Saint Damian alone and not for the rest of the women's order. As soon as he signed his bull of approval, *Solet annuere*, he sent it from his residence down to Saint Damian. Taking the scroll in her hands, Clare kissed it repeatedly. Weeping with joy, she said she was ready to die, and she waited for it, clutching the papal document. But the next morning, when Innocent IV himself appeared, she was feeling very much alive. Clare not only kissed the hand he extended, she kissed his foot, which she was able to do after he placed it upon a wooden stool. She had a final request. To the

---

† Philip the Tall is missing from accounts of these last days. During Clare's canonization process, Sister Cecilia refered to him as "of happy memory;" however, the meticulous Francis of Assisi Early Documents Volume I, page 204 says he died in 1259.

pope's astonishment, she asked him to forgive her sins. Saying that he wished he had as little need of pardon as she, he gave her absolution and he departed, leaving her in peace.

Clare surrendered her soul on Monday, August 11, 1253 as a weeping Leo kissed the foot of her bed. While her sisters sobbed and beat their breasts, the podestà, along with seven knights and a troop of soldiers, arrived to prevent thieves from spiriting her body away.

Two days later Innocent IV led the people of Assisi and his entire court to Saint Damian. One by one the cardinals were allowed to enter the room where she lay. As they filed by her corpse, they placed their rings of office in her dead hands to show their devotion and draw from her power.

Epilogue

CLARE WAS NOT to be buried at Saint Damian. As was the case with Francis, her body was carried to the safety of the Church of Saint George. Since word of her unique, approved rule was supposed to be shrouded in secrecy, Pope Innocent IV may have been surprised when Agnes of Prague requested his permission for her convent to follow it, but he granted it in the last months of his papacy. The community of Saint Damian remained cloistered but it relocated inside the city walls a few years after Clare's death. It exists today in the Basilica of Saint Clare as The Proto-Monastery of the Poor Clares of Assisi.

As for the Lesser Brothers, they continued to argue over the direction of their order until 1266 when Bonaventure, the minister general, a scholar, and future saint, produced a new life of Francis with few mentions of Clare. He then directed that all other written material about Francis be burned, including the first life by Thomas of Celano with its paean to Clare and the women of Saint Damian. However, Leo remained a living testimony to what had been. He filled scrolls with his recollections, some of which served as sources for Bonaventure's work. Before his death in 1271, Leo left them for safekeeping, not with the brothers, but with the convent of Saint Damian. However, they either disappeared or were incorporated into other documents.

More than six hundred years later, in 1893, the French Calvinist pastor Paul Sabatier wrote a biography of Francis that was the fruit of study, research, and skepticism rather than piety. Admiring Francis, he tried to establish him as the first Protestant. The church quickly placed his biography on its Index of Forbidden Books, but his research inspired Franciscans to begin a quest through cobwebbed library shelves for mislaid manuscripts that might reveal the historical Francis. Key ones surfaced. Not everyone, it seemed, had obeyed Bonaventure's order to destroy all documents. Scholarship and the written word, which Francis so distrusted, indicated that the story of Francis and Clare was not quite as it had been represented. Clare's defiance of the pope pierced through the story of her female passivity, like light through pin holes in a shade. Her character and her struggle, once known, can inspire others to persevere despite overwhelming odds.

What did Francis accomplish? Machiavelli wrote in his 1531 *Discourses on Livy* that, because Francis and Dominic had persuaded people to obey the church and not criticize what was evil in it, these saints had encouraged church rulers to behave as badly as they wished. Certainly, Francis did not take reformation as his task. While the church emphasized salvation from sin, he transformed lives by extolling the glory of God.

Early on, Francis captured the imagination of the Western world. Since his death he has spoken to every age, including this secular one, because of his appreciative attunement with the natural world, his esteem for the suffering and the discarded, and his distrust of affluence, which drove him to those who lived on the outskirts of society.

And the official story aside, what if the Roman Catholic Church had allowed Francis and Clare to serve God and humanity in their own way? What if a shrewd Cardinal Hugolino had not seen fit to make use of Francis, and wrest control of his movement away from him? Francis of Assisi would then have had the same impact as Dominic of Huesca, Peter Waldo, or another pious Italian merchant who helped the poor named Saint Homobono of Cremona.

Notes

Abbreviations

FAED: Regis Armstrong OFM Cap. et al. ed. *Francis of Assisi: Early Documents* Vols. I, II, III

CAED: Regis Armstrong OFM Cap. *Clare of Assisi, Early Documents*, Saint Bonaventure, N.Y: Franciscan Institute Publications, 1993

Habig: Marion A. Habig OFM ed. *St. Francis of Assisi Omnibus of Sources*. Quincy, Illinois: Franciscan Press, 1991

Chapter One

3   *illuminate the world* Regis J. Armstrong, CAED, pp. 152, 160

3   *her tiny feet* Chiara Frugoni, *A Day in A Medieval City*, University of Chicago Press, 2005; p. 12

4   *man of few words* Clare's lineage from Gemma Fortini, "The Noble Family of St. Clare," *Franciscan Studies*, Vol. 42, pp. 48-67

4   *heel of Italy's boot* CAED, p. 137

5   *thirtieth birthday* Arnaldo Fortini, trans. Helen Moak, *Francis of Assisi*, New York: Crossroad, 1981, pp. 108, 119

7   *Assisi tax rolls* Arnaldo Fortini, p. 148

7   *in relative peace* William Heywood, *A History of Perugia*, New York: G.P. Putnam's Sons, 1910, p. 34

7   *pope nor emperor* Ugolino Nicolini, *Scritti di Storia*, Napoli: Edizioni Scientifiche Italiane, 1993, p. 59–64

7   *and its debt* Nicolini, p. 333

7   *would have been like* Frugoni, p. 126

8   *never studied letters* CAED, p. 169

8   *prayers she said* CAED, p. 255

9   *not of noble birth* CAED, pp. 137, 141

9   *to be trustworthy* Nicolini, pp. 64–65, 70

11   *in Roman times* Arnaldo Fortini, p. 367

11   *were spent there* CAED, p. 184

12   *watchman recalled* CAED, p. 184

12 *to her skin* CAED, p. 184

12 *obligation to them was done* Caroline Walker Bynum, *Holy Feast and Holy Fast: The Religious Significance of Food to Medieval Women*, Berkeley: University of California Press, 1987

14 *speak out their consent* David Herlihy, *Medieval Households*, Cambridge: Harvard University Press, 1985, p. 81

15 *in abject apology* Marion A. Habig OFM, *Omnibus of Sources*, Quincy, Illinois: Franciscan Press, 1991, p. 486; Arnaldo Fortini, p. 335

15 *gurgles and pips* Habig, p. 1375; Clare's presence and reaction are surmised by the author

16 *the ridiculous Rufino* FAED III, pp.507, 620

17 *came to the city* CAED, p. 256

18 *short and dark* Irene Barbiera and Gianpiero Dalla-Zuanna, "Population Dynamics in Italy in the Middle Ages: New Insights from Archaeological Findings" *Population and Development Review*, Vol. 35, No. 2 (June, 2009), p. 375; "The relics of Saint Clare Exposed in the Basilica of St. Clare," http://www.assisisantachiara.it/wp-content/uploads/2016/10/Reliquie-sr.-Anastasia.pdf, p. 15

18 *five feet five* Steckel, Richard, "New Light on the 'Dark Ages': The Remarkably Tall Stature of Northern European Men during the Medieval Era." Social Science History. Vol. 28. pp. 211-229 https://www.researchgate.net/publication/240740622_New_Light_on_the_Dark_Ages_The_Remarkably_Tall_Stature_of_Northern_European_Men_during_the_Medieval_Era

19 *wandering preacher himself* André Vauchez, *Francis of Assisi*, New Haven: Yale University Press, 2012, p. 34

20 *restoration of the Church of Saint Damian* CAED, p. 182

20 *for fine ladies* FAED II, p. 83

21 *gift of building stones* Marino Bigaroni, "San Damiano," *Franciscan Studies*, Vol. 47, 1987, p. 73 et. seq.

21 *company of Clare's mother* CAED, p. 182

21 *time to act* CAED, p. 259

21 *able to push it open* CAED, p. 259

22 *Francis and to the church* CAED, p. 174

22 *protection of Francis* Maria Pia Alberzoni, "Clare and San Damiano Between the Order of Friars Minor and the Papal Curia," *Greyfriars Review*, 2006, Vol. 20, Issue 1, p. 3

22 *punished by excommunication* CAED, pp. 260, 174 footnote (a)

23 *about four miles away* CAED, p. 174

24 *by no means safe* CAED, pp. 279; 281

24 *resolve of its women* CAED, p. 281

25 *known as Agnes* "Chronicle of the Twenty-Four Generals," *Annales Franciscaines*, Vol. III, p. 175

26 *those of her cities* CAED, pp. 174, 184

Chapter Two

27   *her first marriage* Richard Trexler, *Naked Before the Father: The Renunciation of Francis of Assisi*, Los Angeles: Center for Medieval and Renaissance Studies, University of California, 1989, pp. 10, 26

28   *Church of Saint Paul* Arnaldo Fortini, p. 92

29   *wooden pickling tub* Encyclopedia Britannica https://www.britannica.com/art/interior-design/Late-medieval-Europe

31   *controlled the road* Arnaldo Fortini, p. 115

32   *uneven spaces* Attilio Bartoli Langeli, "Gli scritti di Francesco: L'autografia di un illiterus" *Frate Francesco d'Assisi*. Spoleto: Centro Italiano di Studi sull'Alto Medioeveo (1994) pp. 116–117

32   *Saint George in Assisi* Arnaldo Fortini, p. 95

33   *in the December Liberties* Arnaldo Fortini, p. 98

35   *all kinds of foolishness* Habig, p. 230

36   *there was a doubling* Ulf Büntgen and Willy Tegel, "European tree-ring data and the Medieval Climate Anomaly," 2011, https://www.researchgate.net/publication/228843243_European_tree-ring_data_and_the_Medieval_Climate_Anomaly

38   *to be your guide* Aron Ja. Gurevich, ed. Jacques Le Goff, "The Merchant," *Medieval Callings*, Chicago: University of Chicago Press, 1987, p. 245

38   *did not speak it well* FAED II, p. 73

42   *money purse* Arnaldo Fortini, p. 133, lyrics from James J. Wilhelm, *Lyrics of the Middle Ages: An Anthology*, New York: Garland Press, 1990, pp. 90, 119

43   *honored by all the world* Habig, p. 636

Chapter Three

44   *Vicar of Christ himself* Patrologiae cursus completus Vol. 214, p. 292

51   *called for fighting men* Donald E. Queller et al. "The Fourth Crusade, The Neglected Majority" *Speculum*, Vol. 49, Issue 3, July 1974, pp. 441-443

52   *was named a knight* Arnaldo Fortini, p. 180

52   *and for his knights* Jacques Dalarun, trans. Timothy J. Johnson, *The Rediscovered Life of St. Francis of Assisi Thomas of Celano*, St. Bonaventure University: Franciscan Institute Publications, 2016, p. 2

52   *he was not happy* Dalarun 2016, p. 3; Habig p. 233

52   *bringing out the vision* FAED II, pp. 70-71

53   *six Our Fathers* Henry A. Notaker, *History of Cookbooks*, Oakland: University of California Press, 2017, p.121

53   *people liked him* Habig, p. 230

53   *another had come out* Habig, p. 235

54   *would end up like her* Habig, p. 369

56   *workroom for inspiration* James Bruce Ross, *A study of twelfth-century interest in the antiquities of Rome*, undated, p. 310

56   *pulled him away* Dalarun, 2016, p. 23

57   *chapels and cemeteries* Herbert C. Covey, "People with Leprosy (Hansen's disease) During the Middle Ages," *The Social Science Journal*, 38 (2001), p. 317

59   *their hands in turn* Arnaldo Fortini, p. 206; Habig p. 900; James Walsh,
     Medieval Medicine London: A & C Black, Ltd, 1920 p. 181
61   *among these places* Dalarun 2016, p. 4; Habig p. 907
62   *upon her death* Trexler, p. 28
62   *Peter did this* Arnaldo Fortini, pp. 222, 226

Chapter Four

Main sources for the description of Rome are:

Richard Krautheimer, *Rome Profile of A City 312-1308*, New Jersey: Princeton
University Press, 1980

John Osborne, *Master Gregorius The Marvels of Rome*, Toronto: Pontifical Institute of
Medieval Studies, 1987

66   *who helped him* Arnaldo Fortini, pp. 243, 245; *Archivum Franciscanum
     Historicum* Vol. I, pp. 144–147
68   *first follower of Francis* Habig, p. 373; FAED II, p. 37
69   *shoes on his feet* FAED I, p. 201
69   *style of the leaders* Delcorno, p. 151
70   *went through the town* Habig p. 916
71   *food for all of them* Habig, p. 979
71   *superior holiness* Habig, p. 1834
72   *their neighbors* Habig, p. 921
72   *capable of lying* FAED II, p. 163; FAED I, p. 388
73   *sin as stuffing it* Habig p. 380
73   *published in 1950* Ancel Keys, et al. *The Biology of Human Starvation.*
     Minneapolis: University of Minnesota Press, 1950
75   *as a threat* Dalarun 2016, p. 27
75   *movement would grow* FAED II, p. 40
76   *a suitable way* Habig, p. 1313–1314; p. 1516
79   *to see the pope* Nicolangelo D'Acunto, *Il Vescovo Guido Oppure i Vescovi Guido
     Cronotassi episcopale assisana e fonti francescane"* Melanges de l'Ecole francaise
     de Rome. Moyen-Age, Vol. 108 (1996), pp. 500, 501
82   *break with Rome* Brenda Bolton, *Innocent III Studies on Papal Authority Pastoral
     Care* Aldershot: Variorum, 1995, p. 170
84   *the same bed* FAED I, p. 593

Chapter Five

86   *walk from Assisi* Habig, p. 264
86   *read it once* FAED II p. 311; FAED III p. 515
87   *chapel and four huts* Gregory Paul Caicco, (doctoral thesis, School of
     Architecture, McGill University, October, 1998) "Ethics and Poetics: The
     Architectural Vision of Saint Francis of Assisi" pp. 83–84
87   *planted a hedge* Caicco, p. 83; Habig, pp. 986, 991
88   *jar of oil* Habig, pp. 1178, 985

88 *bark and plants* Dalarun, p. 22
89 *had become obscured* Habig, p. 258–259; Carlo Delcorno, "Origini della predi-
    cazione francescana" *Francesco d'Assisi e francescanesimo dal 1216 al 1226* Assisi,
    p. 151; FAED III, p. 453
91 *joyful in the Lord* Habig, pp. 465–66, 467
91 *good for me* FAED II, p. 787
92 *martyrs of them* Vauchez, p. 98
93 *forest of junipers* Arnald of Sarrant, trans. Noel Muscat, OFM, *Chronicle
    of the Twenty-Four Generals of the Order of Friars Minor*, Malta: TAU
    Franciscan Communications https://books.google.com/books?id=BU-
    n9AAAAQBAJ&printsec=frontcover&dq=chron-
    icle+of+the+twenty+four+generals&hl=en&newbks=1&newb
    ks_redir=0&sa=X&ved=2ahUKEwiK7OvF7orxAhVtneAKHR-
    eCDcMQ6AEwAHoECAsQAg#v=onepage&q=chronicle%20of%20
    the%20twenty%20four%20generals&f=false ;Brother Juniper
93 *returned the animal* Habig, p. 514; FAED II p. 163
94 *service of Christ for a long time* Habig, p. 1011
94 *in 1289* FAED II, p. 103; Vauchez, p. 308
95 *stone pavement* Marina Righetti Tosti-Croce, "La chiesa di santa Chiara ad
    Assisi: architettura" *Santa Chiara in Assisi. Architettura e decorazione* Milan:
    Silvana, 2002, pp. 23-24
96 *Saint Damian and Portiuncula* Maria Pia Alberzoni, *Clare of Assisi and the
    Poor Sisters and the Thirteenth Century*, St. Bonaventure University: Franciscan
    Institute Publications, 2004, p. 38
96 *one of her cousins* CAED, p. 182
97 *holes and tears* Maureen C. Miller, *Clothing the Clergy: Virtue and Power in
    Medieval Europe 800-1200*, Ithaca: Cornell University Press, 2014, p. 141
97 *in his path* Catherine M. Mooney, *Clare of Assisi and the Thirteenth-Century
    Church*, Philadelphia: University of Pennsylvania Press, 2016 p. 25; Arnaldo
    Fortini p. 206
98 *secular clothing* Maria Pia Alberzoni, trans. Edward Hagman OFM Cap, "Clare
    and San Damiano Between the Order of Friars Minor and the Papal Curia,"
    Greyfriars Review, 2006 p. 8 fn 21; Mooney, p. 25; Arnaldo Fortini, p. 206
98 *as great delights* CAED, pp. 58, 146-7, 158
99 *mentioned above* FAED I, p. 594; Habig, p. 1604
100 *source of revenues* Arnaldo Fortini, pp. 367, 368
101 *resulting miracles* Arnaldo Fortini, p. 370
102 *stow away* Habig, p. 274
103 *see its sultan* Habig, p. 275
104 *for the spit* Habig, p. 548
105 *back in another* Habig, p. 480

Chapter Six

Main Sources for the environment of Rome are:

Brenda M. Bolton, eds. W.J. Sheils and Diana Wood, "Daughters of Rome" *Women in the Church*, London: The Ecclesiastical History Society, 1990

Bolton, *Innocent III Studies on Papal Authority Pastoral Care*, Aldershot: Variorum, 1995

Richard Krautheimer, *Early Christian and Byzantine Architecture*, New Haven: Yale University Press, 1986

Krautheimer, *Rome Profile of A City 312-1308*. Princeton, N.J: Princeton University Press, 1980

The Miracles of St. Dominic Narrated by Sister Cecilia: http://www.domcentral.org/trad/domdocs/0006.htm

Zoé Oldenbourg, trans. Peter Green, *Massacre at Montsegur; a History of the Albigensian Crusade*, New York: Pantheon Books, 1962

Jane Sayers, *Innocent III: Leader of Europe 1198-1216*, New York: Longman Group, 1994

111 *cooking on the street* Richard Krautheimer, *Rome Profile of A City 312-1308*, p. 285
113 *at the onlooker* Anne L. Clark, ed. Theodolinda Barolini, "Under Whose Care? The Madonna of San Sisto and Women's Monastic Life in the Twelfth and Thirteenth Century Rome," *Medieval Constructions in Gender and Identity: Essays in Honor of Joan M. Frerrante*, Tempe: Arizona Center for Medieval and Renaissance Studies, 2005 p. 30
116 *not at least in practice* Oldenbourg, p. 39
116 *accused of being a heretic* Habig, pp. 281, 428; FAED II p. 438
117 *fornication and abominations* Oldenbourg, p. 94
117 *has failed to do so* Oldenbourg, p. 95
118 *powerful and resonant* Simon Tugwell OP, *Early Dominicans: Selected Writings*, Mahweh, N.J.: The Paulist Press, 1986, p. 344
123 *From this couple* George L. Williams, *Papal Genealogy: The Families and Descendants of the Popes*, p. 21
123 *in Jacqueline's era* Ferdinand Gregorovius, *History of the City of Rome in the Middle Ages*, New York: Cambridge University Press, 2010, Vol. 4, p. 289
124 *in the Colosseum* David L. Bomgardner, *The Story of the Roman Amphitheater*, New York; Routledge, 2000, p. 222
124 *filorum meorum* Arnaldo Fortini, *Francesco d'Assisi e l'Italia del suo tempo*. Rome: Biblioteca di Storia Patria, 1968, Book II p. 453
125 *visiting near Gubbio* FAED II, p. 321
125 *with great joy* FAED I, p. 249
125 *after Francis's death* FAED II, p. 462
126 *one named Praxeda* CAED, p. 111

Chapter Seven

Main Sources for the Fourth Lateran Council are:

Jessalyn Bird et al. (eds) *Crusade and Christendom: Annotated Documents in Translation From Innocent III to the Fall of Acre, 1187-1291*, Philadelphia: University of Pennsylvania Press, 2013

Medieval Sourcebook: Twelfth Ecumenical Council: Lateran IV 1215

http://sourcebooks.fordham.edu/halsall/basis/lateran4.asp

Jane Sayers, *Innocent III: Leader of Europe 1198-1216*, New York: Longman Group, 1994

127 *presented to Francis* Habig, pp. 293-294
127 *was a zither* https://en.wikipedia.org/wiki/Perdigon#/media/File:BnF_ms._12473_fol._36_-_Perdigon_(1).jpg
127 *he was not happy* Habig, pp. 449, p. 660; https://www.treccani.it/enciclopedia/beato-pacifico/
129 *points out* Vauchez, p. 62
129 *peacock's glorious tail* Habig, p. 450
130 *as long as Francis lived* Habig, p. 458-459
131 *ate a newborn lamb* Vauchez, pp. 271-273
132 *a man of God* Habig, pp. 58, 277-280, 722
134 *recalled him to the Lateran Palace* Habig, p. 1608
134 *Pentecost and Michaelmas* FAED I, p. 580
135 *to live in their own households* Habig, p. 945
136 *honor and obedience* Arnaldo Fortini, pp. 255, 257; D'Acunto, p. 504
136 *friends in Liège* FAED I, p. 578
136 *to be consecrated* John V. Tolan, *Saint Francis and the Sultan: The Curious History of a Christian-Muslim Encounter*, New York: Oxford University Press, 2009, pp. 20-21
137 *spiritual things"* FAED I, p. 579
138 *they deserve."* FAED I, p. 579
139 *quince wine* Vauchez, p. 65; Habig, p. 1602
139 *little bird* Habig, p. 948
140 *as important as preaching* Placid Hermann trans., *XIIIth Century Chronicles*, Chicago: Franciscan Herald Press, 1961, p. 21-23
141 *all were fed* FAED III, p. 51; CAED, p. 161
141 *brethren demonstrate it* FAED III, p. 813
142 *woman's sole* CAED, pp. 148, 160
142 *to fill it* CAED, pp. 140, 271
143 *night's rest* CAED, pp. 160, 272
143 glory from men "The Golden Sayings of Giles of Assisi," Intro xix, https://archive.org/stream/thegoldensayings00robiuoft/thegoldensayings00robiuoft_djvu.txt
143 *animal dung* Habig, p. 418; FAED II, p. 290

144 *section of the city* Christopher Kleinhenz, *Medieval Italy: An Encyclopedia*, London: Routledge, 2004, Florence entry; Franklin Toker, *On Holy Ground: Liturgy, Architecture and Urbanism in the Cathedral and the Streets of Medieval Florence*, Harvey Miller Publishers, 2009, p. 135

145 *Cardinal Priest of Saints John and Paul* Werner Maleczek, *Papst und Kardinalskolleg von 1191 bis 1216*, Wien: Verlage der Osterreichischen Akademie de Wissenschaftern, 1984 p. 130

147 *fruit of the city of Rome* Thomas de Cantimpré, trans. Hugh Feiss, OSB *Supplement to the Life of Marie d'Oignies*, Toronto: Peregrina Publishing, 1990, p. 22

148 *left the peninsula* FAED II, p. 216

149 *for an answer* FAED I, p. 559

149 *to keep it* Hermann, p. 23

149 *November 30* Hermann, p. 41

150 *fierce inhabitants* Hermann, pp. 12, 21–23

Chapter Eight

A major source for this chapter is James M. Powell, *Anatomy of a Crusade, 1213-1221*, Philadelphia: University of Pennsylvania Press, 1990

152 *wrathful God stood by* Bird, Jessalyn et al. (eds) *Crusade and Christendom: Annotated Documents in Translation From Innocent III to the Fall of Acre, 1187-1291* Philadelphia: University of Pennsylvania Press, 2013, p. 126

152 *read their psalters* Arnaldo Fortini, p. 121; Salimbene, Joseph L. Baird, Giuseppe Baglivi, and John Robert Kane. *The chronicle of Salimbene de Adam* Binghamton, N.Y: Medieval & Renaissance Texts & Studies, 1986, p. 75

153 *to join them* Hermann, p. 136

153 *damage done* Arnaldo Fortini, pp. 125, 395

155 *expanse of waves,* Richard Unger, "Difficult Sources: Crusade Art and the Depiction of Ships," Gertwage, Ruthy and Jeffreys, Elizabeth (eds), *Shipping, Trade and Crusade in the Medieval Mediterranean*, New York and London: Routledge, Taylor and Francis Group, 2012, p. 85

157 *to the Crusaders* Paul Moses, *The Saint and the Sultan The Crusades, Islam and Francis of Assisi's Mission of Peace* New York: Doubleday Religion, 2009, p. 109; Powell, p. 161

157 *as interpreters and teachers* Steven Runciman, *A History of the Crusades*, Cambridge University Press, Vol. 3, 1954, p. 144

159 *that man* Geraldine Heng, *Empire of Magic*, New York: Columbia University Press, 2003, pp. 451-452

159 *sultan's offer* Thomas C. Van Cleve, "The Crusade of Frederick II," *A History of the Crusades Vol. 2 The Later Crusades, 1189-1311*, eds. R. L. Wolff and H.W. Hazard, Madison: University of Wisconsin Press, 1969, p. 409

160 *Follow your conscience* Habig, pp. 380, 713

162 *formed a wall* Powell, p. 159

163 *took only Illuminato* FAED I, pp. 605, 609; Habig, pp. 703-705; Arnaldo
     Fortini, p. 396

164 *among wolves* Habig, p. 703

165 *Palm Sunday, 1192* Moses p.68; Thomas Andrew Archer, *The Crusade of
     Richard I 1189-1192*, New York: G.P. Putnam's Sons, 1889, p. 214

166 *trachoma* Habig, p. 1015

167 *patient to wear* Sami K. Hamarneh, *Health Sciences in Early Islam*, San
     Antonio: Noor Health Foundation, 1983, Vol. 2, p. 41

167 *forced on him* FAED III, p. 796

168 *in written form* "What Do Muslims Believe About Jesus?" https://www.islam-
     guide.com/ch3-10.htm

169 *left my Heart* Gril Denis ed. and trans., *La Risala de Safi al-din abi L-Mansur
     Ibn Zafir Biographies de Maîtres Spirituels Connus par un Cheikh Egyptien du
     VII/XIIIème siecles*, Cairo: Institut Francais d'Archeologie, 1986, p. 180

170 *it was reported* Habig, p. 277

171 *most pleasing religion* FAED I, p. 607

172 *not neophytes* Habig, p. 1612; FAED I, pp. 581, 585

174 *after the resurrection* Nicole Chareyron, trans W. Donald Wilson, *Pilgrims to
     Jerusalem in the Middle Ages*, New York: Columbia University Press, 2005, p. 78

174 *Frederick Barbarossa* C.R. Condor, *The City of Jerusalem*, London: John Murray,
     1909, p. 313

174 *to the east* Information on Jerusalem sites is from Conder pp. 317, 284, 290

176 *denounced them* FAED III, p. 793; Hermann, pp 27-29

177 *be incurable* Hermann, pp. 27-28; FAED III, pp. 793, 795

Chapter Nine

182 *outside Assisi* Alberzoni 2004, pp. 39–41, 117, 165

183 *Saint Damian at Assisi* Mooney, pp. 58–59

183 *including the Lesser Brothers* FAED II, p. 54

183 *spirit of Francis* CAED, p. 349

185 *years later* Arnaldo Fortini, pp. 569–570; CAED pp. 146–7, 158, 168

185 *Gasdia* CAED, p. 161

187 *daily life* CAED, p. 144

191 *sinful man* CAED, p. 101

193 *"many popes."* Placid Hermann (trans), *XIIIth Century Chronicle*, Chicago:
     Franciscan Herald Press, 1961, p. 29

193 *Saint Benedict* CAED, p. 101

194 *leave the order* FAED III, p. 399

195 *travel quickly* Raoul Manselli, *St. Francis of Assisi*, Chicago: Franciscan Herald
     Press, 1988, p. 248

195 *horror and chagrin* Habig, p. 389

196 *decamped* Habig, pp. 412, 1492

198 *the Prophet* Tolan, p. 6; for Portugal and Morocco background see Hugh
     Kennedy, *Muslim Spain and Portugal: A Political History of al-Andalus*, London
     and New York: Longman, 1996

198 *as they had done* CAED, p. 158, 162
199 *Cardinal of Ostia* Hermann, p. 29; Habig, p. 383
200 *their disturbers* Alberzoni 2004, pp. 28–30
201 *with sisters* FAED III, pp. 794–95; Habig, p. 1894

Chapter Ten

203 *good for his soul* Habig, p. 1058
204 *you shall obey* Habig, p. 477
204 *in charge* Brooke, Rosalind B. *Early Franciscan Government: Elias to Bonaventure*, Cambridge University Press, 1959, p. 79
204 *to replace them* Habig, p. 419
205 *their reading* Habig, pp. 437, 1163
205 *allowed to lie there* Habig, pp. 484, 485
206 *with meat* Habig, p. 1016
210 *as for them* CAED, p. 58
211 *back to Francis* CAED, pp. 144-145
211 *miserable state* FAED III, p. 795
212 *sit," he said* Habig, p. 414
213 *several times* Habig, p. 279

Chapter Eleven

214 *with him in Perugia* Arnaldo Fortini, p. 290n; FAED III, p. 333
215 *explanation kindly* Habig, p. 424
216 *survives at Greccio* Paul Sabatier, *Examen critique des recits concernant la visite de Jacqueline de Settesoli à Saint François*, Paris: Fischbacher, 1910, pp. 301-304
217 *recommend to me* Habig, p. 1849
218 *that fact* Habig, p. 290; FAED II, p. 7
219 *Saint Peter* Habig, p. 461; *Papst und Kardinalskolleg von 1191 bis 1216*, Wien: Verlage der Osterreichischen Akademie de Wissenschaftern, 1984 p. 137
219 *stay alone* Habig, pp. 1066, 1072
220 *downpour* FAED II, p. 311
221 *simplicity and purity* Habig, p. 1218
221 *Elias's lifetime* Brooke 1959, Plate I
225 *devotions and reflections* FAED III, pp. 797–798
227 *could leave the order* FAED II p. 132; FAED III pp. 127-128
228 *guidance of the Lord* Habig p. 662; FAED II p. 558
230 *wedding bed* Habig, p. 415
232 *into pride* FAED I, p. 126; Habig, p. 1089
232 *knowledge than that* Habig, p. 1089
233 *fallen masonry* Brooke 1959, p. 290
234 *assassinations* Habig, pp. 1601-1602; FAED II, p. 807
234 *when needed* CAED, p. 79
235 *God's word* Habig, p. 527
237 *following it* FAED III, p. 419

237 *his preface* Habig, p. 57

238 *attacking his head* Habig, pp. 416, 1071

239 *Nativity of Christ* www.jassa.org/?p=5152

239 *new Bethlehem* Habig, p. 301-302

240 *the ordained* Habig, p. 517

Chapter Twelve

241 *cook for himself* Arnald of Sarrant, Brother Juniper

242 *gave birth* Habig, p. 282

242 *little dog* Habig, p. 478

242 *their eighties* Katherine Park, "Medicine and Society in Medieval Europe, 500-1500" *Medicine in Society,* Andrew Wear ed. Cambridge: Cambridge University Press, 1991, p. 61

242 *find a way* Habig, p. 102

243 *you have sent me* FAED I, p. 49

243 *order required* 1018 Habig, p. 1018

243 *is impossible* Habig, p. 407

244 Francis's disclaimers, Habig, p. 1019

245 *pagan author* Habig, p. 297

246 *what they did* FAED II, pp. 209, 210

247 *life and knowledge* FAED II, p. 209

247 *as his actions show* FAED II, p. 210

248 *at Portiuncula* Habig, p. 988

248 *no progress* Habig, p. 318

248 *stepped on* Habig, pp. 1027-29

248 *my will is* Habig, p. 512

249 *disgraced clerics* FAED I, pp. 561-564

249 *before all else* André Vauchez, *Francis of Assisi*, Yale University Press, 2012 p. 125; FAED I, pp. 561-564

250 *former troubadour* Mooney, p. 73

250 *kissed his feet* Habig, p. 477

251 *her mattress* CAED, p. 169

252 *the Umbria dialect* FAED II, p. 186

253 *penitent life* FAED, p. 346

254 *pride in it* Habig, p. 442

255 *a new one* FAED II, p. 187

255 *eyes treated* Dalarun 2016, p. 28

256 *one of his eyes* Chiara Frugoni, *A Day in A Medieval City*, University of Chicago Press, 2005, p. 98

257 *felt no pain* Habig, p. 496 ; Philippe Juvin and Jean-Marie Desmonts, "The Ancestors of Inhalational Anesthesia: The Soporific Sponges (XIth–XVIIth Centuries): How a Universally Recommended Medical Technique Was Abruptly Discarded," *Anesthesiology* 2000; Vol. 93, pp. 265–269 https://anesthesiology.pubs.asahq.org/article.aspx?articleid=1945901

258 *could not be trusted* Habig, pp. 310–311

258 *of his woe* Habig, p. 399

259 *graze once again* Yuki Furuse et al. "Origin of measles virus: divergence from rinderpest virus between the 11th and 12th centuries," Virology Journal, Vol. 7 2010, https://www.ncbi.nlm.nih.gov/pmc/articles/PMC2838858 ; Habig, p. 1034

259 *sanctity of this man* Habig, p. 1004

259 *belongs to another* Habig, p. 437

261 *sixty-five percent* FAED II, p. 170

262 *Pacifico would not* FAED II, p. 168

262 *die at Portiuncula* FAED II, p.162

263 *north of Nocera* FAED II, p. 305; Habig, p. 443

263 *unable to purchase* Habig, p. 427

264 *how it will be* Habig, pp. 741, 322; FAED II, p. 119

264 *underwear* Habig, p. 1042

264 *to the Lord* Dalarun 2016, p. 31; Habig, p. 322

265 *on to Portiuncula* FAED II, pp.120–123

265 *heed it* Habig, p. 65

266 *his promise to her* Habig, p. 1084

266 *to joyfully sing* Habig, p. 1264

267 *her journey home* Habig, pp. 1077, 550

268 *reward me* Habig, pp. 322–323; FAED II, p. 387; Dalarun 2016, p. 31

269 *mile at leisure* FAED II, p. 388

270 *used to* Habig, p. 330–332; Vauchez, p. 141

Chapter Thirteen

Main sources for the discussion of the stigmata include:

Jacques Dalarun et al. *The Stigmata of Francis of Assisi: New Studies New Perspectives*, St. Bonaventure, N.Y. Franciscan Institute Publications, 2006

Joanne Schatzlein and Daniel P. Sulmasy, "The Diagnosis of St. Francis: Evidence of Leprosy," *Franciscan Studies*, Annual XXV, 1987, pp. 181–271

274 *inflicted on himself* Habig, pp. 309, 310, 472, 534, 537, 551; Dalarun, 2016, p. 27

274 *Francis's secret kept* Habig, p. 444

276 *textural difficulties* FAED II, pp. 485-491; Vauchez, p. 359; FAED II, p. 489

278 *names of God* Vauchez p. 254; Paul Moses, p. 181

279 *onto his body* Giles Constable, *Three Studies in Medieval and Religious Thought*, Cambridge: Cambridge University Press, 1995, p. 219

281 *Francis and Dominic* Frances Andrews, *The Early Humilitati*, Cambridge: Cambridge University Press, 1999, p. 203; Alberzoni 2004, p. 170

282 *better job of it* Brooke 1959, p. 70

282 *growing among them* Brooke 1959, p. 117; Alberzoni 2006, p. 22

283 *became a leader* Arnald of Sarrant, John Parenti

284 *utter ruin* Lionel Alhhorn, Stupor Mundi, London: Martin Secker, 1912, no. 84; https://archive.org/stream/stupormundilifet00allsrich/stupormundilifet00allsrich_djvu.txt

284 *joy and enthusiasm* Habig, p. 336–340

288 *look to the future* CAED, pp. 103–104

289 *underarm fistula* CAED, pp. 148, 155, 171

289 *come upon you* CAED, pp. 169, 170

289 *bread with him* Habig, p. 1380

290 *had wished* Mooney, p. 74

291 *Privilege of Poverty* CAED, p. 107

291 *sweet and smooth* Mooney, p. 69; CAED, p. 103

292 *could be amended* CAED, pp. 92-100

293 *relics of the Roman Catholic Church* Rosalind B. Brooke, *The Image of Francis: Responses to Sainthood in the Thirteenth Century* Cambridge: Cambridge University Press, 2006, p. 57

293 *inappropriate meal* Brooke 1959, p. 151

294 *day by day* G. F. Karl Evers and Nicolaus Glassberger, *Analecta ad Fratrum Minorum historiam*. Lipsiae: In aedibus Georgii Boehme, 1882, p. 45

295 *chastity as well* The Golden Sayings of Brother Giles, XXVII https://archive.org/stream/thegoldensayings00robiuoft/thegoldensayings00robiuoft_djvu.txt

295 *alchemy took place there* Salimbene, p. 152

295 *movement had changed* Vauchez, p. 152–154; FAED II, p. 478

296 *lock them out* Brooke 2006, pp. 55, 464

298 *Perugia and Spoleto* Brooke 2006, p. 55; Brooke 1959, pp. 138–40

Chapter Fourteen

299 *new burial church* Stephen Van Dijk JP, *The Origins of The Modern Roman Liturgy*, Westminster, Md: The Newman Press, 1960, p. xxv

299 *the subject himself* H. G. Rosedale, *St. Francis of Assisi according to Brother Thomas of Celano*, London: J.M. Dent & Co., 1904. pp. xiii, xiv, xviii; Dalarun, 2016, p. x

300 *remained angry with him* Habig, p. 249; Dalarun 2016, pp. x, xi

300 *Jordan of Giano attests* Hermann, p. 62-64

302 *was included* Brooke 1959, p. 199

303 *care of nuns* Alberzoni 2004, p. 44

304 *food that is vital* CAED, p. 290

304 *excommunicated her* Mooney, p. 102; Alberzoni, Maria Pia, trans. Nancy Celaschi OSF, "Nequaquam a Christi sequela in perpetuum absolvi desidero," *Greyfriars Review*, Vol. 12.2, 1998 p. 82

306 *with greater success* CAED, p. 167

307 *serving sisters* CAED, pp. 67, 68, 70, 76, 92

310 *poverty, simplicity* Dalarun 2016, p. xviii

310 *could do them justice* Dalarun 2016, pp. 5, 86

311 *money for them* Mooney, p. 88

312 *without formal permission* Joan A. Mueller, *Companion to Clare of Assisi Life Writings Spirituality*, Leiden/Boston: Brill, 2010, p. 73; Alberzoni 2004, p. 75

312 *had done his penance* CAED, p. 164: Alberzoni 2006 p. 26;

312 *have been deceived* CAED, p. 109

315 *never studied letters* CAED, p. 169

316 *scribes in the Middle Ages* Mooney, p. 93

316 *treasured gifts* Arnald of Sarrant, note 166

317 *assignments to help them* Mueller, pp. 72-73

317 *he did not approve* CAED, p. 361

318 *brother had given her* Mueller, p. 142

319 *the Lord has called you* CAED, p. 41

319 *agreed to Agnes's request* Codex diplomaticus et epistolaris Bohemiae III. 1 ed. by G. Friedrich https://archive.org/details/CDBIII.1/page/n211/mode/2up

320 *as he said Mass* Mooney, p. 250 footnote 88; Mueller, pp. 149-150; CAED, p. 366-368

320 *human hearts* CAED, p. 45

320 *through contemplation* Habig, p. 249

320 *soul and improve it* FAED III, p. 208

321 *from the Lateran Palace* CAED, pp. 368-374

323 *to their support* Mooney, p. 104

323 *Church of Saint Rufino* CAED, p. 111

323 *Peter and Paul* CAED, p. 375

324 *in her palm* CAED, pp. 152, 160, 163

Chapter Fifteen

327 *enough for you* The Golden Sayings of Brother Giles, XVI, https://archive.org/stream/thegoldensayings00robiuoft/thegoldensayings00robiuoft_djvu.txt

330 *delightful harmonies* Vauchez, pp. 150-151; Brooke 2006, pp. 50-60

330 *be contained* Brooke 1959, p. 202

331 *speak in his stead* The Golden Sayings of Brother Giles, XXVIII, https://archive.org/stream/thegoldensayings00robiuoft/thegoldensayings00robiuoft_djvu.txt

332 *provincial of England* Brooke 1959, *Early Government*, p. 162

332 *Elias's ouster* Brooke 1959, *Early Government*, p. 42; Salimbene et al., p. 150

333 *brothers accompanied him* Maria Pia Alberzoni, "Frate Elia tra Chiara d'Assisi, Gregorio IX e Federico II," *Elia di Cortona tra realtà e mito*, Cortona: Fondazione Centro italiano di studi sull'alto medioevo, 2013, pp. 91-121, http://hdl.handle.net/10807/60637

334 *cannot fall* The Golden Sayings of Brother Giles, XXVIII, https://archive.org/stream/thegoldensayings00robiuoft/thegoldensayings00robiuoft_djvu.txt

335 *walked inside* CAED, pp. 158, 178

335 *Clare blessed him* CAED, pp. 145, 176, 177

336 *cords and habits* Mooney, p. 150

336 *dashed their hopes* Mooney, pp. 129, 132

337 *never formally implemented* Mooney, p. 158

337 *Clare got word to him* Alberzoni, Greyfriars 2006 p. 40

338 *meet the Saracens* CAED, pp. 150, 165, 175, 276

339 *her dearest wish* Mooney, pp. 165-167

340 *September 16, 1252* Mooney, p. 163

340 *meet before God* CAED, p. 49

341 *towns throughout the continent* Neslihan Şenocak, *The Poor and the Perfect:*
     The Rise of Learning in the Franciscan Order, 1209-1310, Ithaca and London:
     Cornell University Press, 2012, pp. 158–159; 237, 247

341 *embellishments to be added to it* Brooke 2006, p. 68

342 *representative on earth* CAED, p. 151

342 *no weakness difficult* CAED, pp. 294–295

343 *clutching the papal document*, CAED, pp. 153, 292

344 *spiriting her body away* CAED, pp. 292–298, 228

345 *last months of his papacy* Alberzoni 1998, p. 113

345 *into other documents* FAED III, p. 199

Bibliography

Alberzoni, Maria Pia. Translated by Hagman OFM Cap., Edward. "Clare and San Damiano Between the Order of Friars Minor and the Papal Curia." *Greyfriars Review* (2006): 1–45.

—— *Clare of Assisi and the Poor Sisters and the Thirteenth Century.* St. Bonaventure University: Franciscan Institute Publications, 2004.

—— "Frate Elia tra Chiara d'Assisi, Gregorio IX e Federico II." *Elia di Cortona tra realtà e mito.* Cortona: Fondazione Centro italiano di studi sull'alto medioevo, 2013. http://hdl.handle.net/10807/60637.

—— Translated by Celaschi, Nancy. "Nequaquam a Christi sequela in perpetuum absolvi desidero." *Greyfriars Review*, Vol. 12.2 (1998): 82–121.

Alengry, Charles. *Les foires de Champagne: Etude d'histoire économique.* Paris: Rousseau, 1915.

Alhhorn, Lionel. *Stupor Mundi.* London: Martin Secker, 1912. https://archive.org/stream/stupormundilifet00allsrich/stupormundilifet00all-srich_djvu.txt.

Anastasia, Sister. "The Relics of Saint Clare Exposed in the Basilica of St. Clare" http://www.assisisantachiara.it/wp-content/uploads/2016/10/Reliquie-sr.-Anastasia.pdf.

Andrews, Frances. *The Early Humiliati.* Cambridge: Cambridge University Press, 1999.

Archer, Thomas Andrew. *The Crusade of Richard I 1189-1192.* New York: G.P. Putnam's Sons, 1889.

Armstrong, Regis. *Clare of Assisi: Early Documents.* Saint Bonaventure, N.Y: Franciscan Institute Publications, 1993.

—— et al. Editors. *Francis of Assisi: Early Documents*, 3 vols, New York: New City Press, 1999-2001.

Arnald of Sarrant. Translated by Muscat, Noel, OFM. *Chronicle of the Twenty-Four Generals of the Order of Friars Minor*, Malta: TAU Franciscan Communications, 2010. https://books.google.com/books?id=BUn9AAAAQBAJ&printsec=front-cover&dq=chronicle+of+the+twenty+four+generals&hl=en&newbks=1&newbks_redir=0&sa=X&ved=2ahUKEwiK7OvF7orxAhVtneAKHReCDcMQ6AEwA-HoECAsQAg#v=onepage&q=chronicle%20of%20the%20twenty%20four%20generals&f=false.

Aubrey, Elizabeth. *The Music of the Troubadours*. Indiana University Press, 1996.

Barbiera, Irene and Dalla-Zuanna, Gianpiero. "Population Dynamics in Italy in the Middle Ages: New Insights from Archaeological Findings" *Population and Development Review*, vol. 35, no. 2 (June, 2009): 367–389.

Barone, Giulia. *Da Frate Elia Agli Spirituali*. Milano: Edizioni Biblioteca Francescana, 1991.

Bartoli, Marco. Translated by Downing, Sr. Frances Teresa. *Clare of Assisi*. London: Darton, Longman and Todd, 1993.

—— *Francis' Nudity*. St. Bonaventure University: Franciscan Institute Publications, 2020.

Beaumont-Maillet, Laure. *Le Grand Couvent des Cordeliers de Paris*. Paris : Libraire Honoré Champion, 1975.

Bertrand, Benjamin Anthony. "Monstrous Muslims? Depicting Muslims in French Illuminated Manuscripts from 1200-1420." Honors Theses. University of New Hampshire, 2015.

Bigaroni, Marino and Van Baer, Agnes. "San Damiano—Assisi: The First Church of Saint Francis." *Franciscan Studies*, vol. 47 (1987):45-97.

Bird, Jessalyn et al. Editors. *Crusade and Christendom: Annotated Documents in Translation From Innocent III to the Fall of Acre*, 1187-1291. Philadelphia: University of Pennsylvania Press, 2013.

Bolton, Brenda. "Daughters of Rome." *Women in the Church*. Edited by Sheils, W.J. and Wood, Diana. London: The Ecclesiastical History Society, 1990.

—— *Innocent III Studies on Papal Authority Pastoral Care*. Aldershot: Variorum, 1995.

Bomgardner, David L. *The Story of the Roman Amphitheater*. New York: Routledge, 2000.

Bonner, Anthony. *Songs of the Troubadours*. New York: Schocken Books, 1972.

Bourquelot, Louis Félix. 1865. *Études sur les foires de Champagne, sur la nature, l'étendue et les règles du commerce qui s'y faisait aux XIIe, XIIIe et XIVe siècles*. Paris: Imprimerie Impériale https://archive.org/details/tudessurlesfoi00bouruoft/.

Brooke, Rosalind B. *Early Franciscan Government: Elias to Bonaventure*. Cambridge University Press, 1959.

—— *The Image of Francis: Responses to Sainthood in the Thirteenth Century* Cambridge: Cambridge University Press, 2006.

Bruzelius, Caroline A. "Hearing is Believing: Clarissan Architecture, ca. 1213-1340." *Gesta*, 31, 2 (1992):83-91.

Büntgen, Ulf and Tegel, Willy. "European tree-ring data and the Medieval Climate Anomaly."2011. https://www.researchgate.net/publication/228843243_European_tree-ring_data_and_the_Medieval_Climate_Anomaly.

Bynum, Caroline Walker. *Holy Feast and Holy Fast: The Religious Significance of Food to Medieval Women*. Los Angeles: University of California Press, 1987.

Caicco, Gregory Paul. "Ethics and Poetics: The Architectural Vision of Saint Francis of Assisi." PhD diss., School of Architecture, McGill University, 1998.

Carney, Margaret. *The First Franciscan Woman: Care of Assisi and Her Form of Life*. Quincy, Ill.: Franciscan Press, 1993.

Chareyron, Nicole. Translated by Wilson, W.Donald. *Pilgrims to Jerusalem in the Middle Ages*. New York: Columbia University Press, 2005.

Ciardi, Anna Minara. "'Per clerum et Populum'? Legal Terminology and Episcopal Appointments in Denmark 1059–1225." *Traditio* 71 2016. doi:10.2307/26421922.

Clark, Anne L. "Under Whose Care? The Madonna of San Sisto and Women's Monastic Life in the Twelfth and Thirteenth Century Rome." *Medieval Constructions in Gender and Identity: Essays in Honor of Joan M. Frerrante.* Edited by Barolini, Theodolinda. Tempe: Arizona Center for Medieval and Renaissance Studies, 2005.

Clareno, Angelo. *Dai poveri eremiti ai Fraticelli.* Rome: Nella Sede dell'istituto Palazzo Borromino, 1990.

Condor, C.R. *The City of Jerusalem.* London: John Murray, 1909.

Constable, Giles, *Three Studies in Medieval and Religious Thought.* Cambridge University Press, 1995.

Cook, Willam R., Editor. *The Art of the Franciscan Order in Italy.* Leiden, Boston: Brill, 2005.

Cooper, Donal. "'In Loco Tutissimo et Firmissimo: The Tomb of St. Francis in History, Legend and Art." *The Art of the Franciscan Order in Italy.* Edited by Cook, William R. Leiden: Brill (2005): 1–37

Cooper, William M. *A History of the Rod In All Countries.* London: John Camden Hotten, 1896.

Covey, Herbert C. *People with leprosy (Hansen's disease) during the Middle Ages. The Social Science Journal* 38 (2001):315-321.

Cusato, Michael F. "Elias of Cortona and the English Friars." *The English Province of the Franciscans (1224-c.1350).* Edited by Robson, Michael J. (2017): 98-108.

D'Alencon, Edouard. "Jacqueline de Settesoli." *Etudes Franciscains* 2 (1899): 5-18, 225-242.

Dalaran, Jacques. *Francis of Assisi and the Feminine.* St. Bonaventure, New York: Franciscan Institute Publications, 2006.

—— Translated by Hagman, Edward. *The Misadventure of Francis of Assisi.* St. Bonaventure University: Franciscan Institute Publications, 2002.

—— Translated by Johnson, Timothy J. *The Rediscovered Life of St. Francis of Assisi Thomas of Celano.* St. Bonaventure University: Franciscan Institute Publications, 2016.

—— et al. Editors. *The Stigmata of Francis of Assisi: New Studies New Perspectives.* St. Bonaventure, N.Y. Franciscan Institute Publications, 2006.

Donovan, Joseph P. *Pelagius and the Fifth Crusade.* Philadelphia: University of Pennsylvania Press, 1950.

Duby, George and LeGoff, Jacques. *Famille et Parenté dans L'Occident Médiéval.* Ecole Francaise de Rome, 1977.

D'Acunto, Nicolangelo. "Il vescovo Guido oppure i vescovi Guido? Cronotassi episco-pale assisana e fonti francescane." *Melanges de l'Ecole francaise de Rome.* Moyen-Age, 108 (1996):479-524.

Delcorno, Carlo. "Origini della predicazione francescana." *Francesco d'Assisi e francesca-nesimo dal 1216 al 1226,* Assisi, 1977.

Evers, G. F. Karl, and Glassberger, Nicolaus *Analecta ad Fratrum Minorum historiam.* Lipsiae: In aedibus Georgii Boehme, 1882.

Fleury-Lemberg, Mechthild. Translated by Leibundgut, Pamela. *Textile Conservation and Research*. Bern: Abegg-Stifung, 1988.

Fortini, Arnaldo. *Francesco d'Assisi e l'Italia del suo tempo* (Book II). Rome: Biblioteca di Storia Patria, 1968.

—— Translated by Moak, Helen. *Francis of Assisi* New York: Crossroad Publishing, 1981.

—— Translated by Sr. M. Jane Frances. "New Information About Clare of Assisi." *Greyfriars Review* 17 (1993): 27–69.

—— *Nova Vita di Francesco d'Assisi* (Book II). Assisi: Santa Maria   degli Angeli, 1959.

Fortini, Gemma, "The Noble Family of St. Clare." *Franciscan Studies*, vol. 42, (1982):48-67.

Friedrich, G. Editor. *Codex diplomaticus et epistolaris Bohemiae* III. 1. https://archive.org/details/CDBIII.1/page/n211/mode/2up.

Frugoni, Chiara. *A Day in A Medieval City*. Chicago: University of Chicago Press, 2005.

—— *Francis of Assisi*. London: SCM Press Ltd., 1998.

Gatti, Isidoro. *La Tomba di S. Francesco nei secoli*. Assisi: Casa Editrice Francescana, 1983.

Gregorovius, Ferdinand. *History of the City of Rome in the Middle Ages*, vol. 4. New York: Cambridge University Press, 2010.

Gril, Denis, Editor and Translator. *La Risala de Safi al-din abi L-Mansur Ibn Zafir Biographies de Maîtres Spirituels Connus par un Cheikh Egyptien du VII/XIIIème siecles*. Cairo: Institut Français d'Archeologie, 1986.

Gurevich, Aron Ja. "The Merchant." *Medieval Callings*. Le Goff, Jacques, Editor. Chicago: University of Chicago Press, 1987.

Habig, Marion, Editor. *St. Francis of Assisi Omnibus of Sources*. Quincy, Illinois: Franciscan Press, 1991.

Hamarneh, Sami K. *Health Sciences in Early Islam*, vol. 2. San Antonio: Noor Health Foundation, 1983.

Hamilton, Bernard F. "Continental Drift: Prester John's Progress Through the Indies." *Prester John, the Mongols and the Ten Lost Tribes*. Hampshire, Great Britain: Valorium (1996):237-269.

Heng, Geraldine. *Empire of Magic: Medieval Romance and the Politics of Cultural Fantasy*. New York: Columbia University Press, 2003.

Herlihy, David. *Medieval Households*. Cambridge: Harvard University Press, 1985.

Hermann, Placid, Translator. *XIIIth Century Chronicles*. Chicago: Franciscan Herald Press, 1961.

Heywood, William. *A History of Perugia*. New York: G.P. Putnam's Sons, 1910.

Hughes, Diane Owen. "Mourning Rites, Memory and Civilization in Premodern Italy." *Riti e Rituali nelle Societa Medievale*. Chiffoleau, Jacques, et al. Editors. Spoleto: Centro Italiano di Studi sull'alto mediovo, 1994.

Johnson, Timothy J. "Clare, Leo, and the Authorship of the Fourth Letter to Agnes of Prague." *Franciscan Studie*s, vol. 62 (2004):91-100.

—— "To Her Who Is Half of Her Soul: Clare of Assisi and the Medieval Epistolary Tradition." *Greyfriars Review* Vol. XI (1997):23–40.

Jorgensen, Johannes. Translated by Sloane, T. O'Connor. *Saint Francis of Assisi*. New
    York: Longmans, Green & Co., 1926.

Juvin, Philippe and Desmonts, Jean-Marie. "The Ancestors of Inhalational
    Anesthesia: The Soporific Sponges (XIth–XVIIth Centuries): How a Universally
    Recommended Medical Technique Was Abruptly Discarded." *Anesthesiology*, 2000;
    https://doi.org/10.1097/00000542-200007000-00037.

Keen, Maurice Hugh. *Chivalry*. New Haven: Yale University Press, 2005.

Kennedy, Hugh. *Muslim Spain and Portugal: A Political History of al-Andalus*. London
    and New York: Longman, 1996.

Keys, Ancel et al. *The Biology of Human Starvation*. Minneapolis: University of
    Minnesota Press, 1950.

Knox, Leslie. *Creating Clare of Assisi: Female Franciscan Identities in Later Medieval
    Italy*. Leiden, Boston: Brill, 2008.

Kleinhenz, Christopher. *Medieval Italy: An Encyclopedia*. London: Routledge, 2004.

Krauthheimer, Richard. *Early Christian and Byzantine Architecture*. New Haven: Yale
    University Press, 1986.

—— *Rome Profile of A City* 312-1308. Princeton, N.J: Princeton University Press,
    1980.

Langeli, Attilio Bartoli. "Gli scritti di Francesco: L'autografia di un illiteratus."
    Frate Francesco d'Assisi. Spoleto: Centro Italiano di Studi sull'Alto Medioeveo
    (1994):101–59.

Lawrence, C.H. *The Friars, The Impact of the Mendicant Orders on Medieval Society*.
    New York: I.B. Tauris & Co. Ltd, 2013.

Lothario dei Segni. Edited by Howard, Donald R. Translated by Dietz, Margaret
    Mary. *On the Misery of the Human Condition*. New York: Bobbs-Merrill Co., 1969.

Maleczek, Werner. *Papst und Kardinalskolleg von 1191 bis 1216*. Wien: Verlage der
    Osterreichischen Akademie de Wissenschaftern, 1984.

—— "Questions about the Authenticity of the Privilege of Poverty of Innocent III
    and the Testament of Clare of Assisi." Translated by Rosen, Cyprian. *Greyfriars
    Review*, 12, Supplement.

Mancini, Francesco Federico et al. Contributors. *La Basilica di S. Maria degli Angeli:
    Storia e architettura*. Electa/Umbrian Associated Publishers, 1989.

Manselli, Raoul. *St. Francis of Assisi*. Chicago: Franciscan Herald Press, 1988.

Miller, Maureen C. *Clothing the Clergy: Virtue and Power in Medieval Europe 800-
    1200*. Ithaca: Cornell University Press, 2014.

Monro, Dana C. "The Children's Crusade" *The American Historical Review*, vol. 19, no.
    3 (1914):516-524.

Montaubin, Pascal. "Bastard Nepotism: Niccolo di Anagni, A Nephew of Pope
    Gregory IX, and Camerarius of Pope Alexander IV." *Pope, Church, and City: Essays
    in Honour of Brenda M. Bolton*. Frances Andrews et al. Editors. Leiden: Brill, 2004.
    http://site.ebrary.com/id/10175336.

Mooney, Catherine M. *Clare of Assisi and the Thirteenth-Century Church*. Philadelphia:
    University of Pennsylvania Press, 2016.

Moses, Paul. *The Saint and the Sultan: The Crusades, Islam and Francis of Assisi's Mission
    of Peace*. New York: Doubleday Religion, 2009.

Nicolini, Ugolino. *Scritti di Storia*. Napoli: Edizioni Scientifiche Italiane, 1993.

Nimmo, Duncan. *Reform and Division in the Medieval Franciscan Order.* Rome: The Capuchin Historical Institute, 1997.

Notaker, Henry. *A History of Cookbooks.* Oakland: University of California Press, 2017.

Oldenbourg, Zoe. Translated by Green, Peter. *Massacre at Montsegur; a history of the Albigensian Crusade.* New York: Pantheon Books, 1962.

Osborne, John. *Master Gregorius The Marvels of Rome.* Toronto: Pontifical Institute of Medieval Studies, 1987.

Park, Katherine. "Medicine and Society in Medieval Europe, 500–1500." *Medicine in Society*, Wear, Andrew, Editor. Cambridge: Cambridge University Press (1991): 59–90.

Peters, Edward. *Christian Society and the Crusades 1198-1229 Sources in Translation.* Philadelphia: University of Pennsylvania Press, 2012.

Peterson, Ingrid J. *Clare of Assisi: A Biographical Study.* Quincy, Ill.: Franciscan Press, 1993.

Petroff, Elizabeth Alvilda. *Body and Soul Essays on Medieval Women and Mysticism.* New York and Oxford: Oxford University Press, 1994.

Pirenne, Henri. Translated by Halsey, Frank D. *Medieval Cities Their Origins and the Revival of Trade.* Princeton, N.J. Princeton University Press, 1974.

Potthast, Augustus. *Regesta Pontificum Romanorum, vol. 1.* Berolini Academy of Berlin, 1874.

Powell, James M. *Anatomy of a Crusade, 1213-1221.* Philadelphia: University of Pennsylvania Press, 1990.

Queller, Donald E. et al. "The Fourth Crusade, The Neglected Majority." *Speculum*, vol. 49, Issue 3, (1974): 441–465.

Righetti Tosti-Croce, Marina. "La chiesa di santa Chiara ad Assisi: architettura." *Santa Chiara in Assisi.* Architettura e decorazione. Milano: Silvana Editoriale, (2003):21-41.

Rosedale, H. G. "Critical Introduction." *St. Francis of Assisi According to Brother Thomas of Celano His descriptions of the Seraphic Father.* A.D. 1229–1257." London: J.M. Dent & Co., 1904.

Robinson, Pascal. "The Golden Sayings of the Blessed Brother Giles of Assisi." https://archive.org/stream/thegoldensayings00robiuoft/thegoldensayings00robiuoft_djvu.txt

Runciman, Steven. *A History of the Crusades.* Vol 4. Cambridge University Press, 1954.

Sabatier, Paul. *Examen critique des recits concernant la visite de Jacqueline de Settesoli à Saint François.* Paris: Fischbacher, 1910.

—— Translated by Houghton, Louise Seymour. *The Life of St. Francis of Assis*i. New York: Scribner, 1894.

Salimbene, Joseph L. Baird, Giuseppe Baglivi, and John Robert Kane. *The Chronicle of Salimbene de Adam.* Binghamton, N.Y: Medieval & Renaissance Texts & Studies, 1986.

Sansi, Mario. "Le Clarisse a Foligno nel secolo XIII." *Collectanea franciscana*, vol. 47 (1977):349-363.

Sayers, Jane. *Innocent III: Leader of Europe 1198-1216.* New York: Longman Group, 1994.

Sbaralea, J.H., Editor. *Bullarium Franciscanum*, vol. 1. https://books.google.com/books?id=GyZGQOBVKRoC&printsec=frontcover&source=gbs_ge_summary_r&cad=0#v=onepage&q=Avvegnent&f=false.

Schatzlein, Joanne and Sulmasy, Daniel P. "The Diagnosis of St. Francis: Evidence of Leprosy." *Franciscan Studies*, Annual XXV, (1987): 181–271.

Schmucki, Octavian. "The Third Order in the Biographies of St. Francis." *Greyfriars Review* 6 (1992): 81–107.

Şenocak, Neslihan. *The Poor and the Perfect: The Rise of Learning in the Franciscan Order, 1209-1310.* Ithaca and London: Cornell University Press, 2012.

Shahar, Shulamith, Editor. *The Fourth Estate: A History of Women in the Middle Ages.* London: Methune & Co., 1984.

Sronkova, Olgá. *Gothic Women's Fashion.* Prague: Artia, 1954.

Steckel, Richard. "New Light on the 'Dark Ages': The Remarkably Tall Stature of Northern European Men during the Medieval Era." *Social Science History.* vol. 28, pp. 211-229.

Storey, Glenn R. "The Population of Ancient Rome." *Antiquity Magazine*, vol. 71 (1997): 966–978.

Thomas of Eccleston. Translated by Father Cuthbert. *The Chronicle of Thomas of Eccleston.* London Sands & Co., 1909.

Thomas de Cantimpré. Translated by Feiss, Hugh. *Supplement to the Life of Marie d' Oignies.* Toronto: Peregrina Publishing, 1990.

Thompson, Augustine. *Francis of Assisi A New Biography.* Ithaca: Cornell University Press, 2012.

Toker, Franklin. *On Holy Ground: Liturgy, Architecture and Urbanism in the Cathedral and the Streets of Medieval Florence.* Harvey Miller Publishers, 2009.

Tolan, John V. *Saint Francis and the Sultan: The Curious History of a Christian-Muslim Encounter.* New York: Oxford University Press, 2009.

Trexler, Richard C. "Francis of Assisi, His Mother's Son." *Studi medievali*, series III, (1995):363-73.

—— *Naked Before the Father: The Renunciation of Francis of Assisi.* Los Angeles: Center for Medieval and Renaissance Studies, University of California, 1989.

Tugwell, Simon, Editor. *Early Dominicans: Selected Writings.* Mahweh, N.J.: The Paulist Press, 1986.

—— "The Original Text of the Regula Hugolini (1219)." *Archivum franciscanum historicum* Vol. 93 (2000):510-513.

Unger, Richard. "Difficult Sources: Crusade Art and the Depiction of Ships," Gertwage, Ruthy and Jeffreys, Elizabeth, Editors. *Shipping, Trade and Crusade in the Medieval Mediterranean.* New York and London: Routledge, Taylor and Francis Group, 2012.

Van Cleve, Thomas C. "The Crusade of Frederick II" A History of the Crusades, Vol. 2 *The Later Crusades, 1189-1311.* Wolff, R. L.; Hazard, H. W. Editors. Madison: University of Wisconsin Press (1969):376-462. https://b-ok.cc/book/848875/17e47d

van Dijk, Stephen J.P. *The Origins of The Modern Roman Liturgy.* Westminster, Md: The Newman Press, 1960.

—— *The Ordinal of the Papal Court from Innocent III to Boniface VIII and Related Documents.* Fribourg: The University Press, 1975.

—— Editor. *Sources of the Modern Roman Liturgy The Ordinals by Haymo of Faversham and Related Documents.* Vol. I, Leiden: E.J. Brill, 1963.

Vasari, Giorgio. *Lives of the Most Eminent Painters, Sculptors & Architects*. London: Macmillan and Co. Vol. 1, 1912.

Vauchez, André. *Francis of Assisi*, Yale University Press, 2012.

Vespierre, Bernard. *Guide du Paris médiéval*. Paris : L'Harmattan, 2006.

Vyskocil, Jan Kapistran. Translated by Buresh, Vitus. *The Legend of Blessed Agnes of Bohemia and the Four Letters of St. Clare*. Cleveland: Micro Photo Division, Bell & Howell, 1963.

Walsh, James. *Medieval Medicine*. London: A & C Black, Ltd, 1920.

Wilhelm, James J. *Lyrics of the Middle Ages: An Anthology*. New York: Garland Press, 1990.

Williams, George L. *Papal Genealogy: The Families and Descendants of the Pope*. Jefferson, N.C. and London: McFarland & Co., Inc., 2004.

Wilms, Jerome. *As the Morning Star: The Life of St. Dominic*. Milwaukee: Bruce Publishing Co., 1956.

Woosnam-Savage, Robert C. and DeVries, Kelly. "Battle Trauma in Medieval Warfare: Wounds, Weapons and Armor." *Wounds and Wound Repair in Medieval Culture*. Tracy, Larissa and DeVries, Kelly, Editors. Leiden, Boston: Brill, 2015.

Index

About the Author

Kathleen Brady is the author of *Ida Tarbell: Portrait of A Muckraker*, for which she was named a Fellow of the Society of American Historians; and *Lucille: The Life of Lucille Ball*. She is featured on many electronic media discussing both subjects. Among her current projects is serving as a Mentor-Editor of The Op-Ed Project.

She is a past co-chair of The Biography Seminar at New York University, a former reporter for *Time* magazine, and a former trustee of her alma mater Saint Bonaventure University, home of the Franciscan Institute, an international center for the study of Francis and Clare and the Franciscan intellectual tradition. She makes her home in New York City.

Contact: www.francisandclarethestrugglesofthesaintsofassisi.com

PHOTO CREDIT: MICHELLE BERGMAN

Made in United States
Troutdale, OR
09/14/2023

12904857R00219